MICROCOMPUTER LANs: NETWORK DESIGN AND IMPLEMENTATION

MICHAEL F. HORDESKI
Consultant, Siltran Digital
Atascadero, California
Lecturer, California Polytechnic State University
San Luis Obispo, California

TAB Professional and Reference Books
Division of TAB BOOKS Inc.
P.O. Box 40, Blue Ridge Summit, PA 17214

FIRST EDITION
FIRST PRINTING

Library of Congress Cataloging in Publication Data

Hordeski, Michael F.
Microcomputer local area networks.

Includes index.
1. Local area networks (Computer networks)
2. Microcomputers. I. Title.
TK5105.7.H675 1987 004.6'8 87-10012
ISBN 0-8306-2888-6

Questions regarding the content of this book
should be addressed to:

Reader Inquiry Branch
Editorial Department
TAB BOOKS Inc.
P.O. Box 40
Blue Ridge Summit, PA 17214

Contents

Acknowledgments

This book would not have been possible without the tireless efforts of those involved in standards development for such organizations as the IEEE, ISA, CCITT, EIA and ANSI. These individuals include Bruce Dilger, Prentiss Yates, Graeme Wood, Chris Wilmering, Earl Witaker, Jay Warrior, Michael Ullman, Don Smith, Garry Stephens, Mark Steiglitz, Kathleen Sturgis, Allan Tanzman, Harvey Shepherd, Seppo Turunen, John Ricketson, Paul Senechal, Dennis Quy, Gene Nines, Toshio Ogawa, Bob Lawler, Samuel Miles, Ronald Martin, Jim Lindgren, Kenneth Jones, Wade Harsy, Dittmar Janetzky, Thomas Phinney, David Carlson, Gunther Martin, Phillip Jacobs, Robert Guzik, Thomas Harrison, Maris Graube, Mel Hagar, Klaus Grund, Robert Harold, Jack Dorsey, Gerhard Funk, Robert Eskeridge, Cesar Doreza, Robert Crowder, Barry Cole, Mark Bauer, Fred Casadei, Dorel Damsker, William Brown, Anthony Capel, Emanuel Delahostria, Steven Cooper, Richard Caro, Steven Dana and many, many more.

Also, there is the support of LAN technology by such institutions as the California Polytechnic State University at San Luis Obispo and individuals such as James Harris, Marc Cooper, Ralph Nicovich and Frank Jansen.

A special thanks to Larry Hager at TPR in New York for his support on this project, and lastly, to Dee at Siltran Digital for the word processing and proofreading of the initial manuscript.

Introduction

Personal computers have revolutionized our lives. In the 1960s, computing was relatively simple; a set of cards was handed over to an operator and a printout was returned in a few hours or the next day. A single error in the control card could cause the program to abort, which would require a resubmittal and the loss of a day or two. This was the decade of the mainframe. The 1970s became the decade of the minicomputer, while the 1980s are emerging as the decade of the microcomputer. Although today's computers seem more complex to use, they are actually much simpler.

The microcomputers that began as the toys of hobbyists are spawning the start of a new era in distributed processing. As this era matures, networks will play a major role in allowing microcomputers to share data transparently across clusters of devices.

The computer revolution has been slowed, however, by an inability to integrate these computers into overall systems. One scenario places microcomputers at the lower level, and host computers at the top. The two are connected by a complex system with numerous branches for the various protocols and data formats. Layers are added to these branches to support differing hardware and operating system requirements.

In many business and industrial applications, isolated, stand-alone personal computers are becoming rare. Connectivity is becoming the key to computing efficiency and productivity in today's information-based society. Computers need to communicate with groups of users and share data sources.

Problems arise when different types of processors are connected together for information exchange. One processor might be foreign to the others and might be connected using an industry standard protocol. The connection could involve a twisted pair, Ethernet, a private network, or a gateway. While today's computers are simpler to use, they can be connected in a variety of ways that appear complex.

An important reason for this is the "knowledge gap" that exists in the area of Local Area Networks (LANs), which have been called the most important topic in microcomputers today. Microcomputer LANs offer end-users a choice they didn't have in the 1960s or 1970s. Hundreds of thousands of existing installations, from the smallest to the largest, can profit from the use of low-cost networks. There is a need to understand what is possible in network applications and how to go about implementing multi-user systems from stand-alone microcomputers. This book was written to fill the need for a clear, comprehensive source of information to help make the right decisions and cut through the confusion surrounding LAN technology and performance.

There are many excellent general-purpose software books that deal with applications that can be used in the business office and home, such as word processing, spreadsheets, and database management programs, but very little useful information is available for connecting computers together. Different hardware and software approaches are needed to deal with such applications as the real-time monitoring and control of industrial processes. The computer user must learn how to specify a system that meets many unique requirements.

This book will allow technologically minded people to apply low-cost computer networks as solutions in office automation and in the control and monitoring of factory production. The book is general in its approach, in contrast to some of the highly specific and narrow books in the past. Some books deal with interfacing computers and digital communications, but they are highly specialized and do not provide the breadth required to evaluate the various systems and techniques available.

Those in office and factory management positions, project/program/department managers, analysts, consultants, planners, engineers, students, and anyone interested in applying microcomputers to networks in order to automate office and factory systems will find something of value in this book. People with little computer expertise, as well as those with a substantial knowledge of computers in office and home applications, will gain important information on the available resources.

After reading this book, you will know what is possible and what tools and resources are most useful. You will know how to go about specifying a system to suit your needs (which is the most common stumbling block), and how to see your efforts through to the completion of the network implementation.

This book will show you how to:

- Determine system requirements and perform design trade-offs between the various technologies such as PBX, baseband and broadband.
- Implement network communication and control protocols based on available standards and equipment.
- Utilize packet and message switching techniques for the maximum benefit.
- Determine the optimum technical and management strategy relative to LANs.
- Evaluate available network hardware and software components.
- Interface local systems to value-added networks.
- Design and build private user networks.

Chapter 1 is an introduction to communications within computer systems, which is basic to understanding modern network concepts and standards. Major topics include address, control, and data busses, CPU-memory-I/O device communication, communications between systems, host/host versus host/slave relationships, handshaking and synchronization techniques, and serial versus parallel communications. Bus standards such as RS-232 and the 488 parallel bus are also introduced.

Protocols and control procedures are introduced in Chapter 2, because they involve some of the most important concepts in computer networks. These include the concepts of resource sharing, distributed computing, communication networks and computer network structures. The important trends are outlined in the concluding section on distributed database management.

The elements of network design include the hardware elements of computer networks, such as terminals, modems, multiplexers, and concentrators (which are the subject of Chapter 3), and the software elements of computer networks, such as addressing, synchronization, flow control, error control, and security. A discussion of network topology concludes this chapter, along with the concept of physical versus logical networks.

The concept of layered network protocols is fundamental to understanding modern network architectures. Chapter 4 relates this concept to terminal/host hardware independence and the layer-to-layer communication between network links and nodes. The functional independence of software and the decomposition of functions into layers are treated as a part of the International Standards Organization model. This chapter provides a basis for understanding the requirements of protocol design for data link, path, and network protocols through the use of examples. Terminal and host interfaces are also treated, along with the problems of network management and internetting.

Communication network concepts are the subject of Chapter 5. It relates the channel characteristics of analog and digital facilities to the determination of channel capacity and bandwidth allocation as well as the bandwidth and media considerations. Other topics include access and transmission delays, switching, interference and errors.

An understanding of LAN Standards is essential in selecting and evaluating LAN vendors and equipment. Chapter 6 considers LAN standards, including Ethernet and IEEE 802. It is concerned with such subjects as logical link control, token bus, and token ring operation.

The importance of packet/message switching is expected to increase in all modern communication system applications. This is the subject of Chapter 7, and includes circuit versus packet switching, routing and path selection, static versus dynamic techniques, congestion control, error control, flow control and packet-switching standards.

Chapter 8 is concerned with network test methods and maintainability. Network tests may be conducted for jitter and bit count integrity. Performance monitoring can include test sequence transmissions, and frame and parity bit checks. Error control is important to maintainability, and includes use of coding techniques for error detection and correction. Some of the important techniques employ convolutional, Viterbi, sequential, feedback and interleaving schemes. Network security also facilitates maintainability, and involves data encryption and authentication techniques.

The planning and implementation of private networks is important to many computer users. This is the subject of Chapter 9, which includes design considerations such as the user profile, the usage profile, and the geographic profile. This chapter illustrates how to evaluate local area network needs using the network profiles to prepare the needs assessment. It also shows how to compare technologies and media, and presents a number of local area network examples, such as Novell's NetWare, AT&T's ISN, Apple's AppleTalk and IBM's PC Network and Token Ring.

Network users must be aware of emerging services such as videotex, teletext, electronic mail and teleconferencing in order to make the best use of these resources. Chapter 10 is concerned with these developments and the future impact of such technologies as digital transmission, digital speech, fiber optics, multiplexing and packet switching.

Chapter 1

An Introduction to Computer Systems and Networks

Computer networks are required by users involved with large or distributed databases. These applications include, but are not limited to, financial institutions, insurance companies, manufacturers, retail firms, distribution outlets, and travel reservation systems. These applications are growing, both in terms of the number of users and the quality of services expected.

The data processing requirements of many businesses require the transfer of data from one location to another. The data processing requirements among these users might differ in such areas as the utilization of computers, performance specifications, and input/output characteristics. Some of the more common data communication processing applications would include:

- Message switching by the processing and communication of messages between points or nodes using limited channel capacity links.
- File management using remote locations for the updating of a centralized file, or other file handling and processing functions from remote locations.
- Inquiry/response systems which are another form of file-oriented systems, in which a remote station makes inquiries of a centralized file but does not change that file.
- Data collection using a remote station to provide updated or current information to a centralized file system.

In the design of such a data communications system, the designer is required to integrate the following system technologies:

- Data Transmission Methods.
- Data Communications Methods.
- Network Structure.

Computer networks may be used to connect laboratory instruments, machine tools, and electronic cash registers. Peripherals such as high-speed text readers, printers, magnetic tape, and disk memories might be required in these applications. Operator input/output functions are usually achieved with a keyboard and CRT display, using wired connections or telephone lines to other locations. In these installations, the scope of the application might change due to the addition or deletion of local nodes or stations.

The larger computers that are used, for example, in insurance companies must deal with large data files holding millions of insurance policies. Magnetic disks and tapes are connected to the computer to access this data. Input/output scheduling can become a major task. In other installations, large computers might be required for high-speed computations. Speed and efficiency in arithmetic computations, beyond what is found in many microcomputers, is needed here.

The typical local microcomputer task is smaller, relatively fixed, and with less need of input/output paths or high-speed efficient arithmetic. Typical input devices include keyboards and industrial sensors. Output devices can include printers, special displays, electric motors, valves, solenoids, and actuators of various types. The local microcomputer might also need to talk to other microcomputers or larger computers, remote terminals, and other peripherals.

The newer microcomputers tend to handle a wider range of tasks. They might have a printing device and a magnetic disk memory to handle the paperwork for a small office—payroll, inventory and other activities that can change from day to day.

The distinction between microcomputers and minicomputers has been constantly changing, with some newer microcomputer overlapping minicomputer performance. This has resulted in many minicomputers approaching mainframe performance. The minicomputer originally offered a modularized approach to computing in a cost-effective package. The microcomputer has taken this approach a step further, mainly through the use of single chip microprocessors.

The continued improvements in electronic communications requires the use of integrated circuits with more and more electronic functions.

This technology has moved rapidly from the early discrete solid-state devices to Very Large Scale Integrated circuits (VLSI). Many early applications of integrated circuits were evolutionary in nature. This resulted in essentially the same type of equipment with improved performance in a lower cost or smaller size. One example is the use of LSI chips in microcomputers in the late 1970s that had essentially the same computing power as some of the larger computers of earlier years. Similar changes in linking computers together were taking place during this period in the office and factory environments, with each succeeding technology generation promising performance advantages over its predecessor. As the degree of office and factory system integration required increases, it becomes necessary to fabricate complete communications systems using techniques and products that simply did not exist before.

ADDRESS, CONTROL, AND DATA BUSSES

The transmission of data in a system of interconnected microprocessors may take place over the main data bus. The structure of these busses may differ. A single, all-purpose, bidirectional structure was common in the first microprocessors, which had fewer external pins. As the number of pin connections increased, microprocessors first used a single 8-bit-wide bus, and then two separate busses: a unidirectional bus for addresses, and a bidirectional bus for data and instruction codes. This *dual-bus* structure with a 16-bit address bus and an 8-bit data bus is standard for 8-bit microprocessors.

A variety of bus structures are used in the 16-bit microprocessors. Some use a single, 16-bit-wide shared data/address bus, while others have separate 16-bit busses for data and addresses.

Most systems communicate with the I/O devices using the bidirectional data bus. If the system has several microprocessors, each may have one or more separate I/O busses. Both serial and parallel I/O busses are used. Almost all microcomputer systems use one bus for both memory and I/O device addresses.

When the information is supplied to the bus from more than one source, *bus driver circuits* must be used to select and control the outputs from each of the sources so they will not interfere with one another. These bus drivers are necessary to:

- Ensure the compatibility between each of the source connected to the bus.
- Control the connection and disconnection of the various sources from the bus.
- Multiplex data onto the bus.

A three-state bus transceiver (bus receiver and a driver) is normally used to link the I/O device line to the bus.

Another major interface is between the microprocessor and the memory. The interface between the microprocessor bus and memory performs three basic functions:

- Ensures compatibility between the bus and the memory.
- Generates the memory address.
- Interacts with the bus-control signals to synchronize data transfer to and from the memory with the operation of the bus.

The interface is as complex as the type of memory and the structure of the bus system requires. Memory interfaces range from general-purpose interface chips to special-purpose, user-designed interfaces. Memory chips are standardized by the organization of the memory arrays into 4-bit or 8-bit words and by the function of the external connections.

A general-purpose parallel I/O interface requires at least one input register, one output register, status bits, and some type of interrupt control. A typical application requires 16 to 24 I/O lines. General-purpose interface chips, therefore, provide several channels. The *channel,* which is also called a *port,* is typically an 8-bit connection that can be used for inputs or outputs.

These chips use a data-direction register to define the port. Each bit of the data-direction register specifies whether the corresponding bit of the port will be an input or an output. A zero in the data-direction register specifies an input, while a one specifies an output. These chips multiplex the connection to the microprocessor data bus into two or three 8-bit ports, including the control lines for the I/O device, with a 40-pin package. A typical device has two ports, each with its own direction register and a status or mode register to indicate the status of each port.

The typical interface device will store the command bits issued by the microprocessor for the port. For each port, the microprocessor will specify if interrupts are to be generated, and which control signals will be used by the port. Whenever a data buffer is filled or emptied, a status bit in a control register is set or reset. To use this interface, the microprocessor executes two basic operations:

- It leads the control registers to specify the mode in which the control signals will operate.
- It loads the direction registers to specify the direction in which the lines of the ports will be used.

This is done for every port in the interface. A data transfer is then performed by a transfer instruction, such as a MOV instruction. Two problems remain to be solved: how the data is transmitted to the internal registers, and how the registers are selected.

The data transmitted by the microprocessor appears on the data bus. The data to be loaded in the various registers is placed on the data bus, and a register selection is performed. This is accomplished by providing an address on the address bus. At least one bit must be used to select the chip and allow the selection of the possible registers. In this way, the microprocessor selects one of the internal registers with the appropriate pattern on the address bus and then supplies the data bits to be transferred into one of these registers via the data bus.

CPU-MEMORY-I/O DEVICE COMMUNICATIONS

In a microcomputer system that communicates with several I/O devices, periodic status checks must be made on each device. These checks, or *pollings,* can result in time lags between the time a device indicates that it's ready to transfer the data and the actual transfer. In some systems, the time spent checking device status is reduced by using a common test line, which signals when a device requires attention. The microprocessor periodically checks the status of this line without having to poll individual devices until one of them signals for service.

The characteristics of polling are:

- Minimal hardware requirements for the interface; usually, no special lines are required.
- Synchronism with program execution. You can predict when a device will be interrogated and how long it will take to service it. No events can occur which tend to disrupt the scheduled polling sequence. By contrast, other techniques, such as interrupts and DMA, are asynchronous.

A disadvantage of polling is the software overhead. Each time that a polling loop is entered, all the devices are checked. In general, most of them will not require service. However, to guarantee that each device is checked within a specified period, the entire loop is executed, even though it might be needless. This results in a waste of processor time. On the other hand, if an interrupt system is used, after an interrupt is accepted the microprocessor must determine which device originated the interrupt—and several devices might generate interrupts simultaneously. For this reason, when multiple devices are connected to the same interrupt line, priorities must be assigned.

Once the interrupt is accepted and the device identified, the service requested by the device must be performed. The microprocessor suspends the program it was executing and branches to an interrupt handling routine, or *handler.* When the required branching address is available, the interrupt is presented to the microprocessor. This is called a *vectored interrupt.*

The execution of the interrupt handler is similar to what occurs in a polling system. Upon the termination of the handler, the program which has been suspended by the interrupt is installed again. This usually requires several instructions from the microprocessor.

When an interrupt-controlled I/O device is ready to transfer data, it may break into the main program. The simplest interrupt system has a single I/O device connected to a single interrupt-request line. A signal on this line causes the microcomputer to jump from the main program to a location in program memory called the interrupt-trap address after:

- The current instruction is executed.
- The current contents of the program counter are stored in the stack.
- The program counter is loaded with the proper program memory address.

Because only one I/O device may generate interrupts, its service routine for the data transfer is loaded into memory starting at the interrupt-trap address. After the completion of the routine, the previously stored contents of the program counter provide the return address back to the main program. Interrupts are inhibited before the service routine starts to prevent multiple interruptions by the same interrupt request.

In some systems, the instruction for the jump back to the main program also re-enables the interrupts. The interrupts are inhibited by setting a mask bit in the microprocessor. Most often, the mask bit is part of the microprocessor's status register, and may be set or reset by the program. The mask bit may be used to prevent the interruption of certain sections of program that must be executed before the next input/output operations occur.

Indirect addressing links allow the service program to be located at an arbitrary position in the program memory. If the interrupt-trap address is in a read/write memory, you can change the program entry point while the main program is going, to vary the response of the system to the interrupt.

The service interrupt and the jump to a subroutinc both cause the contents of the program counter to be saved and then restored to allow the return to the main program. The service program can modify the main program execution if it uses and modifies any registers of the microprocessor. The service program must save and restore the contents of these registers so they will be the same after the interrupt.

The more registers that are used this way, the longer the interrupt response time becomes. More rapid response is achieved by microcomputers designed to facilitate interrupts. Some have two sets of internal registers; the main program uses one set, while the service program uses the other. Other microcomputers use locations in data memory to replace some of the internal registers. A pointer inside the register defines the memory locations. The system will store and modify the contents of the pointer before executing the service program, using a workspace that differs from that used by the main program. After the service program is complete, the pointer register is restored.

The input/output operation might be required to occur at a particular instant or period within an interval. The operation of the I/O device and the execution of the program controlling the data transfer must then be synchronized in real time. To synchronize the I/O device with the program, you can connect an external pulse generator to the interrupt-request line. The program is then interrupted periodically at a known time interval between the interrupts.

Many systems can have more than one source, requiring more than one type of interrupt. These different types of interrupts include:

- External interrupts generated from one or more devices.
- Internal interrupts generated by the microcomputer system to indicate certain conditions or errors, such as power failure, system malfunctions, or transmission errors.
- Simulated interrupts generated by software for use in program debugging or interrupt testing.

The different sources of interrupts might have different service requirements. Some might require immediate attention, while others can wait until the task underway is completed. The interrupt procedure must then:

- Differentiate between these various sources.
- Determine the order in which interrupts are serviced when more than one occurs at the same time.
- Save and restore the contents of registers to assure that the program will continue following multiple interrupts.

Some systems use several interrupt-request lines, each with its own interrupt-trap address. If one source of interrupt is assigned to each line, the system can differentiate between internal, external and simulated interrupts. When several I/O devices use the same interrupt-request line, the interrupt can be recognized either by polling with software or by vectored interrupts using hardware.

Both software and hardware priority schemes can be slow to respond to a high-priority interrupt if it occurs during the servicing of a low-priority interrupt. Individual interrupt mask bits for each interrupt-request line or each I/O device are then used. By setting and resetting these individual mask bits under software control, the interrupt priorities are changed to fit the needs of the application.

Some vectored systems use the microprocessor to define and control the priorities. When an interrupt request occurs, it is transferred to the microprocessor and the address is compared with an interrupt-enabling mask. When the address is equal to or less than the mask, the request is recognized. The mask is then set to one less than the address, and servicing starts. When the address is greater than the mask, the request is simply queued.

DIRECT MEMORY ACCESS

When I/O devices must transfer large amounts of data too quickly to be controlled by the microprocessor, the transfer may be made directly between the device and the memory of the microprocessor system using *direct memory access* (DMA) (Fig. 1-1). Here the transfer is under the control of a DMA controller, which is a dedicated chip or circuit that operates independently of the microprocessor. In a DMA data transfer, the DMA controller takes over control of the microprocessor memory using one of several methods. In general, the following is true:

- An external control line can stop the microprocessor after the current instruction is completed.
- The microprocessor's memory-control signals are disabled while the DMA controller initiates the data transfer.
- As the DMA transfer is completed, the controller resets the halt line so the microprocessor can resume execution.

Processor Accesses Memory
↓
DMA Controller Interrupts Processor
↓
Processor Completes Instruction
↓
DMA Controller Completes Bus Take-over
and Signals I/O Devices to Transmit

Fig. 1-1. DMA operation.

The Cycle Stealing Technique

In the cycle stealing technique, external control lines stop the operation of the microprocessor by suspending the execution within an instruction cycle. The microprocessor clock is stopped while the memory-control lines are disabled. The controller takes over operation and steals several machine cycles to implement the data transfer. As the transfer is completed, the control lines are reset, the clock is started and the microprocessor continues execution of the instruction that had been delayed by the DMA. Microprocessors using dynamic memory usually need to restrict the number of machine cycles that can be stolen so that status conditions are not lost.

Memory Sharing

Another common DMA technique is *memory sharing,* in which the microprocessor is allowed to access the memory only at specific times during a machine cycle. Thus, the memory is available for other devices at the other times. This requires synchronizing the DMA controller with the microprocessor clock.

This type of interleaving reduces the delays in processing that can occur in cycle stealing. In a typical DMA controller chip, the acquisition of the bus for the DMA operation is done with the hold function of the microprocessor.

SYSTEM CONSIDERATIONS

In a typical system, several devices might be connected to the same interrupt line. Then, when an interrupt signal is sent to the microprocessor, it must determine which device caused the interrupt in order to execute the correct service routine.

Several methods can be used. The *software method* uses a polling program to interrogate, in the desired order, each of the devices connected to the interrupt line in order to determine which one is requesting service. The simplest form of this method uses the polling routine to read an interrupt status bit on each device to determine which one caused the interrupt. When a device is found to be requesting service, the routine branches to the appropriate service routine.

The Daisy Chain Technique

Another software-driven method which requires some additional hardware uses the daisy chain technique to identify the device. The method is based on devices connected end-to-end. After preserving the register information, the microprocessor generates an interrupt-acknowledge, which is gated to device A. If device A generated the interrupt, it places its identification code or number on the data bus where it is read by the microprocessor. If it did not generate the interrupt, it propagates the acknowledge signal to device B. Device B then carries on the procedure. This physical arrangement of devices is the daisy chain.

Hardware Methods

Hardware methods are more efficient in processing overhead. The software techniques are simple in terms of the connections required, but tend to require appreciable time from the processor, greatly increasing the overhead for implementing interrupts. The hardware schemes make use of a hardware device to automatically supply the address of the correct interrupt handling routine. This results in automatic interrupt-vectoring.

In the basic vectored interrupt system, it is the responsibility of the I/O controller to supply the interrupt and to identify the device causing the interrupt. It might even supply the branching address for the interrupt-handling routine.

When the controller only supplies the identity of the device, it then becomes the software's task to look it up in a table which holds the branch address for each device. While this allows simpler hardware, it does not achieve the fastest performance. The best performance is achieved when the microprocessor receives both the interrupt and the branch address. It can then branch to the required location in memory and start servicing the device immediately.

Another design problem is to determine which I/O device should be granted service in the event of simultaneous interrupts. Priority schemes, in their simplest form, assign a fixed priority number to each device; zero is given the highest priority, one is next, and so on down to the lowest device.

The priorities can be enforced in hardware or in software. Software enforcement of priorities requires a routine for checking the status of the devices and servicing the device with the highest priority first. Enforcing priorities using hardware can also be implemented, using interrupt controller chips. These typically supply a masking register along with the required interrupt-management logic.

SERIAL INTERFACE DESIGN

A number of computer devices are designed to accept data using a single signal and ground wire pair, using a bit-serial format. Seven bits, which represent characters or digits, are usually sent one bit at a time in synchronism with a clock signal that the device provides.

The serial port usually consists of the two single-bit serial-data busses, linked to the serial-input and serial-output lines of a shift register which is 16 bits long. The serial shift register is then loaded or read via parallel input and output lines, and shifted one bit at a time under software control. The serial port is commonly used as the asynchronous serial-data communications interface for devices such as printers. The internal shift register performs the parallel-to-serial and serial-to-parallel code conversion under program control. Typical integrated circuit chips for this task include the UART devices.

A UART (Universal Asynchronous Receiver Transmitter) converts a serial input into a parallel output; it might simultaneously convert a parallel input to serial output. These devices are normally used for low- to medium-speed applications. Their main function is the serial/parallel conversion needed for the serial data link.

On the input lines of the UART, the digital signal appears as a sequence of zeros and ones. The UART is supplied as eight parallel bits. In order for the UART to determine that there are several zeros or ones in succession, rather than one, it uses the timing from an external clock. The clock is always synchronized with the serial signal. Each pulse of the clock (one half-period) identifies the presence and the duration of a bit. Three successive clock pulses can then identify three zeros or ones in sequence in the input signal.

The receiver portion of the UART assembles 3-bit words. These are output on an 8-bit port to the data bus. The UART can also accept an 8-bit input signal from the data bus and serialize it onto an output line using the clock.

The UART has three sections: receiver, transmitter, and control section, as shown in Fig. 1-2. The receiver operates on the serial input and

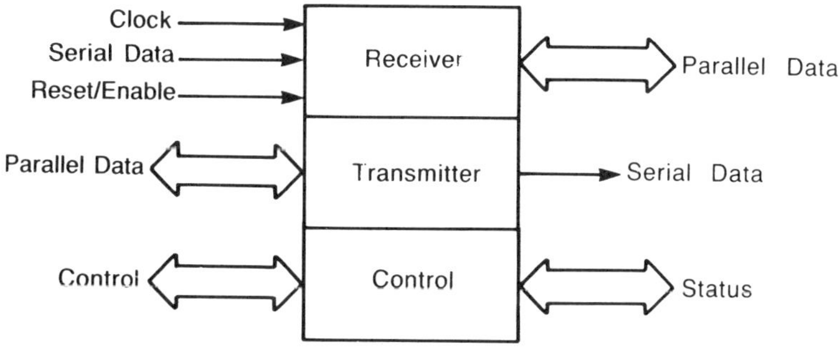

Fig. 1-2. UART structure.

supplies an 8-bit parallel output as discussed. The transmitter section receives an 8-bit parallel input and, using the clock, supplies a serial output. The control section interprets the control signals from the microprocessor and implements the required control functions. It also supplies the status and control outputs to the microprocessor.

The UART provides the designer with a number of standard functions. It can be used to manage the start and stop bits as well as verify the correct transmission of data, using parity techniques. In 8-bit serial transmission, each 8-bit character might be framed by a start bit and two stop bits. The UART may then strip the characters from its start and stop bits and retain only the 8-bit data. During transmission, it adds the required start and stop bits to the output data stream.

Parity Checking

Parity checking adds an extra bit, which is then used to verify the correct transmission of the data. The parity bit can be used to detect when a data bit has changed. The number of ones in the word is counted, and if this number is odd, and if you are using even parity, then the parity bit is zero. If the parity were odd, the parity bit would be zero. Thus, when using even parity, the total number of ones contained in the word is also even.

If any of the bits were to change during the transmission, the parity detecting circuit would reveal this. This type of detection technique is used for single-bit errors. Techniques are also available for detecting multiple-bit errors.

Because single-bit parity techniques solve most of the problems normally encountered in serial data transmission, they are often used. Most UARTs implement parity detection or generation using a control word. Most can implement odd or even parity, and the length of the word handled may be either five, six, seven, or eight bits. The stop bits may be one, two, or sometimes one and one-half.

BUS STRUCTURES

In this chapter, the basic schemes and hardware available for handling simple input/output communications have been examined. The combinations of communications lines that tie the computer network together determine the *bus structure.*

The basic structure of the computer network depends on the arrangement of signal lines that the system elements use to communicate with one another. This, in turn, determines how the various devices will interface with each other.

The most fundamental bus structure links each device in the system to the processor using unique signal lines. This type of structure is simple to implement, but quickly becomes expensive because of the number of connections required.

Most computer systems use some form of *multiplexed structure* in order to reduce the total number of connections. There are two types of multiplexed bus structures which are based on the shared bus concept. These are the daisy chain and the party line structures.

The daisy chain structure passes data through each system element until it arrives at the correct device, as discussed earlier in this chapter. Each device acts as both a source and acceptor on the bus.

In the party line structure, each device is connected to a single bus through triple-state buffers. The bus may be undirectional, but more often a bidirectional bus is used, so data can pass both ways among the various sources and acceptors. Most computers use the bidirectional party line structure for the main data bus, but the number and structure of the busses differs. A single, all purpose, bidirectional structure was used in the first microprocessor.

Most microprocessors, in the early days of computing, used a single 8-bit-wide bus that evolved into two separate busses: a unidirectional bus for the addresses, and a bidirectional bus for data and instructions. This dual-bus structure, using a 16-bit address bus and an 8-bit data bus, became the standard for 8-bit microprocessors. Several different bus structures have been used for 16-bit microprocessors. Some have used a single, 16-bit-wide shared data/address bus, but most have separate busses for data and addresses.

Most microcomputers communicate with the I/O devices through the bidirectional data bus. When the system has several microprocessors, each might have one or more separate I/O busses, while other busses are common to all. Both serial and parallel I/O busses are used. Most single microcomputer systems use a single bus for both memory and I/O device addresses.

Bus Design Considerations

Because the information is supplied to the bus from more than one source, bus-driver circuits must be used to select and control the outputs from each source so they do not interfere with each other. The bus driver functions include:

- Ensuring the compatibility among the sources connected to the bus.
- Controlling the connection and disconnection of different sources from the bus.

- Multiplexing the information onto the bus from the various sources.

A triple-state bus transceiver which functions as a receiver and driver is normally used to link the I/O device line to the bus.

Many devices operate in real time, and demand joint, asynchronous control of the data flow through the interface. Some of these devices are also electromechanical, and cannot provide the speed of response necessary to keep up with the rest of the system. In these cases, buffers or special-purpose controllers must be used.

These interfaces can contain circuits for certain functions peculiar to the particular type of device. For example, a keyboard display interface would require matrix encoding, and perhaps parity-generating, functions. A printer interface requires message formatting, character storage, and print-head control, and timing functions. The communications require serial-to-parallel/parallel-to-serial conversion, parity generation and message formatting.

The concept of the intelligent bus interface can reduce some of the costs required to implement special-purpose interfaces. The typical intelligent interface consists of a separate processor system, which uses a limited instruction set that tends to emphasize I/O control and interface operations rather than the usual type of general-purpose instructions. The interface processor system uses a bus that is compatible with the host microprocessor system. It has extensive I/O handling facilities along with data and program memories. The intelligent system interface allows the user to program the interface functions required by a particular I/O device, rather than assembling and connecting additional hardware for this task. Also, by releasing the host processor from many I/O tasks, an improvement in system performance is achieved.

Bus Standards

Bus standards define the way two subsystems are to interface. The use of a standard electrical interface tends to assure that various equipment designed by different agencies will function together in a system.

Most microprocessor bus structures are compatible with other devices in that particular microprocessor family. The characteristics of some of these microprocessor bus structures for 16-bit microprocessor units are considered here. Of particular interest are the bus contention techniques. The Intel Multibus is designed for interfacing Intel's 8080, 8085 and 8086 devices. A bus *arbiter* is used to control access to the bus, and the control scheme uses a master-slave concept. A master processor takes control of the bus, and the slave devices act upon the commands provided by the master.

An asynchronous handshaking protocol is used to allow units of various speeds to use the bus. Intelligent slave processors are allowed, which cannot control the bus, but are added to obtain more processing power. Multiple masters can exist if connected in a daisy chain or a parallel priority. The device coordination techniques used in the multiprocessor environment include:

- The bus arbiter, which determines the device that may use the bus during the next cycle.
- A bus lock signal, for the blocking of interrupts and requests by the other processors.
- Synchronization to an external event, which makes use of a WAIT instruction and the input signal.
- Bidirectional request/grant lines, which are used to share the local bus between the host and other processors using a handshaking sequence of request, grant, and release.
- A semaphore technique, used for locking devices and processes.

The Z8000 uses two major techniques for multiprocessing. A first-in-first-out (FIFO) buffer communication module is used to operate each processor as a separate system. The module passes messages through the buffers to achieve the system communications. The processors are loosely coupled and high-speed resource sharing is generally not possible.

A second technique uses two signals to achieve a daisy chain global priority. A processor examines the bus for a busy condition, and, if the bus is free, the processor places a request in the chain. The result is reported as a flag. The time used to operate this type of mechanism does not allow high-speed communications.

The multimicroprocessor environment makes use of the following techniques:

- Multiprocessor control and output instructions.
- Control signals for bus request, bus acknowledge, multimicro in, multimicro out, and segment traps.
- A bus arbitration mechanism.
- Asynchronous bus communications using the FIFO scheme.
- A semaphore technique to synchronize software processes.

In a 68000 multiprocessor environment, each processor can use a local bus along with local memory and peripherals. A global bus connects the local busses together using bus arbitration modules. The result is not a true multiprocessing system, but a connected group of microcomputer systems.

Any access involving the global bus takes longer than a local access. Access from the global bus to a local bus is done using a DMA operation. With a fixed priority system for the global bus, a processor with low priority might not get a global transaction started or completed.

Multimicroprocessor operation employs the bus arbitration modules, and signals for bus request, bus grant, and bus grant acknowledge for arbitration. This type of bus arbitration tends to be powerful, but the master/slave type of protocol used can result in system bottlenecks as the number of processor increases.

SERIAL BUS STANDARDS

There are several types of almost universally used external bus standards that allow connections of computers, peripherals, and communications equipment. These standard bus interfaces can be grouped into two major categories: serial interfaces that transmit and receive data one bit at a time, and parallel interfaces that send and receive data using groups of bits. The serial standards tend to be more general than the parallel standards, because they do not have to specify the number of bits in a word. The parallel interface standards specify a fixed word size, and words having nonstandard lengths might need to be treated using special techniques. The major advantage of parallel transmission is the higher throughput.

RS-232

A popular serial interface standard is tne RS-232C Interface for modems and data terminal equipment (DTE). RS stands for *recommended standard,* while the C indicates that this is the third version for the standard. This standard defines 20 distinct signals, as shown in Table 1-1.

The RS-232 bus standard was originally designed to interface DTEs and modems. Other equipment might not use all the signals, and not all devices will operate together without some modifications.

The standard defines 13 different combinations of the 20 signals. The simplest interface for a send/receive terminal requires at least three signals: Signal Ground (AB), Transmitted Data (BA), and Received Data (BB). The device at the other end of the transmission link might also require a Clear-to-Send (CB) signal before it can transmit the data.

Terminals that use the RS-232C standard use a 25-pin male connector (DB-25) which mates with a corresponding female connector (Fig.

Table 1-1. The Symbols for the Twenty RS-232C Interface Signals.

Symbol	RS-232C Signals
AB	Signal Ground
CE	Ring Indicator (Modem to DTE)
CD	Data Terminal Ready (DTE to Modem)
CC	Data Set Ready (Modem to DTE)
BA	Transmitted Data (DTE to Modem)
BB	Received Data (Modem to DTE)
DA	Transmitter Signal Element Timing (DTE to Modem)
DB	Transmitter Signal Element Timing (Modem to DTE)
DD	Receiver Signal Element Timing (Modem to DTE)
CA	Request to Send (DTE to Modem)
CB	Clear to Send (Modem to DTE)
CF	Received Line Signal (Modem to DTE) Detector
CG	Signal Quality Detector (Modem to DTE)
CH	Data Signal Rate Selector (DTE to Modem)
CI	Data Signal Rate Selector (Modem to DTE)
	Secondary Channel
SBA	Secondary Transmitted Data
SBB	Secondary Received Data
SCA	Secondary Request to Send
SCB	Secondary Clear to Send
SCF	Secondary Received Line Signal Detector

1-3). Because this standard was originally developed to interconnect terminal equipment and modems, when the standard is used to interconnect other kinds of equipment, such as computers, the modems used to interconnect the RS-232 devices might have the wrong connector types. Then, a null modem is required. This is a pair of identical connectors with the Transmitted Data pins wired to the Received Data pins.

Other control signals might also have to be wired to produce the proper operating conditions. A terminal that is required to recognize the

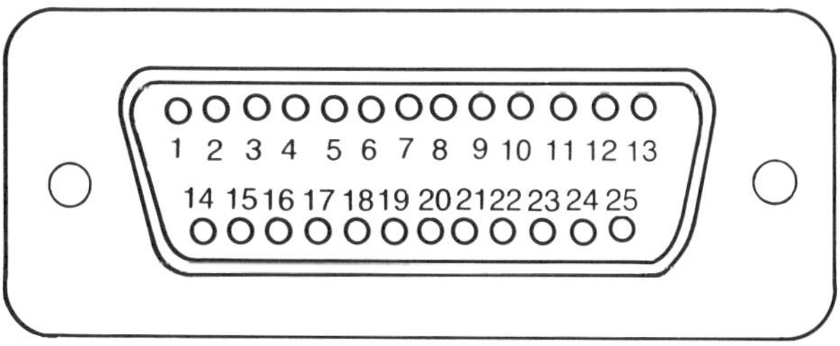

Fig. 1-3. 25-pin RS-232 connector.

Clear-to-Send (CB) signal might also produce a Request-to-Send (CA) signal. Wiring these two pins together assures that the terminal will operate with equipment that might not produce a Clear-to-Send signal.

Because the RS-232C standard does not specify the shape or spacing of the pins on the connector, a terminal could use any connector that had 25 pins, and still conform to the standard. In practice, this does not occur because most devices use the DB-25 type of connector originally used in Bell telephone modems.

The RS-232 standard has been in use for many years, and has emerged as one of the most successful standards in industry. However, its electrical specifications were defined in an earlier period of integrated circuit technology, and the logic levels might not be compatible with many recent products. Most contemporary logic uses a single positive five-volt supply, while RS-232 uses two equal voltages of opposite polarity in the 5- to 25-volt range.

RS-422-A, RS-423-A, RS-499

In an effort to resolve this incompatibility, the Electronic Industries Association (EIA) introduced two other standards, RS-422-A and RS-423-A, that use five-volt positive levels. These two standards differ only in the electrical characteristics of the interface signals; the functions remain essentially the same as those for RS-232C.

Other disadvantages of the RS-232 standard are excessive radio-frequency interference (RFI), crosstalk, and limited speed. The maximum rate of about 20,000 bits a second is insufficient in many applications. Another newer standard, RS-449, can be used for data rates to two megabits a second, and cable lengths to 200 feet, compared to 50 feet for RS-232. It also uses ten more signals compared to RS-232, as shown in Table 1-2.

This standard requires two connectors: a 37-pin unit (DB-37), used for the modem-DTE interface, and a 9-pin unit (DB-9), used as the secondary channel (Fig. 1-4). In most applications, a single DB-37 connector is used.

The RS-449 standard was designed to replace RS-232C. Equipment which conforms to the RS-449 standard requires an adapter to mate to RS-232 devices. Some interfaces might require cables with 36-, 9-, and 25-pin connectors to interconnect the various mixtures of equipment. The RS-449 standard adapter requires resistors for the logic conversion. The loopback control signals are used as shown in Fig. 1-5.

The serial interface trades efficiency for the general-purpose characteristics of an interface in which any number of bits can be transmitted

Table 1-2. The Symbols for the Thirty RS-449 Interface Signals.

Symbol	RS-449 Signals
SG	Signal Ground
SC	Send Common
RC	Receive Common
IS	Terminal in Service
IC	Incoming Call
TR	Terminal Ready
DM	Data Mode
SD	Send Data
RD	Receive Data
TT	Terminal Timing
ST	Send Timing
RT	Receive Timing
RS	Request to Send
CS	Clear to Send
RR	Receiver Ready
SQ	Signal Quality
NS	New Signal
SF	Select Frequency
SR	Signaling Rate Selector
SI	Signaling Rate Indicator
SSD	Secondary Send Data
SRD	Secondary Receive Data
SRS	Secondary Request to Send
SCS	Secondary Clear to Send
SRR	Secondary Receiver Ready
LL	Local Loopback
RL	Remote Loopback
TM	Test Mode
SS	Select Standby
SB	Standby Indicator

in any order in either the synchronous or asynchronous mode. A major reason for using RS-232 has been the wide range of equipment that can be connected using this interface. Many computers have an RS-232 compatible I/O port, and almost all data terminal equipment uses RS-232 interfaces. They are also common in tape drives, and other low-speed peripherals such as printers. Because overall peripheral compatibility is often a major consideration, the flexibility afforded by RS-232 results in its current widespread popularity.

THE 488 PARALLEL BUS

Parallel transmission through the device interface overcomes the low throughput of serial transmission. One widely used parallel standard is alternately known as the General Purpose Interface Bus (GPIB), the Hewlett-Packard Interface Bus (HP-IB-1972), the IEEE-488 Bus (IEEE

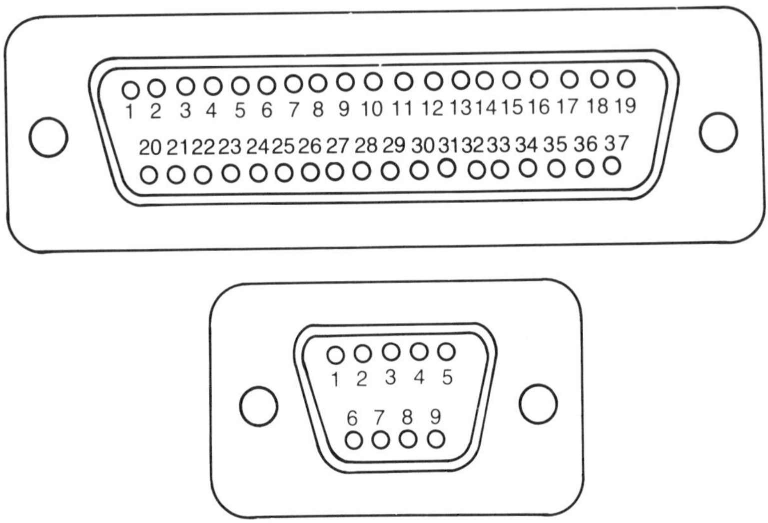

Fig. 1-4. 37-pin and 9-pin RS-449 connectors.

Standard 488-1975), or the ANSI bus (ANSI MC1-1975). This standard was originally developed by Hewlett-Packard in 1972 for interfacing some of the first programmable electronic test equipment. It was later adopted by both the IEEE and the American National Standards Institute (ANSI) in 1975 and revised by the IEEE in 1978.

This standard is useful as the physical layer for test-equipment connections, and there are many bus-compatible devices, including computer

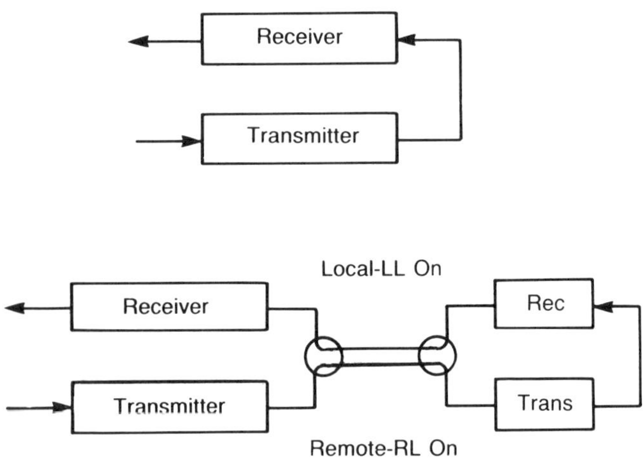

Fig. 1-5. RS-449 loopback tests.

Table 1-3. The IEEE-488 Bus and Its Interface Signals.

Data Interface Management Bus	Data Byte Transfer Control	Data Bus 8 Lines EI01-DI08
IFC—Interface Clear ATN—Attention SRQ—Service Request REN—Remote Enable EOI—End-Or Identify	DAV—Data Valid NRFD—Not Ready for Data NDAC—Data Not Accepted	

peripherals. The 488 bus supports data transfer rates to one megabyte. The 24-pin cable has eight parallel data lines (that use an asynchronous bit-parallel byte-serial format) and eight control lines, as shown in Table 1-3. Devices that interface to the bus use a male plug (Fig. 1-6). The cables use both male and female plugs at each end, which allow multiple devices to be connected in a daisy chain. Up to 15 devices can share the bus. Devices are allowed to talk, transmit data, listen, receive data, and/or control the bus.

Devices can be separated by up to 20 meters, but for maximum speed, cable lengths should be one meter or less for each device connected to the bus.

Every device on the bus is assigned a control address. A listener can respond only to the messages addressed to it. Control devices might force a talker to send data to the desired listener by issuing the proper address.

The 488 bus has a number of advantages over a serial interface such as RS-232. It is faster and more efficient, with the data being transferred eight bits at once. The eight-bit bus is also compatible with many microprocessors and has a greater channel capacity. A single 488 channel can accommodate as many as 14 devices.

Many products, however, have not adopted the 488 bus. This is partly due to the apparent complexity of the required control sequences. The

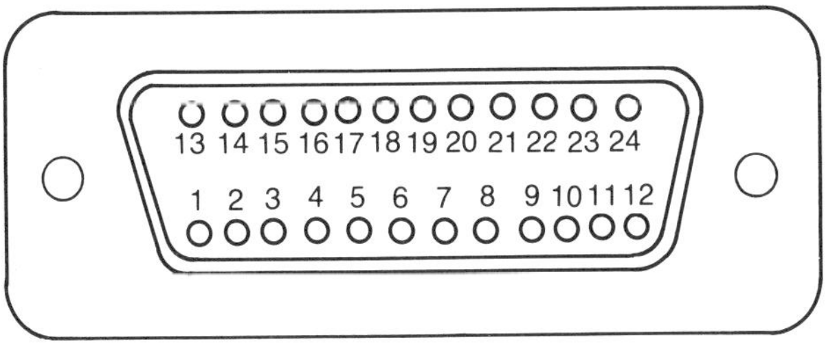

Fig. 1-6. IEEE-488 24-pin connector.

sequential control patterns were costly to implement in the past, and the availability and lower cost of the one-chip universal asynchronous receiver transmitters (UARTs) forced the adoption of the RS-232 type of serial interfaces in many products. Since this time, many products that facilitate the use of the IEEE bus have appeared, including single chip ICs like the 68488 that contain most of the circuits needed to interface to the 488 bus. The only additional circuits required are the bus transceivers.

IEEE-488 bus controllers are also available that relieve the computer from many of the detailed transactions required to transfer blocks of data using the 488 bus.

REVIEW EXERCISES

1. Supplying an input or output facility requires, at the minimum, a latch. Discuss how it is usually economical to provide bidirectional facilities using an I/O interface chip like a PIO. Describe a typical system design in which PIOs or UARTs are connected to the microprocessor busses.

2. Discuss device connection to the data bus and the connection to the address bus for the chip and register select inputs.

3. Describe the essential operation of the three input/output scheduling techniques and the interface devices that are used to provide the required input/output facilities.

4. Why are interrupts used to obtain a faster response time from the microprocessor system when it is required to service I/O devices? Discuss two problems that might occur.

5. Discuss the three basic functions required between a microprocessor and memory.

6. An interface device has two sets of four internal registers; three pins are provided for internal register selection. Show how these signals may be used to select one of the registers if they are connected to the address bus. Design an address decoder that will select the internal registers to be read or written into. The register sets include an input latch, output latch, direction register, and status register.

7. What are the main characteristics of the polling technique?

8. Discuss three basic general-purpose I/O interfaces.

9. A nonprogrammable hardware interface performs the basic bus-interface functions and includes interrupt-request control logic. Discuss how it operates as a parallel I/O port.

10. A hardware programmable interface includes decoding logic, addressable parallel I/O ports and interrupt-control logic. Discuss how ex-

ternal wiring can be used to determine the address, data direction, and width of each port, and control the operations.

11. A general-purpose interface is software-programmable. The software determines how the interface is structured, and operates from the contents of a control register, loaded by the program. The interface also includes a data-direction register, which allows the function of individual I/O lines to be selected by software. Show how this may be accomplished.

12. What are the advantages and disadvantages of a pure serial interface?

13. What is the main use of the RS-232 and 488 busses in LANs?

14. What is the advantage of using a 488 bus controller?

Chapter 2

Data Communications

Data transmission technology provides the means for transmitting signals. In telephone communications, there are various grades of line, such as low-speed voice or broadband, and various types of line, such as private, switched, or WATS. There are also a number of alternatives to telephone communications, including microwave or satellite transmission.

Data communication uses about one-third of the public telephone network, and this percentage is growing. The rate of growth of data communications is affected by a number of factors, including:

- Communications costs.
- The number of systems and procedures available.
- Alternative transmission technologies.
- Regulatory and competitive factors, which have changed rapidly in recent years as a result of massive changes in the structure of the telephone industry.

Two basic types of data communications are direct data transmission and concentrated data transmission. Direct data transmission uses a single line, or *channel,* for the transmission of data. This system is the simplest to implement, and is suitable for handling a predetermined volume of messages. If more than one user requires the communications line, then some form of multiplexing must be used. This includes the various techniques of frequency-division-multiplexing (FDM) and time-division-multiplexing (TDM).

Concentrated data transmission makes use of the store-and-forward concept for the handling of messages. Techniques include message switching and packet switching.

In message switching, a message is accumulated in a register or other storage device until a complete message has been assembled. It is then transmitted to the proper destination when a data channel is available. Message switching thus differs from channel switching, in which no accumulation or storage takes place. In channel switching, if a line or data link is not available, the service request is repeated.

Packet switching depends on the formation of messages into a *packet,* or group with a predetermined length. The communication processor plays a major role in packet data communications. Some of the functions required are:

- Scheduling.
- Data compression.
- Polling.
- Buffering.
- Data link control.
- Code conversion.
- Formatting.

Some of these have been introduced in Chapter 1. Many of these functions can be performed by software routines, but dedicated techniques are more efficient and cost effective for many applications.

Microcomputers may be used to perform many of the utility functions in a data communication system. These include protocol handling, error code generating and checking, packet and message formation, receiver/transmitter control, synchronization, and automatic repeat request (ARQ) or forward error correction (FEC). Microcomputer software can also be used to provide multiple access control in time-division, frequency-division, space-division, and code-division systems.

PACKET COMMUNICATIONS

In a packet communication system, data communication is based on the transmission of message packets. The two basic forms of packet communications are packet switching and packet broadcasting.

In *packet switching,* short bursts of data are sent through the communication network to the destination. These groups of packets are tagged with a destination address, and switched through the network nodes until the proper destination is reached.

Packet broadcasting requires the simultaneous transmission of a packet to several remote stations. Each station uses decoding circuits, which decode each incoming packet to determine if it is addressed to that station. Packet broadcasting can act as a radio broadcasting communication system, and can be implemented with satellite transmission networks.

Wide area data communications links are commonly established using either a public dial network or private circuits leased from one of the available carriers. Neither of these carrier selections actually uses a true wire connection when long distances are involved. The long-haul components of these networks involve microwave satellite, high-speed coaxial, and other trunk technologies. Most of these trunk portions of the link are immune to interference. Copper wire is used at the ends of the links, and this is where most of the data interference problems occur.

Satellite transmission has several advantages. The communication costs are independent of the transmission distance. The data transmission employs broadcasting techniques rather than switching techniques. Data rates to 30 megabits per second can be realized. A disadvantage is the time delay as the signal is transmitted.

Packet broadcasting may also be implemented on wire channels, then the system can use both ground-based broadcasting and satellite-based channels. Data is transmitted to the satellite from the earth station in bursts, and a repeater on the satellite receives the transmissions and broadcasts them over an area of the earth's surface. The ground stations in this area intercept the broadcasts, decode the address information, and select the packets labeled for their destination.

Typically, a microcomputer is implemented in a packet-switched data communication network as the data link interface processor. The basic functional structure is shown in Fig. 2-1.

The communication processor links the transmission lines with the buffer memory, which is connected to the master or host processor. The microcomputer may use one or more data strobes to transfer data onto the data link. A data transfer acknowledge (DTACK) is used to indicate that a transfer is complete. An address strobe signal indicates that a valid address is on the data link and an enable clock is used to synchronize data transfers. A valid peripherals address signal may be used to indicate that a destination is being addressed.

In a packet bus system, the destination nodes request and receive information in discrete units of packets. This allows a complete task to be requested. The bus is released and free while the task is assembled for transfer in the packet format.

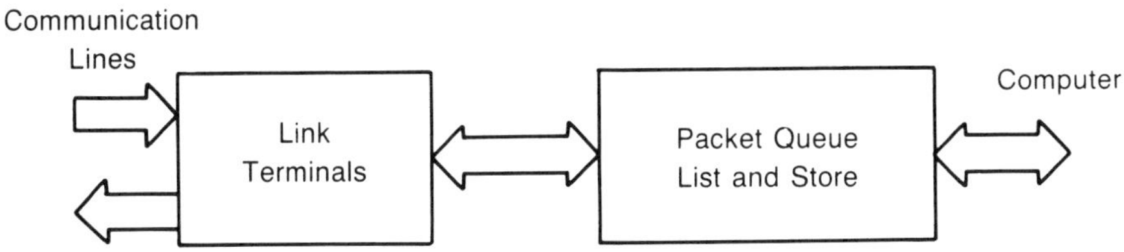

Fig. 2-1. Data link processor.

The data link interface might require the following operations:

- Serial/parallel conversion.
- Error checking, such as arithmetic check sums and cyclic redundancy checks.
- Encoding the header and frame information on outgoing data and decoding the header and frame information from incoming data.
- Assembling the data into packets.
- Handling the link and synchronization control requirements.

The processor performs the packet handling functions based on a protocol flowchart. From the information given in the flowchart, the system designer codes the software programs to perform the desired operations. The programs can then be stored in ROMs to be called by system control or user commands.

COMMUNICATIONS SYSTEMS

Before considering the design of a typical communications link processor, a discussion of communications in general terms will be beneficial, starting with the telephone switching systems.

An important area of computer networks uses switched telephone networks. This application of data communications is growing, and reaches every facet of our lives.

A telephone switching system provides the communication links between lines in response to subscriber requests. These systems can range in size from the private automated branch exchange (PABX) with under 100 lines, to the central office or tandem system, with tens of thousands of lines.

In a central office switching system, the main elements of the system are the switching network and the processor. The switching network allows for selectively interconnecting the two-wire paths by internal junction circuits. The interconnections provide the path between a subscriber station and a trunk that connects to other central offices.

The requirements in the telephone switching system include the peripheral and administrative functions. Microcomputers are often used to implement the special call facilities of the system and to control administrative routines. These are the routines that periodically perform the diagnostic checking throughout the system in an attempt to determine the presence of malfunctions.

The central processor acts as the centralized data processing facility which implements the various telephone, maintenance, and administrative functions of a telephone switching system. The central processor can be divided into five sections:

1. The control system, which acts as the main processor.
2. Program memory.
3. Call memory.
4. The signal processor or auxiliary processor.
5. The signal processor call memory.

The control system has three main functions: data processing, input and output communications, and maintenance. It usually has two independent sections for reliability. These independent sections are configured to perform all of the system functions. In the normal operating mode, both sections carry on the same functions on the basis of duplicated information. This is known as the *in-step mode.* Only one of the two independent sections can alter the system status or control the execution of telephone functions at a given instant. The two independent sections provide the control and maintenance information to the rest of the system on a mutually exclusive basis.

The control system performs data processing functions in accordance with the program stored in the memory. In response to the program, the control system processes data obtained from the call memory, and generates and transmits signals for the control of the other system units. The call memory is a word-organized random-access memory in which the more volatile system information is stored. The information is written into or read from the call memory by the control system.

Because information in the call memory is changed at the normal system operating speed, the more volatile system information is stored here. This information can include:

- Call signaling requirements.
- Information involving changes in the directory or line equipment numbers.
- Changes in subscriber classification.

- System administration.
- Subscriber and trunk busy/idle data.
- Network path busy/idle data.
- System work lists and queues.

The signal processor implements the repetitious input and output system operations which, if performed by the control system, would limit the call-handling capacity of the overall communications system. Although the signal processor is independent, it is still subject to the commands of the control system. It communicates to the control system the information necessary to perform the data processing required for the call processing and system maintenance functions.

The call memory of the signal processor is a word-organized random-access memory. The program for controlling the signal processor and the data upon which the processor operates are stored here.

Each signal processor network in the system is associated with a separate call memory system. If more than one signal processor network is used in the system, a corresponding number of call memory systems are also used. The type of information stored in the signal processor call memory usually includes the control program for the signal processor, which is used when the signal processor system is not under the commands of the control system, and the data generated and used by the signal processor system for its own programmed operations.

The information stored in the call memory tends to be a mixture of instruction words and data words. The typical types of data stored are:

- Information relating to calls, such as the supervisory changes of state information, which is received from the switching network and administrative circuits of the switching system.
- Information relating to calls received from the central control system for processing by the signal processor system.
- System work lists and queues.

Microcomputers can be used at various points in the system to perform specific processing functions that might have been previously performed by a central processor on a periodic basis, including all of the testing, supervisory, and administrative routines.

Several different bus and cable systems can provide the communication paths for transmitting the control signals and information between the various elements of the control system and between the control system and other sections of the switching system. The bus system normally uses two duplicate busses, which are called bus zero and bus one. Each of these uses a number of pairs of conductors that can be transformer-coupled between the sources and destinations. The data is transmitted over a bus in parallel.

Multiconductor cables provide the bidirectional communications paths between the different sections of the central processor and the other parts of the switching system. The conductor pairs of the cables may be either transformer-coupled or directly connected.

These considerations reflect a bottom-up synthesis approach, which can lead to problems in the design at both the hardware and software levels. The goals of the communications system must meet the user needs, and they must be specified before centralization or decentralization of functions can be made. After the overall system design has been specified, other issues relating to the operational specifications can be considered, including the following categories for communications functions:

- The physical communication means (direct wire, telephone link, microwave and fiber-optics).
- The protocols for reliability, error checking and security.
- The rates compatible with the system devices.

The user interface in these systems can provide a wide range of capabilities, including active reports, logs, alarms, and interactive message communications, and a database for analysis and record-keeping.

COMMUNICATIONS PROCESSING

Consider a typical communications processor, in which digital speech encoding is often an important part of the facilities in the switched telephone network. The digital transmission of communications data can require a basic processing configuration, as shown in Fig. 2-2. The computer acts as an interface processor.

A typical communications processor might have its circuit elements distributed on several printed circuit boards (PCBs). These could be mounted in a common chassis, housed within a cabinet or EMI enclosure. The control PCB might be located directly on an operator control panel. Another physical configuration would separate the boards as required by the particular application or facility. These circuits provide the communications functions discussed below.

A bus driver provides the output buffers for the data, control, and address signals to the external devices. It also provides priority-seek logic to permit orderly handling of service requests from individual line

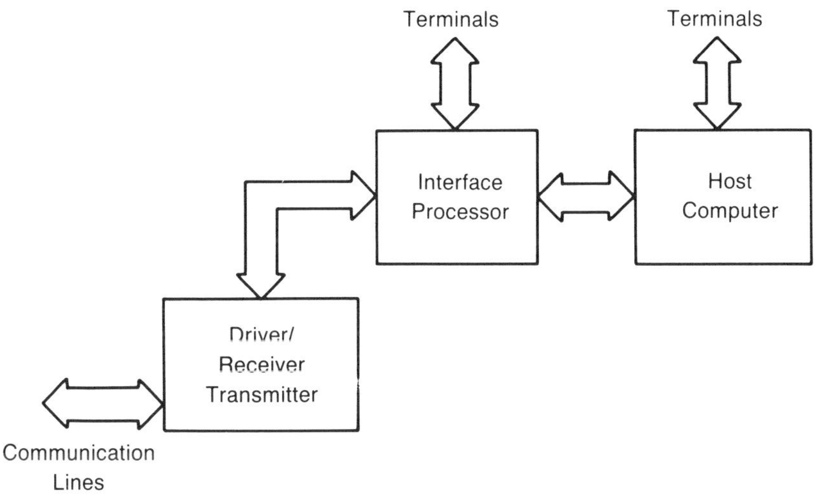

Fig. 2-2. Basic communication processor.

adaptors, as well as the timing, control, and command decode signals required to interrogate each line adaptor. A crystal-controlled clock provides the required asynchronous bit rates.

An interface board provides the communication ports, which might be independently programmable, in format, parity, mode (asynchronous/synchronous), and clock rate. The controller might be a general-purpose microcomputer which uses its control programs to execute control tasks, including a number of predetermined operations on the interface data.

The control panel functions are often similar to those shown in Fig. 2-3. Here, the signals are received and transmitted in an asynchronous mode over the port.

Within the asynchronous data stream, each character of data is transported in a binary bit "frame." This frame has a start bit to signal

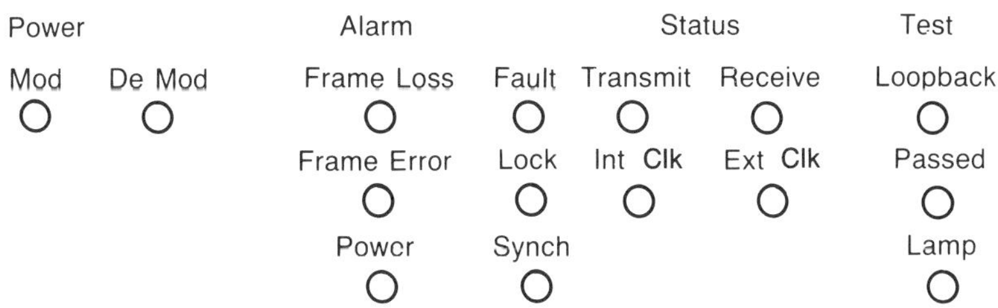

Fig. 2-3. Typical communications control panel.

the beginning of the frame (or character), a stop bit to signal the end of the frame, five to eight data bits to encode the character in binary, and an optional parity bit that encodes the count of zeros and ones for error detection.

The start bit tells the receiving device to begin looking for ones and zeros. The start bit is always preceded by a low voltage signal on the data line (mark) which delineates the beginning of a start bit. The stop bits signal the end of a frame. Stop bits follow the parity bit, and may be one to two bits in length. The slower the speed of transmission, the more stop bits required for end-of-frame recognition.

Embedded in the heart of every character frame are the data bits. The collective binary value of the data bits corresponds to a value assigned to an ASCII character. Another code, such as EBCDIC or Baudot, would be handled in the same fashion, with different binary values corresponding to different characters. When a message switch is activated, a corresponding indication on the panel or display might begin blinking until specific operational conditions occur.

If a device is in the slave computer mode, then the master computer must enable the activation. A signal will then be sent back to the master computer to notify it that a specific device has been activated and enabled.

Many asynchronous systems append a parity bit following the data bits, for error detection. Parity bits trap errors in the following manner: when the transmitting device frames a character, it counts either the number of zeros or ones in the data bits, and appends a parity bit that corresponds to whether the count in the data bits was even or odd. The receiving end also counts the data bits (zeros or ones) as it receives them, and compares the computation to the parity bit. If an error is detected, a flag can be set and retransmission may be requested.

The transmitter structure tends to be similar to that shown in Fig. 2-4. The transmitter converts the parallel data from the decoded inputs into a serial word which contains the start, parity, and stop bits. A holding register is used for the input of data, and, when the transmitter register is empty, the data is transferred for output after all of the selected conditions have been satisfied. The selected conditions and reset line are monitored by the receiver for compatible transmit/receive operation. When a control switch is activated, the switch input is decoded, and this data is used to load the transmitter-holding register.

When an asynchronous communications interface adapter (ACIA) is used, there is also a control register and a status register, which hold information about the status of the transmissions. This information is then read by the processor. There can also be an interrupt signal, which interrupts the microprocessor.

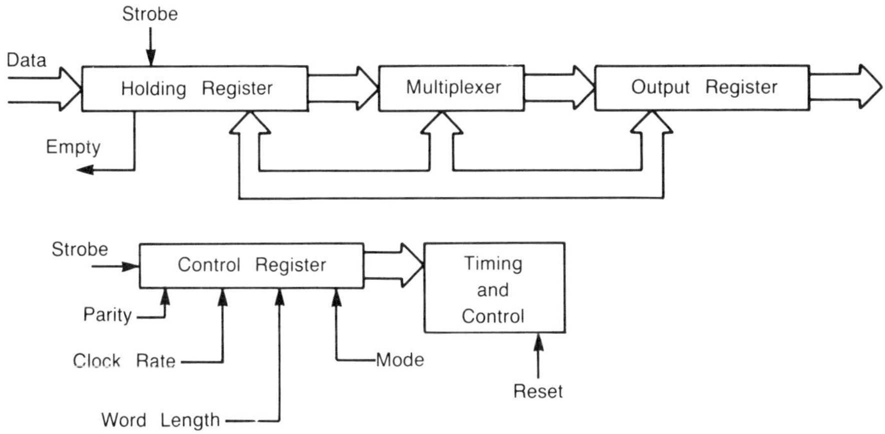

Fig. 2-4. Typical transmitter structure.

When the microprocessor reads the status register, it does so by selecting the chip and setting the register select lines into the chip. It is usually looking for either a message that the transmit-data register is empty and needs another byte from the microprocessor, or that the receive register is full and has a byte that the microprocessor can read. The messages are bits in the status register. The right-most bit (bit zero) might be labeled "Receive-Data Register Full," and bit one labeled "Transmit-Data Register Empty."

In the case where the microprocessor has to send three bytes of information to the ACIA, it would send the first byte, then keep checking the status register until the Transmit-Data Register Empty bit becomes one, indicating that the first byte has been transferred to the transmit-shift register, and the second byte can now be sent to the transmit-data register. A loop might be used that continually reads the status register in the ACIA until it comes back with the empty message.

Two other signals, called Request-to-Send (from the ACIA to the device) and Clear-to-Send (from the device to the ACIA) may also be used. The ACIA monitors these signals, and will not attempt to send bits unless it knows that the device on the other end is ready.

The ACIA also checks for certain error conditions. If the data being received has a parity bit with each byte, the ACIA can check if one of the bits in the byte was lost. The ACIA can also add parity bits to outgoing bytes. The sum can be even or odd parity, and the number of bits per byte can be selected to be seven or eight.

Either one or two stop bits comes with the byte that the ACIA transmits or expects to receive. These are at the end of the byte, and are selected by the bits sent to the control register. The bits in the control register are also used for enabling or disabling interrupts from the ACIA to the microprocessor when the Transmit Data Register Empty condition occurs, and for the operation of the Request-to-Send signal to the device on the other end. You can also set the ACIA to expect a data bit, when receiving, every time a clock pulse arrives from the device. In any case, the start bit is set and the data is transferred to a transmit register where it can be sent over the transmitter output line. Loading the transmit register empties the holding register to allow a new word to be decoded and loaded for transmission.

A typical receiver structure is shown in Fig. 2-5. The receiver converts a serial word with start, data, parity, and stop bits into parallel data while checking parity with the transmitter. Proper code transmission is verified by a parity check and the receipt of a valid stop bit. Word length select and reset lines may also be used to coordinate the transmit/receive operation.

When a character is ready to be received by the receiver section, the data stream* is monitored for a valid start bit. Then, the receiver register is loaded and assembly begins by sampling the center of each successive data bit of the character. The parity is checked, and, if it is wrong, the character is ignored and a transmit-error bit is sent. If the parity is correct, then the receiver section monitors for a valid stop bit. The character may then be loaded into a holding register where the address is decoded.

Parity checks might not provide enough security in some applications, because noise or extraneous bits can be interpreted incorrectly as single parity bits. Although the probability of this occurring might appear to be low, in some applications the risk associated with its affects are sufficient to require the use of other methods of error checking.

In this section, the specific operations of a typical communications processor have been discussed. Because many practical applications of this nature are rooted in large systems of communication nodes and links, this discussion also pertains to the various requirements for a large number of LAN applications.

---

*Computer data streams are simply sequences of electrical highs and lows, (ones and zeros), but the ability to differentiate ones and zeros allows us to code virtually anything. A simple eight-bit sequence of ones and zeros can produce any number from zero to 255. These binary values are set to a corresponding character set. The character set includes all of the letters and numbers, punctuation, and control characters. As a result, every time a computer receives a binary value, it interprets it as a character.

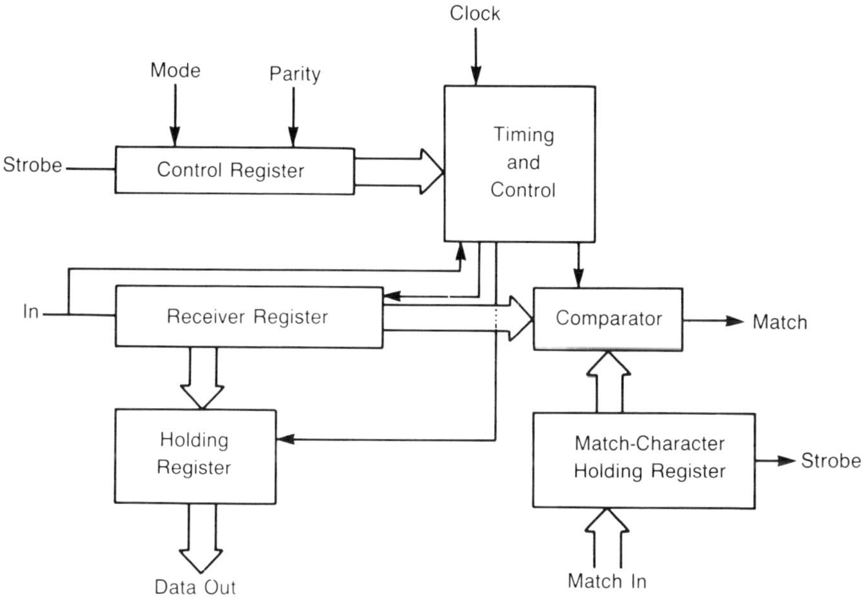

Fig. 2-5. Typical receiver structure.

HOST/SLAVE MODES

In the *slave mode,* the communications processor manages the interface between the master computer input/output messages and the network ports, which can consist of synchronous receive/transmit line pairs. The processor is controlled by commands from the master computer. However, certain control functions may override master computer directives. Some of these may become operations only if enabled by the master computer (Fig. 2-6). Line-status and problem notices are usually returned to the master computer. Figure 2-7 shows the basic data paths of the slave mode. The message transfer is between the master computer buffers and communications ports.

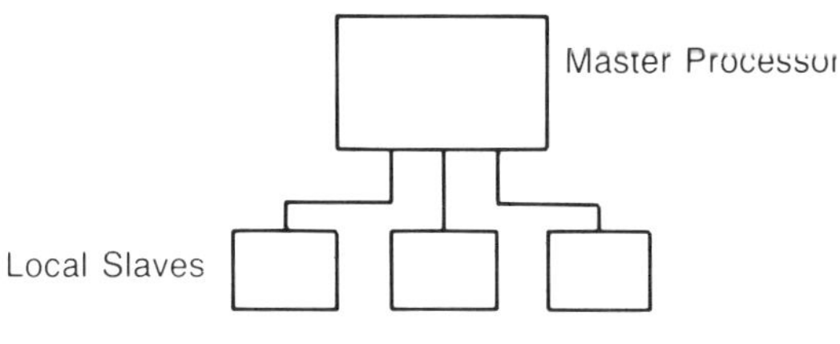

Fig. 2-6. Hierarchical architecture.

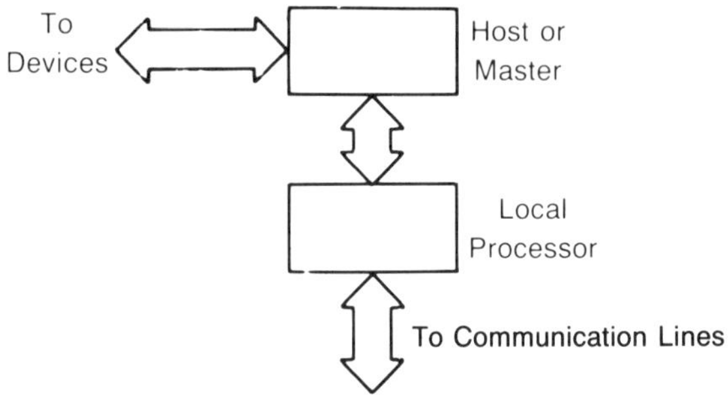

Fig. 2-7. Slave mode communications paths.

The processor memory may use a direct memory access (DMA) to the computer. This DMA function can be used to fetch command packets, store response and problem notification packets, and transfer message data to and from the master computer. External devices may interrupt the master computer after placing responses in the master computer memory, at the completion of buffer transfers, and at other strategic times in the processing. A software program is used to initialize the interface ports with the appropriate clock modes, character widths, and other parameters. The external device prepares a status register which is read by the master computer during the interrupt.

In the *host processing mode,* the processor manages the interface between the external devices and the network receive/transmit lines. The devices are controlled through the operation of the host processor. Figure 2-8 shows the data paths used in this processing mode. Message transfer is between the external devices and the ports. The receive and transmit baud rates can be selected by the user. The processor will detect alarm signals from the external output device and take the appropriate action. Communications to and from the external devices is usually in

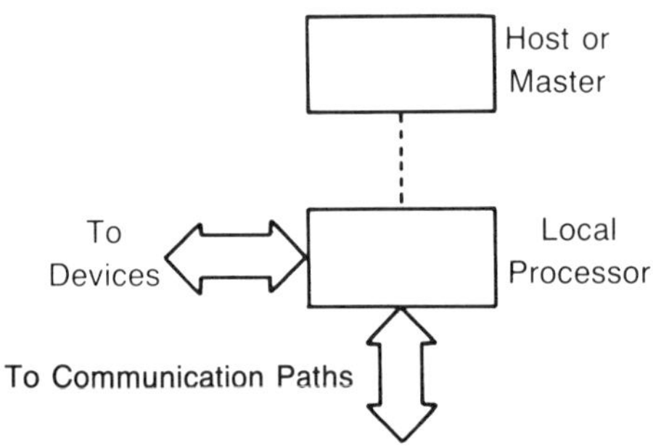

Fig. 2-8. Host mode communication paths.

ASCII code. The transmission code and character width are the same for receive and transmit, and may be selected by the user.

In the host mode, system status and problem conditions are indicated using control panel lamps or a CRT screen. A switch is typically used to select the desired mode of operation, and it is sensed only after a device RESET. If the slave mode is sensed, processing is stopped until a RELEASE command is issued by the master computer. A switch might also be provided for a SELF TEST facility in the host processing mode. This switch is also sensed only after a device RESET occurs. It places the selected port in a loop condition, allowing the data received from an input device to be transmitted to an output device.

A RESET sets all programmed functional settings to zero, and forces the switch settings to be used in the slave mode or host processing mode. An interrupt is generated in the slave mode to indicate that a reset has occurred.

The following indicators may be used to indicate problems:

- INVALID MESSAGE.
- INVALID SELECTION.
- PARITY ERROR.
- INPUT ERROR.

Switches might be provided for either bit-step clocking with one clock pulse per bit, or character-step clocking, with one clock pulse per character. You can also select the character size and transmission code used. Incoming data from the ports is converted from the code selected. The bit rates for the transmit and receive functions can be selected, as can the parity for the transmit and receive lines.

ERROR CHECKING

One critical aspect of communication system design is speed. For example, the amount of time and storage requirements for an error checking test like the cyclic redundancy check calculation is relatively high because of the great number of operations required per character. Processing time requirements can place a constraint on the transmission speeds which can be used. Table 2-1 indicates the difference in processor time and storage requirements for this type of error checking operation, compared to a simple arithmetic checksum test.

When a simple arithmetic checksum is not adequate, you can use either vertical or longitudinal redundancy checking, which involves adding a bit or block to the message rather than computing the polynomials

Table 2-1. A Comparison of Processor Time and Storage Requirements for Error-Checking Techniques.

	Maximum processing time per character (relative)	Program storage requirement (bytes)
	Typical Input Operation	
Arithmetic Checksum Test	0.45T	440
Cyclic Redundancy Check	1.10T	530
	Typical Output Operation	
Arithmetic Checksum Test	0.28T	270
Cyclic Redundancy Check	1.40T	350

required for the cyclic redundancy check. The system might use a diagnostic mode, in which the program executes diagnostic tests to isolate hardware faults. These tests might operate only under master computer control.

Protocol

The program will also manage the protocol. During a message transmission, this includes the insertion of the appropriate block frame control characters. During a message reception, this includes the deletion of block frame control characters.

Normally, the protocol used defines the error checking method. A packet protocol can be checksummed by the transmitter or receiver. The packets can be numbered in sequence and checked for an out-of-order packet because they can be encoded to allow the detection and correction of errors. The actual implementation of an error scheme should be based on the type of service to be offered, the allowable system delays, and the bandwidth characteristics of the actual circuits involved.

A basic packet protocol requires that a SYNC flag be checked. If it is not, then a synchronization routine is entered to synchronize the operation. A receive flag is checked next. The packet-receive flag is set as a start-of-text character is received, and remains set while the message is received. As each character in the message is processed, the receive flag is set, while the end-text flag is not set. This indicates that the characters being received are part of the message.

Some checking schemes use a transparent idle flag, which is a specific bit sequence that can occur in the middle of a message as data. To avoid confusion between data and an idle protocol character, any idle bit-sequence in a message is repeated. These repeated sequences are detected and translated into the correct data that they represent. If the transparent idle flag is not set, the character count is incremented, and, if the maximum character count has not been reached, the current checksum is calculated. The checksums are updated for each character that is received, and the total checksum is compared with the transmitted check digits.

Packet techniques allow traffic to be in an asynchronous time-sharing mode on the communications lines. This allows the traffic to be concentrated on the higher speed channels. There is also the capability to route the traffic around failed channels, and to bypass congested channels.

The system discussed in these sections could be a node with several links in a network. It requires the system memories or registers to log the messages, and buffers are provided if a destination is not ready to receive a message. Each message is reassembled and checked before it is forwarded on. This allows messages with different priority levels or security classifications to receive the proper treatment. The complete system might involve a substantial amount of processing and storage.

NETWORK CONCEPTS

In the ideal distributed system, the intercommunication between the processors is reduced to a minimum. They might not always interact with each other, but they will participate in the exchange of data in word or block formats. Each processor acts as a controller to completely control a part of the process. Some of these systems might also be qualified as multiprocessor systems.

A *multiprocessor system* involves the use of more than one central processing unit in the system configuration. The advantages in a multiprocessor system include:

- Greater system efficiency and utilization of system resources.
- Increased system capabilities in responding to real-time events.
- Improved fault tolerance and a greater capability to react to malfunctions and errors.

Most systems involve a number of processors, used in the peripherals and other system components. Each of these may function as an interface device. Instructions are sent to these devices by the controlling processor. The processors residing in the peripherals and other devices essentially act as slaves.

When there is one main processor and a number of slave microprocessors, the system becomes a distributed system rather than a true multimicroprocessor system. A multimicroprocessor system refers to a system in which any number of processors may assume the role of a master. This might involve a complex interconnecting operating system to synchronize the operation of the system. The cost of developing complex operating systems, capable of synchronizing a number of processors operating simultaneously, is high. A high unreliability for the system is also implied, because there is no proof that the system will operate correctly under all circumstances. The usual philosophy is to simplify and allocate the hardware resources as needed. The recommended implementation has been to use dedicated processors wherever needed, and to synchronize their operation as loosely as possible, in order to simplify the overall system operation. This results in lower costs, greater simplicity, and improved reliability.

A range of communication techniques is available for local and distributed or wide-area system implementations. Any device that is primarily concerned with the transmission of data over a carrier, whether local or long distance, may be considered a data distribution device. Within the local category of data distribution devices are line drivers, local multiplexers, and modem eliminators. The wide-area category includes modems (both dial-up and leased line types), multiplexers and modem control device.

What follows is an outline of some of the issues in local and distributed networks. Typically, the cost-effective organization for distributed intelligence in many applications is a hierarchical architecture, as shown earlier in Fig. 2-6. The main issue in the design of such a system is the distribution of intelligence within the hierarchy for a particular application.

In some cases, it is best to centralize the decision-making and control functions within the master, or main, processor. This scheme would place the local devices under complete control of the master, with an attendant increase in the communications and computation demands at that level. For other applications, it is conceivable that complete decentralization of control functions is best. The local units would operate as independent agents, performing local control. The trade-off between centralization and decentralization of intelligence in such a system is a key issue that affects the hardware and software design. This trade-off is made from the identification of user needs and system requirements.

In a hierarchical network, each device that is connected to the bus might communicate with the others by means of a message buffer located in a common memory. When one device transmits information to another, it stores a message with the information in the common memory, or receiver. The system that is to be implemented might provide the interprocess communication in the form of message routing and process scheduling. The system could recognize three types of tasks: priority tasks, message tasks, and periodic tasks. The priority tasks are scheduled as system events. These usually include all of the input/output and real-time clock computational needs. An interrupt or a system reset are examples of events that would produce the scheduling of one of these tasks.

A significant measure of a system's power and flexibility can be attributed to the design of its bus. The bus structure must allow for the relationships between the various system devices. It must support a priority-based network. In such a configuration, each device contends for bus controls, and the devices resolve contention via a priority line. This allows an increased number of devices without incurring the timing overhead of a pure serial network. When a pure serial bus control network is used, the maximum bus transfer rate is always reduced.

Serial data transmission is characterized by transmitting one data bit at a time between two devices. The flow of the data can follow one of three transmission modes: simplex, half duplex, or full duplex. Simplex only allows data flow in one direction, half duplex allows data flow in both directions (but not both simultaneously), while full duplex allows for simultaneous two-way transmissions.

The bus would provide its own clock, which may be derived from the processor clock. The bus clock provides the basic timing reference for resolving bus contention among the multiple bus requests. This allows devices with different speeds to share resources on the same bus. The actual transfers proceed asynchronously with respect to the bus clock.

The transfer speed is a function of the transmitting and receiving devices alone. This technique prevents slower modules from being hampered in gaining control of the bus, but it does not reduce the speed at which the faster modules can transfer data via the same bus. Thus, there is no decrease in throughput.

Because the individual devices in a common bus system can be very flexible, you can either tailor each device to perform one specific function, or make them all the same and completely interchangeable. Each unit is self-contained, and becomes even more powerful because of its interconnection to other units. The system can be as powerful as you want, because you can limit or expand modules to suit the requirements. If necessary, you can dynamically reconfigure the system by changing module program, which enables the system to work around any module that is not operating properly.

Any device failure in a pure serial link cannot be corrected or overcome by the other units. This architecture should not be used in a system whose operation is critical and must be maintained at all times.

The use of a serial link is not limited only to hardwired operation between processors. A modem or radio frequency link can be used. One example is a weather-recording system that collects data on rainfall, wind speed, temperature, and the time of day. It analyzes the data, and, at a predetermined time, the information is passed to another processor via a modem. This system can collect and analyze data from several remote processors. All remotes are responsible for their own instrument control, data analysis, storage, and communication. The serial link provides a system of self-contained units which operate with one remote talking at one time.

Common-bus architecture lets the devices talk to each other on shared lines, using a common system memory. One way of sharing memory requires the use of a status word in memory. When a device wants the resource, it reads the status word to check if service is available. But if two devices want service at the same time, a problem might exist. One device can read the status, and then a second device can read it without it being changed. Both units think they have the bus. One way to solve this problem is to use a test-and-set instruction. The test-and-set employs an increment, so an available resource is not allocated twice.

If the resource is not ready and the device must wait while another device requests it, a *deadlock* might exist, where both devices wait for the key to a resource supposedly held by the other. To avoid a deadlock, the system can be programmed such that the resource can be used immediately after a request. The program can sense the inactivity of a resource, and release it on the basis of task priority. In some cases, it might be necessary to structure the entire system to minimize deadlock on the bus.

The deadlock situation can be worse in a private-bus system. It is even more complex in a common-bus system that also uses a private bus. This system takes the best features of a common bus, while minimizing the drawbacks. Each private-bus link uses its own local memory, but also has access to the system devices, as in a common-bus system.

DATABASE MANAGEMENT SYSTEMS

A distributed database management system (DBMS) offers three major advantages over a centralized system:

1. It is more reliable, because it is made up of multiple computers at multiple locations. It is not susceptible to total system failure when one computer breaks down.

2. In a distributed system, data can be stored in locations in which the data are frequently used. This allows the access to be faster, and communication costs lower.
3. A distributed system lends itself more readily to increases in database capacity. If more processing is needed to accommodate increases in database size or usage, new sites can be added to the network.

A *database management system* is a tool for storing and retrieving formatted data. The collection of stored formatted data (which is called a *database*) may be accessed by a group of users, and many of the facilities of a DBMS are designed to allow interference-free sharing of common resource. The collection of data has an internal structure (the *format*) which is known to the system, and which is used in retrieving the data. This format (which is also referred to as the *data model*) differs among the various systems.

The Relational Database

A common data model is the *relational* model. It is simple in concept, but powerful, and it has been used since about 1970. A database in the relational model is a set of relations. You can think of a relation as a table, such as shown in Table 2-2. The rows are called the *tuples* of the relation, and the columns are called *attributes.*

A fundamental operation of all database management systems is the selection of a subset of the database that meets a specified criterion. In relational systems, such criteria are usually expressed in a form called *relational calculus.* Consider a query like: "What was the home state of President Kennedy?" Using the relations of Table 2-2, this question would be expressed by the following statements:

1. Define a variable to range over the relation PRESIDENTS.

Table 2-2. Two Relations: Elections-Won and Presidents. The Columns Are Attributes and the Rows Are Tuples.

ELECTIONS-WON	YEAR	WINNER-NAME	WINNER-VOTES
	1956	Eisenhower	447
	1960	Kennedy	303
	1964	Johnson	486

PRESIDENTS	NAME	PARTY	HOME-STATE
	Eisenhower	Republican	Texas
	Kennedy	Democrat	Mass.
	Johnson	Democrat	Texas

2. Request from the HOME-STATE attribute all those tuples in which the attribute NAME equals KENNEDY.

The system will select those tuples in the range of the variable which, when tested, yield a true value. In general, these qualifications include Boolean combinations of the various conditions.

A more complicated expression is required to deal with a query such as: "In which election years was a Republican from Texas elected?" This query has the following form:

> Extract the YEAR attribute from any ELECTIONS-WON relation whose WINNER-NAME attribute matches the NAME attribute of a tuple in the PRESIDENTS relation if that tuple has a HOME-STATE of Texas and a PARTY equaling Republican.

A wide range of questions can be expressed using these types of constructions. In addition to query capabilities, relational database systems also have facilities for updating, inserting, and deleting tuples, as well as for defining the database.

Consider the means by which this functionality is achieved in a distributed system. There are various questions on issues like the following:

- Whether the distributed structure of the database is visible or invisible to users.
- The characteristics of the communication network that connects the distributed DBMS sites.
- The nature of typical distributed applications.
- The data model supported by the system.

The general system architecture of a distributed DBMS is shown in Fig. 2-9. The system consists of a collection of independent computers, each of which supports a portion of the overall database. These computers are interconnected by a communication network. Users are permitted to enter transactions at any of the computers. These transactions may reference data stored at a remote site, in which case the system accesses the data through the network.

Redundant and Nonredundant Systems

The system may or may not permit data redundancy. In a nonredundant system, the database can be partitioned among the various

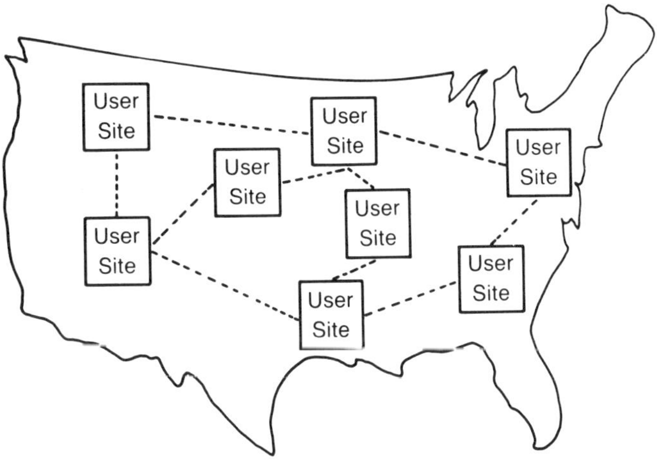

Fig. 2-9. A distributed database management system.

sites in the network, but no data item is stored at more than one site. In the redundant system, subsets of the database stored at different sites may overlap, resulting in the same data item being stored at more than one site in the network.

The use of the nonredundant approach simplifies the system design significantly. Although most implementations use this nonredundant approach, redundancy provides improvements in all of the areas which we seek to enhance through distribution. This includes reliability, because without redundant data, a failure at a particular site will cause the failure of all applications that require the data stored there, even though other nodes of the system are operational.

Access efficiency is also affected, because in a nonredundant system each data item must be stored at exactly one node. If data items are accessed frequently from geographically dispersed locations, substantial communication delays might be incurred in accessing the data. A system that includes redundancy can reduce the time of retrieval by storing the data at several sites. In some inventory applications, for example, a file might receive frequent accesses from both New York and California. If the file is stored in only one location, there will be a substantial amount of long-distance communication. In a redundant system, the file could be stored at both locations and accesses to the data would be much quicker and less costly.

The redundant-data approach also allows more flexibility in increasing the database capacity. Parts of the database that are accessed frequently can be stored at many local sites using fast storage methods, while those parts that are needed occasionally can be stored at an archival site using less expensive, slower storage methods. Additional database sites can be added to accommodate increases in database activity. In a nonredundant system, on the other hand, increases in activity of certain data could require an upgrade of the site at which that data was stored.

The Visibility of the Distribution

Another area of concern in the relational model is the visibility or invisibility of the distribution to users. In many systems, it is assumed that users who access or update data are not required to specify the location of the data or of redundant copies. In these systems, users enter queries and updates into the distributed DBMS in the same manner as in a nondistributed system.

The data distribution is kept invisible because distribution is a database design issue, and, in order to maintain data independence, users need not be aware of it. With redundant updates, invisibility is needed because the consistency of the database depends on keeping all redundant copies of data up-to-date and identical. This responsibility should not be left to the users.

DATABASE DESIGN CHARACTERISTICS

The characteristics of the computer network required vary widely, and can include:

- Ethernet-like networks, which are high-bandwidth, low-delay networks suitable for short distances.
- Packet-switched networks such as ARPANET. These have lower bandwidth and higher delay than Ethernet-like media, and are usable over much longer distances.
- Point-to-point leased circuit configurations. These networks typically support lower bandwidths than Arpanet, but incur lower delays.
- Broadcast networks, either radio broadcast networks like Aloha, or broadcast networks employing satellites.

These communication techniques cover three orders of magnitude in bandwidth, and over six orders of magnitude in delay.

There are other considerations that have a significant effect on the distributed DBMS design, including the following:

- The feasibility of propagating control information to all of the database sites in real time.

- The feasibility of posting updates to all copies of redundant data in real time.
- The trade-offs between the cost of moving data from site to site for processing complex queries, and the cost of performing the extra computations locally.

Directory Management

Directory management is another important area of database management systems. The directory, or *schema*, is used to define the database being managed. This frees the user or application program from the need to supply this information, and it simplifies the database structure. The directory typically contains the following information:

- The logical structure definition, including the names of relations and their domains.
- The physical structure definition, which includes the data field formats.
- The file statistics.
- Accounting data, including who has access to the file.

In a distributed database, an additional item of directory information—the location of each piece of the database in the network—is required. The DBMS must have access to this information in order to process user requests as it executes the accessing strategy and accounts for the resources used.

Directory management schemes can be divided into two types:

1. The nonredundant approaches, in which each directory entry is stored in only one location.
2. The redundant approaches, in which each entry may appear in several places.

The nonredundant approaches include centralized, distributed, and hybrid configurations.

In the *centralized* scheme, the complete directory is stored at one site. This requires access to the directory site for every retrieval or update. The *distributed* technique allows each site to have directory entries for the data stored at that site. Local accesses can proceed using the local directory. A request requiring access to remote data must be sent to all sites to determine which one has the required data. The *hybrid* approach partitions the network into several sections, and employs a centralized directory in each part.

In a redundant system, centralization assumes an approach which might be considered a combination of the centralized and distributed nonredundant systems. Each site has its local data, but each central site has a complete directory. The nonlocal sites may appeal to a single site to determine the location of the remote data. Using the distributed approach, each site has the complete directory stored locally. User transactions can be started without a remote reference, but directory updates must be posted to every site. Many hybrids are possible. The most typical would allow an arbitrary subset of the directory to exist at each site. This allows a large degree of flexibility, but requires a multi-layer directory to tell the system where the parts of the directory are stored.

Another consideration that determines the type of directory management scheme is the retrieval frequency. A high frequency of directory retrievals promotes both redundant directories and distribution. The directory update frequency is another factor. A high frequency discourages redundancy and encourages centralization because each change must be posted to every copy of the directory. Reliability is also a factor, tending to encourage both redundancy and distribution.

Up to this point, comments regarding directories were concerned with the issue of system access. Consideration must also be given, however, to the problems concerning the allocation of the pieces of the database to sites in the network. This is usually referred to as *file allocation,* and can be expressed as variants of the following problem:

Given: A description of user demand for service (stated as the volume of retrievals and volume of updates from each node of the network to each file) and a description of the resources available to supply this demand (stated as the network topology, link capacities and costs, and the node capacities and costs).

Determine: An assignment of files to nodes that does not violate capacity constraints and minimizes total costs.

Consider a system of two sites in which the bulk of the communication costs is incurred between the nodes that store the relations involved. A file allocation scheme which places all the relations involved in one query at a single site will be less expensive than one in which these relations are distributed.

Another problem with file allocation is the synchronization cost involved in updating redundantly stored data. This cost might dominate update costs (particularly for costs measured as delays), depending on the synchronization scheme, the mix of update traffic, and the database design.

REVIEW EXERCISES

1. Discuss the differences between message switching and packet switching.

2. Describe how a FIFO communication module runs each processor in a network as a separate system and passes messages through buffers to achieve system communications. If the processors are loosely coupled, why is high-speed resource sharing not possible?

3. A system communications technique uses two signals in a daisy-chain global priority. A process examines the bus for a busy condition. If the bus is not busy, the process places a request into the chain. The result is reported with a flag. Why does the time required to operate this mechanism rule out high-speed communications?

4. Discuss how multiprocessor operation can use the following feature:

    a. Special multiprocessor control and output instructions.
    b. Signals for bus request, bus acknowledge, and input/output and control.
    c. Bus arbitration mechanisms.
    d. Asynchronous communications using a FIFO.
    e. A semaphore to synchronize software processes.

5. In a distributed system environment, each processor uses a local bus with local memory and peripherals. A global bus connects the local busses together using bus arbitration modules. Can this be operated as a multiprocessing system? Discuss how access from the global bus to a local bus can be obtained by a DMA operation. If the priority on the global bus is fixed, what problems might be encountered by a processor with low priority?

6. Describe the operation of a typical communications serial transmitter.

7. What are the advantages in systems that use more than one central processor?

Chapter 3

Elements of Network Design

The components of a data communications network that have direct contact with the physical telecommunications transmission facilities are the modems, multiplexers, and concentrators. The circuitry, intelligence, and features that have evolved in these devices over the past several years has been revolutionary. In this chapter the basic principles of operation will be considered, along with the techniques that have allowed the use of existing transmission facilities.

THE MODEM

The term *modem* was coined from the terms MOdulator and DEModulator. These devices convert, or *modulate,* a signal into another form. For example, an analog tone is modulated for transmission, and demodulated into a digital signal at the receiving end of the transmission line or link. A device that does this is a true modem. There are other devices, such as modem eliminators and short haul modems, that do not actually perform the modulation and demodulation functions, but are still called modems because they are employed in the same way as true modems. These *null modems* and *modem eliminators* are essentially cable adaptors for connecting terminals or personal computers together using the RS-232C interface.

The rate in data symbols sent per unit of time is called the *baud rate.* The speed at which modems operate is given in bits per second (bps).

The data rate that is transmitted is given in bauds (data symbols/second). It might be equal to the bit rate, in modems operating at 1200 bps, or below it, depending on the modulation method used. The concepts of modulation have their roots in analog communications.

Modulation Methods

One of the major reasons for the widespread use of AM (amplitude modulation) is the relative ease of achieving the modulation and demodulation functions. Modulation in large commercial transmitters is performed via plate modulation. This involves controlling the plate of the output tube with the modulating signal while the carrier is injected at the grid. Smaller transmitters utilize all solid-state devices for throughput, with the similar technique of collector-modulation of the output transistor.

Detection of AM can be performed by passing the modulated waveform through a diode and then a filter to recover the audio signal. A simple AM receiver requires only a tunable antenna, diode, resistance-capacitance (RC) filter, amplifier, and transducer. The performance of such a simple receiver can vary widely, depending on signal conditions.

Most commercial receivers employ the superheterodyne principle for improved sensitivity, selectivity, and fidelity. This involves shifting the received radio frequency signal down to an intermediate frequency, and performing all recovery operations in this mode.

Frequency modulation (FM) provides a means of achieving improved discrimination against noise and interference. Improved performance is gained, however, at the expense of increased bandwidth and circuit complexity. Modulation of FM can be achieved by either direct or indirect methods. Indirect methods require the modulating signal to be integrated and then used to phase-modulate the carrier. Direct methods employ a carrier oscillator which is directly controlled by the modulating frequency. Monaural audio frequencies occupy the zero to 15 kHz band; these are modulated by the exciter and amplified by the transmitter.

FM stereo broadcasting utilizes multiplexing techniques to achieve channel separation via a single FM carrier. In the matrix method, the sum and difference frequencies are obtained by an analog summing and phase-shift network; the difference frequency is amplitude modulated at 38 kHz with a balanced modulator, which produces upper and lower sidebands. A pilot signal is added to allow detection of stereo broadcasting. The detection of FM stereo can also be accomplished by either matrix or time-division multiplex (TDM) methods.

Pulse amplitude modulation (PAM) is basically the same as a sampled data system. The sampling switch is usually an analog switch or analog multiplexer. Analog inputs are switched into a common transmission line by a time-sequence generator. One switch channel might be used to transmit the clock signal for synchronization during demultiplexing. The demultiplexing circuit is functionally equivalent to the multiplexing circuit, with all operations performed in reverse.

Pulse duration modulation (PDM) can be achieved from PAM by using a voltage-controlled oscillator or multivibrator (VCO) or (VCM), which converts the amplitude of the pulse train to the modulation percentage of a fixed amplitude pulse. Another method of PAM to PDM involves combining the PAM pulse train with a triangular wave, or sweep, and then clipping this signal with a level detector to produce PDM.

Pulse-position modulation can be derived from PDM by differentiation followed by clipping. PPM allows conservation of signal power at the cost of increased bandwidth.

An important application of pulse code modulation (PCM) is now found in modern data communications systems. Binary coded data is converted to frequency shift keyed (FSK) signals for transmission over a telephone link by a modem. Modems are then used to convert the transmitted PCM-FSK signals to binary data. Multiplexing is achieved by frequency-division multiplex (FDM) of the transmission signals or by TDM of the binary signals before transmission.

Data Communication Trends

Prior to the 1968 Carterphone decision by the FCC, hardwired connections to a common telephone link were not allowed. Data communications through the telephone network was accomplished with devices such as acoustic couplers, which interfaced via audible tones with the telephone headset. Since 1968, independent manufacturers of data communications equipment have vigorously pursued this previously closed market, resulting in rapid technological growth and increased customer acceptance.

Digital signals are transmitted by selecting one of a number of waveforms. The typical transmitter function, as shown in Fig. 3-1, is to convert a string of data symbols (the binary digits or bits) into a sequence of physical symbols representing the data. The function of the receiver is to make the correct decisions on the sequence in order to allow the recovery of the data.

The characteristics of the channel through which the data is transmitted dictates the nature of the physical methods used to represent the data. Voice-grade telephone channels were originally designed to transmit analog voice signals in the frequency band of 300 to 3000

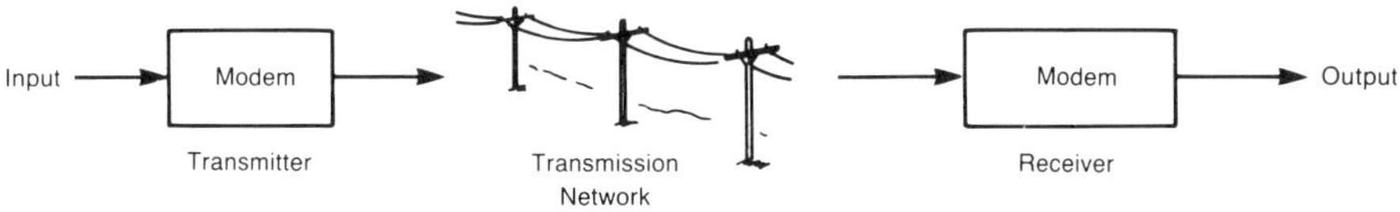

Fig. 3-1. Basic point-to-point data link.

hertz. The signals used in modems must fit into this band and operate with the various limitations of the channel.

A major cost item in providing long-distance interconnections is the cost of transmission. Private leased facilities from a common carrier such as AT&T can be used, or the public network, as in the direct-distance dialing (DDD) telephone facilities can be used.

Data communications tends to be "bursty" and nonsymmetric. There are significant quiet periods when little or nothing is sent, and the volume of data sent in one direction might be much larger than that sent in the other direction. Many devices generate data which uses only a fraction of the capacity of a voice-grade telephone channel. Because the cost of the channel per unit of time is independent of the data rate up to the channel capacity, it is useful to employ techniques that allow a number of low-speed devices to share a channel, and smooth the "bursty" and statistical fluctuations common in data communications, so the transmitted data rate more closely represents an average than a peak.

THE MULTIPLEXER

Multiplexing is commonly used to achieve both of these objectives. Using multiplexing, a modem with a capacity of 4800 bits per second could be used for the transmission of sixteen 300 bps terminals, as shown in Fig. 3-2. A cost saving can be achieved with most present-day tariffs and equipment costs. If the terminals are active only five percent of the time, which is typical, a statistical multiplexer could be used. It could handle up to 320 terminals, because 320 × 300 × 0.05 = 4800 bps. This type of intelligent multiplexer has a lower cost than the lines and modems that would otherwise be required to support 320 terminals. These intelligent multiplexers are usually designed with programmable microcomputers that include a memory. These can be programmed for

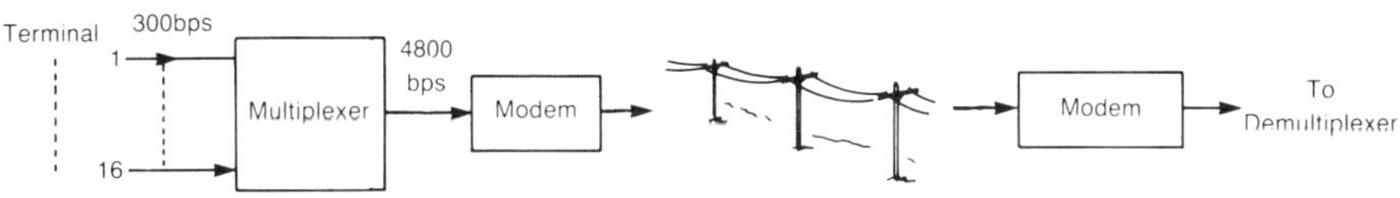

Fig. 3-2. Multiplexing on a point-to-point data link.

data compression and other intelligent functions, such as automatic speed changing, protocol conversion, system diagnostics, and error control.

THE CONCENTRATOR

In the past, a concentrator referred to devices which not only performed multiplexing to one output port, but which had a processor that would perform switching and routing to several output ports, as well as the data compression, code conversion, error control, and protocol functions.

The use of a concentrator today is the same as that of a front-end processor: it relieves the main, or master, processor of some of the more routine communications tasks. Today, intelligent statistical multiplexers have the capability to perform most of the tasks previously performed by concentrators, while the concentrator now functions as the switching node in large networks and provides multiplexing, switching, network management and link protocol functions.

MODEM TYPES AND EVOLUTION

In the 1970s, most modems operated in the voice-band at speeds of less than 300 bps. Almost all of these were manufactured and installed by the Bell System, which has since been broken up. There are now several million modems in use, supplied by many different independent manufacturers. Speeds of 300 to 16,000 bps are available, with features that include handshaking, bandsharing, multiplexing, data compression, unattended autodial, and diagnostics.

True modems are classified as either asynchronous (with no clocking) or synchronous, which requires synchronizing the data stream to a clock. Asynchronous modems usually operate at speeds below 1200 bps, sending a character at a time. Modems operating above 1200 bps are almost always synchronous.

Half duplex, or HDX, refers to a modem that will operate in both directions, but only one direction at a time, so the modem must be switched from the transmit to the receive mode. A full duplex, or FDX, modem will operate in both directions at the same time. Some of the limited distance, short haul, modems that are available will operate on wire-pairs of up to 20 miles.

Originally, many modems were acoustically coupled into the telephone lines using a handset transducer. Some of the newer devices (which are not true modems but actually line drivers), operate at baseband, without modulation, directly into the telephone lines. Modems can be grouped into the following types:

- Low speed—less than 600 bps.
- Medium speed—1200 to 4800 bps.
- High speed—greater than 9600 bps.
- Wideband—bandwidth over 16,900 bps.
- Short haul—for limited distances.
- Line drivers—modem eliminators, without modulation.
- Acoustic couplers—telephone headset couplers.

Modems are also grouped in terms of their mode of transmission. This may be point-to-point or multidrop, half duplex or full duplex, two-wire or four-wire. The type of lines on which modems are operated is also a factor. This includes dial-up lines, leased telephone lines, or twisted pairs which may be leased or owned.

Two-wire lines are commonly used in connecting to the dial-up public system. The transmit and receive signals are sent together on a single pair of wires, and are usually separated by a transformer in a balanced bridge configuration.

Most long-haul sections of the telephone network use a four-wire configuration. This provides two independent channels for the transmitting and receiving functions, as shown in Fig. 3-3. The four-wire configuration is subject to echo problems, and, for voice-grade channels, echo suppressors might be used if the echo delay exceeds 150-200 milliseconds. Echo suppressors provide an additional attenuation in the direction that is not currently being used. Thus, if the modem is operating in full duplex, echo suppressors cannot be used. Most modems provide the necessary disabling tone, which is a 400 millisecond single-frequency of 2010 to 2240 Hz.

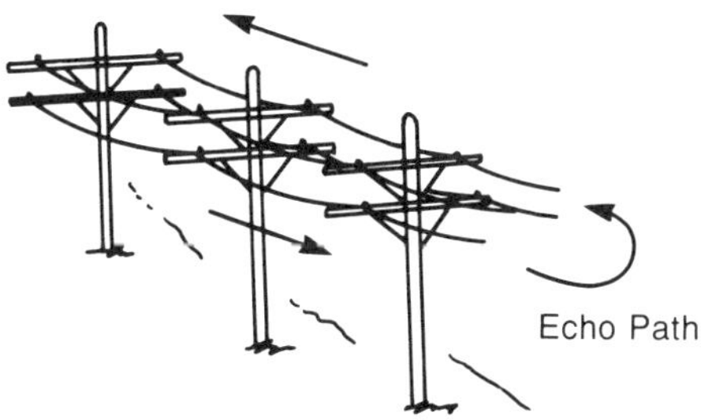

Fig. 3-3. 4-Wire transmission.

Polling

Multidrop modems employ a master modem that polls a number of remote tributary modems in a defined sequence. The master modem and the polled modem communicate during any single transmission. The polling time is a function of the response time of each modem to send when polled. This response time is normally less than 10 ms, and represents the time interval between when the request-to-send (RTS) is received from the data terminal equipment (DTE), and when the clear-to-send (CTS), to which the modem responds, is sent back to the DTE. This is shown in Fig. 3-4.

Polling can also be used with the dial-up network, but the total dialing and connect time might be greater than 20 seconds on leased four-wire lines.

FEATURES OF MODEMS

Modems can be stand-alone modular units, printed-circuit boards (PCBs), or large-scale integrated (LSI) chip sets. The LSI chip sets are used by many manufacturers in modem racks, terminals, multiplexers, concentrators, and personal computers. The stand-alone modems are usually self-contained with a power supply, and are packaged with function and error lights. Typical features include:

- Automatic Call Units (ACUs) that store numbers which can then be dialed automatically.
- Operation at more than one baud rate and compatibility with other modems currently in use, such as the Bell 212.
- Switching of the line between data mode and voice mode.
- The use of a standard interface which is used to pass data, control, and autodial instructions from a terminal or personal computer.

Even many newer, less-expensive modems have automatic dialing.

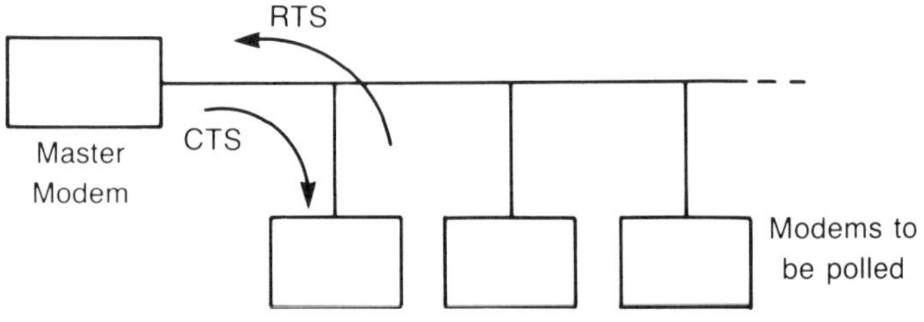

Fig. 3-4. Modems to be polled in a multidrop configuration.

In the past, automatic dialing for modems used on the DDD network required the use of a separate ACU. This was a stand-alone unit with its own interface to the modem and to the computer.

Autodial

Autodial can be used with polling or as a dial-up back-up feature when a leased line opens. Some of the autodial modems use a list of numbers, which are programmed by the user through an RS-232C interface. The dialing may be terminal-keyboard controlled or controlled by software. The directory may be stored in nonvolatile EPROM so it is retained even after a power shut-down. A linking feature is also available that replaces the first number dialed with the next number if the first call is unanswered or busy. This provides a simple method of least-cost routing.

Inverse Multiplexing

Inverse multiplexing and multiport operation are other relatively new features. Multiport, or split-stream, operation is a type of multiplexing which is done at the input to the modem. It permits several different data streams of the same or different rates to be combined into one signal.

The V.29 modems, which operate at 9600 bps, have this feature. Multiporting allows four 2400 bps independent data streams to be combined into one 9600 bps output. Other combinations are also possible, such as the input of two 2400 bps and one 4800 bps streams.

Inverse multiplexing allows several voice-band modems to be used with several lines for transmitting a single data stream at a higher rate than can be accomplished with a single line. As an example, a 19.2 Kbps data stream can be split using inverse multiplexing by sending the odd bits occurring at 9.6 Kbps through a 9.6 Kbps modem and a voice-grade line, while the even bits are sent through another 9.6 Kbps modem and a second voice-grade line. This is shown in Fig. 3-5. If the input data rate is less than 19.2 Kbps, and one or both of the modems is multiport, the excess can be sent through the other modem ports.

An incentive for using inverse multiplexing is the gap that appears in the available channels above 14.4 Kbps. Another advantage is fail-soft back-up. If one line fails, the other can continue at a reduced rate.

Problems sometimes occur in the reconstruction of the bit stream from the two or more lines used, because there might be various changing propagation delays. This can require some form of elastic buffering or dynamic alignment of the bit streams. When one path is over hundreds or thousands of miles of terrestrial wire, and the other is routed by satellite facilities, delays of close to one second are possible.

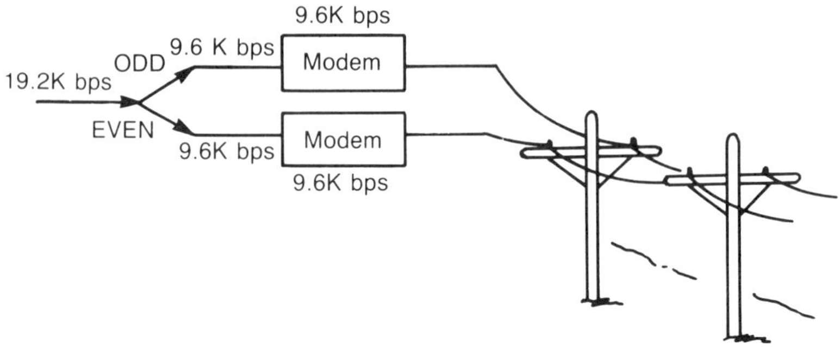

Fig. 3-5. Inverse multiplexing.

Many of the HDX modems have a low data-rate reverse channel which can be used for signalling and/or automatic repeat-request (ARQ) acknowledgments in link protocols. Some modems can also alternate data and voice on a single line. Other features can include synchronous-to-asynchronous conversion, and elastic buffering, which allows the input rate to differ from the output rate.

Modems use a number of diagnostic features. One common technique is to monitor both the local and remote modem, as well as the line, by using a remote digital loopback. This can be used to test the modem-line combination and to make a fault isolation of the lines. Other diagnostic techniques include an internal eye pattern generator that may be used to check the amount of phase jitter and noise. Almost all modems have built-in and standardized handshaking protocols to establish the initial synchronization.

AT&T-Type Modems

Many modems are compatible with those manufactured by AT&T. These are known as the AT&T or Bell type of modem. Many of these are listed in Table 3-1. The following abbreviations are used:

FSK — Frequency Shift Keying. Typically a mark is represented by one frequency and a space as another frequency.

PSK — Phase Shift Keying. The use of two or more phases to represent a sequence of marks and spaces.

QAM — Quadrature Amplitude Modulation. A combination of PSK and amplitude-shift keying, as shown in Fig. 3-6.

QPSK — Quaternary Phase Shift Keying. A four-level PSK also called differential 4-PSK.

Table 3-1. AT&T or Bell-Type Modems.

Type	Date Rate (bps)	Transmission Mode	Clocking	Modulation Method
102 A,E,F,J	0-300	HDX or FDX	Async.	FSK
113, A,B,C	0-300	HDX or FDX	Async.	FSK
201, A,B,C	2400	HDX	Sync.	QPSK
202 B	1200 DDD 1800 leased	HDX	Async.	FSK
208 A,B	4800	HDX	Sync.	PSK
209 A	9600	HDX	Sync.	QAM
212A	300 or 1200	FDX	Async.	QPSK

The Bell 103 is a full-duplex modem that uses frequency-shift keying and bandsharing in two separate portions of the voice telephone band (Fig. 3-7). In the originate mode, the transmitter sends a 1270 Hz tone for a mark. ("One") and a 1070-Hz tone for a space ("zero"). At the same time, it receives marks and spaces in the high band at 2225 Hz and 2025 Hz. This is done for the reverse data path on the same voice channel. The modem at the other end is "reversed" in that it receives in the low band and transmits in the high band. This type of originate-and-answer handshaking allows full-duplex operation.

The Bell 113 is similar to the 103. They are compatible with each other, and either has the ability to receive as well as send. The 113A and C versions are designed for the originate mode, as discussed above, and the 113B is designed for the answer mode.

The Bell 201 is a half-duplex synchronous modem which operates at 2400 bps using differential PSK (Fig. 3-8). It is often used on 4-wire multidrop applications, because it has delay time of about 8 ms between the request-to-send command and the clear-to-send response.

The Bell 202 is a half-duplex modem which operates with FSK at rates up to 1200 bps on dial-up lines, and 1800 bps on leased lines (Fig. 3-9). It can be used in multidrop leased lines with polling, because the response time is about 10 ms. These modems contain a low-rate reverse channel which can be used up to 75 bps. This modem has been used for

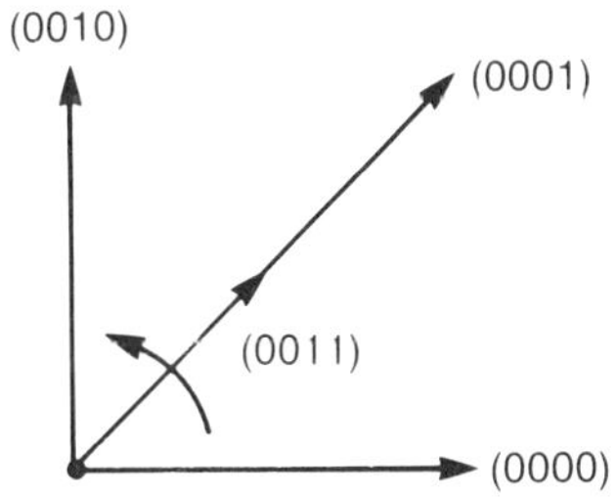

Fig. 3-6. Quadrature amplitude modulation.

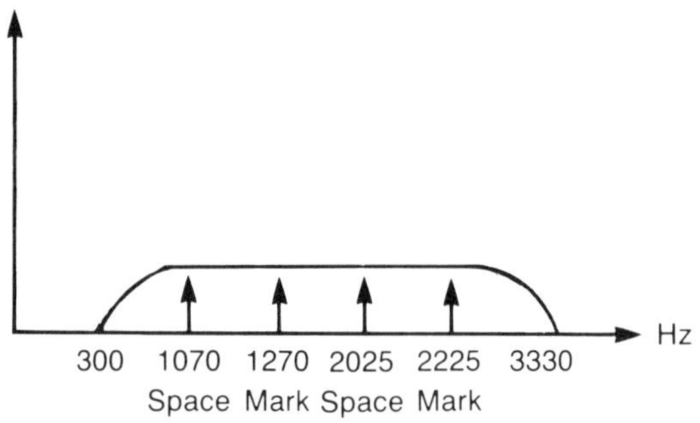

Fig. 3-7. Bell 103 frequency sharing.

acoustically coupled modems in the past, but, due to distortion and background noise problems of the telephone handset, at the 1200 bps data rate it is generally not acceptable.

The 208 and 209 units operate at 4800 and 9600 bps. They use a system of tribit and quadbit amplitudes and phases, as shown in Fig. 3-10. The higher data rates are often used in:

- The support of multiplexed data.
- High-speed file transfers.
- Graphics communications support.
- The transmission of compressed speech and data simultaneously.
- Digital facsimile.

The Bell 212A is a full-duplex modem for speeds up to 1200 bps. It uses Quaternary Phase Shift Keying (QPSK) as shown in Fig. 3-11,

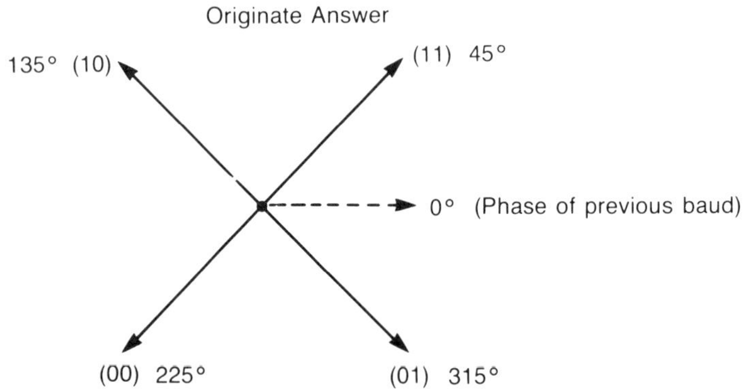

Fig. 3-8. Bell 201 differential phase-shift keying.

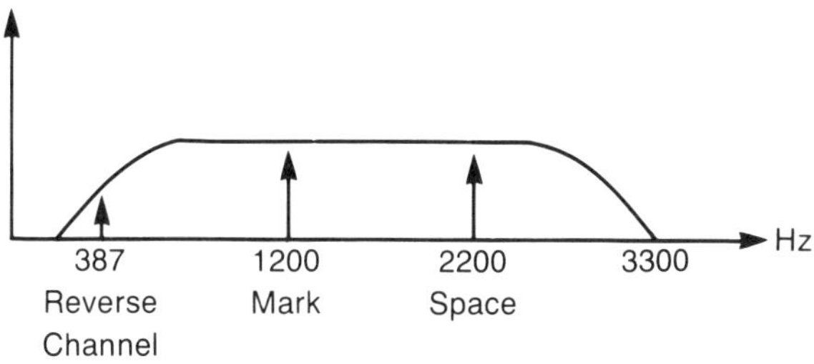

Fig. 3-9. Bell 202 frequency sharing.

and is compatible with the type 103/113 devices. It will automatically switch speeds between 1200 and 300 bps, and perform the required asynchronous-to-synchronous conversion.

Many manufacturers provide modems which are compatible with the 103, 113 and 212. Other standards in use include the CCITT V.21, which is a recommendation for 200 bps FDX modems in the switched telephone

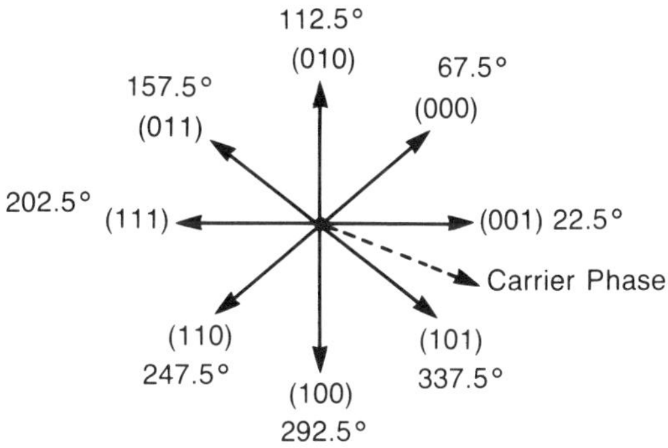

Fig. 3-10A. Bell 208 phase-shift keying.

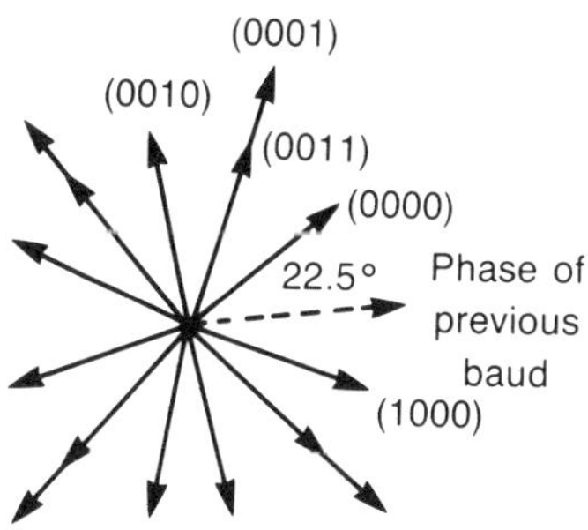

Fig. 3-10B. Bell 209 phase amplitude system.

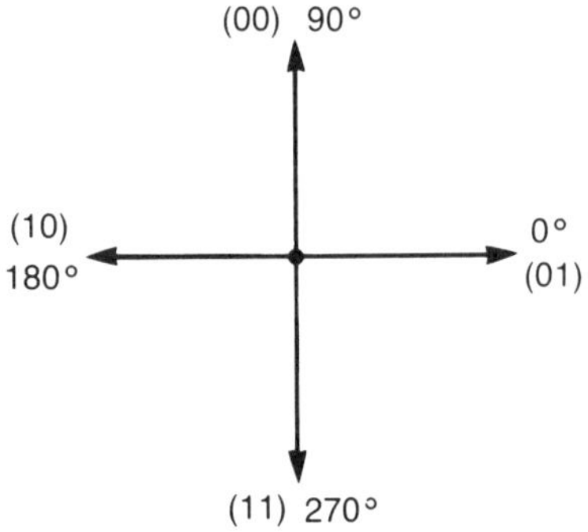

Fig. 3-11. Bell 212A phase-shift keying.

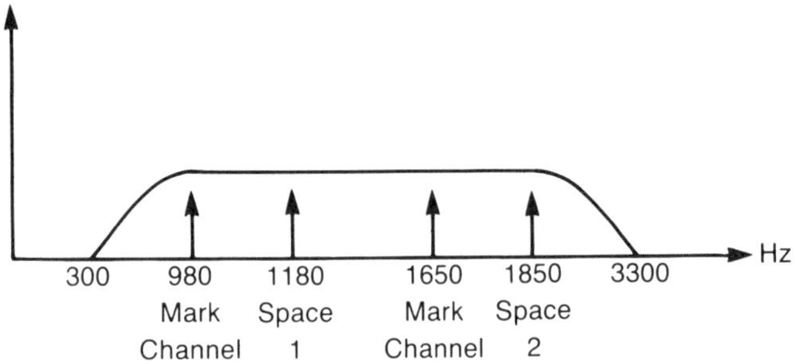

Fig. 3-12. CCITT V.21 frequency sharing.

network. It is similar to the Bell 103 scheme, as indicated in Fig. 3-12. CCITT V.23 is a recommendation for 600 to 1200 bps HDX modems. Its characteristics are shown in Fig. 3-13.

At the higher rates of 4800 and 9600 bits per second, many modems are also compatible with the CCITT international standards designated

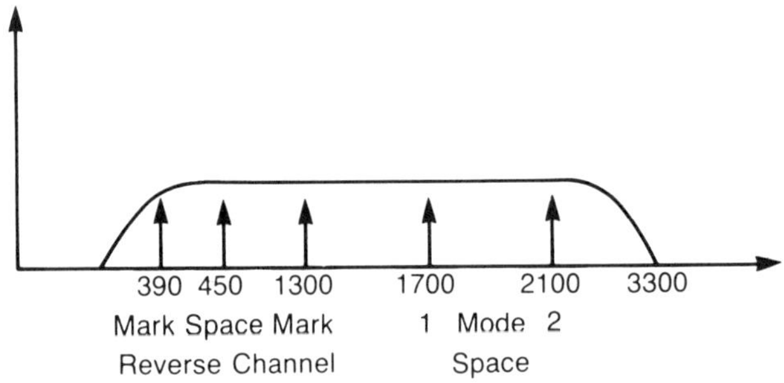

Fig. 3-13. CCITT V.23 frequency sharing.

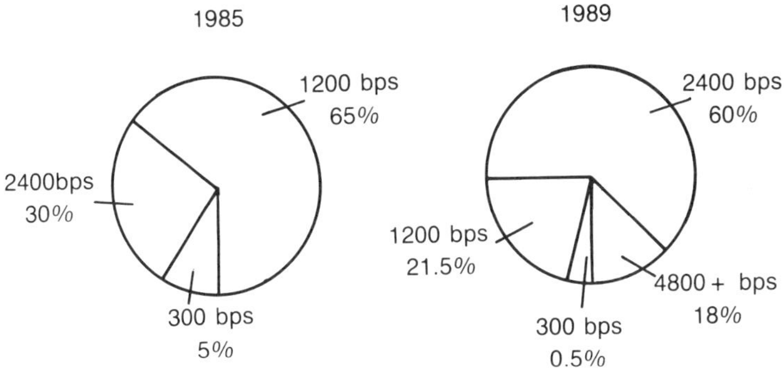

Fig. 3-14. Modem trends.

as V.27 (U.S. Federal Standard 1006), and V.29 (Proposed Federal Standard 1007). CCITT V.22 is another standard for use at 2400 bps on dial-up lines. The trends in modems are illustrated in Fig. 3-14. Although the maximum theoretical transmission rate on voice-grade lines is about 30 Kbps, the techniques required are expensive, and include the use of special modulation, automatic equalization and phase-tracking.*

CONNECTING MODEMS TO THE NETWORK

The physical connections for modems and DTEs have been standardized, and a 25-pin RS-232C/V.24 interface is almost always used. This represents the lowest, or physical-layer, protocol used in the International Standards Organization (ISO) model for the Open Systems Interconnect (OSI) reference standard for computer networks. The RS-232C standard was described in Chapter 1. According to the United Nations Consultative Committee on International Telegraphy and Telephony (CCITT), which publishes international standards, V.24 is considered virtually the same as RS-232C.

The physical interface protocol of the ISO model specifies pin connections, functions, and electrical characteristics, including voltage and current levels and recommended cable types and lengths. Figure 3-15 shows the basic ISO model, and Table 3-2 illustrates the differences between the EIA-RS-232C and CCITT-V.24 designations.

When polling is inadequate, modems can be arranged in networks. They are often used in this way in both standard and statistical time-

*Modems which can evaluate such parameters as the quality of the line, and adjust speeds accordingly, have been operated at speeds greater than 21000 bps.

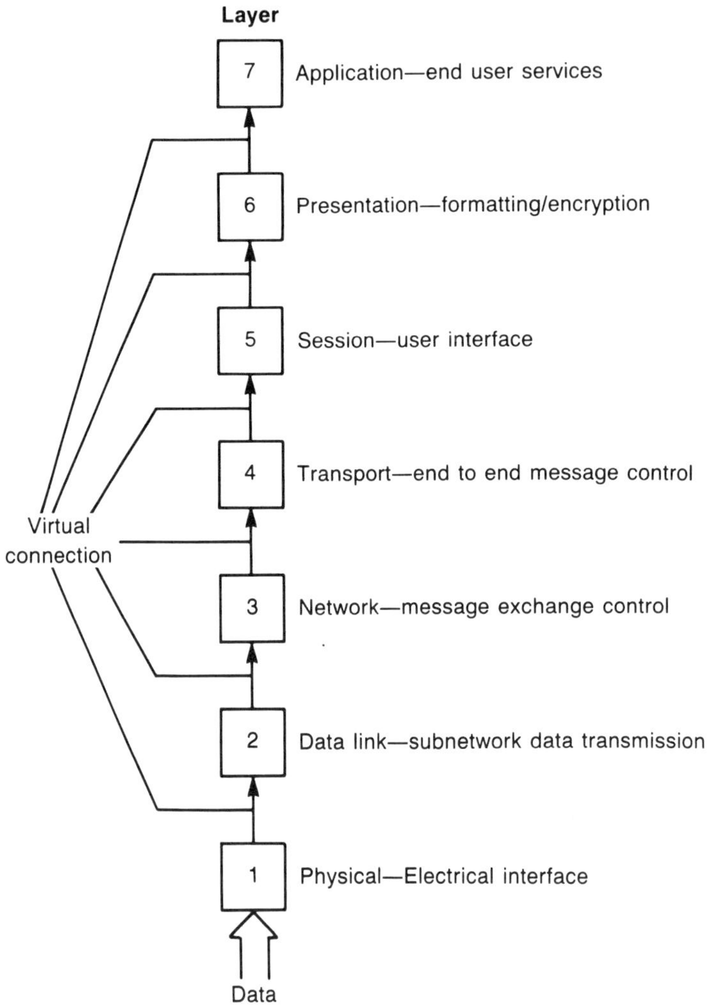

Fig. 3-15. In the ISO model for Open Systems Interconnection (OSI), data passes physically through layer 1, all other layers transfer information through virtual connections.

division multiplexing applications that require master/slave configurations.

Some modems operate at frequencies above the voice band in an FDX mode, on telephone lincs in a local area network that is unique to a particular building or facility. In these installations, the lines are unloaded, and band-limiting filters are not installed by the telephone company except where the lines are connected to the public network. Some of these modems operates with FSK 9600 bps data at about 40 MHz in one direction and about 75 MHz in the other direction. This type of modem can also be used in an analog PBX to provide a low cost voice/data local-area network.

Multiplexers in Networks

The main reason for using multiplexing is to save line and modem costs through the sharing of a common channel. Multiplexing is commonly used by the common carriers in their networks for voice transmission. This is a type of trunk multiplexing which differs from the data multiplexing used in most local networks.

The original use of multiplexing goes back to early radio and telephone communications, when a transmission medium, such as a

Table 3-2. RS-232/CCITT V-24 Interfaces.

DB Pin	EIA RS232C Circuit	CCITT-V-24 Circuit	Description
1	AA	101	Protective Ground
7	AB	101	Signal Ground/Common Return
		102a	DTE Common
		102b	DCE Common
2	BA	103	Transmitted Data
3	BB	104	Received Data
4	CA	105	Request to Send
5	CB	106	Clear to Send
6	CC	107	Data Terminal Ready
22	CE	125	Ring Indicator
8	CF	109	Received Line Signal Detector
21	CG	110	Signal Quality Detector
23	CH	111	Data Signal Rate Selector (DTE)
23	CI	112	Data Signal Rate Selector (DCE)
24	DA	113	Transmitter Signal Element Timing (DTE)
15	DB	114	Transmitter Signal Element Timing (DCE)
17	DD	115	Receiver Signal Element Timing (DCE)
14	SBA	118	Secondary Transmitted Data
16	SBB	119	Secondary Received Data
19	SCA	120	Secondary Request to Send
13	SCB	121	Secondary Clear to Send
12	SCF	122	Secondary Received Line Signal Detector
		141	Local Loopback
		140	Remote Loopback
		142	Test Indicator
		116	Select Standby
		117	Standby Indicator
		126	Select Transmit Frequency

broadcast band, was subdivided into channels, with each channel occupying a distinct frequency.

MULTIPLEXING METHODS

Multiplexing involves obtaining multichannel capability from a single resource. Multiplexing can be achieved in either the frequency domain (frequency-division multiplexing, or FDM), or the time domain (time-division multiplexing, or TDM).

FDM

Frequency-division multiplexing normally involves modulation techniques which multiply the message function by a higher-frequency sinusoid, referred to as the *carrier.* The sinusoidal carrier, with its unique and discrete spectrum, allows noninterfering broadcasts of many communications channels or stations; also, simple selection of sinusoidal carriers is possible with simple tuned circuits.

The detection or demodulation of AM can be accomplished by either synchronous (or product) demodulation using a balanced modulator or frequency converter, or noncoherent methods, such as envelope detection, using a simple dc diode peak detector. Product demodulation does not tend to distort the output message; however, noise effects are additive and might mask the output for low levels of input signal. At high signal-to-noise ratios, envelope detection approximates product demodulation, however, at low signal-to-noise ratios (less than 6.6 dB) the output message is distorted beyond recognition. This property is known as the *AM threshold effect.*

By eliminating the presence of the carrier when the message function is zero, transmission power is reduced with no reduction in information transmission. This technique is known as *sideband suppression,* and is popular for applications where power conservation is important.

Frequency modulation results in superior noise and interference immunity compared to AM, but at the cost of increased bandwidth. FM is also more sensitive to perturbation of the transmission media than AM methods. Typical bandwidth expansion ratios (message signal/carrier) are ten for commercial broadcasting, and one hundred for transcontinental microwave relay links.

Phase modulation does not enjoy wide usage compared to frequency modulation because of the implementation requirements of a precise phase reference, and the limitations on the peak frequency deviation.

Double-sideband suppressed-carrier (DSSC) or single-sideband suppressed-carrier (SSSC) are more appropriate for limited bandwidth applications. DSSC and SSSC with synchronous detection can be superior to ordinary AM under conditions of low signal-to-noise ratios. Ordinary AM with synchronous detection is normally not used because of implementation difficulties.

SSSC-FM (frequency modulation of a carrier by single-sideband subcarriers, which are amplitude modulated by the message function) has been utilized for long distance telephone communications. Recent installations, however, use digital transmission because of its superior performance characteristics. SSSC-FM has been used by telephone companies to transmit 600 or more voice channels on a single RF carrier.

Examples of other FDM multiplexing methods include FM-FM, FM-AM and FM-PM, which have been used for RF telemetry systems.

TDM

Time-division multiplexing requires the desired messages to be sampled, and the samples to be transmitted sequentially. Each sampled message channel occupies the entire baseband bandwidth. Sampling a continuous signal requires a minimum sampling frequency of twice the signal bandwidth, to allow reconstruction of the original waveform without loss of information. This relation holds for an ideal band limited signal that contains dc components. The amplitude, or duration, of the samples may be modulated by the message function, resulting in pulse-amplitude modulation (PAM) or pulse-duration modulation (PDM).

The message samples can also be represented in a digital format, resulting in pulse-code modulation (PCM). Digital message representation offers higher resolution compared to analog methods (PAM) and PDM) even under the ideal analog conditions of high signal-to-noise ratios. It also offers greater noise immunity because of easily recognized pulses, each of which form only a small part of the message. These advantages are gained at the expense of a large baseband bandwidth and deleterious effects upon recovered-message quality because of the decision-making requirement. The former is generally not a problem except for wideband noise considerations, and the latter is specifiable and adaptable to error correcting codes.

To transform a continuous message to digital format, it is necessary to divide the sampled analog signal into a number of finite intervals. This process, which is called *quantizing,* introduces error because of the difference between the quantized intervals and the sampled analog signal. This error can be reduced by increasing the number of quantizing increments (n) and can be expressed by the following relation:

$$\text{error} = (2^n - 2)^2$$

At the low end of the dynamic input range, the number of quantizing levels is small, and the quantizing error may be large compared to the input signal. To overcome this effect, nonuniform quantization can be used by either nonlinear spacing of the quantization levels or logarithmic compression of the input signal followed by uniform quantization.

After amplitude quantizing, it is necessary to digitize, or convert, the information into a binary format. Errors can occur whenever a zero or one is interpreted incorrectly because of background noise, and an incorrect word is coded. Total converter noise is dependent on the type of circuit used, and should be less than one quantization level. Conversion noise and quantization noise are independent, and are added on an rms basis. Thus, the actual signal-to-noise ratio due to conversion equipment alone will be approximately 3 dB less than the quantization noise.

D/A converters are basic to the digital conversion process, because they are also used when converting analog signals to digital format in A/D converters. To convert a binary number to an analog voltage, binary weighting factors are added by using operational summing amplifiers and resistor-ladder networks. Semiconductor switches activated by the digital input are generally used to obtain the appropriate weighting factors. Errors occur from resistor and reference voltage tolerances. The total output voltage error is usually less than the voltage attributed to the least significant bit (LSB). The analog-to-digital conversion process cannot be more accurate than the analog conditioning circuits, and the total analog error should be less than the quantization error.

One basic method of analog-to-digital conversion requires the analog input to be compared to a time varying reference while pulses are stored in a binary counter. If a linear ramp is used as a reference, errors due to ramp linearity and comparator resolution allow accuracies of within about one percent to be obtained. Higher accuracies are achieved by using modifications of this method.

One variation uses a D/A converter after the counter to obtain a staircase voltage waveform. Errors are then dependent on D/A accuracy and comparator resolution.

Successive approximation converters compare on a bit-by-bit basis instead of by continuous counting. Starting with the most significant bit, a decision is made to determine if each bit is zero or one. This method is much faster than the counting type of converter, which requires 128 counts for a seven-bit number.

Sample-and-hold circuits can be used to prevent errors due to *aperture time*, which is the time period (usually equal to the conversion time) when the analog signal might change from its initial value. Another method to reduce aperture-time errors is to use the track-and-hold circuit which follows the analog signal until commanded to hold.

DIGITAL TRANSMISSION

Various binary waveforms can be used for digital transmission including:

- Unipolar two-valued signals, which utilize a comparator set at one-half the signal amplitude.
- Bipolar non-return-to-zero (NRZ) signals, which have the advantage of zero average current.
- Return-to-zero (RZ) signals, which use one-half of the bit interval only, and may be either unipolar or bipolar.
- Manchester, or split phase coding, used where high accuracy is required. A change from a high to low signal in the middle of a bit time signifies a one, while a change from a low to high signal in the middle of a bit time is interpreted as a zero.
- Differential encoding, or Kineplex, which operates via bit transitions with waveform transitions occurring only during transmission of a one.

For transmission with a carrier, the digital bits can be used to control (modulate): amplitude (signal or no signal), which is called on-off keying or amplitude shift keying (ASK); frequency, which results in frequency shift keying (FSK); or phase, resulting in phase shift keying (PSK).

By adding redundance in the form of extra digits to a word, error detection and correction is possible. Increasing the minimum distance between distinct message words increases the bit capability for error detection and correction. Parity checks can also be used to increase the minimum distance between words by determining the number of ones in a word. Parity can be determined by applying an exclusive OR to all digits, which is compared to a parity check bit added to a word to allow error detection.

Any broadband signal can be divided into distinct nonoverlapping channels. Each of these channels can then be put to a separate use. The individual signals can be separated by the proper filtering at the receiving end. This technique, which is called frequency-division multiplexing (FDM), continues to be the most common way for efficient transmission over expensive, wideband long-haul trunks for analog voice transmission.

The FDM system is usually made up of a number of 4-kHz units of the total band, with each unit carrying one analog voice channel. A stack of twelve 4-kHz channels is known as a *group,* a *supergroup* is formed from 60 voice circuits, and 10 supergroups make a *mastergroup,* with 600 voice circuits.

When a long-distance voice-grade line is used, the modem likely to be located along the path is assigned to one of the 4-kHz frequency channels.

The T-Carrier System

Newer trunk systems use digital time-division multiplexing. This T-carrier system uses pulse-code modulation (PCM) to digitize each voice signal to 64 Kbps. A digital TDM hierarchy is used. The multiplexing hierarchy used in North America is listed below:

1. Twenty-four Kbps and 64 Kbps channels are grouped in a 1.544 Mbps T-1 carrier.
2. Four T-1 carriers are grouped to form a 6.312 Mbps T-2 carrier.
3. Seven T-2 carriers are grouped into a 44.736 Mbps T-3 carrier.
4. Six T-3 carriers are grouped into a 274.176 Mbps T-4 carrier.

The T-3 and T-4 carriers, then, contain 672 and 4032 independent 64 Kbps channels. These carriers are used on microwave, coaxial and fiber-optic systems in networks designed primarily for voice communications. Similar techniques which are not usually compatible exist on other continents. These are examples of multiplexing done by the common carriers internal to their networks. To the user of data communications, the signals might be multiplexed or even sampled and digitized, but it is still a connection that provides all the characteristics of a voice-grade line.

The first multiplexing techniques for data transmission with voice-grade used FDM, and the data on each channel used binary FSK. The voice channel was divided into FDM subchannels such as shown for CCITT R.39 in Table 3-3.

To avoid interference, the tones are ± 30 Hz from the center frequency, which, for channel one, is 420 Hz:

$$420 + 30 = 450 \text{ Hz for a MARK}$$
$$420 - 30 = 390 \text{ Hz for a SPACE}$$

At 75 bps, 24 channels will fit in the voice band, at 150 bps, only 12 channels will fit, and at 600 bps, only two channels can be used. The military uses a different standard for frequency assignments, as shown in Table 3-4.

Table 3-3. CCITT 4.39 Frequencies for FDM Multiplexing.

Channel Number	75 Baud/bps Spacing 120 Hz FSK ± 30 Hz	150 Baud/bps Spacing 240 Hz FSK ± 60 Hz	600 Baud/bps Spacing 1440 Hz FSK ± 240 Hz
1	420	480	1080
2	540	720	2520
3	660	960	
4	780	1200	
5	900	1440	
6	1020	1680	
7	1140	1920	
8	1260	2160	
9	1380	2400	
10	1500	2640	
11	1620	2880	
12	1740	3120	
13	1860		
14	1980		
15	2100		
16	2220		
17	2340		
18	2460		
19	2580		
20	2700		
21	2820		
22	2940		
23	3060		
24	3180		
25	5300 < Out-Of Band		

Table 3-4. MIL STD-1888 Operating Frequencies for FDM.

Channel Number	110 Baud Spacing 170 Hz FSK ± 42.5 Hz	200 Baud Spacing 340 Hz FSK ± 85 Hz
1	425	510
2	595	850
3	765	1190
4	935	1530
5	1105	1870
6	1275	2210
7	1445	2550
8	1615	2890
9	1785	
10	1955	
11	2125	
12	2295	
13	2465	
14	2635	
15	2805	
16	2975	
17	3145	
18	3315	

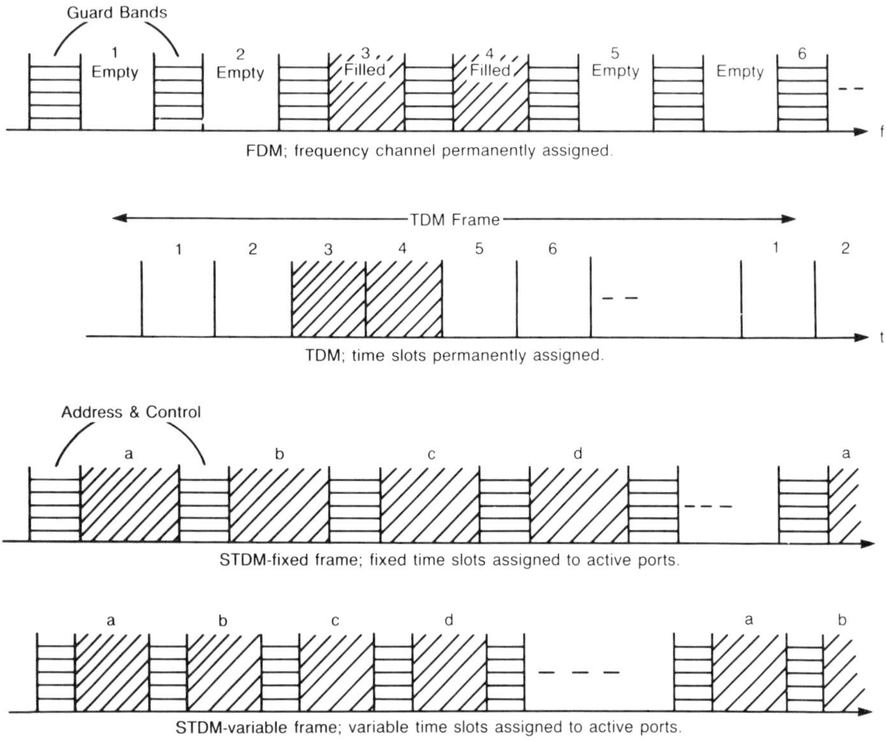

Fig. 3-16. Multiplexing techniques.

FDM has been replaced almost entirely by time-division multiplexing, with statistical time-division multiplexing (STDM) for data transmission. The major differences between these multiplexing techniques is shown in Fig. 3-16.

STDM

The use of microcomputers and resident communications software has advanced the multiplexer into a device that does much more than multiplexing. STDM is now the preferred technique.

FDM does not require separate modems, because each channel essentially operates as a subvoice-grade FSK modem. TDM assigns slots which are repeated every frame. These slots are divided among the terminal ports on a fixed basis. If a 9600-bps modem has 32 slots per frame, then the average output rate of each slot is:

$$9600/32 = 300 \text{ bps.}$$

If asynchronous terminals with 8-bit ASCII characters are used, with two bits for start and stop bits, then each time slot supports:

$$\frac{300 \text{ bits/second}}{10 \text{ bits/character}} = 30 \text{ characters/second.}$$

Most asynchronous terminals receive asynchronous data at 10, 15, or 30 characters/second. If manual keyboard-entry is used, a fast average is five characters per second, or 60 words per minute. Thus, at least 50 percent of the time will be spent transmitting idle characters, with much capacity and bandwidth to spare. In most common-carrier networks computer-controlled switching reacts to the demand, and assigns channels according to the traffic fluctuations. FDM suffers from this inefficiency when the channels are fixed.

TDM is more efficient than FDM, because it does not require guard bands, and operates directly in digital form. STDM improves on this by incorporating the statistics of the data transfer into the allocation of the channel use. Increases of greater than one order of magnitude are possible.

STDM uses a variable, instead of a fixed, assignment of the time slots. Ports that do not require full capacity do not receive a full slot. Although some channel space must be reserved for the required address and control data that must be used for statistical multiplexing, the total space is small in comparison to that usually taken up with idle bits.

STDM may be fixed-frame or variable-frame, where both the size of the slots and the frame depend on the data. They may support asynchronous or synchronous data, or both. Buffers are required, as is also the case with TDM.

A modem is required with TDM to interface with a voice-grade line. Almost all STDMs include at least one built-in modem and one or more microprocessors for preprogrammed and programmable functions. These multiplexers are known as smart, or intelligent, MUXs.

INTELLIGENT MULTIPLEXERS

STDMs have been available since the mid-1970s, and their major features are designed to improve link utilization.

In addition to the intermittent statistical characteristics of data traffic, there are other statistical characteristics, such as the nonuniform distribution of the frequency of character occurrence, that can be used by applying data-compression techniques to improve bandwidth utilization.

Improvements can be achieved by applying deterministic techniques to:

- Start and stop bits
- Control symbols
- Filler characters used for synchronization
- Flags and trailers
- Acknowledgment waiting times

STDM can improve transmission efficiency by a factor of 10 for asynchronous data, and by a factor of two to six for the different types of synchronous data transmission. The higher figure applies to character-oriented protocols, such as IBM's Binary Synchronous Communication (BSC). The lower figure applies to bit-oriented protocols, such as Synchronous Data Link Control (SDLC) or High-Level Data Link Control (HDLC).

For asynchronous data transmission, the improvements expressed as the percentage of time saved are as follows:

- Stripping off start/stop bits and reinserting at the other end: 20%.
- Operating in a balanced HDX mode: 50%
- Optimizing the character duty factor: 200-800%
- Compressing text: 50%

When a combination of all techniques is used, a 1000% reduction in the time needed to transmit a given amount of information is possible, which is a change of one order of magnitude.

For synchronous data, there can be no moving of start/stop bits or changing of the character duty factor. Some protocols require FDX operation, which requires text compression and the possible removing of redundant frame overhead, resulting in the lower figures for synchronous data.

The concept of data compression is simple. In a sequence of data, some symbols will occur much more frequently than others. In English, for example, a space will occur about 17 percent of the time, while the more common lowercase letters such as e, t, a, i, and r occur collectively about 30 percent of the time. Less common occurrences include the uppercase letters of J, Z, and W, which will occur less than 0.1 percent of the time.

The basic technique involved in data compression is to use less bits for those letters that occur more frequently. Instead of using the same number of bits, such as seven plus one parity used in ASCII, to all characters, fewer bits can be used for the most frequently occurring symbols, and a larger number for the rarer symbols. This will result in an average length that will be smaller.

Special coding is required in data compression to uniquely decipher a string of variable-length codewords because, without separators, the prefix of any codeword that represents a character must be distinguished from a shorter codeword representing another character. These codes, known as *Huffman codes,* provide a way to reduce the average number of bits and characters to a minimum.* Huffman coding may use either tree-search algorithms or storage tables.

Overflows

There are other problems due to the use of variable-length coding. Special handling of encoding and decoding is required for the variable frames. This includes buffering for all incoming data, and results in additional delays with the possibility of blocking, if the buffers should become filled due to an overload.

In conventional time-division multiplexing, each channel has a fixed time slot. Fixed frames are transmitted continuously between the multiplexer and demultiplexer. Each of the time slots that represent an inactive channel must be filled with an idle character to maintain the proper framing. You have seen that transmission efficiency can be improved with statistical time-division multiplexing (STDM) by dynamically allocating transmission bandwidth to whichever terminals are active at any time. As the data arrives at the statistical multiplexer, it is placed in a buffer that has been assigned for each active channel. The frames of data are assembled as the data is removed from these buffers.

Overflows could occur during peak traffic periods unless the terminal equipment is signaled to cease transmission. Transmission flow control on incoming channels can be utilized with either in-band or out-of-band traffic control signals. In-band signals are typically nonprinting control characters, which are transmitted to the terminal as if they were data characters. Out-of-band traffic control is achieved by using special control signals on the separate control lines available in the data terminals.

When the terminal equipment continues sending data during overloads, buffer overflow can occur. The buffer might attempt to re-

---

*See, for example, *Information Theory and Reliable Communications,* R. G. Gallagher, John Wiley, 1968, and, for the use of Huffman codes in statistical multiplexers, *Data Communications,* June, July/August, 1976, articles by G. D. Forney, R. W. Stearns, and W. Y. Tao.

cover from overflow by dumping the data of one or more of the terminals, transmitting a DATA LOST message to the affected terminal, and, possibly, disconnecting the terminal.

When the total buffer utilization drops below a preset overload condition, the flow control can be released by either in-band or out-of-band signals to allow the transmission to be resumed.

SPEECH INTERPOLATION WITH STATISTICAL MULTIPLEXING

A type of statistical multiplexing can be applied to voice channels. These techniques are known as *time assignment speech interpolation* (TASI) for analog transmission, and *digital speech interpolation* (DSI) for digital transmission. Both techniques fill the quiet gaps in one channel with speech from other channels. The bursts of speech must be directed into the proper channel-time slots. Typically, digital signal processing using PCM is employed along with buffers for speech storage and microprocessor control for the switching functions.

Speech interpolation has been used in the U.S. Bell System and by COMSAT and European telephone companies. Typically, 48 voice channels are concentrated into 24 transmission channels in North America, and 60 voice channels are multiplexed into 30 channels in Europe. The basic operation is similar to that used for the statistical multiplexing of data. The incoming speech is recognized and stored in buffers assigned to the voice channel. The buffer memory is of variable length. The stored speech is transmitted in bursts as bandwidth becomes available. The buffer is then returned to a pool for further use. Control signals are used to direct the use of the buffers.

High levels of speech activity can cause buffer overflow, resulting in the loss of speech segments. This loss is called *clipping* and presents a serious limitation in speech interpolation systems. The usual control algorithms for its prevention involve systematic techniques for dropping noncritical segments and reducing the data rate in digital interpolation systems.

Design Issues

The effects of delays due to queueing and blocking from buffer overflow can be difficult to predict. Buffer overflow is not often encountered, because most STDMs provide enough storage. Queueing delays can also be minimized by designing for overloads.

The typical treatment is to assume that the data traffic from all the active sources is homogeneous (pooled buffers) and that a steady-state statistical equilibrium has occurred, so you are beyond startup and any gross traffic changes.

Consider an STDM switch (Fig. 3-17) in which the average arrivals from each of these homogeneous sources is X bps. Also, let there be N sources which fill F slots in the STDM frame. The multiplexer requires Ts seconds to service each source, as it delivers C bps, which is its capacity. Let A equal the average number bits in an active buffer. Then:

$$Ta = A(X)$$

which is the time required to accumulate A bits arriving at X bps.

To assemble a frame, a complete scanning cycle is required. The total time delay is made up of the sum of the time to unload the active buffers and the time to scan all N sources. The total frame overhead, OH, must be considered, in bits, as well as the offered load, L.

The total delay, Td, is the sum of the queueing delay, OH ÷ (C – L), plus the time required to transmit a frame that contains a total of F bits at C bps, plus the processing delay, Tp. Thus, the following formula is used for the STDM time delay:

$$Td \cong \frac{OH}{C - L} + \frac{F}{C} + Tp$$

Typical delay curves are shown in Fig. 3-18, with OH = 16 bits, F = 512 bits, and Tp = 10 ms. Suppose C is 9600 bps and the aggregate average load, L, is 8400 bps. The delay then approaches 100 ms, as shown in curve A.

The effects of overhead and frame buffer size are dependent on the load. In general, as the load approaches the system capacity, the delay

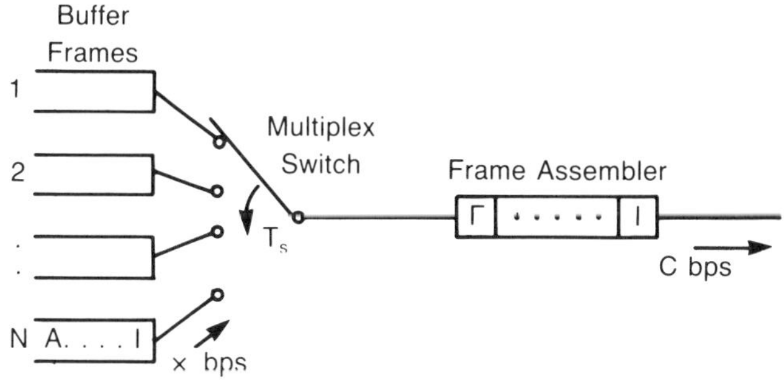

Fig. 3-17. STDM model.

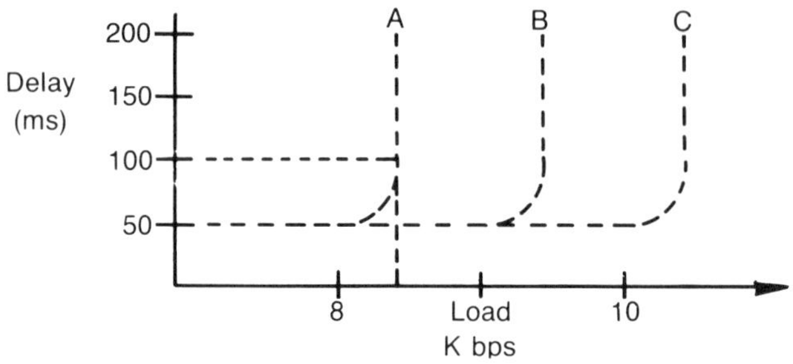

Fig. 3-18. STDM delay.

becomes very large. This is the usual queueing curve, which indicates that, if the aggregate arrival rate is very close to the next maximum service rate, the queue will begin to grow very rapidly. It is not possible to maintain a stable queue when the load is greater than the capacity.

The overhead has a major effect on the delay. For a specified delay, the overhead sets the maximum load, or throughput, that the STDM can handle. This effect of overhead is shown in curves B and C. If the data compression is 30 percent (curve B), then the effective capacity is 9600/(1 – 0.3), or 13.7 Kbps, and the delay is reduced to about 50 ms, which is more than a 30 percent reduction from no data compression. The actual capacity would have to be greater than 14 Kbps to achieve the type of delay without data compression, as shown in curve C.

A major contributor to the frame overhead is the intermultiplexer frame form used by the STDM. A typical format is to use a structure similar to the SDLC and HDLC level-two link protocol, as shown in Fig. 3-19. This contains the following features:

- Opening and closing flags.
- Multiplexer addresses required for networking.
- Frame numbers for ARQ error control.
- Active terminal addresses.
- Cyclic redundancy checks (CRCs) for error detection.

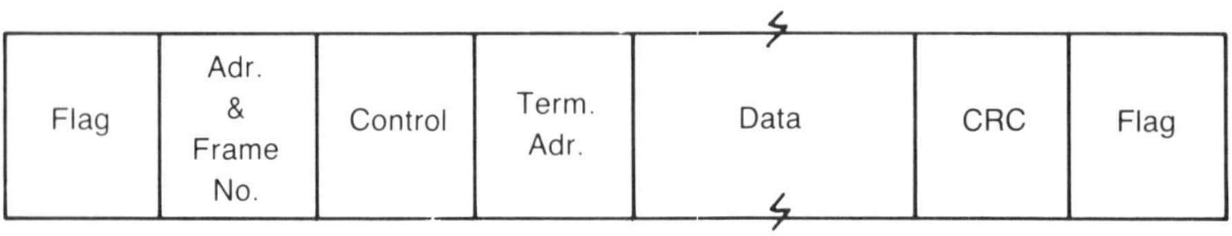

Fig. 3-19. SDLC and HDLC type of frame.

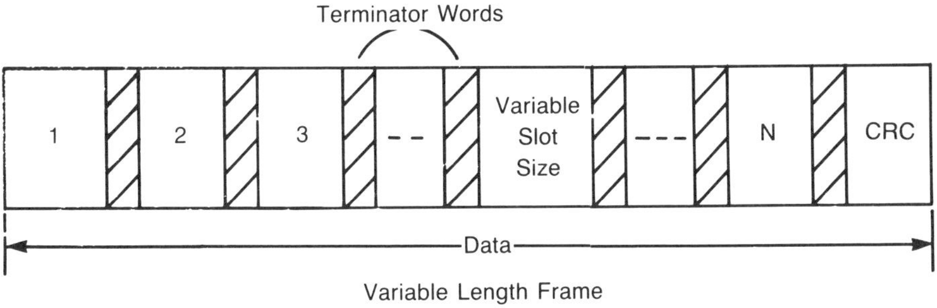

Fig. 3-20. Variable length frame.

The sum of these can add up to almost 60 bits, and can result in a delay of about 300 ms.

The frame formats may use either direct addressing to indicate which terminal is active, or indexed addressing, which signifies the relative position of the active terminal after the current one. Indexing reduces overhead for high traffic conditions, because a smaller address field is required.* A frame format that does not require explicit addresses or byte counts is shown in Fig. 3-20. This format uses variable-length Huffman-coded characters with a slot for each active and inactive source.

When characters are to be queued in an active buffer, any of them that are Huffman coded, up to a maximum, are placed in the slot reserved for that source. If the slot is not filled to its maximum, then a *terminator code* is inserted. The terminator is part of the Huffman code, so it can be distinguished from the other characters. The inactive slots will contain only the terminator code.

This technique used no terminal addresses, due to the unique decoding of the Huffman codes, while allowing data compression. It is useful for high loading factors.

The average aggregate data rate cannot exceed the capacity of the data link, but the aggregate peak rate may exceed the capacity for short periods of time, provided that the buffers are large enough to hold the difference.

---

*Additional considerations can be found in *A Study of Asynchronous Time Division Multiplexing for Time Sharing Computer Systems,* W.W. Chu, AFIPS Fall Conference, 1969, "On the Analysis and Modeling of a Class of Computer Communications Systems," W.W. Chu and A.G. Konheim, IEEE Transactions on Communications, June, 1972, and *Computer Communication Network Design and Analysis,* M. Schwartz, Prentice-Hall, 1977.

Control of the buffers is usually performed by the microprocessors in the STDM. This might include pooling of the total buffer space among the ports. Pooling allows a flexibility and efficiency that cannot be achieved with fixed allocation. A disadvantage of pooling is decreased reliability, because the system is now vulnerable to a single failure. The solution is to separate the ports into groups which share the buffer spaces. As long as the buffer is large enough to accommodate peaks in the aggregate traffic load, its effect on delay and throughput will be small.

Most STDMs operate on asynchronous data, but a few are designed to use synchronous data, in formats such as BSC, SDLC, and HDLC. STDMs normally conduct an automatic check of each block sent. If an error is found, the data is not acknowledged as correct by the receiving multiplexer. An automatic request for retransmission (ARQ) is then sent. Some adjustments are possible to the ARQ demands to improve throughput.

Intelligent STDMs

Intelligent STDMs can provide such features as:

- Automatic terminal speed recognition.
- Port configuration control.
- Protocol intervention.
- Protocol transparency.
- Detailed operator reports.

These operator reports are generally menu-driven, and include:

- Local and remote diagnostics.
- Alarms and status.
- Message statistics.
- Processor and buffer utilization.
- ARQ retransmission rates.
- Terminal and channel states.

Some of these intelligent STDMs have several hundred input ports, with data rates varying from 50 bps to 9.6 Kbps, and trunk ports that operate at 9.6, 14.4, 19.2, or 64 Kbps, with switching and routing capabilities.

A number of architectures are in use. Several of these multiple microprocessor configurations are shown in Fig. 3-21. Typically, a high-speed front-end microprocessor controls most of the centralized functions, such as routing, diagnostics, and report generation.

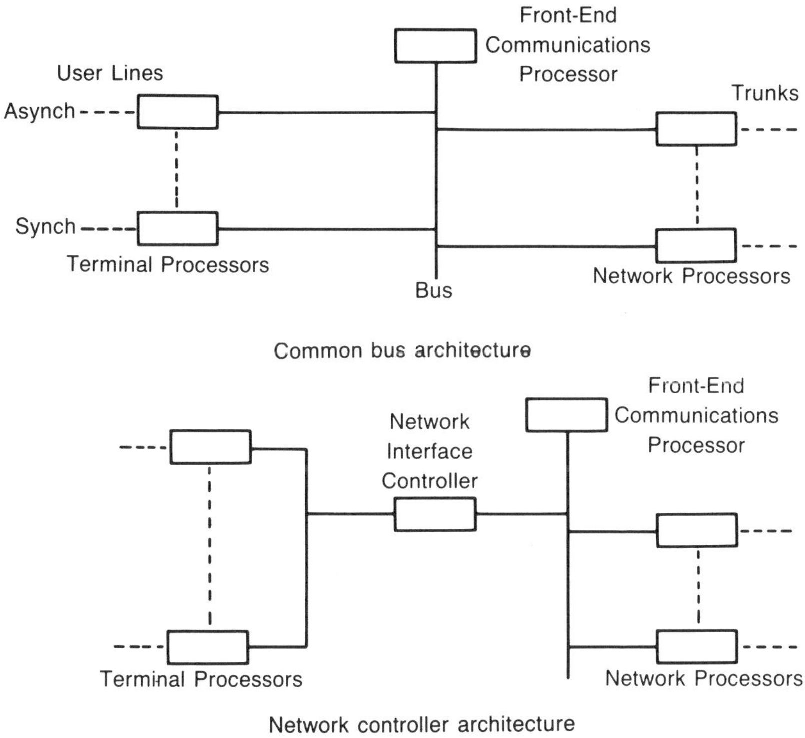

Fig. 3-21. Intelligent STDM architectures.

The individual terminal processors usually have about 32 to 64K of memory for programs and buffers. Each of these processors will handle about 16 ports. If synchronous capability is allowed, this is usually done with a separate processor. A network processor may be used to format the intermultiplex frames and handle the intermultiplex protocols. This processor might also be called a network interface controller (NIC), or similar term. It is used on the composite terminal traffic to coordinate scheduling with the front-end processor, to reduce contention among the terminal processors. There are many variations in these designs.

Concentrators

A concentrator is a device that collects data traffic from a number of sources and transmits them through a greater number of facilities or trunks. Originally, concentrators were programmable units that had somc storage and forwarding capacities, as well as switching capabilities. This is similar to today's intelligent STDMs, which are difficult to distinguish from traditional concentrators. Some intelligent STDMs are even more versatile than many concentrators.

Most current concentrators are used to handle the Level 3 protocols in the ISO-OSI reference standard, such as CCITT X.25, as well as the Level 2 data link control protocols. This makes the concentrator more like a network node, because it performs such functions as switching, routing, flow control, load leveling, polling control, and traffic monitoring.

A typical application that shows the use of STDMs, concentrators, and front-end processors in a distributed network appears in Fig. 3-22. The use of leased or dial back-up telephone channels requires modems, which might be an integral part of some devices. If Dataphone Digital Service (DDS) lines are used, a Data Service Unit (DSU) is required.

In a typical distributed communications configuration, each port has localized processing for such functions as ARQ retransmissions and node-to-node synchronization. These may be processed by network port processors. Other functions, such as character detection, dial-connection handshaking, and adaptive data compression are handled by terminal port processors. The removal of these processing functions from the main processor provides more processing power for building frames and supplying network-routing algorithms. Typically, an improvement in character-handling performance by a factor of three to four can be achieved. The number of ports supported is greater, because the data

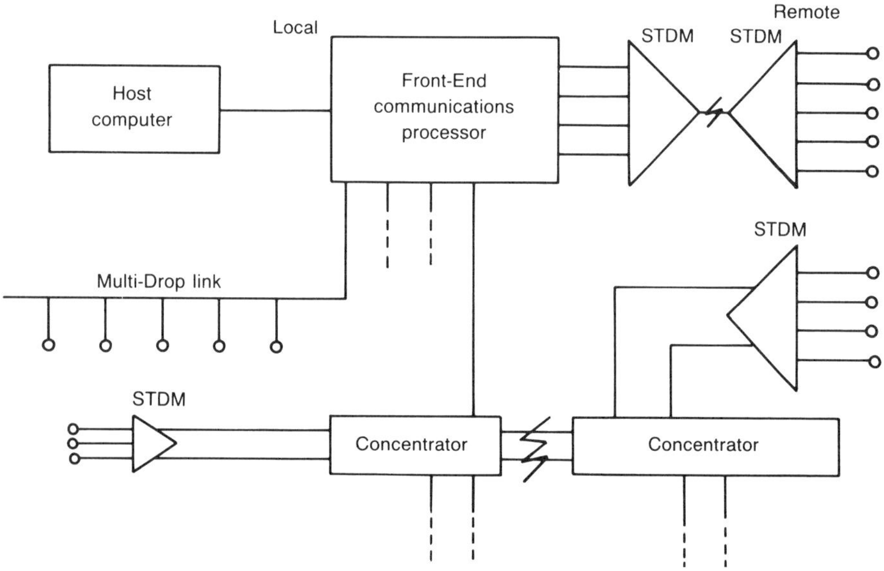

Fig. 3-22. A typical distributed network.

buffering is distributed. Incoming characters are processed locally and then buffered in a FIFO, which generates an interrupt to the main processor. When the interrupt is serviced, the characters are taken from the FIFO via the interrupt, greatly reducing the main processor overhead per character.

A routing table can be used to build the network port frames. This is updated as links are removed or become congested.

Dynamic routing implies that each new call requires a connection. Whenever a network link fails, or becomes congested, calls are reestablished without data loss, provided the buffers are not exceeded. Interprocessor communication is necessary to guarantee end-to-end data integrity and flow control. This can be accomplished by control packets, which are routed through the network by any available path, using a protocol such as CCITT X.25 for the packet switching.

A modular structure for both software and hardware is useful, so that additional features can be added as needed.

The delay characteristics of concentrators are similar to those discussed for STDMs. The architecture, software, and features vary widely. The optimal cost-effective use of concentrators requires careful consideration to questions of network topology, traffic considerations, network management, and the changing technology. A branch office, for example, might need to link several terminals to the main computer at the head office. Using a network with separate leased data links would require a modem for each device. In addition, the cost of the telephone lines, as well as the problems of reliability and data management, must be considered. The answer is usually STDMs or concentrators.

REVIEW EXERCISES

1. Define and discuss the various types of modems available.
2. Diagram a multiplexing system for 32 300-bps terminals.
3. How does a concentrator differ from an intelligent STDM?
4. Define the following terms: true modem, short-haul modem, line driver, half duplex and full duplex.
5. How are echo suppressors used?
6. Draw a flow diagram for polling a master and six modems in a multidrop configuration.
7. Describe inverse multiplexing. How is it used?
8. Discuss how the ISO-OSI model will affect the teleprocessing approaches of organizations around the world. Consider error-controlled strategies, line sharing (multiplexing and concentration), data link and

higher level protocols, as well as advanced public and private network approaches, including packet switching architectures.

9. What is the difference between data multiplexing and trunk multiplexing?

10. Diagram the analog FDM and the T-carrier TDM systems.

11. What are the advantages and disadvantages of fixed frame and variable frame multiplexing?

12. Describe how future teleprocessing systems might differ in their physical interface to signal converters. Scrutinize the economic and technical characteristics of telecommunications facilities, and include signal conversion devices for analog and digital transmission applications.

13. Why should particular emphasis be placed on strategies for distributed processing?

Chapter 4

The Elements of Protocols

The word *protocol* has been borrowed from common usage to describe computer communication behavior. In noncomputer terms, it describes social behavior, such as the orderly exchange of greetings. In computer communications, it has a similar meaning; it describes the order of events required to establish data connections and exchange data between computing equipment, as illustrated in Fig. 4-1.

Consider the simple example of a town meeting. If all those in the audience spoke simultaneously, the chairperson (and the rest of the audience) would struggle to hear everything, and much of the information would be lost. For this reason, meeting protocol requires a process of raising hands or standing in order to speak. This results in the orderly exchange of information among the participants.

If computers are to exchange information, some form of protocol is required in order to create a path for exchanging the information. The physical path is analogous, in digital communications, to the path connecting the two devices.

BASIC PROTOCOL CONCEPTS

The protocol represents the logical abstraction of a process to allow different machines to share information. The function of protocols in data communications requires the establishment of:

- Conventions, requirements, or specifications.

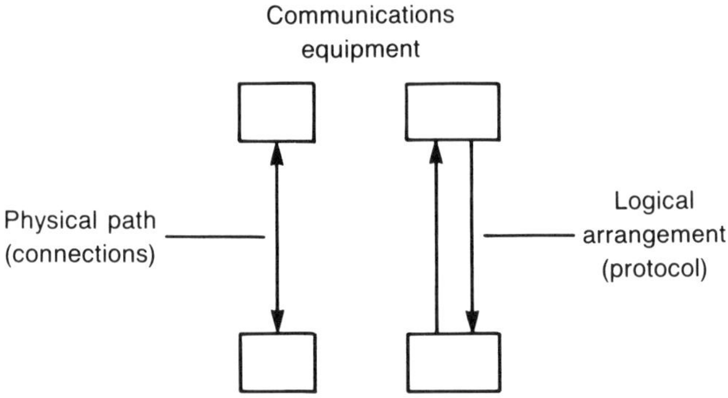

Fig. 4-1. Communications protocol.

- A standard communications path.
- A standard data element.

Conventions

Conventions are needed for starting and stopping the data exchange through the path. An important requirement for the data path is that errors in the data stream need to be detected. The control of the traffic flow through the path might be simple or complex, or there might be no traffic control at all.

The protocol convention can determine the nature of the data representation, the format and speed of the data representation over the communications path, and the sequence of control messages that are sent. A control message might be a simple "hello" which initiates a session or connection, it might be some or other supervisory or control step. Messages can range from a single bit to a complex string of bits, like those control messages that are used to start and stop data traffic.

The fundamental concept behind the use of standards is to give communication users more flexibility in selecting and interconnecting equipment. Standardization can result in reduced system development time and lower maintenance costs, and allows for expansion as communications needs change.

One of the basic elements of a communications protocol is the concept of handshaking, which refers to the controlled two-way transfer of data across an interface. The sequence of interlocking steps required to interface two devices is similar in some ways to a handshake between people, which usually signals the beginning of the transfer of some information.

Communications Paths

The protocol can also include a standard communications path between the computing devices. This often involves translating the physical realities of a path between two devices into a more useful *virtual* communications path, which is more suited to the characteristics of both pieces of equipment. The virtual communications path might require several items to be specified. One of these is an addressing structure for the path, which allows the communications between devices. A level of priority might also be required among devices seeking to send messages over the same path.

Data Elements

The protocol can establish standard data elements for use in communication over the path, creating a virtual data element which is exchanged between devices. The use of this virtual data element can allow two devices to swap character streams. These streams, or strings, can range from a simple command or set of data to an entire file. The file might represent a program, a job, or a graphic image.

Consider an application in which there are three different kinds of data sources, such as different mainframes or minicomputers. Suppose these source devices need to exchange data with three different types of receivers: text terminals, graphics terminals, and personal computers. Unless a standard shared protocol is used, nine different protocols are required to allow all the possible connections, as shown in Fig. 4-2A. Each of these protocols will serve a special purpose. A better solution for interconnecting equipment is to employ a standard protocol which would require only a six-connection implementation (three sources plus three receivers). This is illustrated in Fig. 4-2B.

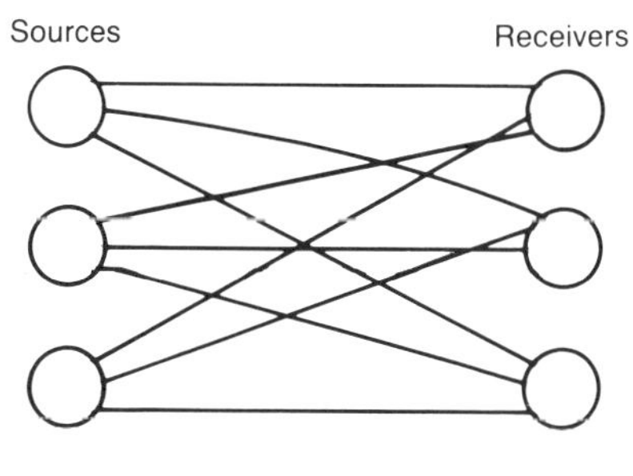

Fig. 4-2A. Nonstandard implementation requires nine unique connections.

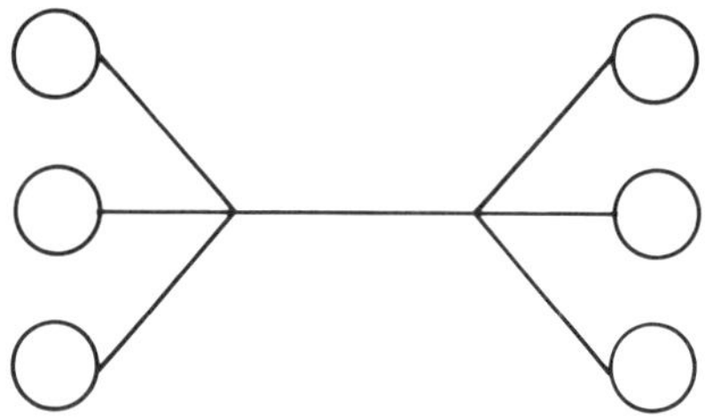

Fig. 4-2B. Standard implementation requires six connections.

Levels of Protocol

There are several differences between using a single level of protocol and several levels of protocol in a hierarchy. A one-level protocol has the advantage of being simple to implement. Most one-level protocols are application-dependent special-purpose protocols, and they work best when used in this fashion.

Multilevel protocols allow the separation of functions, which are required in a complex system. In this way, the responsibility for resource management can be segregated into different areas as required by the different resources. A multilevel protocol also support modular changes in the network, because each level of the protocol acts as a separate module. Multilevel protocols are more flexible, because special-purpose protocols can be substituted or used in parallel with the standard protocols as required. Thus, the multiple levels can be general, while maintaining the advantages of single-level protocols for special applications.

Another consideration is whether the protocols should be transparent to the user, or whether they should perform a virtual communications function. A *transparent protocol* is not noticed by the user. It exists to provide a function that the user does not need to control. The advantage of the transparent protocol is that it makes user operations simpler. A *virtual protocol* performs a tangible service, such as creating a virtual file, but the virtual protocol exists only as a logical entity. It has no physical existence.

If two protocols of different levels communicate, the lower-level protocol must first accept the data and control information from the higher-level protocol before performing any functions on it. The lower-level protocol usually treats both thc data and control information as data, adding its own set of header and trailer controls.

As the data moves through the protocol levels, it collects similar control-data envelopes. a host-to-host protocol will accept the application data from the user program and add its own control information. As the data travels further, the link control procedure will add more information. This layering of protocol hierarchy is not unlike the nesting of the levels in a complex operating system.

Note that there are fundamental differences between protocols and interfaces. Protocol is the set of rules for communications between similar processes, while interface is often used for the set of rules between dissimilar processes. As discussed earlier, an interface is the physical connection between two devices or processes, while a protocol is a logical concept. Consider a system with an interface between a host computer and a switching node. In this system, there may be a host-to-node protocol and a host-to-host protocol, as shown in Fig. 4-3.

Protocols can be used for a variety of functions. In most networks, more than one protocol is employed, with each protocol supplying a specialized set of functions.

NETWORK APPLICATIONS

A typical network is made up of subnetworks (such as the switching modes), transmission facilities, and subscriber equipment, including hosts, terminals, and front-end processors. The transmission equipment can include the multiplexers and switches, which allow data to travel over the network.

There might be specified levels of performance which are necessary for certain network applications and functions. This can include resource

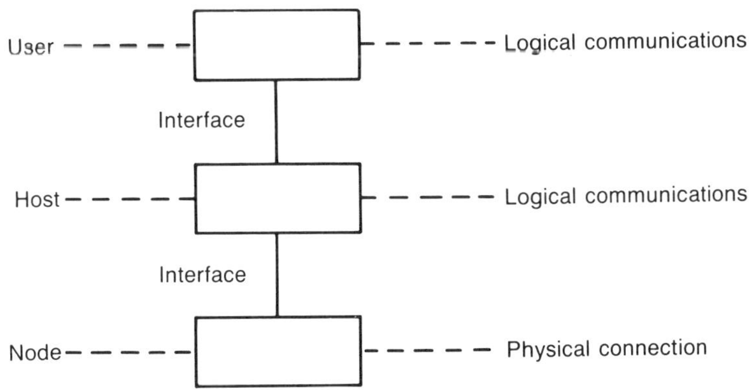

Fig. 4-3. Interfaces and protocols.

sharing among hosts, terminals, and other equipment on a cost-effective basis.

The protocol design is often the key to effective resource sharing among the network devices. This is because most processes within the host computer communicate with other host processes, or with processes in terminal handlers, via a specified protocol. In a similar way, the network transports data using low-level protocols.

Virtual protocols are usually employed in complex systems in which higher-level protocols are built on top of the lower-level protocols. The virtual communications are then established by the lower protocols. An end-to-end protocol is often used to control the overall integrity of transmission.

Link Control

The link control procedures for Level 2 of the International Standards Organization (ISO) model can be considered as the core protocol for most networks, because it is the most basic. The important link control procedures used today have the following features in common:

- Sequencing.
- Flow control.
- Data transparency.
- Connection and disconnection.
- Error control.
- Failure recovery.

The most common link control protocols are HDLC, SDLC, and BSC (BiSync). The HDLC protocol is the most common in new designs of these three.

A key feature of link control procedures is the provision for data transparency. Because both data and control messages travel through the link, it is necessary to distinguish the data bits from the control bits. The link control protocol must be able to tell when and where a data block begins and ends without restricting the data content. The protocol does this by assigning a control meaning to certain data patterns. The beginning of a block of data will be flagged with some specific pattern of ones and zeros.

The two most common methods for achieving data transparency are *bit stuffing* and *byte stuffing*. Bit stuffing is used in HDLC and byte stuffing in BySync. Byte stuffing uses a pair of characters, while bit stuffing uses a series of eight bits.

The transmitting hardware adds bytes or bits that the receiving hardware removes, preserving the transparency of the original pattern of data. One simple technique is to double the required control byte, so when the receiving hardware recognizes two control bytes in a row, one of them is automatically removed. Both bit stuffing and byte stuffing work in a similar way.

Connection and disconnection are also done in the link control procedure. When a connection is established, the devices involved in exchanging information might also exchange various types of identification. This is also the time when various parameters of importance to the data exchange will be set, including provisions for disconnection and reconnection if errors should occur.

The link control technique for recovering from failures usually requires some form of periodic test of the link operation. If the link becomes inoperative and fails the test, both ends of the link must have recovery procedures. Both ends must know that the link is not operational, even though, physically, there might be a problem in only one direction. After both ends are notified that the link is malfunctioning, they can begin to establish a new virtual connection. This mechanism must be fail-soft, so that the link can continue functioning in spite of any errors in transmission of data or control information.

Error control is that property which allows the link control to perform the failure recovery and to achieve accurate communications under normal operating conditions. The link control procedure does this through the management of transmission errors.

A variety of methods are used for error control. A common approach is to use an error-detection mechanism for each transmitted message, requiring retransmission by the source if the receiver does not acknowledge the proper error-free reception. The retransmission can be initiated by either a negative acknowledgement from the destination, if the message is not received, or by a positive acknowledgement, if the message arrives but contains errors. A timer in the source might also be used to retransmit messages when positive acknowledgments are not received within a specified period of time. Positive acknowledgments are more trustworthy, because the negative acknowledgments themselves might be lost.

One of the most basic ways of detecting errors is parity checking. One bit of the data is reserved to give the parity, based on the number of ones or zeros in the data string. More complex techniques for uncovering errors include computing the cyclic redundancy checksum (CRC) and similar summations.

If a block does contain errors, the destination device might ignore it. Then, after a predetermined amount of time, (usually the time required to receive a positive acknowledgement), the source can retransmit the block. The source might identify each of the blocks it is transmitting by some control number. This number typically sequences, or counts, from zero to some set limit, and then recycles. The destination can use this sequencing to detect missing or duplicate blocks. Messages with numbers lower than the lowest expected number, or higher than the highest, indicate duplicates.

Traffic Sequencing

Traffic sequencing is not a primary function of link control, but it is used to ensure that the traffic leaving a particular link is in sequence with the traffic entering.

A large switching network might have many links, and sequencing is more efficient if it is done at the final destination. Large centralized networks often use sequencing at the link control level. The blocks are assigned a unique sequence number, which is used to detect missing and duplicate blocks. It also maintains status information to the sender and receiver. Many early systems had only one or a few links, which worked well with the existing link control procedures, which were designed for only one link between the host computer and the peripherals. As these systems grew in complexity, they outgrew the original link control sequencing, which was never replaced.

Flow Control

Flow control is concerned with matching the sender's transmission rate to the receiver's capability to accept traffic using the link control procedures. One of the basic techniques requires the explicit allocation of resources. The receiver explicitly notifies the sender that it can accept traffic. A designated storage area is usually reserved for messages to be transmitted.

Many flow-control techniques use some form of *feedback.* In one system, the sender transmits messages until the receiver begins to reduce the amount of allocated space. A simpler flow control which is used in some systems consist of on/off control, with its limited efficiency. In other systems, the receiver tells the sender the specific transmission rate that can be supported. This is designed to prevent the receiver from becoming overloaded with traffic. The flow-control mechanism then allocates the number of messages to the sender based on the receiver's instantaneous reception rate. This requires some knowledge of the *window* in which a limited number of messages can travel from source to destination to approximate the flow control.

Flow control can also be performed through error-control mechanisms. One simple technique involves not sending positive acknowledgments. This provides a flexibility that is not possible with simple on/off control. Error control messages are used in ARPANET, the Defense Department's international packet switching network, to provide flow control.

Another type of flow control within the link control requires the discarding of messages when they cannot be accepted. This method relies on a higher-level of protocol to retransmit the messages at a later time.

Most statistical multiplexers utilize the CCITT X.25 Level 2 link protocol procedure.* This procedure calls for transmission of information in variable-length frames. The fields within the frame are:

- A flag to synchronize the demultiplexer with the rest of the information in the frame.
- Addressing to indicate the source or destination of a particular message.
- A control field to identify the type of message.
- A variable-length field into which the data is packed.
- A cyclic redundany check (CRC) to perform error detection.

The error-checking procedure involves a retransmission of the frame in error. Each frame is held in buffer storage until an acknowledgement is received from the other end of the link. Table 4-1 shows the control byte used.

---

*The major international standards are defined by the CCITT (the Consultative Committee on International Telephone and Telegraphy). The CCITT has specified four levels of protocol between equipment:

1. Level 1 is the physical or plug interface between DTE and DCE. The current standards for this interface include the RS-232, 449 electrical interfaces and others.
2. Level 2 describes the link-control procedure. An example of this protocol is high-level data link control (HDLC).
3. Level 3 is the network control protocol. The X.25 protocol is the international standard at Level 3.
4. The host-to-host protocol exists at Level 4 and is used to connect one DTE to another on an end-to-end level.

Table 4-1. X.25 Link Access-Level Control Byte.

Format	Command	Response	Coding 1 2 3 4 5 6 7 8
Information	I		N(R) P* N(S) 0
Supervisory		RR	N(R) F* 0 0 0 1
		RNR	N(R) F 0 1 0 1
		REJ	N(R) F 1 0 0 1
Unnumbered	SARM		0 0 0 P 1 1 1 1
	DISC		0 1 0 P 0 0 1 1
		UA	0 1 1 F 0 0 1 1
		CMDR	1 0 0 F 0 1 1 1

*Poll/Final

Commands:

I = Information
SARM = Set Asynchronous Response Mode (''Start'')
DISC = Disconnect

Responses:

RR = Receive Ready
RNR = Receive Not Ready
REJ = Reject
UA = Unnumbered Acknowledge
CMDR = Command Reject

Sequence Numbers:

N(R) = Receive
N(S) = Send

HOST-LEVEL PROTOCOL

The host-level protocols usually have several levels. At the lowest level, a host-to-host protocol performs the end-to-end communications between processes on different computers. The computers may be on different networks or within the same network.

At the host-to-host level, the required network services vary greatly. Multiple destinations, nonsequenced service, low delay, or high reliability might be among the important requirements. The host-level protocol characteristics will depend on the type of interprocess communication desired, the network interface needed, and the services available to support the host level. The level above the host level is often labeled as the application level, or the user level.

Layering, as you have already seen, involves separating the protocol functions into different levels. Some of these levels are independent, and some support others. For example, TELENET for virtual terminals is supported by the host-to-host level in ARPANET.

The use of levels can simplify the access to each one, and allow the network to access services at several different levels, as shown in Fig. 4 4. The utility of this concept depends, in a large part, on stable, well-defined interfaces between the protocol levels. This allows the levels to be changed without affecting the interface, allowing service to evolve with the existing protocols. Thus, service interruptions are minimal when upgrading is required.

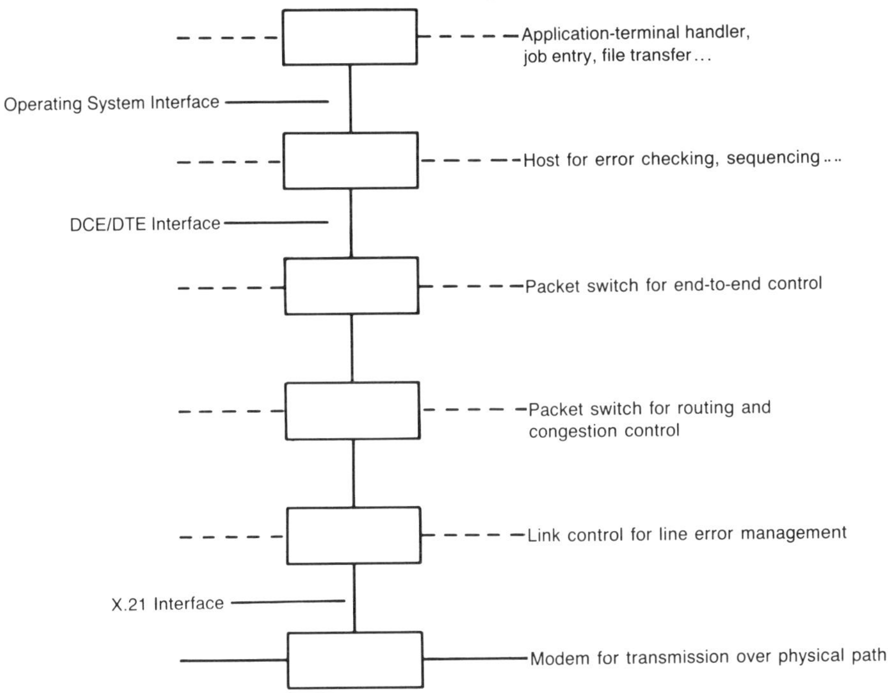

Fig. 4-4. Protocol layering.

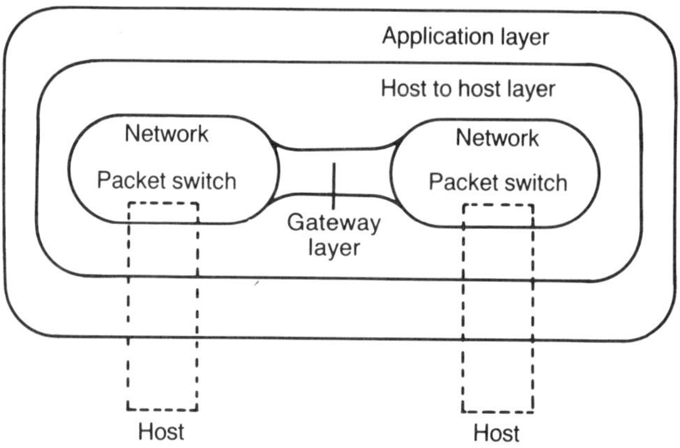

Fig. 4-5. Protocol shells, layers and networks.

Symmetry is an important principle in protocols. The ends of each level are connected, and form contours at each level, as shown in Fig. 4-5. Contours that do not match indicate that the ends are in the wrong layer. This becomes even more of a problem in distributed systems where there might not be any single site in control.

The operation of sequenced full-duplex point-to-point protocols is relatively common, even in the use of multiple networks. Multipoint services such as broadcasting to several processes or conferencing are emerging, based upon experiences with shared satellite channels, ring nets, and Ethernet in cooperative distributed protocols.

The protocol must work correctly even when the systems work concurrently. Consider ARPANET, where there is a host/host protocol (TCP) adjacent to the Network Voice (NVP). The former supplies point-to-point interprocess communication, while the latter carries compressed speech over a low-delay nonsequenced network datagram service. Cooperation between the systems must exist even though they remain essentially independent. This is in contrast to the master/slave relationship that was discussed in Chapter 2.

The objective of independence usually requires some form of separation of control and data. This separation of control and data, or data transparency, is achieved (as discussed earlier in this chapter) through bit-stuffing or special frame characters. In some standards, such as the X.21 standard, different electrical leads are used for control and for data. In other standards, a special format is used to distinguish information from control bits.

The case for symmetry is evident when comparing an electronic mail service with public-switched telephones. With the mail system, two people can simultaneously send information which crosses in the system without adversely affecting communication. In the telephone system, two calls can collide when both are dialed simultaneously, making the information exchange impossible until someone hangs up. The telephone system represents an asymmetrical protocol based on the master/slave model. Such a system does not mix with symmetric ones, because it cannot support any other. These mixed protocol systems are subject to many potential problems.

Some of the basic tenants of protocol design, such as requiring different protocol levels to operate independently with common objectives, might appear to be wasteful and inefficient. A typical example is flow control, which promotes duplication. However, this repetition in different levels is needed for the sharing and protection of resources within the levels.

Synchronization is required to maintain the state of each of the ends of a protocol in close correlation. Flow control is a type of sequencing mechanism.

Resource management takes on the form of flow control when the resource to be controlled is buffer space. Resource sharing is typically achieved using some form of multiplexing where a common address structure allows access to the resources.

Uniformity must exist in such areas as the process of port addressing and the allowable data format to allow communications between processes. A number of common conventions are used, such as paired agreements between hosts. In general, resource-sharing is more effective when a single standard is used for host/host communications. Uniformity can be maintained by translating one host protocol into another. Then, the translator becomes a part of the system as the shared convention. A number of different mechanisms might be needed to complete the translation and relate the objects and operands from one protocol to another. This technique can result in many potential conflicts, but translation might be the only practical solution where certain parts of the network cannot be modified.

In a broadcast system, where all processes hear all transmissions, the distributed control protocols must allow cooperation. They must be able to run the same control or decision-making algorithms against the same data. The usual positive acknowledgement schemes quickly become unwieldy, because a single broadcast could require thousands of acknowledgments. True broadcast protocols exist for packet-speech conferencing. These are real-time systems where a few packets are not a great problem, so data acknowledgments are not used.

A similar situation occurs in applications where synchronized real-time connections, which may be broadcast, drive input/output devices. These include joysticks, lightpens, and other tracking devices which might require a virtual graphics protocol for different process connections. Synchronization is important so the user can view the motions and created images while hearing the related text. Without synchronization, the display might not be coordinated with the text.

Other protocol considerations include encryption for privacy, priority selection, reliability, and the delay mechanisms that might be used for the scheduling of messages or packets.

THE ISO-OSI MODEL

Communication can be considered a high-level function, supported by a connection, which is a lower-level function. This multilevel hierarchical system of data networks is evident in the International Standards Organization (ISO) model for communications networks. The ISO reference model for Open Systems Interconnection (OSI) is composed of seven layers and it attempts to define a network as a group of manageable pieces with well-defined interfaces. The model defines the overall structures, functions, and relationships among the layers and their interactions, but it does not define the specific protocols required to implement the functions within each layer.

Each layer of the model communicates with a corresponding peer at the other ends of the connections. A physical connection only exists at layer one; layers two through seven communicate with their peers using virtual connections established in software. These layers exchange information through the layer-to-layer interfaces, because each layer has only a virtual connection to its peer. Only layer one exchanges data directly through a connection with its peer.

The use of layers and their interfaces provides a structure that allows the protocols that implement a layer to be changed without affecting other layers. This allows changes in technology to be implemented on a layer-by-layer basis.

The concept of layers in the OSI model can also be related to the existing telephone network. The caller initiates a session by dialing a telephone number (the network address). An acknowledgement follows, when the called party answers. The caller does not need to know how the network locates and rings the called party's phone, or how the information travels from one mouthpiece to the distant party's earpiece, as long as it is transported without errors. The local and long-distance networks might use a combination of satellite, microwave, fiber-optic, or copper-wire links, as long as the physical connections that make up each data link are compatible at the connecting ends.

Related Protocols

The communication between the stations on a LAN can use various medium access control mechanisms, such as CSMA/CD and tokens, various physical configurations, including the type of cable used, and the topology, such as bus and ring. All of these fit within the two lowest layers of the OSI reference model. The protocols required define the interface between the network and the data link control layers as well as the internal operation of the data link and physical layers. These protocols are required to control the access to a shared resource at these layers.

Other protocols are required for the total operation of the network. These include terminal interfacing, host interfacing, network management and control, internetting, and higher-level protocols. The relationship of these protocols is shown in Fig. 4-6.

TERMINAL INTERFACES

At this level in a local network the need exists to establish connections to the host computers in the network. A terminal command language can provide the opening and closing of connections. After the connection is provided, the terminal will appear to be in a transparent mode so the characters entered at the terminal can be forwarded to the host.

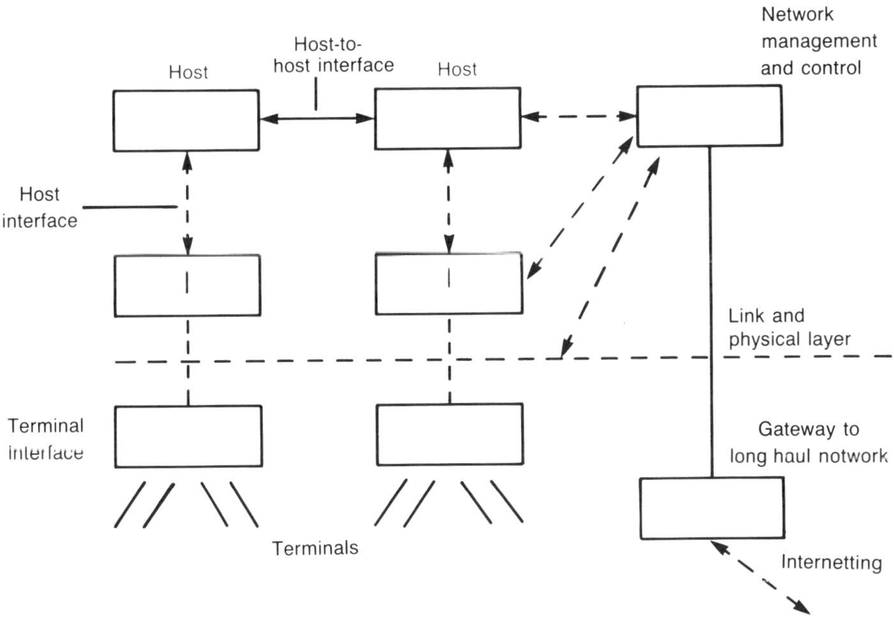

Fig. 4-6. Related LAN protocols.

These commands will also allow the setting of communications parameters and the determination of the status of parameters and connections. These parameters include such variables as speed, data forwarding, and echoing.

An interrupt capability might be used to bypass the data stream. This is equivalent to the hard-wired line that will interrupt a program that was discussed in Chapter 1.

These features are similar to those covered in CCITT Recommendations X.28 and X.29 for interfacing asynchronous terminals to packet switching networks.

Virtual Circuits

In a connection from a terminal to host, as shown in Fig. 4-7, a virtual circuit will exist between the terminal interface unit and the host interface unit. The virtual circuit protocol will be required to coordinate the sequencing of data, flow control and error control, and other functions between the two devices. These functions are at the transport layer.

Unique protocols might be used, while still meeting the requirements of IEEE 802. Equipment from different vendors is unlikely to operate at the transport layer unless a common transport protocol is used, such as the ISO transport protocol, the Xerox Network Systems (XNS) protocol, or the Department of Defense Transmission Control Protocol (MIL-STD 1778). XNS is used in some personal computers, where it operates with Ethernet.

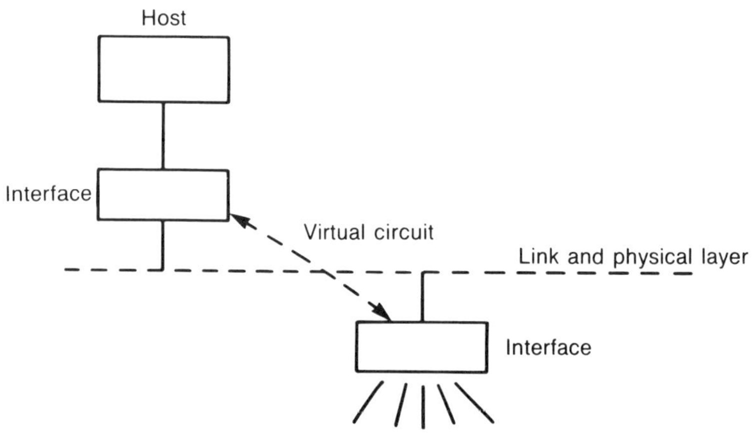

Fig. 4-7. Terminal to host protocol with virtual circuit.

Host Interfaces

The two major techniques for interfacing host computers to a local network are: terminal emulation and multiplexing.

Terminal emulation uses separate physical terminal ports. The network appears to the host as a collection of terminals, each with its own port. When a terminal requires a connection, it is assigned an available port by the interface unit. This approach is simple because it can be used with any host that supports terminals. An overhead exists for the host in the flow control required for the terminal ports. This can be done with ASCII XON/XOFF flow-control signals or RS-232 RTS/CTS modem control signals. This approach also limits the network to terminal access, and the host cannot initiate connections or communicate with other hosts.

A multiplexed host interface allows many logical connections using a single high-speed physical connection. The physical interface allows access to the host's bus, and is unique to the particular host.

Software in the host is required to demultiplex the connections. This software must be compatible with the transport and session layer protocols of the remote devices communicating with the host. These interfaces allow process-to-process applications, such as file transfers between hosts on the network.

Terminal emulation interfaces were used in most early local network products. These supported only terminal-to-host communications. High-speed multiplexing interfaces are now available using Ethernet for the network and busses such as Multibus or Unibus, for the host.

NETWORK MANAGEMENT

The practical operation of a local network depends heavily on the capabilities built in for such functions as fault isolation and maintenance. Fault isolation and diagnostics are necessary to locate faults in broadband or baseband cable systems. There should also be a capability to detect faulty interface units.

The capacity to modify software in the interface units is also needed, allowing new releases of software to be installed and the address of stations to be changed. These functions could be performed locally at a single station or remotely from a network center.

Other management functions include the collection of statistics, and access control. This latter function is concerned with who is allowed to use the network. *Session keys* are one method of access control. These keys are issued to devices that need to encrypt data, and the key expires at the end of the session.

Although local network standards can allow equipment from different sources to coexist on a local network, network management standards are required for the practical operation of a network involving a mix of vendors' equipment. These network management protocols span several layers, and are not confined just to the two lowest layers inside the network.

INTERNETTING

Local area networks will usually be connected to long-haul networks via interfaces to Private Branch Exchanges (PBXs), modems, or packet switching networks. A typical modem interface is shown in Fig. 4-8.

This interface is similar to a terminal emulation interface to a host. A terminal user will establish a virtual connection to the modem interface, and, by issuing commands to the modem, a circuit-switched connection will be established to a remote host or another network. The interface will manage flow control and buffer data.

The connection of packet-oriented local area networks to long-haul packet switching networks can be made in one of two ways. First, the gateways can operate at the datagram protocol level, where each packet is treated as a self-contained unit and forwarded on to the next network. This is called a *nontranslating* gateway.

Second, the gateway can operate at the virtual circuit level, connecting virtual circuits through the two networks. Here, the gateway deals with the required functions, such as sequencing and error control of the data on a virtual circuit. This is called a *translating* gateway.

In either type of gateway, the protocol requirements include routing, message size, addressing, flow control, and acknowledgments. These

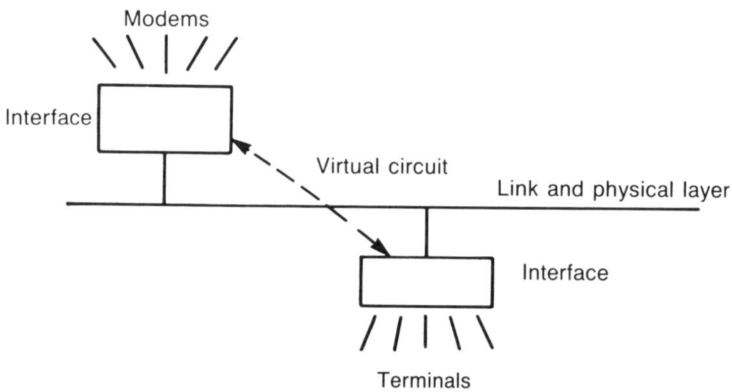

Fig. 4-8. Modem interface.

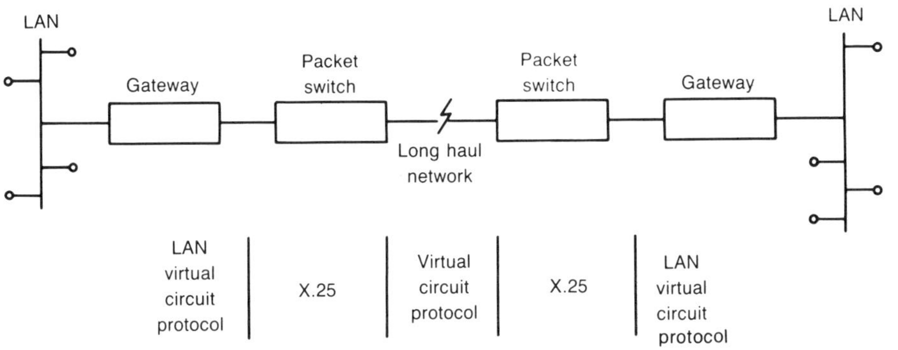

Fig. 4-9. Long-haul network interface with a virtual circuit gateway.

requirements will be determined by the choice of a datagram or virtual circuit gateway.

In the connection of a local network to a long-haul network with a datagram gateway, the compatible protocols at the transport level and above are used in the two networks. The virtual circuit management functions, such as flow control, sequencing, and duplicate detection, are performed on an end-to-end basis. The gateway operates at the internet level, and routes each packet independently.

The connection of a local network to a long-haul network with a virtual circuit gateway is shown in Fig. 4-9. The virtual circuit approach allows incompatible transport-level protocols to be used in the two networks. The virtual circuits are connected end-to-end in the gateway. Sequencing, flow control, duplicate detection, and retransmission are done by the gateway.

Major differences in the two protocols can present problems. Virtual circuit gateways, while performing translation, might be adequate for low-speed terminal-to-host connections, if the terminal user can intervene in special circumstances. Host-to-host communications require other techniques. Datagram gateways with compatible transport protocols have been employed with the XNS protocol.

REVIEW EXERCISES

1. What is the main function of a protocol?
2. Discuss how handshaking can be accomplished on an RS-232 interface.
3. Determine the number of unique protocols required for a system of four sources and eight receivers if protocol sharing is not used.
4. What is the difference between a protocol and an interface?

5. What is a virtual protocol?

6. What functions is a link control protocol concerned with? How can it achieve data transparency?

7. Discuss error-control methods for a link-control protocol.

8. Describe some methods for flow control in a link-control implementation.

9. What is the advantage of protocol layering?

10. Draw a connection shell for three networks with a common gateway, where three-way communication is not possible because the protocol layers do not all match.

11. Draw a detailed protocol layer that could be used in the system shown in Fig. 4-5 based on the ISO-OSI model.

Chapter 5

Communication Networks

Local area networks are a departure from the hierarchical structures of mainframe computers caused by the evolution of computing systems. As computers and memory systems have become smaller, more powerful and less expensive, the trend has been away from the hierarchical structure, toward a more distributed structure. Before the advent of inexpensive microprocessors and memory chips, processors and their memories were centrally located. The terminal equipment used for input and output were unintelligent devices. These "dumb" terminals were only required to change the received signals into visible characters and convert the keystrokes into transmitted signals.

These mainframe systems required a large investment in both initial and maintenance costs, and usually many hours of programming time were needed before even a simple application was in operation. Compatibility between different manufacturer's equipment was practically nonexistent. It was unlikely that another vendor's equipment would be purchased unless it was to be used as a completely independent system. Most computers used different chips and architectures with proprietary protocols for input/output between the processors and peripherals. Often, there was a new standard for each new product.

The terminals were usually located in the vicinity of the computer room. They were connected with direct hard-wired links, which provided low-error transmission at relatively high speeds using synchronous transmission. Terminals at remote locations were usually serviced using facilities leased from the public telephone network. The public telephone circuits are designed for voice service, and have limited data-carrying capabilities. The error rate can often exceed 10,000 times the error rate that is experienced on direct links. The cost of the leased circuits can also be high, although it can be reduced by using multiplexing to service several terminals, as discussed in Chapter 3.

The microcomputers and minicomputers of today are designed with flexible architectures, to serve a broad range of applications. The lower investment required allows smaller units in the corporate structure to be tailored to the needs of smaller user groups. These systems are now deployed in increasing numbers, and software applications are available to serve a wide range of functions. More users now access the computer, and they require access from workstations located closer to their desks. This is accomplished mostly with asynchronous terminals that require less-complex protocols than synchronous terminals. The software and the terminals are available through a number of vendors, and users often have a wide range of choice.

The asynchronous terminal interface that has become standard is RS-232. It is designed to support terminals located near the host. This standard, which is known as V.24 by the International Telegraph and Telephone Consultive Committee (CCITT), supports transmission at rates up to 19.2 Kbps, up to a distance of 50 feet.

Remote terminals require devices known as *data circuit terminating equipment*, or DCEs, as shown in Fig. 5-1. Installations with an analog PBX for voice transmission require modems, as discussed in Chapter 3. The modems condition the data signal for transmission through the voice channels. The data rate is usually limited by the bandwidth of the voice channel. At a rate of 19.2 Kbps, a 24-line by 80-character display can be updated in less than one second.

Transfers of large files with several million bits normally demand higher speeds. The ports of many computer systems can supply data at

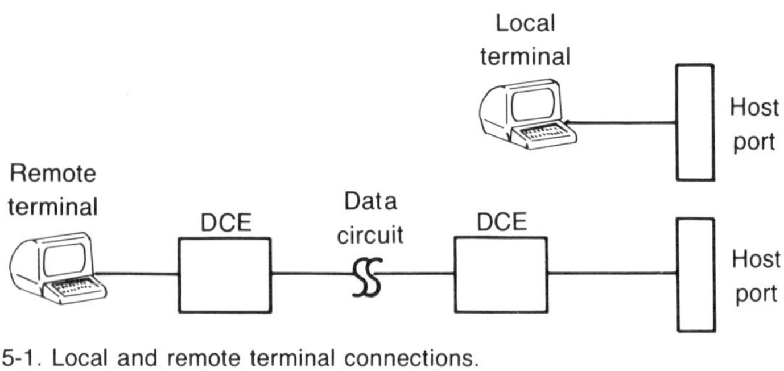

Fig. 5-1. Local and remote terminal connections.

rates up to 50 Mbps. Higher rates might also be required for high-resolution graphic applications.

DATA AND VOICE COMMUNICATIONS

The U.S. public switched-telephone network connects over 170 millions users. The switched network's appearance of uniformity and general ease of use make it a prospective model for any hypothetical data network. One reason for the public telephone network's ease of use is that the interfaces have been completely standardized. This includes the telephone equipment, the wiring, the numbering system, and the signals provided to users during calls, such as the dial, busy and ringing tones. Note also that the internal operation of the network appears to be transparent to the user. After the dialing sequence has been completed, the network assumes the responsibility for routing the call and maintaining the connection without user assistance.

The standardization of the voice system is due primarily to government regulation through the years, as well as the industry domination by a single supplier, the former Bell System. Even with the recent deregulation of the industry, these standards remain, and equipment that is designed accordingly will operate properly on the network.

Local communications products have evolved in a freer environment characterized by diversity. Many proprietary data communications standards exist which are largely incompatible. Some of these even vary from one product line to another. These differences include:

- Binary codes used to represent information.
- Transmission formats.
- Addressing and routing.
- Data rates.
- Wiring.
- Connection set-up procedures.

The connections are the paths for data exchange. To the communicating parties, a connection appears to be a physical path dedicated solely to their use. Not all connections might be supported by a distinct physical path, however. Using multiplexing, a single pair of wires can support a number of simultaneous virtual connections, all on the same physical connection. These virtual, or logical, connections are often used for data exchange among processors in a common computer system. The software process and the user cannot distinguish these virtual connections from hard-wired links.

Bauds

When data transmission rates are expressed in bits per second, these indicate the rate of data transfer exactly. The baud rate refers to the rate of transitions occurring on the transmission line. This is not always equal to the bit rate, because there are a number of ways to represent bits as transitions on a transmission line.

Some techniques, such as nonreturn-to-zero, or NRZ, encoding, use a single baud per bit, while others, such as Manchester encoding, require two bauds per bit. Some encode more than one bit with each baud, and the baud rate of a data stream might be higher or lower than the bit rate. The bandwidth required to transmit at a given rate is then dependent on the encoding scheme used. The bit rate is expressed in bits per second and the signalling rate is expressed in baud. The signalling rate rarely differs from the bit rate by more than a factor of two to four when wire transmission is used.

Character Codes

The two most widely used standards for representing characters and print-control information in digital systems are the American Standard Code for Information Interchange (ASCII) and the Extended Binary-Coded-Decimal Interchange Code (EBCDIC). ASCII is used by many asynchronous terminals, and EBCDIC is used in a wide range of IBM and IBM-compatible equipment. Code conversion is one of the functions performed by Layer 6, the presentation layer, of the ISO-OSI model.

ANALOG AND DIGITAL SIGNAL CONCEPTS

Most of the early PBXs were used for analog voice traffic. These analog signals appear to be continuous (Fig. 5-2A) because the signals may take on all possible values between the lowest signal level and the highest. Binary or digital signals have only two possible values, representing the binary digits (or bits) zero and one (Fig. 5-2B). Digital signals can be used to encode any desired number or letter.

Fig. 5-2A. Analog signal.

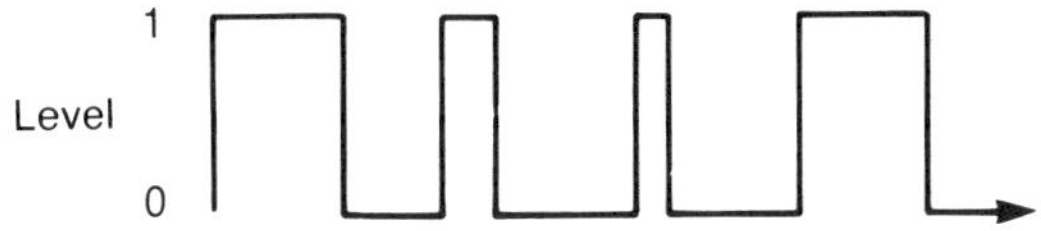

Fig. 5-2B. Digital signal.

These letters or numbers can be represented by analog speech signals. A group of bits is often used to represent a binary number or letter. The bits correspond to the value of the signal at a given instant. The specific values represented by a group of binary numbers can be assigned according to any desired scale, with either fixed steps between successive values (a linear scale) or variable steps (a nonlinear scale).

The analog telephone converts variations in sound pressure into variations in an analog electrical signal. The number of variations that occurs sets the frequency of the signal. The speech that is produced can be considered the summation of a number of pure tones that occur simultaneously. The difference between the maximum and minimum frequencies represents the bandwidth.

The human voice contains signals of 100 Hz to 5000 Hz. The telephone system limits these frequencies to 300 Hz on the low end and to about 3500 Hz on the high end, producing a bandwidth of about 3200 Hz. This is enough for the transmission of recognizable speech.

Analog speech can be represented in digital form following the steps of sampling and analog-to-digital conversion. The continuous analog waveform is sampled at regular intervals of time, and the analog values are converted into binary numbers. A common coding technique is pulse code modulation (PCM), as shown in Fig. 5-3.

The sampling theorem requires that a signal of limited bandwidth must be sampled at twice its highest frequency to reproduce the original signal (for speech, this is about 8000 times per second. The assignment of a discrete binary number to each sample produces an error known as the *quantization error*. This is the difference between the actual value of the analog sample and the nearest value encoded by one of the binary numbers.

The quantization error is reduced by using a scale with more bits

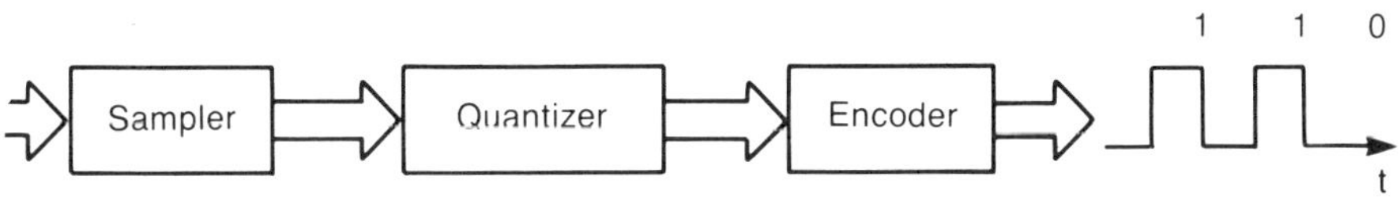

Fig. 5-3. Pulse code modulation.

per sample, which produces smaller steps. The standard scale for speech encoding in North America is called *u-law 255*, which is an 8-bit nonlinear scale. (European countries use an algorithm known as A-law.) The bit rate, or bandwidth, required for PCM speech signals with this scale is:

$$8 \text{ bits} \times 8000 \text{ samples/second} = 64{,}000 \text{ bits/second} = 64 \text{ Kbps}$$

CIRCUIT SWITCHING AND PACKET SWITCHING

Circuit switching and packet switching are two basic techniques used for allocating bandwidth. Circuit switching is often used to control and route voice traffic. Control is via a centralized hierarchical mechanism which requires a global knowledge of the network's configuration. Packet switching is often used with data traffic. It is suited to distributed control mechanisms which require little information about the network configuration as the data moves from source to destination.

Although the use of circuit and packet switching differs, the hardware for each form of switching can often be used to support the other. For a number of applications, a hybrid system might be the optimum solution.

If a circuit represents a route or path between certain parts or devices, then circuit switching provides a means to establish a connection. The data pattern remains fixed in time and space, and the path is fixed until the circuit is disconnected. To establish a circuit-switched connection, it is first necessary to locate an available data path, assume control of it, and then allocate it to the exclusive use of the communicating parties. This is the circuit set-up overhead.

Circuit switching is more efficient when the communicating parties exchange a large amount of data relative to the data that must be exchanged for the set-up overhead. After the connection is made, there is generally no additional overhead required to maintain it. The bandwidth and other resources are dedicated until the connection is broken. This type of circuit is efficient only if all of the allocated bandwidth is used.

Circuit switching is useful for voice conversations that tend to be long (usually several minutes) compared to the set-up overhead, which is usually several hundred milliseconds. Thus, the ratio between the data transmission time and the set-up overhead is several hundred to several thousand.

Packet switching uses the available bandwidth only when there is data to be transmitted. This more efficient use of bandwidth requires more processing overhead for the transmission of each packet. The packets are formed by adding information to the beginning and end of

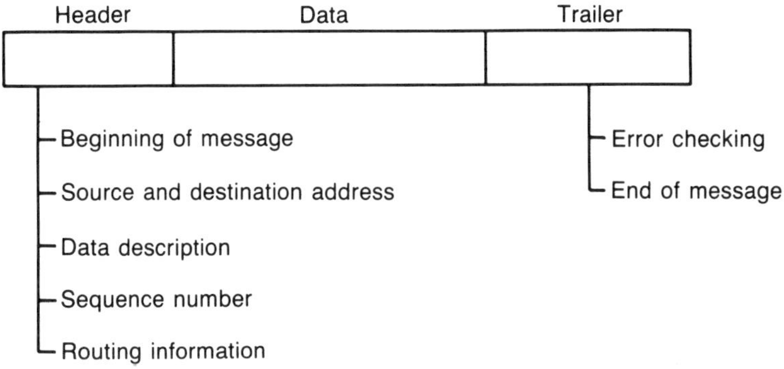

Fig. 5-4. A data packet.

each group of data. This is illustrated in Fig. 5-4. A packet header identifies the source of the data and its destination. It might also identify the nature of the data, and even provide billing and accounting information. The trailer contains the error checking which is done to test for the presence of incorrect symbols that might have produced during the transmission.

Packet switching is a type of message switching where the length of each transmission is limited to the maximum packet size. Longer messages are broken down into a number of packets, which are reassembled into the original messages on the receiving end.

Packet switching is more efficient in transaction-oriented applications, in that bursts of data must be exchanged during the small period of time that the different units are logically connected during a session.

An example of such an application is a distributed database as discussed in Chapter 2. The communications costs for this type of application with packet switching are more likely to reflect the actual amount of data transmitted, rather than the total connection time. Packet switching is also more suitable to systems in which the users switch rapidly and often between a number of applications or are in communication with multiple applications simultaneously.

Delay Considerations

In addition to the relative efficiency of packet or circuit switching for a given application, a major concern is the delay experienced between the time a device is ready to transmit data and the time the data is received at the destination. The total delay is made up of the transmission delay and the access delay.

Transmission delay is the time required to send a message through the media. This delay is a direct function of the distance required to send the message, and an inverse function of the bit rate for both packet and circuit switching.

Access delay is the time that it is required to access the transmission system before transmitting data. In circuit switching, the circuits allocated to a connection are immediately available to the users following the initial set-up time. In packet switching, an access delay can occur prior to the transmission of each packet if the system is in use, or if other users waiting have a higher access priority.

Certain classes of packet networks, such as those that use token passing, have a deterministic maximum delay that may be incurred by a single user. This is a function of the number of users and the distances between them. Other networks, based on the CSMA/CD access method used in Ethernet, have a maximum delay that is probablistic. The probability of a long delay might be minimized by restricting the number of users, but it is theoretically possible for the delay to increase to the point where no data gets through.

The use of protocols at the third and fourth layers in the OSI model can provide virtual connections, which act as circuits for packet switching. Fast circuit switching is also available in circuit-switched systems. It uses a circuit set-up procedure whose delay is much less than the usual 100 to 500 milliseconds.

Space-Division Switching

Most early manual and electromechanical PBXs employed space-division switching networks. These systems provided a unique dedicated physical path for each conversation. A full-duplex physical path was used for the duration of the call, which was carried by continuous analog signals.

Space switches are arranged to connect a number of inputs (N) and outputs (M). If a single-space switching network is to provide simultaneous connections between each input and any available output, a matrix of N × M switching elements is needed. Thus, to connect 200 users to any of 200 devices would require 40,000 bidirectional switching elements.

In most voice applications, the probability of each user needing service at the same time is low. So, most voice PBXs provided fewer paths than needed to connect each input to any other line or trunk. When all available switch paths become filled, the calls are blocked until a path becomes free. This is known as a *blocking system*. A nonblocking system is one that allows all possible combinations of lines and trunks, simultaneously. These systems are usually not used in voice service.

The probability that a user will be blocked from service can be expressed as a function of the number of lines connected to the system and the average traffic in each line. The total traffic is the number of calls multiplied by the average duration of each call, which is expressed in seconds for a one-hour period. Each call is then equivalent to *3600 call-seconds* or 36 ccs (hundred call-seconds).

For many business applications, a majority of the lines might require less than 6 ccs of traffic during the busiest hour. If the switching system has 3600 ccs capability, it is nonblocking for 200 users, because the system can support 100 two-way connections of 36 ccs traffic.

Digital Switching with Data Busses

A data bus in a PBX is a high-bandwidth data path that is shared among a number of devices, which can include voice stations, data terminating equipments (DTEs) or personal computer/workstations (PCs). These devices gain access to the bus through bus interfaces, which provide the device ports, as shown in Fig. 5-5A. Most digital PBXs use these data busses to concentrate data before switching operations are performed. The switching operations can be done in a switching network connected to the bus, or in the bus itself. These centralized busses are known as short busses. They are relatively inexpensive and can use parallel transmission to support very high bandwidths.

Communications between the user device and the bus can be through a link between the PBX port and the device. The data bus might operate at a high rate in order to support many users, but the bandwidth of an

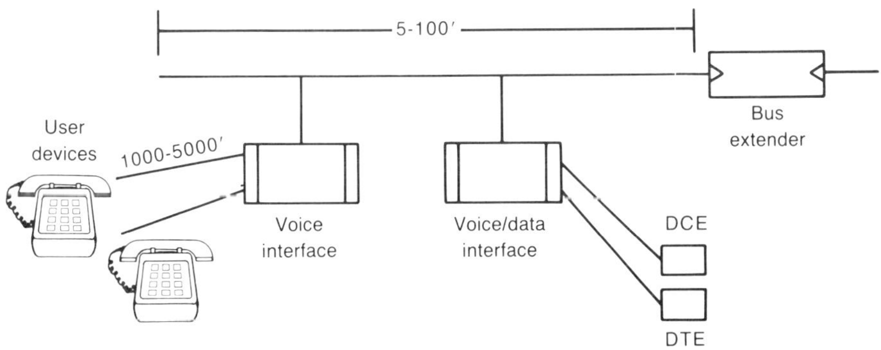

Fig. 5-5A. Short bus used for PBX systems.

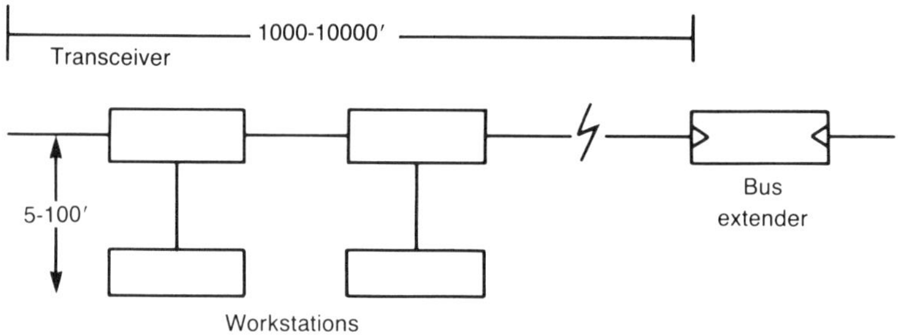

Fig. 5-5B. Long bus used in broadband and baseband LANs.

individual link to a device might be much lower. The links can operate at rates required to support a certain class of device types.

Long distributed busses with the full bandwidth are used as shown in Fig. 5-5B. This is the type of bus often used in baseband and broadband local area networks. Long busses might use serial transmission over a single cable to reduce wiring costs.

DATA COMMUNICATIONS REQUIREMENTS

Data communication requirements are quick to change, and this has been fueled by the emergence of networks that can be used to connect computer-based systems to geographically dispersed users. Current data services are provided, in part, by modems operating over analog channels using a frequency-division multiplex (FDM) hierarchy. Rates up to 9600 b/s can be supported over a single voice channel. Higher data rate modems require proportionally larger FDM bandwidths.

Digital transmission facilities can be used to handle data requirements more efficiently. However, the early implementations of PCM for digital telephone applications did not include direct data interfaces, and modems were still required to provide the necessary conversion for the interface of data with a PCM voice channel.

PCM channels can be used with modems at rates up to 9.6 Kbps, but not all of the bandwidth is used. It is more efficient to have the data channels directly multiplexed with PCM channels. A single 64 Kbps PCM channel could be multiplexed to six channels of 9.6 Kbps data. This type of submultiplexing of 64 Kbps channels is common in digital transmission facilities.

The organization of emerging data transmission networks is based on the existing terminology and interface standards. The basic schemes to interface between data terminal equipment (DTE) and data circuit terminating equipment (DCE) in a data transmission network is shown in Fig. 5-6. The DTE is the user device, typically a computer, while the DCE is the communication equipment, often a modem or multiplexer, that connects the user to the network. The interface is made up of three types of signals—data, timing and control—and by the different levels of organization required for the network application.

The timing signal required depends on the type of DTE used. You have seen that asynchronous terminals transmit data characters that are separated by start-stop pulses. These pulses allow the receiving terminal to identify the beginning and end of each character. With this scheme, no timing line is required between the DTE and DCE.

Synchronous and Asynchronous Transmission

With synchronous transmission, characters are transmitted continuously in blocks without start or stop pulses. The transmitting and

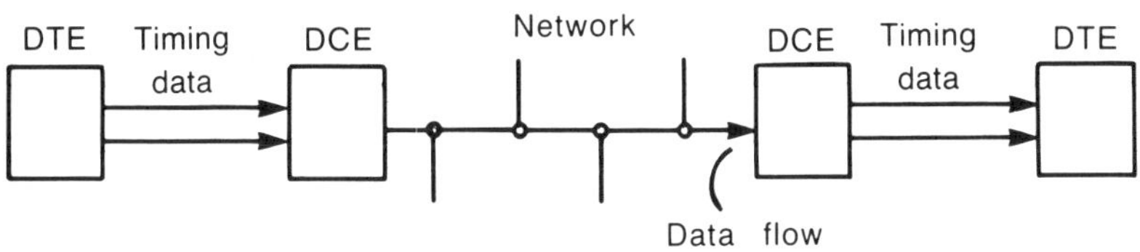

Fig. 5-6A. Codirectional timing.

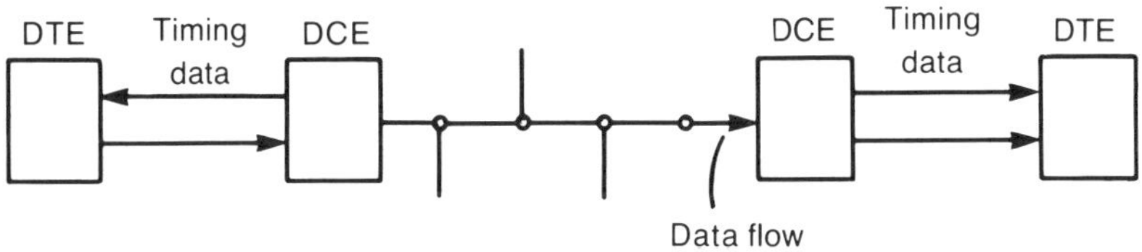

Fig. 5-6B. Contradirection timing.

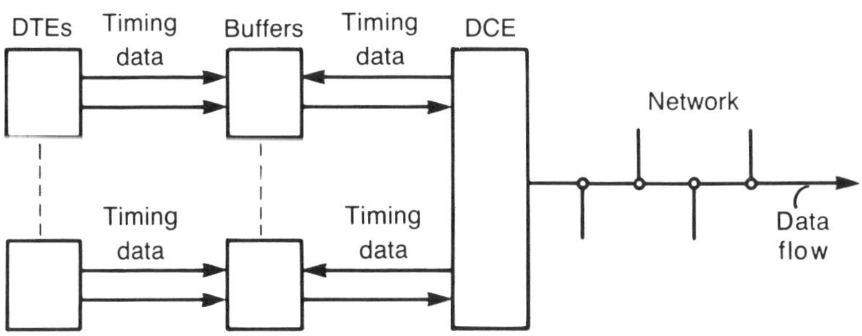

Fig. 5-6C. Buffered timing.

receiving terminals are required to operate at the same speed so the receiver can decode which bit is first in a block of data. There are a number of schemes used for the timing lines in synchronous transmission:

• *Codirectional timing*, which requires the DTE to supply a timing line to synchronize the DCE frequency source to the DTE.
• *Contradirectional timing*, which requires the DTE to be slaved to the timing of the DCE.
• *Buffered timing*, which uses buffers that allow each DTE to operate from its own timing source. The buffers compensate for the differences in data rate between each DTE and the DCE.

The buffered technique is often used when the line interfaces with several different terminals. The buffers can be a part of the DTE or DCE, and must be large enough to allow slip-free operation for some specified period of time, depending on the application.

Asynchronous data transmission is normally used for data rates below 19.2 Kbps, and it is used in most ASCII terminals. The internal timing references, or clocks, of the transmitter and the receiver run independently. The transmitter initiates a transmission by sending out a start bit. It then transmits data at fixed time intervals. The receiver detects the start bit, and samples the data stream at fixed time intervals. The transmitter and receiver must be set for the same bit rate in order for the data to be interpreted correctly. Following the start bit, the transmitter might send a single byte with one or more stop bits to indicate the end of the data.

The use of these short bursts of data allow the receiver to resynchronize its clock at the beginning of each transmission. Longer data streams need a higher clock accuracy in order to remain synchronized.

Synchronous transmission is more suitable for long, uninterrupted bit streams at higher speeds. The clock information is encoded along with the data, and the receiver adjusts its clock rate accordingly. A Manchester-type of code, which provides two transmissions per bit, is used to send long streams of data without requiring resynchronization. Synchronous standards group the bits logically into frames with an easily detected pattern to mark the frame boundaries. The receiver then scans the incoming stream for the pattern which it uses for synchronization.

In the T1-D3 standard, 24 PCM-encoded 64 Kbps voice channels are multiplexed into a single 1.544 Mbps stream. Each frame holds an 8-bit sample from each of the 24 voice channels, plus a framing bit for synchronization. The framing bit alternates between zero and one. The resulting 193-bit frames are repeated 8000 times each second to achieve the 1.544 Mbps rate.

Rates for continuous synchronous transmission range from the T1 1.2 Kbps up to the T4 rate of 274.176 Mbps. T1 transmission is often used between PBXs and hosts.

Synchronous transmission can be used for transmitting blocks of data, in which the beginning of the data stream is used for synchronization. IEEE Standard 802 defines rates of one, four, five, 10, and 20 Mbps for synchronous transmissions. The errors in these block transmissions can be checked using a block-check character (BCC) or cyclic redundancy code (CRC) at the end of the transmission.

Voice-Grade Channels

The voice-grade channel for telephone communications has evolved during the past century. A worldwide network of close to one billion telephones exists. These are connected through a variety of trunks, including wire and fiber-optic pairs and cables, microwave and millimeter wave repeaters, and satellites. Connections range from complex electromechanical switches to programmed electronic switches.

Because the network already exists, and the addressing and internal signalling schemes are essentially standardized, it is possible to access almost any location. In the early days of data communications, this network seemed to be a logical choice for providing data communications over extended distances.

The telephone network evolved with the purpose of providing quality voice communications. It was not originally designed for the needs of data communications which have occurred only recently (Table 5-1).

The emphasis on voice transmission resulted in sectioning the transmission medium into 4000 Hz units. Filters were used to obtain a flat response over each 4000 Hz band. Voice quality is essentially

Table 5-1. AT&T (Bell) System Equipment for Data Transmission.

Series	Class	Characteristics
100	subvoice-grade lines	Low Speed (0-300 bps) Serial
200	voice-grade lines	Medium Speed (1200-9600 bps) Serial
300	group band and T-1 lines	Wideband (19.2, 40.8, 50, 230.4 Kbps, 1.344, 1.544 Mbps)
400		Parallel
500	submultiplexed T-carrier	DDS (2.4, 4.8, 9.6, 56 Kbps)
600		Acoustic Coupler, Special-Purpose
800		ACU, DAS, Channel-Terminating Units
900		Test Equipment

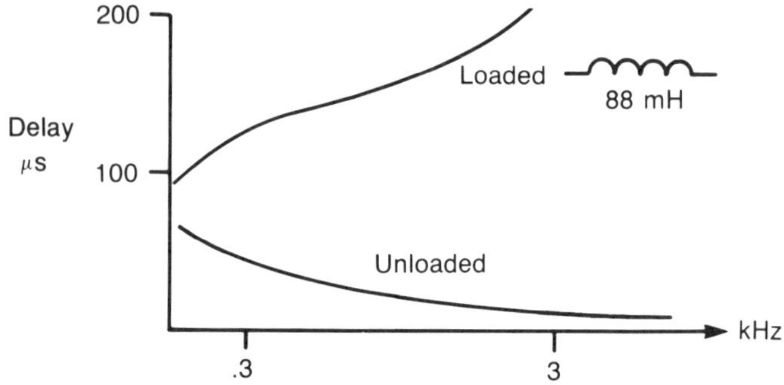

Fig. 5-7. The effects of loading coils on the voice band.

unaffected by variations in phase delays, so no consideration was given to this delay, which can greatly affect data and image transmission.

The twisted-wire pairs in cables are also conditioned with loading coils. These inductors are placed about a mile apart in a cable to flatten the frequency response. They produce a large differential delay in the voice band (Fig. 5-7).

Another problem is the use of echo suppression for two-wire to four-wire conversions. Suppressors are added to reduce the undesirable echoes by attenuating the reverse direction of the transmission.

The transmission of high-speed data is greatly affected by the techniques used to enhance voice quality. If leased lines are used only for data transmission, the loading coils and echo suppressors can be removed. In the United States, a voice-grade leased channel (the 3002 channel) can be obtained for data communications. It has the characteristics shown in Fig. 5-8. Note that there are a wide variety of

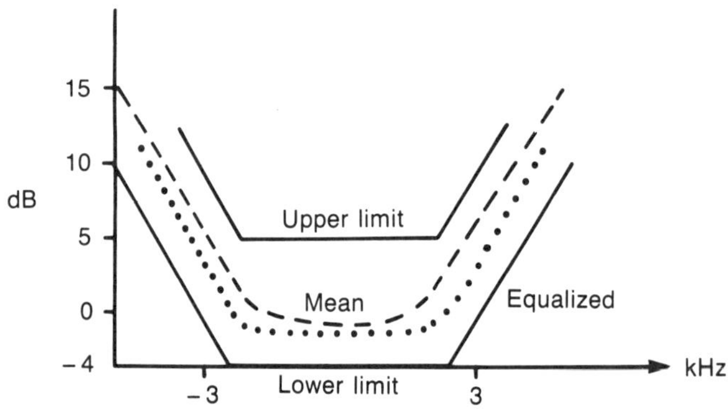

Fig. 5-8. Attenuation characteristics of voice-grade 3002 channels.

attenuation curves possible, depending, among other factors, on how the line is routed.

A fixed equalizer can be used to compensate for the variation in frequency. A compromise equalizer will adjust to the line and attempt to maintain the relative phase delay constant over the band. At rates below 2400 bps, a fixed compromise equalizer or a manually adjustable equalizer might be satisfactory with the proper modulation. At higher rates, the effects of frequency response can be much more severe, resulting in interference that can make the proper coding and decoding impossible. Even an adjustable equalizer cannot help much under these conditions. Thus, for almost all data applications above 2400 bps, voice-grade lines must be used with automatic tracking and adaptive equalizers to account for the line variations.

At the higher data rates, variations of the basic frequency-shift keying (FSK) modulation technique are used to enhance the data rate/bandwidth ratio. Other problems at high speeds include noise, phase jitter due to frequency conversions in the analog multiplexer chains, echo effects, phase and gain shifts due to the momentary loss of the carrier signal, and harmonic distortion from nonlinear amplification.

Conditioned lines are available for an additional monthly fee. These are leased lines that have some controls for data transmission. One of these is the C-conditioned type of line, which has a tighter envelope on attenuation and delay than the basic 3002 line. This is shown for attenuation in Fig. 5-9. There is more control on attenuation and the differential delay over the voice band. A D-conditioned line is also

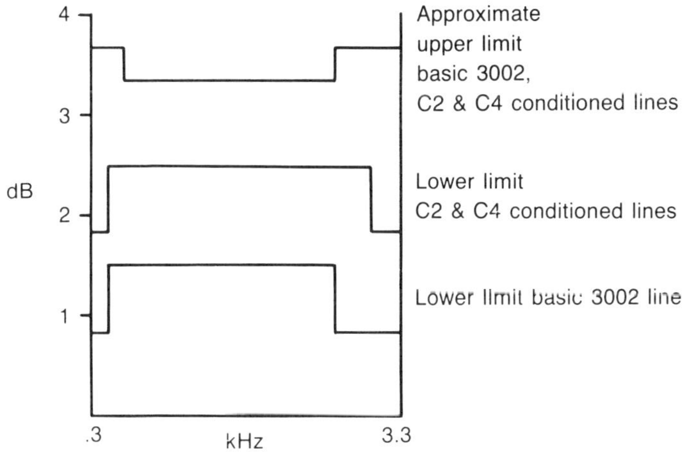

Fig. 5-9. Conditioned line characteristics.

Table 5-2. Problem Areas Controlled by Conditioning.

Problems	Basic 3002 Line	C-conditioned	D-conditioned
Attentuation Distortion		Controlled	
Delay Distortion		Controlled	
Signal/Noise Ratio			Controlled
Harmonic Distortion			Controlled
Impulse Noise			
Frequency Shifts			
Phase Jitter			
Echo Effects			
Phase Shifts			
Gain Shifts			

available. Many problem areas, however, are not controlled by conditioning, as shown in Table 5-2. The areas not controlled under the tariff specifications as shown in the table are subject to the variability of local and regional internal practices.

The different delay specifications for the C1, C2, and C4 classes of conditioning are shown below:

C1	C2	C4
to 1kHz: 1 to 2.4μs	to 0.5kHz: 1 to 2.6μs	to .3kHz: 1 to 2.6μs
to 1.75kHz: 0.8 to 2.6μ	to 1.5kHz: 0.6 to 2.6μs	to .5kHz: 0.8 to 2.8μs
	to 3kHz: 0.5 to 2.8μs	to 1.5kHz: 0.6 to 3μs
		to 3kHz: 0.5 to 3μs

For data rates of 14.4 and 16 kbps, or in areas where the lines are noisy, D-conditioning might be required, because it affects the signal-to-noise ratio and harmonic distortion.

C-conditioning is often ineffective except at the lower rates, so a large number of modems operating at up to 4800 bps have built-in equalization and might not require conditioning.

INTERFERENCE AND ERRORS

Data transmission involves the transmission of symbols at some specified rate. The receiver has the task of interpreting these symbols using its internal program or logic to make the proper decisions, even though noise and timing problems (which might cause an error in deciding the correct symbol) are always present to some degree.

Data transmission is not the same task as is required in analog transmission where the fidelity of the waveform must be maintained.

What is required here is the proper decision, so that one symbol is not confused with another one. The *intersymbol interference* (ISI) which causes this confusion occurs when a short finite-duration pulse is transmitted into a band-limited channel. The pulse becomes a time-dispersed signal, so it is longer than its original duration and is delayed, as shown in Fig. 5-10.

This effect occurs because the frequency components of the pulse are differentially attenuated and differentially delayed, due to the limited frequency response of the channel. The higher frequency components will be delayed more than others, thus, the output pulse is spread and dispersed over a different time frame. These dispersed responses will tend to interfere with one another, creating the intersymbol interference.

The principle method of evaluating this intersymbol interference, which is the major problem in high speed data transmission on band-limited channels, is to use a superposition of a string of symbols as observed at the output of the channel, called the *eye pattern*. Typical eye patterns are shown in Fig. 5-11.

BANDWIDTH LIMITATIONS

The bandwidth of a transmission line is a function of its length, because the transmitted signal is attenuated as it propagates along the medium. The losses are dependent on the transmitted frequency, and usually increase rapidly above the cutoff frequency of the media. In practice, the data rate is affected by the transmitter and receiver characteristics and the environment in which the cable is placed. The effects of interference and cross-coupling can be especially important in unshielded cables.

The relationship of bandwidth to distance for voice-grade media (VGM) is shown in Fig. 5-12. The T1 digital link, for example, supports full-duplex digital transmission at a rate of 1.544 Mbps for distances up to 2000 feet, using two pairs of voice-grade connections. For shorter distances, higher data rates are possible.

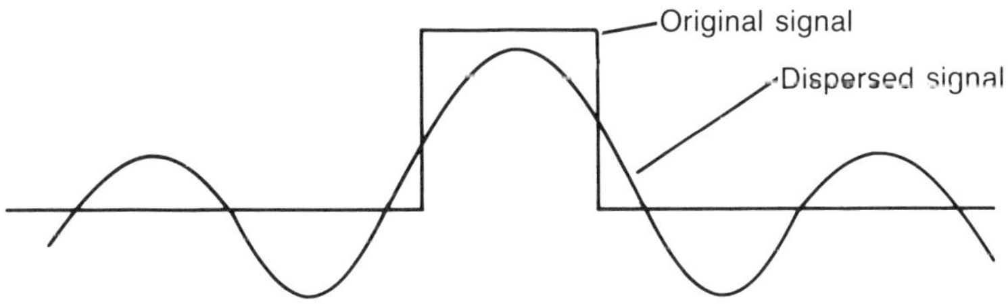

Fig. 5-10. Time dispersion in a band-limited channel.

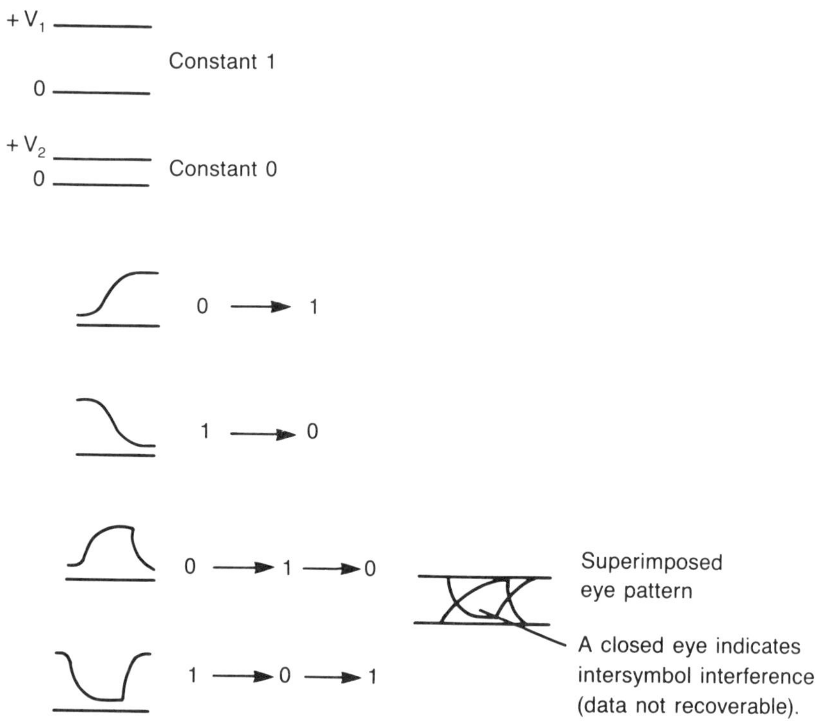

Fig. 5-11. Eye patterns.

WIRING SYSTEMS

Wiring topology and specifications are a critical part of any LAN implementation. Many existing buildings are wired for voice service, and

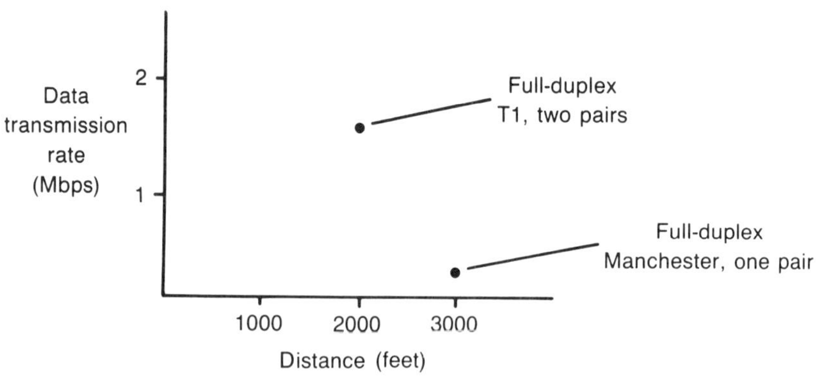

Fig. 5-12. VGM bandwidth.

most PBX systems use a star topology. The star PBX, or home-run wired system, uses dedicated wires that run from the user's workstation to the PBX. The number of wire pairs required for each station depends upon the services provided and the type of transmission used.

Buildings are usually wired uniformly with the same number of wire pairs. Most PBXs are installed with two or four pairs of wire between the PBX and the user workstations. Most PBX wiring is 24-gauge insulated solid-copper wire in unshielded twisted pairs. This is commonly known as telephone grade or VGM.

The use of VGM allows a wide range of common tools and accessories for cable distribution, termination and testing. The techniques are familiar to a large number of telephone technicians, and are less costly to install and maintain than most other types of cabling. Coaxial cables can cost 10 to 15 times as much per link per unit length.

The star topology provides an advantage in flexibility compared to ring or bus-oriented topologies. The star configuration makes it relatively easy to relocate a user, because only one connection is affected, and there is a single point to aid testing and troubleshooting.

In a local area network, one station must be able to send a message to any other station. Exceptions might be made for various reasons, such as privacy or security restrictions. To connect all nodes directly to all other nodes would be costly, and adding or deleting nodes would quickly become a complex procedure. If the network provides a shared communication medium for the interconnection of stations, then it

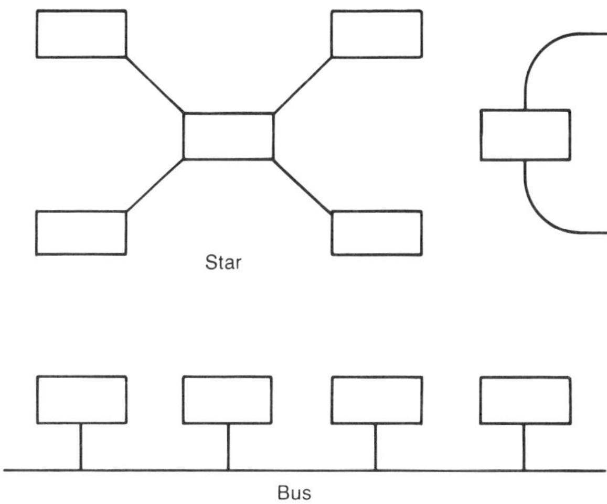

Fig. 5-13. PBX topologies.

becomes desirable to minimize the logic and computation required by each station to make routing decisions.

Typical network topologies include the star, ring, and bus, as shown in Fig. 5-13. These structures allow uniform and effective network control strategies.

There is an important difference between the physical and the logical topology. A physical bus could use a logical ring control structure, and other combinations are possible.

REVIEW EXERCISES

1. How is speech represented in digital format?
2. Discuss the advantage of virtual connections.
3. What is the difference between the bit rate and the baud rate?
4. What is quantization error? How can it be reduced?
5. Discuss the use of circuit switching versus packet switching. Describe how packet switching would function in the distributed database of Chapter 2.
6. Draw a diagram for a space switch with four inputs and four outputs.
7. An application requires a maximum of 10 ccs. If the switching system has 10,800 ccs capability, what is its nonblocking capability?
8. What are the differences between long and short busses? Where are they used?
9. Discuss the use of codirectional, contradirectional and buffered timing.
10. Discuss the use of asynchronous and synchronous transmission.
11. Draw a diagram describing the T1-D3 synchronous standard.
12. How are voice-grade channels conditioned?

Chapter 6

LAN Protocols

In this chapter the current standards for local area networks (LANs) are introduced. The protocols used in LANs refer to the Open Systems Interconnection (OSI) reference model. The evolution of LAN standards began with Ethernet, and evolved to the current IEEE 802 standards, which cover several types of LAN configurations.

Local network protocols support a variety of combinations of topology, transmission medium, signal encoding technique, and data rate. Protocols and standards for LANs involve more than just the protocols internal to the local network. Standards for interfacing the terminals and computers to the LAN are also necessary, as are the protocols for network management and control operations. The applications that are supported on the LAN are also likely to require transport and higher-level protocols.

LAN PROTOCOLS AND THE OSI MODEL

In terms of the OSI reference model, the protocols internal to a local network occupy the two lower layers: the physical layer and the data link layer.

Physical layer protocols cover the mechanical, electrical, functional, and procedural functions. RS-232 defines:

- A standard 25-pin connector.
- Specific electrical signal levels.

- The assignment of functions to the pins.
- The procedures for initializing communications, and sending and receiving the data.

The data-link layer protocol provides functions, such as error control and access control, on a logical data link. Many local network protocols resemble HDLC at the data link layer. HDLC uses a cyclic redundancy checksum for error detection, and polling to control which station has access to a multipoint link.

In local networks, where many stations can share a common communications line, several access-control schemes are used, including a contention scheme, known as carrier-sense multiple access with collision detection (CSMA/CD), and token-passing schemes, which are related to polling. This is summarized for point-to-point lines as shown below:

OSI Reference	Protocol for Point-to-Point	Control for Local Area Network
Physical	RS-232	Baseband or Broadband Signals
Data Link	HDLC	CSMA/CD or Token Passing

THE EVOLUTION OF ETHERNET

An experimental Ethernet was first reported in 1976. A major step for the evolution of LAN standards began in 1980 with the release of the Ethernet specification by Digital Equipment Corporation (DEC), Intel, and Xerox. The 1980 Ethernet specification was concerned with the two lower protocol layers of the ISO Model.

The Ethernet specification received acceptance as an industry standard for local area networks by a number of independent vendors. A number of products appeared for Ethernet networks as a result. The concept of an open system, which allowed interoperability among different vendor's equipment was an important step in the development of LANs. Ethernet controller boards became available in 1982 and Ethernet controller chips, based on large-scale integration, appeared shortly thereafter.

At the physical layer, Ethernet uses coaxial cable which does not exceed a few kilometers in length, and a topology known as *dendritic*, which is similar to a branching nonrooted tree. Baseband signaling is utilized at a data rate of 10 million bits per second (Mbps). (The first experimental Ethernet used 3 Mbps signaling.)

At the link control layer, a contention-based channel-access protocol is employed. This is the carrier-sense multiple access with collision detection (CSMA/CD) technique. This layer also defines a frame structure for messages similar to that used in HDLC.

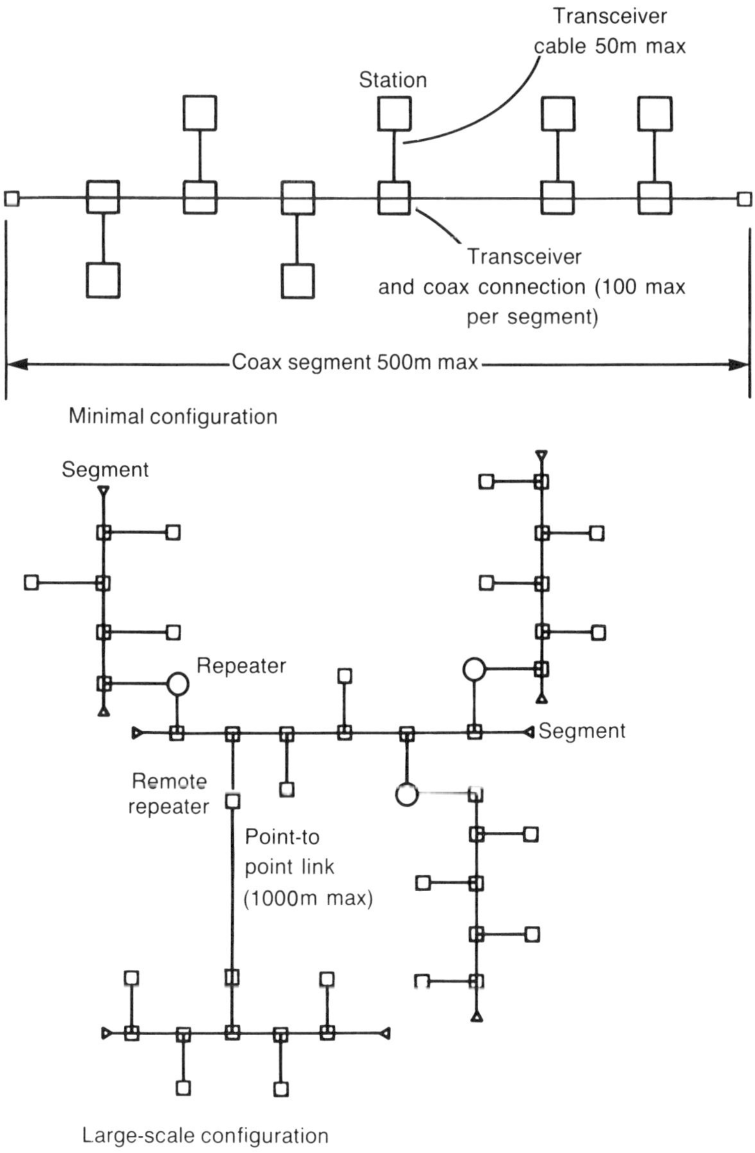

Fig. 6-1. Ethernet configurations.

Typical Ethernet configurations are shown in Fig. 6-1. The minimal configuration consists of a single segment of coaxial cable of up to 500 meters. The user devices—workstations or host computers—are connected to the main cable using an access or transceiver cable that can be up to 50 meters in length. Most of the Ethernet protocol logic is implemented in the workstation.

The access cable is connected to the main cable using a transceiver, which performs the signal transmission and reception. The propagation delays are short, and the transceivers are able to detect collisions by comparing the outgoing and incoming signals. Transmission is halted when collisions are detected.

A local network of more than 500 meters uses multiple segments which are connected with repeaters. The repeater retransmits every message with a small delay which acts to cancel out the distance limitation of a single segment with the baseband signaling employed. In a large building, one segment could be vertical up a utility shaft, with segments spread out for each floor as shown in Fig. 6-2. A single segment can contain up to 100 stations.

A point-to-point link is used to connect segments that might be some distance apart. This can be up to 1000 meters in length, and acts as a repeater divided into two sections. The interconnected segments appear to be in one logical space to the CSMA/CD protocol. A maximum of two repeaters can be in the path between any two stations.

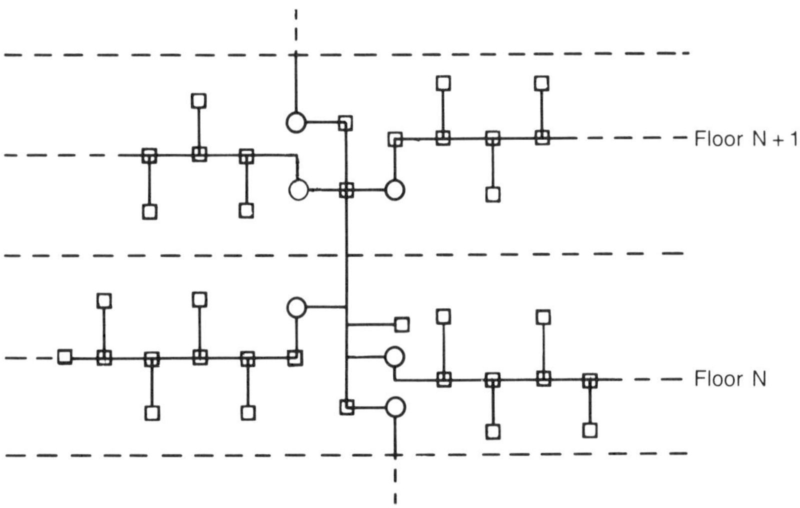

Fig. 6-2. Typical multi-story configurations.

The Ethernet standard is now one of the options within the IEEE 802 local network standards. There are a few modifications from the revised 1980 specification. The final Ethernet specification will be considered as part of the IEEE 802 standard.

THE IEEE 802 LOCAL AREA NETWORK STANDARD

The IEEE began its project 802 for local area network standards in 1980. The general concept for this project covers the two lower layers of the OSI reference model and the interface to the network layer.

The data link layer is divided into two sublayers: a logical link control sublayer similar to HDLC, and a medium-access control (MAC) sublayer, such as the CSMA/CD protocol used in Ethernet.

An access unit interface takes the place of the transceiver cable in Ethernet. It is defined between the component containing both the link layer and physical signaling and the physical medium attachment to the transmission media.

The IEEE 802 standard is actually a family of standards. This is shown below:

LINK LAYER:	IEEE 802.2 LOGICAL LINK CONTROL		
PHYSICAL LAYER:	IEEE 802.3 CSMA/CD BUS	802.4 TOKEN BUS	802.5 TOKEN RING

A common portion exists at the logical link control sublayer, and the three main options involving the MAC sublayer and the physical layer allow:

1. A CSMA/CD access protocol on a bus topology.
2. A token access protocol on a bus topology. (In a token access protocol, permission to transmit, which is the token, is passed from node to node through the network. A node can transmit only when it possesses the token.)
3. A token access protocol on a ring topology.

Along with the three major options, there are a number of suboptions for different transmission media, signaling methods and data rates. The following list summarizes these options:

CSMA/CD

Baseband 50 ohm coax	Broadband 75 ohm coax
Manchester coding	
10 Mbps	2, 10 Mbps

Token Bus

Single Channel 75 ohm coax	Broadband 75 ohm coax
Continuous and Coherent FSK	Multilevel, Duobinary AM/PSK
1, 5, 10 Mbps	1, 5, 10 Mbps

Token Ring

Baseband 150 ohm twisted pair	Baseband 75 ohm coax
Differential Manchester	
1, 4 Mbps	4, 20, 40, Mbps

The Logical Link Control Sublayer

There are two types of operations possible using the logical link-control procedures:

Type 1—connectionless.
Type 2—connection-oriented.

Type 1 is similar to a datagram in that there is no need for the establishment of a logical data link. There is no acknowledgment, flow control, or error recovery, and either individual or group addressing may be used. In Type 2 operation, a logical data link is established, acknowledgments are provided, and only individual addressing is allowed.

Two classes of logical link control are allowed:

Class I—Type 1 operation only.
Class II—Both Type 1 and Type 2 operation.

All stations support connectionless operations, but only Class II stations support both connectionless and connection-oriented operations.

The logical link control sublayer includes:

- An interface service specification to the network layer above.
- The logical link control procedures.
- An interface service specification to the medium access control sublayer below.

The interface service specification to the network layer defines the calls for an unacknowledged connectionless service. This is the datagram type of service, in which the stations exchange data units without establishing a data link connection or acknowledgments. A connection-oriented service is an option.

The logical link control procedures have their roots in the asynchronous balanced mode used in HDLC and ADCCP (ANSI X3.66). These have been extended for the multistation, multiaccess environment of LANs. In the point-to-point or multipoint configurations supported by HDLC/ADCCP, all transmissions are to and from a primary station.

In a local network, a logical data link is possible between any pair of stations, and a single station can have multiple data exchanges simultaneously with several different stations. This type of exchange is accomplished via a port address to a higher-level protocol within the station. The format of the logical link-control protocol data unit is shown below:

Dest. SAP	Source SAP	Control	Info
1 Octet (8 bits)			

The destination service access point (SAP) and source service access point represent individual addresses, although the first of these can be used as a group address. The control field is for the commands and responses. Connectionless data exchanges use an unnumbered information (UI) command. Connection-oriented data exchanges use an information (I) command and response, along with receive ready (RR), reject (REJ), and receive not ready (RNR) commands and responses.

The CSMA/CD Access Protocol

The carrier-sense multiple access with collision detection (CSMA/CD) access protocol is one of the options in IEEE 802. This option relates to the ISO layers as shown below:

LOGICAL LINK CONTROL	MAC Service Specification
MEDIUM ACCESS CONTROL	MAC PS Service Specification
PHYSICAL SIGNALING	PS/AU Interface Specifications Assess Unit Interface
PHYSICAL MEDIA ATTACHMENT	Baseband MAU Broadband MAU
MEDIUM	

It contains:

- The media access control (MAC) service specification.
- The MAC sublayer with CSMA/CD.
- A physical signaling (PS) layer service specification.
- The interface specification between the physical signaling layer and the access unit (AU).
- The physical medium attachment unit (MAU) with baseband and broadband options.

CSMA/CD protocol can be summarized as follows:

1. The MAC sublayer constructs the frame from the data supplied by the logical link control.
2. A carrier-sense signal at the physical layer is monitored for traffic.
3. If the response is positive, then transmission is deferred.
4. If the response is negative or clear, frame transmission is initiated after a fixed delay of 9.6 microseconds for a 10 Mbps system, to provide recovery time for other stations.
5. The medium is monitored by the physical layer for collisions.
6. A collision-detect signal is sent to the MAC sublayer, in the event of a collision.
7. Collision handling begins with a bit sequence known as a *jam*. This sequence is 32 bits for a 10 Mbps system, and it is transmitted to ensure that the duration of the collision is sufficient to be noticed by the other transmitting stations.
8. Transmission is terminated and a retransmission is attempted

after a random delay.

9. If repeated collisions occur, the retransmission is repeated, but the random delay is doubled with each attempt. This is called *binary exponential backoff.* The delay interval is doubled for each of the first ten retransmissions, and then stays the same up to the 16th retransmission.

10. The retransmission is abandoned after 16 tries, and an error condition is signaled.

A collision will occur if several stations attempt to transmit at the same time, and their signals interfere with each other. A collision window time is allowed during the initial part of transmission before the transmitted signal has had time to propagate to all stations and a return signal propagate back. The time to acquire the medium is thus based on the round-trip propagation time of the physical layer. After the collision window has passed, the station will have acquired the medium and subsequent collisions will be avoided.

The retransmission delay is a function of the slot time that exceeds the round-trip propagation time and the jam time. In a 10 Mbps baseband system, the slot time is equal to 512 bit times. The backoff delay will be an integral number of slot times.

The Media Access Control Sublayer

The services provided by the MAC sublayer allow the local logical link control sublayer to exchange data with other sublayers. The MAC sublayer defines the procedures of the CSMA/CD protocol and the MAC frame structure.

The functions provided by the MAC sublayer are equivalent to the major functions provided in a data link layer protocol. First, it provides data encapsulation via framing, addressing, and error detection. Second, it provides medium access management, with allocation performed using collision avoidance, and contention resolution for collisions.

The MAC frame format is shown below:

Preamble	Start Frame	Dest Addr	Source Addr	Length Count	Data	PAD	FCS
7 Octets	1	2 or 6	2 or 6	2			4

The preamble is a seven-octet field which is used for synchronization and power-up reset. Next, a delimiter indicates the start of a valid frame. The start frame delimiter field is the sequence 10101011. This is followed by the destination address and the source address for the frame.

The address fields may contain either two or six octets, but the source and destination addresses must be the same size for all stations on the network. The destination address may be either an individual or a group address. The group address may be either a multicast-group address, for a group of logically related stations, or a broadcast address, for a set of stations. If the destination address uses six octets, it may be local or global. Because the global addresses will be unique, they must be assigned from a master list. The length field is two octets long, and it indicates the number of data octets in the data field.

The data field will use a logical link control frame format with destination SAP, source SAP, control, and information. When the length of the data unit is less than the minimum required by a particular implementation, then the data field can be extended by a group of extra octets known as PAD. If 10 Mbps baseband is used, then the minimum frame size is 512 bits.

The frame check sequence (FCS) field uses a 32-bit cyclic redundancy check (CRC) which is computed as a function of the destination address, source address, length, data and PAD fields.

The MAC frame format is similar to the original Ethernet specification, except the addresses are always six octets in Ethernet. Also, Ethernet uses a type field instead of the length field, which is composed of two octets, to identify a higher-level protocol.

PHYSICAL SIGNALING AND THE ATTACHMENT UNIT INTERFACE

The MAC sublayer communicates with the physical signaling sublayer using the primitives defined in the service specification. The Data Terminal Equipment (DTE) containing the data link and higher-level protocols can be physically separate from the Medium Attached Unit (MAU) connected to the transmission medium.

The DTE and MAU are connected by a cable with specifications defined in the attachment unit interface (AUI). This interface allows the DTE to be used with the specified types of transmission media. It also permits the DTE to test the interface, the interface cable, and MAU, and the medium. It consists of four circuits with separate data and control lines for each direction, along with power and grounds in a 15-pin connector.

The same framing and preamble are used for the transmission of data across the AUI as defined in the MAC sublayer. The AUI will support data rates of one, five, 10, or 20 Mbps with a cable of up to 50 meters in length.

Manchester Coding

Manchester coding is used for the transmission of data through the AUI. This type of coding combines the data and clock into a single bit stream, as shown in Fig. 6-3.

A transition to the inverse state always occurs in the middle of each bit period, while the signal state during the first half of the bit period indicates the data value.

The Medium Attachment Unit

The medium attachment unit (MAU) for a baseband coaxial system is patterned after the original Ethernet specification. The signaling rate is 10 Mbps, with up to 500 meters of coaxial cable in a single segment. The total number of MAUs on a segment cannot exceed 100.

Multiple segments are connected with repeaters using a bus topology, as discussed previously for Ethernet. There can be up to two repeater units in the path between any two MAUs.

Collisions are detected on the coaxial cable when the signal level on the cable exceeds the value allowed by two transmitters. The maximum cable connection path for a point-to-point link is 2500 meters, and the data propagation delay for a repeater must be less than 7.5 bit periods.

The 50 ohm coaxial cable is normally marked with color rings every 2.5 meters. The MAUs are then attached at these points to keep the signal reflections to a minimum. The connections are made with a piercing tap connector, or by cutting the cable. The shield of the trunk coaxial cable should be effectively grounded at only one point of the cable.

BROADBAND NETWORKS

Broadband networks use the same types of coaxial cable and components used in community antenna television (CATV) systems. The signal capability of these systems can exceed 300 MHz.

Broadband systems use a tree topology and employ splitters, as shown in Fig. 6-4. The root of the tree is called the head-end. The signals are applied to the cable at directional taps and travel in a single direction.

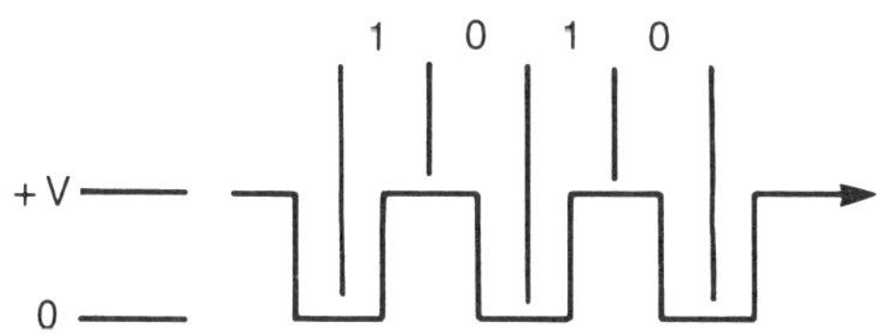

Fig. 6-3. Manchester coding.

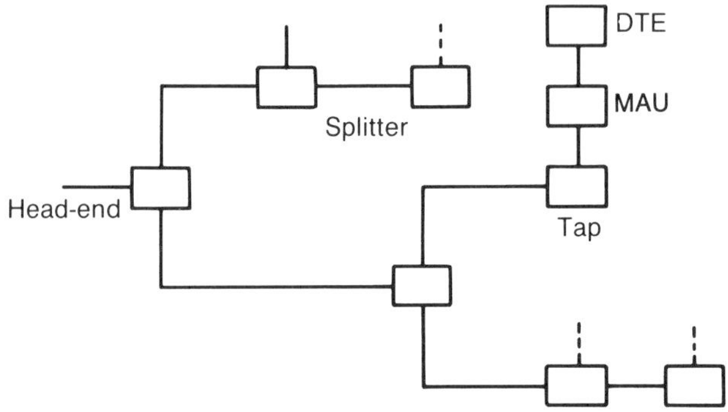

Fig. 6-4. Broadband network tree.

Either a dual-cable or a single-cable system can be used. The dual-cable system uses two parallel cables in a tree configuration which are looped together at the head-end. A MAU transmits on the inbound cable to the head-end, and there the signal is looped to the outbound cable and broadcast to the other MAUs.

A single-cable system uses different frequencies for each direction of transmission. If the frequency range is halved, the lower half of the frequency range is used for inbound transmissions and the upper half for outbound transmissions. A modulator at the head-end shifts the inbound signals up in frequency and retransmits them on the outbound cable. The transmitter and receiver will use different frequencies in this type of system. Dual-cable systems normally do not use a head-end modulator with separate transmitter and receiver frequencies.

Broadband systems use 75 ohm coaxial cable. The trunk sections are generally aluminum sheathed. The signal levels are calculated during the design based on the attenuation of the cable lengths and the number of taps and splitters. Amplifiers are used to maintain the signal levels. With the proper placing of these amplifiers, the system can have a maximum length of several kilometers from the head-end.

Collision detection cannot be based on the signal levels because of the variation in signals along the different points of the cable. Collision detection is usually done with a bit comparison. A copy of the transmitted frame is kept by the MAU, and this is compared with the received frame. A match is required for a specific time window in order to acquire the cable. If other MAUs are transmitting, then the window will not be reached.

Data rates range from one to 10 Mbps, and frequency allocation is performed in units of 6 MHz, as done for television channel bandwidths.

THE TOKEN BUS PROTOCOL

The token access protocol using a bus topology is similar to the CSMA/CD concept, but it does not use a distinct MAU which is physically separate from the DTE.

Token Bus MAC Sublayer

The frame format used in the token bus MAC sublayer is similar to that used in the CSMA/CD bus, as shown below:

Preamble	Start Frame Delimit	Frame Control	Dest. Address	Source Address	MAC Data	FCS	End Frame Delimit
1 or more Octets	1	1	2 or 6	2 or 6	0-8191	4	1

A preamble is used by the receiving modem to acquire the signal and perform a phase lock. The preamble pattern will be a function of the modulation technique and the data rate. The duration must be a minimum of two microseconds.

The start frame delimiter is an octet that is distinguished from the data. The frame control is an octet that indicates the class of frame being sent. These include:

- MAC control frames for token functions.
- Logical link control data frames.
- MAC management data frames.

Each frame has two address fields: a destination address field and a source address field. The addresses may be either two or six octets in length, but all addresses on the network must have the same length. The destination address can be an individual, group, or broadcast address. The source address is always an individual address. Addresses with six octets can be globally administered.

Depending on the class of frame specified by the Frame Control field, the MAC Data field can contain LLC protocol data, MAC management data, or MAC control frames. The frame check sequence (FCS) is the same as used in the other IEEE 802 options. The end delimiter is an octet that is distinguished from data to determine the end of the frame check sequence.

Token Bus Access

The right to transmit the token is passed among all the stations in a logical circle or ring. Each station knows the address of the station from which it got the token (predecessor), and the address of the station that should get the token next (successor). The predecessor and successor addresses must be dynamically determined and maintained. The token is passed from station to station in numerically descending order. The numerical address of a station does not necessarily relate to its physical position on the bus.

When the station has completed the data transaction and the required maintenance functions, it passes the token to its successor. After transmitting the token frame, the station checks the bus. If it detects a valid frame following the token, it assumes that its successor has the token and is transmitting. If a valid frame is not detected, it attempts to recover the token.

If a valid response is not detected after sending the token the first time, successive fall-back steps are taken to recover the token. The token-passing operation is tried a second time, and, if there is still no response, the sending station assumes the successor is inoperative.

A *Who Follows* frame is then sent to the failed successor's address in the data field of the frame. The network stations compare the value of this with the address of their predecessor. The station that achieves a match sends its address in a *Set Successor* frame. The station holding the token uses this address, and the failed station is bypassed on the logical ring.

If there is no response to the *Who Follows* frame, the frame is sent again. If there is still no response, the station sends a *Solicit Successor 2* frame, naming itself as the destination. If any operational stations respond, they will be added to the logical ring with a controlled-contention process based on response windows.

The response window defines the time interval during which a station must hear the beginning of a response from another station. The window is a controlled interval of time following the transmission of a MAC control frame in which the station sending the frame pauses to detect a response. If the station detects a transmission start during this window, it will continue to listen to the transmission, even after the response-window time expires, until the transmission is complete.

All stations in the ring periodically send *Solicit Successor* frames specifying a range of station addresses between the frame source and the destination address. Stations with an address within this range may elect to enter the ring by responding to the frame.

The sender of a *Solicit Successor* frame transmits the frame, and waits for a response in the response window after the frame. The responding stations send requests to become the next station in the logical ring. When the frame sender detects a valid request, it allows the new station to enter the ring by changing the address of its successor to the new station, and passes the token along to the new successor. Initialization is handled as a special case of adding new stations using a timer.

If multiple stations should respond to a *Solicit Successor* frame, an arbitration method is necessary to identify a single responder. A *Resolve Contention* frame is used, in which the responding stations must choose two-bit value, and then listen for either zero, one, two, or three slot-times. The process is repeated until only a single responder is left.

A priority system is used to prevent any single station from monopolizing the network. Data frames are assigned a service class representing one of four priorities. The priority system allocates the network bandwidth to the high priority frames, and sending the lower priority frames only when there is sufficient bandwidth. The bandwidth is allocated by timing the rotation of the token around the logical ring.

Each class is assigned a target token rotation time, and, for each class, the station measures the time it takes the token to circulate around the logical ring. If the token returns to a station in less than the target rotation time, the station is allowed to send frames of that particular class until the target rotation time has expired.

If the token returns after the target rotation time has expired, the station is not allowed to send frames of that priority. A token hold time is also used to limit the number of high priority frames that can be transmitted before passing the token.

Token Bus Physical Layer and Medium

The three types of physical layer and medium that can be used for the token bus are:

- Single-channel phase-continuous FSK.
- Single-channel phase-coherent FSK.
- Broadband bus.

Phase-continuous FSK is a type of frequency-shift keying in which the translation between the signaling frequencies is continuous, rather than the shift of one frequency by another.

Phase-coherent FSK is a type of frequency-shift keying where the two signaling frequencies are integrally related to the data rate. The transitions between the two signaling frequencies are made at zero crossings of the carrier waveform.

In the broadband bus, the medium is the 75 ohm coaxial-cable system. A single-cable split configuration or a dual cable is allowed. Signals are transmitted toward the head-end, and then retransmitted on the outbound cable or channel. Multilevel duobinary AM/PSK modulation is used, in which the carrier is amplitude modulated and phase-shift keyed. Duobinary signaling allows the data to be transmitted with a reduced frequency spectrum. Multilevel duobinary uses several distinct amplitude levels to represent the data. A three-level duobinary system is used, which provides a signal rate of about 1 bit/Hz.

The data-signaling rates are 1 Mbps, 5 Mbps, and 10 Mbps. The required channel bandwidth are 1.5, 6, and 12 MHz. The channels have a difference of 192.25 MHz between the inbound and outbound channels.

The medium consists of a long, unbranched, trunk cable which uses tee connectors and short drop cables. The extension to a branched trunk requires repeaters which are used to span the branches. The tee connectors are nondirectional, and the signal from a station propagates in both directions along the trunk cable. The trunk cable is a 75 ohm CATV-type coaxial cable, and the drop cable is 35 to 50 ohm cable, which may not exceed more than 35 cm in length.

For the phase-coherent option, the medium is 75 ohm cable similar to that used in CATV. Branching is accomplished with splitters, and the trunk cable is connected to the drop cable with nondirectional taps. Extensions use repeaters connected in the trunk cable. Data-signaling rates are 5 Mbps and 10 Mbps. The 5 Mbps rate uses signaling frequencies of 5 MHz and 10 MHz, while the 10 MHz data rate uses signaling frequencies of 10 MHz and 20 MHz.

For the phase-continuous case, the data-signaling rate is 1 Mbps using differential Manchester encoding. The modulation carrier uses a center frequency of 5 MHz, varying smoothly between the signaling frequencies of 3.75 MHz and 6.25 MHz with transition times of 100 nanoseconds.

TOKEN RING

The token ring uses a token medium access control with a ring topology instead of a bus topology. The token ring standard is depicted on the following page:

	Logical Link Control	MAC Service Specification
	Medium Access Control	Token Ring Protocol
Drop Cable	Physical Control	Physical Layer and Medium Options
Trunk Cable	Trunk Coupling Unit	Trunk Cable

The medium access control uses the token ring protocol, and the trunk coupling unit is inserted in the trunk cable.

Token Ring MAC Sublayer

The media access control frame format for the token ring is shown below. The format is similar to the token bus.

Starting Delimiter	Access Control	Destr Addr	Source Addr	Info	FCS	Ending Frame Delimiter

The starting delimiter is a unique bit pattern which indicates the beginning of a frame. Next, the access control field identifies the frame data either for medium access control or logical link control. The token passing depends on the bit pattern in this field.

The destination and source addresses can be either two or six octets, but all of the stations on a network must have the same address length. The destination address can be an individual or group address. The six octet addresses can be globally or locally administered.

The information field will hold the logical link control data, or the parameters required for a control frame. The CRC is 32 bits as in other options.

The ending frame delimiter indicates the end of a frame. There are two bits in this frame that are used for station management. If the frame is repeated by a station whose address matches the destination address, then the *Address Recognized* bit in this frame is turned on. If the frame

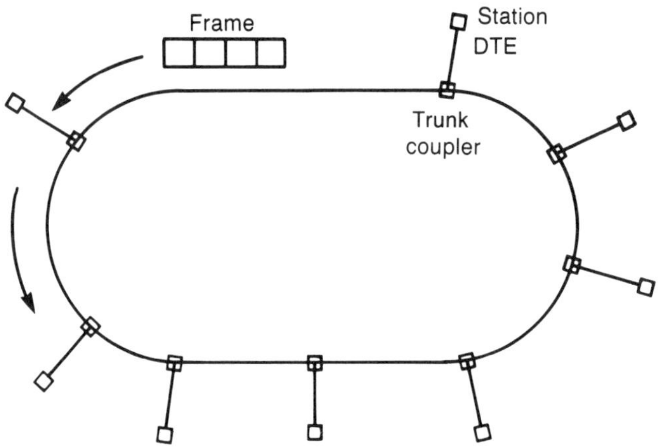

Fig. 6-5. Token ring.

is copied successfully at the destination address and the FCS balances, then the *Frame Copied* bit is turned on.

The operation of a token ring is shown in Fig. 6-5. The physical connections of the medium establish a logical connection of active stations on the ring. The token allows a station to transmit frames. Each station on the ring repeats the data that it receives.

The frames traverse a complete revolution of the ring, returning to the source station, which removes the frame. A station passes the token to its physical successor if it has no more data to transmit, or if the token-holding timer has expired.

When the destination address matches the address of a receiving station, then the station sends the frame to its logical link control layer. The frame is repeated on the ring, with the two bits in the ending frame delimiter set, if appropriate.

Token Ring Physical Layer and Medium

There are two physical layer and medium options that can be used for the token ring. For low cost, 150 ohm, shielded twisted pairs with data rates of 1 Mbps or 4 Mbps can be used. Baseband signaling is used with differential Manchester coding.

For higher data rates, coaxial cable can be used. This allows data rates of 4 Mbps, 20 Mbps, and 40 Mbps. Baseband signaling with differential Manchester coding is also used.

REVIEW EXERCISES

1. What is the relationship of Ethernet to the ISO model?
2. Draw an Ethernet configuration for a five-floor installation with two segments of ten nodes on each floor.
3. What are the major differences between IEEE 802.3, 802.4, and 802.5?
4. Discuss a datagram type of service.
5. Draw a flow diagram for CSMA/CD protocol.
6. What is the maximum delay time used for collision handling with binary exponential backoff if the initial delay is two microseconds?
7. Discuss the use of a collision window in CSMA/CD.
8. What is the slot time in a 10 Mbps baseband CSMA/CD system?
9. What is the function of the PAD field in the MAC frame of a CSMA/CD system? How does this MAC frame differ from Ethernet?
10. What is the maximum data propagation delay for a repeater in a 5 Mbps baseband MAU?
11. How can collisions be detected in a broadband network?
12. What are the main characteristics of the token bus protocol? How does it differ from CSMA/CD? How are link failures handled?
13. What is the target token rotation time? How is it used?
14. Draw a phase diagram for phase-continuous FSK, phase-coherent FSK, and multilevel duobinary AM/PSK.

Chapter 7

Packet/Message Switching

The beginnings of store-and-forward communications have their roots in the batching of messages on some media to be transported long distances. The media for store-and-forward systems evolved with paper-tape and Teletypewriter technology.

Messages could be sent from one Teletype to another over a leased-line network. Intermediate Teletype machines recorded the messages on paper tape and electronically forwarded them by relaying the paper-tape messages to the next intermediate or destination Teletype.

In these electromechanical store-and-forward systems, the messages were created "off-line" and manually edited on the paper tape. The Teletypewriters, with their automatic send/receive capability, acted as a typical message-switching center. The sender would dial up a message-switching center and transmit the contents of a message from the paper tape. The message-switching center would receive the message, punch it out on the tape, and acknowledge the message receipt. The message center was required to have a knowledge of the topology of the entire network so that it could use this knowledge to decide which Teletypewriter messages should be forwarded.

The messages were batched together for forwarding, and routing decisions were made manually by the operators. The Teletypewriters were not all part of the same electromagnetic network, but could have been part of a specific network, such as a circuit-switching network or a radio network.

The advent of electronic computer systems eliminated the manual switching and forwarding operations. Computer-controlled switching and memory functions were used to temporarily store the messages in transit. AUTODIN I, an early message-switching system, appeared in the mid 1960s. It was used by the Defense Communications Agency in its packet switching network.

In this system, the messages were entered by an operator in a format defined by a standard called JANAP 128. This format was interpreted by the AUTODIN I message switches. The messages were sent from switch to switch in short blocks.

The maximum message length accepted by the store and forward portion of the system was 550 blocks. The procedural limitations for message length were defined in JANAP 128. Messages were segmented for transmission into blocks of 80 characters, exclusive of control characters. In certain message types, blocks of 79 or less characters were permitted, provided that the last character of such a block was followed by the special control character, End of Medium (EM). Each block was transmitted, preceded, and followed by framing control characters. The typical message consisted of three parts: the header block or blocks, a variable number of text blocks, and a single (end-of-message) block. Provision was made in JANAP 128 for an exceptional message type which consisted of a single block.

A log of messages was kept at each switch, and buffer storage was provided to hold messages if a destination terminal was not ready to receive them. Each message was reassembled at each switch and checked for errors before it was forwarded to another switch.

In any system such as this where there is a range of priorities on each message and many destinations, the entire process requires a substantial amount of computation and storage, and results in extended transit times.

Packet switching on point-to-point circuits, or radio or satellite channels is similar to the older message-switching systems, but there is less transmission delay and a greater flexibility to recover from intermediate switch failures.

A major difference between packet switching and circuit or message switching can be illustrated with Fig. 7-1. This shows the typical delay for message delivery that occurs when the circuit must be set up before the message can be transmitted.

Message switching reduces this delay by allowing immediate transmission. The transit time is reduced even further by dividing the message into smaller packets, and sending the smaller packets in a store-and-forward manner via intermediate packet switches to the final

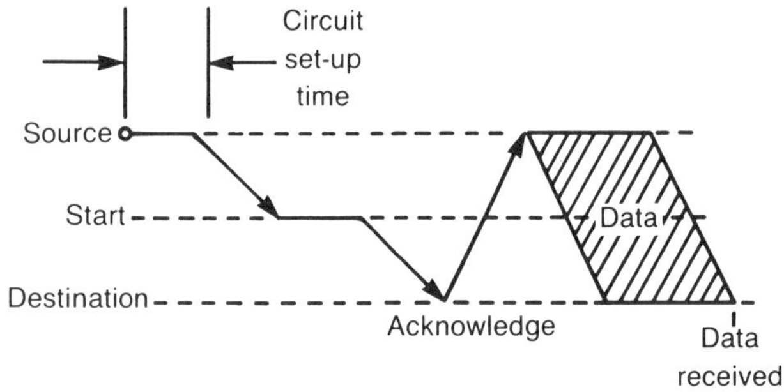

Fig. 7-1. The effect of circuit set-up time.

destination. The fragmentation and reassembly of packets into messages can be done by the packet switching system or by the user computers.

Facilities such as sequencing, error control, routing, fragmentation and reassembly, flow, and congestion control might often appear to be independent of each other. However, these can all interact when they are implemented in a packet switching system.

SEQUENCING

Sequencing is a function of the type of service offered by the packet network which can be either a datagram or virtual circuit. The datagram type of service does not provide any prior association among the datagrams in the network. Each is delivered independently of the other, and there is no enforced relationship between the order in which one computer enters datagrams into the network and the order in which these datagrams are removed from the network and delivered to the user.

Most public or commercial networks offer a sequenced service in which the packet switching computers maintain the order of packet delivery to match the order of packet entry into the network. This provides the virtual circuit between the sender and receiver. The major difference between a real circuit and a virtual circuit in packet networks is the variable transit delay that usually occurs in a virtual circuit.

Private networks might offer a datagram service alone or with a virtual-circuit service. The CIGALE network offers only datagram, while ARPANET offers both types of service. The Canadian DATAPAC network offers a virtual-circuit service, but it is built on top of an underlying datagram network.

ERROR CONTROL

Error control in point-to-point store-and-forward systems often uses a hop-by-hop acknowledgement technique. The basic concept is shown in Fig. 7-2.

As packets are sent from one node to the next, they will be retransmitted by the sending node if an acknowledgment has not been received after a specified time window, or if a negative acknowledgment is sent by the receiver.

Lost packets can be detected by:

- Numbering them sequentially and checking for out-of-order packets which can trigger a negative acknowledgment.
- Checksumming by the sender and the receiver.
- Encoding the packets so that errors can be detected and corrected. Errors that cannot be corrected can cause the packet to be rejected.

The selection of an error-detection-and-correction technique will depend on the type of service, the delay and the bandwidth of the circuits used.

Consider a negative-acknowledgment-only technique. Let each packet be checksummed by the sending packet switch. The checksum is then appended and sent with the packet. The receiving packet switch will verify the checksum and send a negative acknowledgment if an error is detected. The source switch is required to keep a copy of a packet it sends in case a negative acknowledgment is received.

Without a positive acknowledgment, the sender can assume that if there is no response after a timeout window, the packet must have arrived. This technique depends on a fixed round-trip delay from the sender to the receiver and back. A risk exists, because the link from receiver to sender might have become inoperative after a negative acknowledgment was initiated or before the packet arrived.

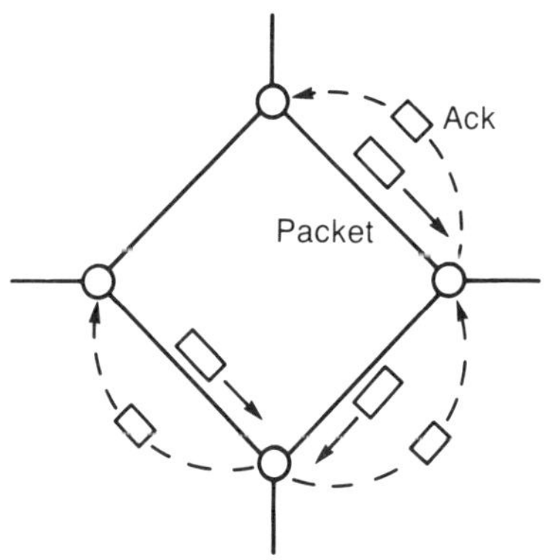

Fig. 7-2. Packet-switching model.

A positive acknowledgment scheme with retransmission after a timeout avoids these problems. Negative acknowledgments can also be used with this scheme to speed up retransmission.

To improve the channel utilization, several packets are transmitted before a response is expected. The pipeline is always full of packets, and each must be identified in order to be positively or negatively acknowledged.

Error control with multiple packets depends on the sequencing used. In the TYMNET system, the sequence of packets is based on the hop-by-hop technique as they move from source to destination. When a packet is received in error, or is missing, the receiver sends a negative acknowledgment and does not forward any more packets until the missing packet is received.

The CIGALE and ARPANET networks use a sequenced delivery on an end-to-end basis. These source-to-destination packet switches do not attempt to maintain sequence during the store-and-forward transit. In order for multiple packets to be in transit from switch to switch, these networks divide the physical link between switches into a set of logical links. (Typically eight links are used. For long delay channels, however, 16, 32, or 64 logical links might be used.)

The sending packet switch assigns a packet to a logical link that is not in use. Upon assignment, the logical link becomes busy. The logical-link number is carried in the packet so that it can be uniquely acknowledged. Only one packet at a time occupies a logical link, but the many logical links allow the sender to transmit many packets before having to receive an acknowledgment.

The receiver will acknowledge the logical-link receptions by sending back an eight-bit to 64-bit word which shows the logical links being acknowledged. Without the hop-by-hop sequencing, the logical link can be reused as soon as it has been acknowledged, independent of any other logical links.

It is possible for more than one copy of the same packet to be sent to the receiver on a given logical link. The receiver must be able to detect this, so the duplicate is not treated as a new packet. This can be done by labeling a packet with both its logical-link number and a color or group.

Let a packet be labeled with its link number and the color red. The red packet is retransmitted until an acknowledgment is received for a red packet on the logical link. The logical link then becomes idle again. A new packet can then be sent on the logical channel. It is labeled with the logical-channel number, but this time it is colored green. If a red acknowledgment arrives at the sender, it will be ignored, because the sender is now awaiting a green acknowledgment. If a red packet arrives at the receiver, it might be acknowledged, but then discarded. Other labels could be used, such as even and odd or zero and one. This technique does not preserve the relative order of all packets sent on the physical channel, because each link is treated as an independent unit.

LINE CONTROL STANDARDS

Line control is concerned with the methods used to reliably transport frames of data from one unit to another. A popular standard is the High Level Data Link Control (HDLC) procedure. This standard is closely related to the Synchronous Data Link Control (SDLC) procedure from which it is derived, and is also known as the Advanced Data Communications Control Procedure (ADCCP). The basic format of an HDLC frame is shown in Table 7-1.

A frame is signaled or flagged to the receiver by the presence of the FLAG sequence. Protection against the unintentional signaling of the FLAG sequence is accomplished by stuffing a zero into the data stream after any sequence of five one-bits. The receiver deletes a zero which follows five ones, after it detects the occurrence of a FLAG sequence.

The end of a frame occurs when the next FLAG sequence occurs. The value of the preceding 16-bit frame checksum is compared with the checksum generated as the frame arrives. The checksum verification and bit-stuffing functions are available in the form of integrated circuit chips.

The HDLC procedures also include such functions as sequencing, flow control and error control. The link initiation and disconnect utilizes the following:

- A Set Asynchronous Response Mode (SARM) command.
- An Unnumbered Acknowledgment (UA) response.
- A Disconnect (DISC) command.

A Poll/Final (P/F) bit is used in both commands and responses. In the command frames, it is used as a Poll (P) bit, and when set it requires

Table 7-1. Basic HDLC Frame Format.

FLAG	0 1 1 1 1 1 1 0	
ADR	Address	
CTL	Control	
DATA	Data	
FCS	Frame Checksum	16-Bit Cyclic
FCS	Frame Checksum	Redundancy Check
FLAG	0 1 1 1 1 1 1 0	

a response. In response frames, it is used as a Final (F) bit and acknowledges the command poll.

The usual mode of operation in HDLC is an asymmetric primary-secondary mode, in which one side issues commands and the other responds. There is also an asynchronous balanced mode (ABM), in which both sides can act as primary and secondary, with each side issuing and responding to commands from the other.

FLOW CONTROL

Flow control in a store-and-forward packet switching network is concerned with the rate at which packets flow from one packet switch to the next. Procedures such as HDLC usually achieve this by limiting the number of packets that can be unacknowledged at any time. The control field format for HDLC is shown in Table 7-2.

The frames are expected to arrive in sequence, so N(R) is only incremented if the expected frame arrives. When a receiver has no outgoing information frame to send, a receiver-ready (RR) supervisory frame can be sent to indicate the next frame expected. When an unexpected frame number arrives, the receiver might respond with a supervisory reject (REJ) response, to indicate the number of the frame expected. The receiver can stop all transmissions from the sender with a receiver-not-ready (RNR) response. This can be terminated with an RR frame.

Table 7-2. The Control Field Format for the HDLC.

Format	Commands	Responses	Encoding 1	2	3	4	5	6	7	8
Information	I			N(R)[1]		P		N(S)[2]		0
Supervisory		RR		(N(R)		F	0	0	0	1
		RNR		N(R)		F	0	1	0	1
		REJ		N(R)		F	1	0	0	1
Unnumbered	SARM		0	0	0	P	1	1	1	1
	DISC		0	1	0	P	0	0	1	1
		UA	0	1	1	F	0	0	1	1
		CMDR	1	0	0	F	0	1	1	1

<Poll/final>

[1]N(R) is the frame number of the next frame expected.

[2]N(S) has a range from zero to seven which identifies the frame number in a repeating modulo = 8 sequence.

The two primary flow control mechanisms are the RNR control, and the limitation of seven unacknowledged frames (which can be extended to 127 frames if required by the round-trip delay).

The error control scheme also limits the number of unacknowledged packets. When buffers are saturated, packets will not be accepted and they might be discarded without acknowledgment. The sender must retransmit them later. The sender, however, might be involved in sending new packets, so delays might occur.

Another possible problem with HDLC in a packet network is the fixing of a sequencing relation on packets being transported from one switch to another. Some networks might not require a set packet sequence on a hop-by-hop basis, and this can cause transit delays when errors occur.

Flow control is necessary for allocating the flow of packets through the network. It is generally necessary to control the rate at which new packets are sent along on a hop-by-hop basis, and there might be a requirement to control the introduction of packets into the network by limiting those bound for certain destinations from one source. This is essentially an end-to-end type of flow control, with the ends at the source and destination packet switches. The need for this control is related to the buffer space available at the destination.

These requirements are often dynamic, so the destination packet switch sends permission to the source packet switch. If the requirements are more static and can be predicted, buffers can be allocated for the lifetime of a virtual circuit. In some networks, a pool of buffers is shared, and statistical calculations are made to control the amount of flow for a given buffer allocation. In asynchronous systems, the measurement and control of rate of flow is difficult to implement, because it depends on levels of protocol outside the basic packet switching network.

CONGESTION CONTROL

Flow control generally refers to the point-to-point procedures between adjacent packet switches, while congestion control considers the aggregate network resources and attempts to keep them from becoming saturated. A common problem is that each individual source/destination flow may be accommodated, but the aggregate might overtax the total network resources. A congestion-prone system has a throughput delay, as depicted in Fig. 7-3.

The throughput rises with the traffic, and the delay grows until the throughput reaches a maximum. This is the *saturation point*. Ideally, the delay would increase with increasing load. In the congestion-prone system, the throughput is reduced with increasing load until it reaches

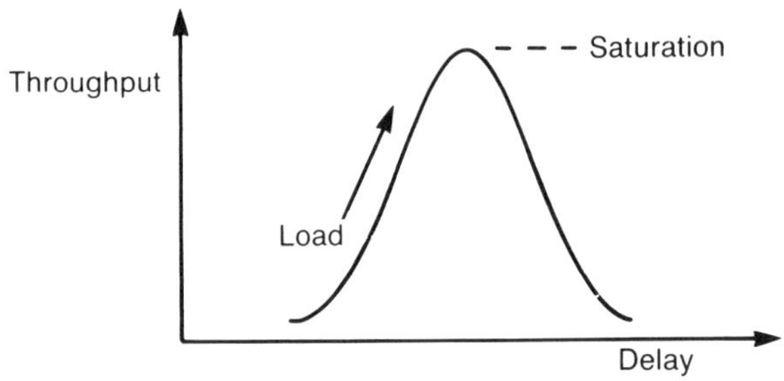

Fig. 7-3. A congestion-prone system.

zero and the delay becomes infinite. This has the same effect as stopping traffic on a freeway during rush hours.

The technique used in the CYCLADES/CIGALE network discards packets as buffers begin to fill. This type of strategy is simple to implement, but creates havoc when congestion occurs.

Congestion begins with the first pair of packet switches that cause saturation. Because the discarded packets must be retransmitted, the delay increases unless the traffic needs drop fast enough to prevent the congestion mode.

Congestion control can be based on a fixed number of packet carrying slots. Packet switches may not accept a packet unless there is an empty slot for it. The problem then becomes how to distribute the empty slots to those switches that need them. The empty slots can be treated like empty taxis, with some of them waiting at packet switches while others must move among other packet switches. The disadvantages of this concept are:

- The extra overhead that is created.
- The slot maintenance that is required.
- The possibility of local congestion aborting the control.

The buffers of each packet switch can also be partitioned into groups, where the number of groups depends on the maximum number of hops required to forward a packet from source to destination. The routing algorithm attempts to group the packets according to the number of hops they have taken. The concept is to protect those packets which have traveled part way by providing a "waiting station," in the form of a buffer. Each group is given a buffer, and, if there are no loops in the routing, the system should not deadlock. However, there must be a fall-back strategy to account for nodes so they do not cause a complete shut-down.

Deadlock is the point where all throughput stops, and the system comes to a halt. If the routing algorithm in a store-and-forward system should cause the traffic flowing in opposite directions to flow through two adjacent packet switches, then each switch can become filled with packets destined for the other, and communication stops. The more conservative schemes that use buffers which are reserved by fixed preallocation are generally subject to deadlock, and even the more adaptive techniques that can be employed are not completely free of deadlock. Even when deadlocks are avoided, severe degradations in performance can result from poor congestion-control algorithms.

Traffic patterns with long packets in one direction and short ones in the other tend to degrade throughput for the short packets. The acknowledgments are delayed in the long-packet direction by the long packets, even with the piggybacking of acknowledgments on return traffic. If a fixed limit is placed on the number of packets that need to be acknowledged at one time, then the short-packet side will not fully utilize the channel; it cannot keep the pipeline filled.

FLOW CONTROL OPERATION

The model for a packet network can be considered a pool of resources. Each user must acquire a part of these resources, in the proper sequence, in order to accomplish the required task, which typically is the transfer of data from source to destination. When the competition for the resources is unrestricted and uncontrolled, the following problems can occur.

Inefficiency because of conflicts. Conflicts can be between two or more users, or because a user acquires more resources than strictly needed, thus starving other users. When two users transmit simultaneously on a random-access channel, the data becomes garbled and the channel is wasted. Another cause of wastage is the unnecessary acquisition of buffer resources. Consider a multi-node network with several host-to-host connections. The buffers at the junction nodes might rapidly become filled by additional traffic demands. Packets on the way to the additional destinations will be rejected due to buffer overflow, and throughput to these destinations will be reduced to zero. The introduction of new traffic will cause a total throughput decrease due to buffer capture.

Unfairness due to uncontrolled competition. Some users, because of their relative position in the network, might be able to capture a larger share of resources than others and thus receive preferential treatment. An example of this occurs in a network where some node pairs, because of the higher value of some of the line speeds along their connecting paths, tend to capture the buffer pools.

Congestion, which is a direct consequence of wastage.

Because wastage in an uncontrolled network increases in proportion to the offered traffic, there will be an optimum offered load beyond which the wastage is higher than the potential gain in throughput. Beyond this optimum, the network is congested. Operation of the network under congested conditions can result in deadlocks. These will occur when each user in the network has acquired part of the resources necessary to complete a task and does not want to release them, while waiting for the remaining resources to become free. When a deadlock develops, throughput drops to zero, because no task can be completed. Deadlock created by heavy traffic between nodes might cause the packets flowing between the nodes to fill up the available buffers. Throughput will then also fall to zero, because the packets currently at one node cannot be transferred to another, because of the lack of free buffers ready to receive them.

Flow control can prevent these problems by properly regulating and blocking the flow of packets internally in the network, as well as at network entry points. Flow control usually requires some exchange of information between the nodes, along with some exchange of commands to implement the control strategy. This results in channel and processor overhead.

Flow control usually requires the reservation of resources to individual users or types of users, and this reduces the benefits achieved compared to complete resource sharing. The gain in efficiency due to flow control is offset by the loss in efficiency due to the limited sharing and overhead that occur. This is shown in the curves of Fig. 7-4. The ideal throughput corresponds to perfect control with zero overhead. This ideal throughput increases linearly until it reaches the theoretical network throughput. In an actual control procedure, the throughput values are lower than in the ideal curve, due to control overhead. An uncontrolled system follows the ideal curve for low loads, but for higher loads, it quickly collapses into deadlock.

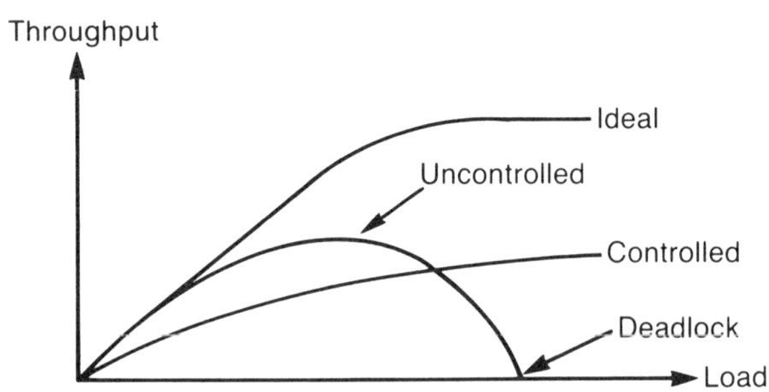

Fig. 7-4. Flow control performance.

Flow control provides safety at high loads, at the cost of reduced efficiency. This reduction in efficiency is due to higher delays at the lower loads and lower throughput capacity at the saturation level.

Flow Control Levels

At the lowest level in a packet network is the link protocol, which serves to transport the packets across the physical links. One function of this protocol is involved with flow control. This is the dropping of packets when the receiving node is not ready. The sender will then retransmit the packet after waiting an appropriate time. The receiver might use commands such as RNR (receiver not ready), in HDLC and SDLC.

There are two types of physical links: the internal, or node-to-node links, and the network access links. These require a node-to-node protocol and a network access protocol. The node-to-node or link protocol is typically HDLC, SDLC, or X.25 level 2.

Moving up the hierarchy, there is the entry-to-exit (ETE) protocol, which allows the transport of single and multipacket messages from the entry to the exit node. Here, flow control is involved with the regulation of input traffic using buffer allocation and time windowing, as well as the sequencing and reassembly of multipacket messages at the exit node.

At the highest level of network protocol is the process-to-process or transport protocol, which involves the delivery of packets using the virtual connection between processes. The goal here is to regulate the flow to achieve the most efficient use of network resources without buffer overflow.

Networks that use virtual circuits have another level of protocol below the process-to-process level. This is the virtual-circuit protocol, which specifies the rules for establishing, maintaining, and closing virtual circuits. The protocol normally uses a selective flow control on a connection-by-connection basis. A virtual-circuit implementation requires the assignment of a fixed path for each connection at setup time. A part of the packet header is used to identify the packets belonging to a connection. Routing maps are implemented at the intermediate nodes at set-up time; these are used to route the packets.

Datagram networks do not require any circuit set-up before transmission, because each packet carries all the information required to travel to its destination. Selective flow control is not possible in datagram networks, because the information required for each connection is fixed in the header and is not inspected by the intermediate nodes.

Node-to-Node Flow Control

Node-to-node flow control is also known as store-and-forward flow control or hop flow control. A main part of its operation is to block the traffic to a node that is congested. This is usually done by discarding packets at the congested point. The packets are then retransmitted later, after a specified timeout.

The link will act as if it were blocked, until the congestion is cleared. In HDLC and SDLC, instead of discarding packets, transmission is blocked using a receiver-not-ready (RNR) command. When the congestion is cleared, the receiver issues a receiver-ready (RR) command to reopen transmission.

Congestion can be defined as the lack of free buffers. If packets are accepted until all of the buffers are full, a deadlock can occur. This deadlock is known as *direct store-and-forward deadlock.* It can be avoided by placing a limit on queue length. This strategy eliminates direct deadlocks, because the packets directed to a destination are not allowed to have access to the entire buffer pool. This type of strategy is used in ARPANET.

The other type of deadlock that can occur in packet networks is *indirect store-and-forward deadlock.* This situation will occur in a ring topology even when there is a limit imposed on the queue length. If all queues are filled to their maximum, a deadlock will occur. The required solution is a structured buffer pool, as shown in Fig. 7-5.

The nodal buffers are organized in a hierarchical structure and, at level zero, there is a pool of unrestricted or common buffers. From level one to level n (where n is the maximum number of hops on any network

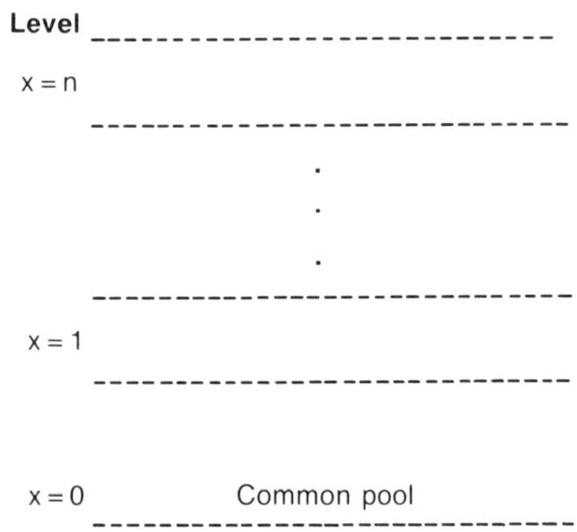

Fig. 7-5. Structured buffer pool.

path) the buffers are reserved for specific classes of packets that have covered x hops. Under heavy load conditions, the buffers fill up from level zero to level n. When the buffers at a specific level are filled up, the arriving packets for that level or greater are discarded.

This technique eliminates store-and-forward deadlocks of both the direct and indirect type. It does, however, require a large buffer space and extra processing to maintain the structured buffer pool.

Another technique for recovery from indirect store-and-forward deadlocks requires two overflow buffers which are used only when a deadlock is detected. Packets compete for the overflow buffers and the contention between packets is resolved by issuing a priority to each packet. The lowest-numbered packet will eventually be delivered to its destination, thus freeing a regular buffer and resolving the deadlock. The traffic will then move through the network using regular buffers. There is some buffer wastage and some processing overhead during the overflow period.

Network Access Flow Control

Node-to-node flow control prevents deadlock, but it does not prevent network overload, because it is used only after the internal queues have grown relatively large. The network operation might be deadlock-free, but it still tends to be inefficient when traffic demands exceed network capacity. It might be more effective to control the introduction of packets into the network. This is called network access flow control.

This scheme attempts to regulate the input of packets into the network based on local or global congestion measurements. Like node-to-node flow control, it is supported by a network access link protocol, discarding packets when the network is congested, and retransmitting via RNR and RR commands. The most basic scheme consists of admitting or rejecting input traffic based on the amount of storage available at the entry node. A pool of buffers can be used, with limits on the number of buffers that can be occupied by input packets.

It might be more effective to anticipate congestion using buffer occupancy rates collected from the internal nodes in the network. A congestion table can be used, where each node regulates its input packet rate on the basis of the tabled information. A count of buffers available at each node is stored and updated in much the same way that routing tables are updated in a distributed routing system. The input rate to each destination is regulated based on the information obtained, which is a measure of the overall network congestion.

In another scheme, a fixed number of permits are circulated among the nodes. (SNA uses end-to-end sessions to provide both network flow control and access control.) A permit scheme is used with permits that are dedicated to a single user. A packet may leave an entry node only when it captures a permit passing through it. The packet carries the permit through the network and releases it at the destination. The number of permits at an entry node must be large enough to satisfy demand and maintain fairness.

Node-to-node control does not protect from overload, while access control does not protect from deadlocks. Both are required for efficient and reliable network operation.

PACKET FORWARDING

Packet forwarding is a process that takes place at each intermediate node in the path. It involves testing the header of each incoming packet and placing the packet in the proper output queue. Both virtual-circuit and datagram forwarding mechanisms can be used. In the virtual-circuit mode, the packet header holds the connection data. The intermediate nodes hold a routing table for the assignment of the route to be used. Both the connection data and route are fixed at connection set-up time.

In the datagram mode, the complete route might be stored in the routing label of each packet header, or only the destination node might be carried in the header, in which case the next hop is determined by the routing-table.

ROUTING

In a store-and-forward system that is not fully connected with all packet switches having direct communication links to all other switches, the routing algorithms determine the optimum sequence of switches through which a packet is forwarded to reach the desired destination. Most packet-switched networks attempt to minimize the delay or the number of hops required to reach the destination.

Fixed routing uses routes that are preselected, with routing tables for possible failure of a link or switch. When a failure occurs, the proper routing table is selected and loaded from memory. Packets could also be routed to all of the neighbors and duplicates issued through the use of tables recording the identity of recently forwarded packets.

Consider the TYMNET system, which selects a route when a user logs in. A central supervisory computer checks the current routings already in operation and attempts to optimize the traffic flow and minimize the delay for the new user. When a failure occurs, the users log in again and a new routing table is used.

In TRANSPAC and TELENET, a route is selected when a customer requests that a virtual circuit be set-up. The hop-by-hop routing of the virtual-circuit set-up request determines the route of the virtual circuit. When a failure occurs, the virtual circuit is reset and the user must request that a new one be set up. These nondynamic alternate routing schemes usually confine themselves to recovering from failures.

In dynamic, or adaptive, alternate routing such as that used in ARPANET and DATAPAC, the routes are dynamically selected on a packet-by-packet and hop-by-hop basis. The packet switches exchange delay and traffic load information among themselves and change their routing decisions accordingly.

The dynamic routing schemes are more prone to anomalies due to loops in the routing mechanism. A number of strategies for dealing with the looping problem exist. A certain amount of testing can be done to verify that the routes are loop-free before using them. This becomes a cycle-time problem for the rate at which the routing might have to change.

Algorithms that allow multiple routes to be used simultaneously to increase the effective bandwidth present the problem of determining the number of routes from source to destination in the presence of line and switch failures.

The measurement of delay or queue length at packet switches in ARPANET and several other networks indicates that the bursty nature of packet-systems results in information with large swings and a high potential for oscillation. Basing any routing decisions on these measurements can introduce severe oscillations in network behavior, especially if congestion is approached. If the congestion is local, then routing around it might be preventive. But, if it is due to excessive traffic entering the entire network, alternate routing might only compound the problem.

Distributed routing algorithms can be defined using the following:

- Deterministic control with fixed routes. (Precomputed tables are employed which can be manually selected to deal with line or node failures.)
- Isolated control based on local information without sharing information with adjacent packet switches.
- Distributed control, where each packet switch makes its own decisions but propagates information of importance to other nodes. (DATAPAC, ARPANET)
- Centralized control with route-making decisions made by a single central unit (TYMNET).

The major problems in any routing scheme is keeping it stable under all normal operating conditions and not introducing loops, and devising a method to propagate the required information to or among the packet switches before conditions have changed and have made the information obsolete.

Regardless of the scheme used, there is a loss of time, bandwidth, buffer space, and other network resources to move routing information through the system. Routing can affect flow and congestion control. As you have seen, a routing algorithm that causes loops can lead to network congestion. If substantial network resources are required for routing, the network will become less useful for communication traffic.

In some distributed systems, the routing computation is performed in parallel by all the nodes, in a cooperative manner, based on partial status information which is exchanged between the nodes. Centralized systems might employ a network routing center (NRC), which assembles the global status of the network, computes the minimum delay routes, and distributes the routing tables or routing commands to the nodes. There are also mixed systems, which combine features from some or all of the other types. An example would be the integration of centralized and isolated routing.

The basic building blocks common to all the possible techniques include:

- Network status monitoring.
- Network status reporting.
- Route computation.
- Route implementation.
- Packet forwarding.

The network status variables required for the routing computation are the topological connectivity, the traffic pattern, and the delay. In order to acquire local connectivity, each node monitors the status of adjacent lines and/or nodes by monitoring the line traffic or by periodically interrogating its neighbors. The local traffic load can be monitored by measuring the average of instantaneous queue lengths, the average flow on outgoing links, or the incoming traffic from external sources.

Global status requires full network connectivity and traffic pattern information. It can be acquired by correlating the local status information from all nodes in the network.

Partial status is the status measured relative to a given node. It is at an intermediate level between local and global status. It represents the status of the network as seen by the node and includes all the information necessary for a routing decision at that node.

The isolated system policy is based on local status information. The distributed system policy is based on partial status information, and the centralized system requires local status acquisition at all nodes as well as global status information at the NRC.

The network status measurements can be processed locally or forwarded to a collection center for further processing. In a centralized system, local measurements are periodically reported to the NRC and combined there to produce the global status. In a distributed system, the local measurements are combined with the information received from neighbors to provide the partial status of the network as viewed from that node. The partial status is then communicated to the neighbors. In the isolated system, measurements are processed and used locally with no exchange of status information between nodes.

In an isolated system, a node derives routing information from the length of its local queues. A basic scheme is to select the output link with the shortest queue, regardless of the final destination of the packet.

In the flooding technique, the node routes a copy of each transit packet to its neighbors. This technique is extremely insensitive to failures, because it will always deliver a copy of the packet to a reachable destination. The disadvantages are poor line efficiency and the presence of loops.

These problems can be reduced by combining a local adaptive policy with a static routing policy. The static policy is used to establish a priority among the outgoing links. The traffic is then distributed among primary and secondary routes according to queue lengths rather than following fixed proportions as in a static, multipath policy. The combined static and local adaptive combination has good adaptivity to load fluctuations, but the adaptivity to failures tends to be poor, because the underlying policy is static.

Distributed, adaptive schemes employ distributed routing computation with routing information exchange among the neighbor nodes. These adaptive schemes must be able to rapidly adjust to changes in network topology and traffic pattern. For a typical medium-sized network of five to 20 nodes at a 9.6 Kbps linespeed, the algorithm should converge in a few seconds.

In a centralized routing system, the network routing center (NRC) is responsible for global network status collection, route computation, and route implementation. The NRC might be a nodal processor with special software, but more often it is a host computer with the storage and processing capability required to store the network topology and traffic information and to compute the optimal routes. The system can implement individual paths on a call-by-call basis using a virtual-circuit approach, or a periodic distribution of routing tables can be made from the NRC to all the nodes.

Distributed routing becomes more attractive beyond certain network sizes while a centralized system has several advantages over distributed and isolated system:

- It allows some type of flow control of the incoming traffic. (In TYMNET, the NRC monitors the loading in the network and calls can be rejected when a specified limit is exceeded.)
- It eliminates routing computation requirements at the nodes.
- It permits a more accurate optimization of the routes which reduces problems due to loops and oscillations that can occur when the network state is not completely known.

The disadvantages of centralized systems include:

- The increased traffic overhead in the proximity of the NRC due to the periodic status reporting from the nodes and the routing of commands from the NRC to the nodes.
- The lack of system reliability, because if a single NRC is used, the entire network is lost when an NRC failure occurs.

A hierarchy of NRCs can be used which continuously monitor each other. If one should fail, another can take over. Four NRCs are used in TYMNET.

PACKET ROUTING CONSIDERATIONS

The objective of the routing procedure is to transport the packets using minimum-delay paths from the source to the destination. The packet delays can be optimized in the following two ways:

User optimization. The individual delay for each source-to-destination traffic requirement is optimized. Each source-to-destination requirement is optimized independently until a competitive equilibrium is reached. This approach is most often used in adaptive routing situations with distributed decision-making.

System optimization. The average system delay is optimized and averaged over all of the node pairs. The paths between all source-to-destination pairs are optimized jointly according to a common objective, the overall average delay. This approach is generally used in static routing situations where the traffic is not subject to sudden changes. Decisions are generally centralized.

Static and Adaptive Routing

If the network topology is not subject to changes, such as those due to failures and modifications, and the traffic inputs can be characterized by Poisson processes with a constant mean (stationary processes), then the optimal routing solution becomes a static solution with a set of fixed paths between the node pairs. The traffic between each source-destination pair could bc distributed on several paths simultaneously in such a way that the proportions do not vary with time.

Most network environments are dynamic and change with time, and the user traffic might fluctuate rapidly depending on demand. An adaptive routing scheme can react and adjust to these changes. The userfulness of such a scheme is related to its response time, which is a measure of the rate at which it can track and adjust to traffic and node changes. If these changes occur at a low rate with respect to the network transmission rates, a periodically refreshed static scheme can be used.

Static routing schemes are often used to evaluate networks, where they are useful in predicting throughput and delay for a given topology. To simplify the performance of adaptive routing schemes, the routing is approximated with static routing and the traffic is approximated with a stationary environment.

Dynamic Techniques

In static policies, the primary concern is the computational properties of the algorithms and how well they work in distributed environments. The focus is on the type of information exchanged between the nodes. The amount of overhead introduced by the routing messages and the routing computations becomes more critical in dynamic applications, because these affect the time required to converge to a solution. The impact of line and node failures also becomes more critical.

In a static or quasistatic routing environment, the time between traffic pattern changes is much larger than the average transmission time, and the routing computation can be done in a background mode, at a slow update rate, without affecting network performance.

The dynamic network environment assumes that the time between traffic changes is comparable to the time required to measure such changes, to compute new routes, and to implement the routes. A prompt recovery is also required from failures. These can be restated as follows:

- Under time-varying traffic conditions, the system must adjust to load fluctuations and provide minimum delays.
- After a failure, the system must minimize the time to recover to a stable condition.

It is also desirable that, at steady state, the adaptive system converge to the optimal static routing for the existing traffic pattern.

Adaptive routing requires a procedure that dynamically updates the routing tables according to changes in the network. This procedure can include:

- The detection of the status of the network by the measurement of link idle time or link queue lengths.
- The computation of the routes.
- The implementation of the routing tables.

Critical issues in the adaptive system include line and processor overhead. The overhead places a constraint on the frequency of routing updates and affects the performance during transient traffic conditions and the time to recover from failures.

Route Computation

The route selection will generally be based on the minimum delay to destination, computed from the network status information available at the node. In an isolated system, each node knows the state of its own queues and holds a list of preferred output links which are ranked in some priority for a particular destination. Routing can begin with the highest priority link, until the queue exceeds a specified limit. Then the next link in the priority scheme is used.

In a distributed system, each node uses the partial status information to compute the minimum-delay route to each destination. This route is then used for that particular destination.

In a centralized system, the NRC maintains a global network status and periodically computes the optimal routes between all node pairs. The most common method for storing the routing information in the nodes is to use an N X n matrix, where:

N = total number of nodes
and
n = number of neighbors of each node

The routing tables are either computed locally in distributed systems or provided by an NRC in centralized systems.

In these table implementations, the packets in the same end-to-end user session can use different paths. In order to maintain sequencing, one of the following techniques is required.

The use of virtual circuits. Routes are selected on a session-by-session basis, depending on the present link utilization and connectivity. These are then implemented by loading the proper routing maps in intermediate nodes on the route.

Explicit path routing as used in the IBM Standard Network Architecture (SNA). Each node computes the shortest paths to each destination. At the beginning of a session, the origin node selects a path based on the load. The selected path and the destination are stored in the header of each packet. The next node on the path uses this with its own table to map the path into its table. Thus, all packets follow the route selected by the origin node and there is no need for specific routing instructions at the intermediate nodes for each session, as employed in the virtual-circuit system.

Source routing. The source node has knowledge of the complete paths to all destinations. The entire route is stored in the header of each packet. If multiple paths are available, the source node might balance the load by distributing packets on different paths or route the packets for the same session all on the same path, as done in the explicit path method.

In general, table updating must be coordinated among the nodes such that it proceeds sequentially from the destination to the origins. A node cannot update its tables until it receives the proper information from its neighbors "downstream." The proper sequencing of updates can be interrupted by line errors and link or node failures. When this happens, loops might occur in the traffic flow, causing deadlocks.

A slow algorithm convergence will cause only part of the total traffic to be deviated from the old routes to the new, shortest route. A quasistatic scheme generally becomes unsuitable for dynamic applications when the traffic fluctuation period is comparable to the routing update cycle, and when the link and node failure rates cannot be neglected.

It is relatively easy to compute and dynamically update the shortest single path from each node to all destinations, while it is much more difficult to compute and distribute the traffic over multiple paths. A common solution to the minimum-delay problem is the shortest-queue-with-bias algorithm, as used in the ARPA network. Each node maintains a delay table with the estimated delay from node to destination. The adaptive policy attempts to send packets on minimum-delay routes. Each node periodically updates its own delay table using the delays measured on its output lines and delay information received from neighbor nodes. A bias term is added to reduce looping effects.

The major problem in this scheme is effectively splitting the traffic on multiple paths during sustained loads. If heavy traffic exists between two nodes, it might require the simultaneous use of more than one route. The system can select only one route at a time between updates, and, within each update interval, one of the routes is alternatively filled up to capacity, while the other is idle. This not only represents an inefficient use of resources, but it can also cause looping.

ROUTING AND FLOW CONTROL CONSIDERATIONS

Computer network resources can generally be shared, and coordination is required among the user devices to allow for efficient and fair utilization. This coordination is provided through the network procedures or protocols which function as the rules governing the access to resources, the establishment of connections, and the exchange of data through the network.

The communication resources are those required for the transfer of data in the network. These include the channels, switching processors, data buffers, and the protocols that govern them. These make up the communications *subnet*.

One of the key advantages of data networking compared to dedicated connections is the extended sharing of common facilities among a population of random users with bursty requirements. The protocols supervising the sharing of these resources are referred to as internal protocols, because they operate within the subnet boundaries. Those protocols that involve external processes, such as the end-to-end protocols and network access, are referred to as external protocols.

The function of the routing and flow-control procedures is to control the traffic within the network with the goal of maximum data transfer efficiency. Functions such as error protection, sequencing, and duplicate detection might or might not be provided by other protocols.

The routing protocol should provide the best collection of paths between sources and destinations, given the traffic requirements and the network configuration. The selection of the best path might depend on the traffic and the existence of constraints not always related to performance, such security or internal policy.

The traffic requirements and network configurations will change with time, and, because the system must quickly respond to link and node failures, the routing protocol must be adaptive, so that it can adjust the routes to the varying conditions.

The routing protocol attempts to optimize the network resource utilization as long as the traffic can be accommodated by the network. If the traffic exceeds the network capacity, the network inputs must be regulated to reduce the total load to an acceptable level. This regulation mechanism is often provided by the flow control procedure.

The throughput in an uncontrolled network will increase for increasing traffic, up to the system capacity. Beyond this point, there will be a sudden collapse in performance, leading to possible deadlocks. The flow control system should seek to prevent this degradation, or at least improve performance, so that deadlocks that might arise because of congestion will occur well outside the expected performance limits.

The detection of *inaccessible nodes* is required to avoid network congestion due to undeliverable packets. Inaccessable nodes are those which cannot be reached from a given node because they have failed, or because the links leading to them have failed and caused them to become isolated.

Congestion control is the result of the cooperation of several levels of protocol, from the link level to the end-to-end level. Each of these protocols contributes to flow control while performing other functions, such as error protection and sequencing.

The routing protocol and the flow-control protocol can be treated as separate functions. Flow control determines when to block the data traffic at an entrance or at a point within the network, while routing selects the optimum path to the destination. Strong interactions between the two protocols exists in some packet subnets.

In a virtual-circuit subnet, a path is established, and resources along the path are allocated at the connection setup time. The routing protocol is responsible for selecting the optimum path that has the resources to support the connection. If there is no available path, the connection is not made, which is a part of the flow control. In a datagram network, these functions are much more independent.

ADDRESSING

At each protocol layer, except for the physical layer, there will always be more than one potential destination, so there is a requirement to identify the destination of a packet of data. The typical approach to addressing in a layered architecture is to create a hierarchical address space.

A host which is physically attached to a packet switch through a shared local loop will have a unique link address. The interface between the packet switch and the local loop will also have a unique address, because it is one of many in the system.

In a host, there might be several operating programs or processes. These will have logical input/output channels, or ports, which must have unique addresses if the data communicated through the network and the protocol layers are to reach the desired destination. In order for the data to travel through multiple networks, they will require distinct identifiers. The hierarchical address scheme might partition the total or global address space as shown below:

.NETWORK.
.HOST.
.PROCESS.
.PORT...

There are three essential concepts which lead to strong and efficient addressing. This is the distinction of names, addresses, and routes.

A *name* identifies what something is. It could identify a service, such as an inquiry service or an electronic message service. It could also identify a particular host computer or network branch.

An *address* identifies where something is relative to other items. An address would indicate which packet switch a host is connected to for example while a *route* identifies the path used to get there.

The assignment of names, addresses, and routes in a network can be static or dynamic. Names are usually more static than dynamic, while routes tend to be the opposite. Addresses fall within these ranges.

Addresses can be virtual or physical. In a physically addressed network, such as ARPANET, the address identifies which packet switch the host is attached to, and which port of that packet switch. ARPANET internally assigns routes to addresses dynamically. When a host is reattached to a different port number, the host address changes.

In a virtually addressed network, the packet switches rely on a table which shows the correspondence between the virtual addresses and the physical addresses. The hosts can then be attached to more than one physical address while using only a single virtual address. Several virtual addresses can map to the same physical address, permitting these virtual hosts to be emulated by a single physical host. The cost of this flexibility is larger routing tables.

PACKET-SWITCHING STANDARDS

Most of the efforts to standardize the various aspects of packet switching and related data communications are the result of such groups as the International Telecommunications Union (ITU), which is responsible for the Consultative Committee for International Telegraphy and Telephone (CCITT). The CCITT is involved with developing voluntary international standards for communication, while another group, the International Standards Organization (ISO), has the responsibility for developing computer and data-processing standards.

In the United States, agencies such as the National Bureau of Standards and the American National Standards Institute provide technical support to the CCITT and ISO, and formulate standards for the federal government. Federal Information Processing Standards (FIPS) are one example.

Protocol Layering

In a networking environment, the term "protocol" has come to mean both a format and a set of procedures that are commonly agreed to for the purpose of achieving communication. It is useful to consider a horizontally partitioned layering of functions which must be performed to realize an application running on a store-and-forward network. Layering of protocols is the result of a stratification of functions among the different parts of the system.

One of the more comprehensive attempts to use layering to define a communication systems architecture was undertaken by the International Standards Organization (ISO), Technical Committee 97, Subcommittee 16 on Open Systems Architecture. The objective of TC97/SC16 was to define the function and layering of a set of protocols to permit the interoperation of systems which are built independently

Application
Presentation
Session
Transport
Network
Link
Physical/electrical

Fig. 7-6. ISO open systems architecture.

but to the same architectural standards.

The protocol layers which resulted are shown in Fig. 7-6. The layers are representative of the software and hardware required to obtain service from a packet-switching network. At the lowest level is the physical or electrical standard, including the type of connector, voltage levels, and the definition of each connector lead. The link level is representative of a procedure like HDLC. This layer of protocol is used to move blocks of data from the data termination equipment (DTE) to the data communication equipment (DCE). In most packet networks, the host computers are considered DTEs and the packet switches as DCEs.

The relationships of these protocols to the DTE and that which is reflected to the DCE is shown in Table 7-3.

The network protocol is the set of procedures that allows the host to send and receive packets on the network. It typically includes provisions for addressing, network control messages, and the setting up of virtual circuits if these services are available. The transport layer provides DTE-to-DTE services such as sequencing, flow control, duplicate detection, and multiplexing. The session layer of protocol is intended to control the access to the host services. This is the layer that implements the user log-in mechanisms. The presentation layer provides the mechanisms for mapping between specific user terminals to generic or virtual terminal characteristics. The application layer deals with the specific user applications such as text editing, message handling, and query/response actions.

Table 7-3. The Relationship of Protocol Layers to the DTE and the DCE.

	⋮	
DTE	Transport	Host
	Network	
	Link	
	Physical	
	!	
	Physical	
DCE	Link	Packet switch
	Network	
	Internal network procedures	
	DTE/DCE Protocols	

TYMNET

A virtual-circuit policy is used in TYMNET, which is the packet network supporting the communications requirements of TYMSHARE. In TYMNET for each connection request between a user and a remote host, a control packet is first sent by the origin node to the NRC that acts as the supervisor. This control packet holds the source, destination, and password information.

After the password is verified, the NRC determines the minimum-cost path for the virtual circuit. Each link in the network has a cost factor associated with it, which depends on the link bandwidth and load, as shown in Table 7-4. The link becomes overloaded when the number of virtual circuits carried on it exceeds a specified quantity.

After the path has been determined, the NRC allocates the buffers and sets up parameter tables at each intermediate node along the path, to create the virtual circuit. After receiving the parameter table entries, each node sends an acknowledgment to the NRC. After all the acknowledgments are in, the NRC informs the users that the connection has been established and data transfer may start.

The link-load information can be updated by the NRC after each circuit allocation change, but the network topology is initially acquired using a network takeover phase. Here, the NRC first sends a command to its own node to obtain the node's capacity, the capacity of its links, the table entries, and neighbors. The command is then sent to the neighbors, which are also taken over, and the procedure continues until no more nodes are left. If link failures occur, they are reported to the NRC and the topological map is updated. The virtual circuits that are affected by a failure must generally be reinitialized by the user.

In packet radio networks, the role of the network routing center can be played by the station. The station can use a network connectivity initialization procedure similar to the takeover scheme used in TYMNET.

Transport Protocols (ARPANET)

ARPANET used one of the earliest transport protocols. The

Table 7-4. TYMNET Cost Factors.

	Approximate Cost Factor		
Line speed bps	**Normal**	**Overloaded One Way**	**Overloaded Both Ways**
9600	1.0	2.6	4.2
7200	1.1	2.7	4.3
4800	1.2	2.8	4.4
2400	1.6	3.2	4.8

communications subnet of switching computers provided a datagram message-oriented service, and the requirement for additional connection-oriented service appeared early. Because of the sequenced message delivery, the host-host protocol concentrated on flow control interruption, multiplexing, and simple, convenient addressing. In combination with the initial connection protocol (ICP), it allowed many connections to various services to be supported.

The host-host protocol set an important trend in protocol specification. The format and procedures for message exchange between the protocol machines was exactly and completely specified, but the interface between the user and the protocol was only functionally specified. This allowed implementations of the protocol to be tailored to different machines, while the different machines were still able to talk to each other.

The user interface was stream-oriented, with flow control in both bits and messages provided by control messages. A single control connection was used, while data messages were sent on individual connections.

The French Cyclades network appeared later than ARPANET, and it used a simpler communication subnet. A transport station (TS) was developed, which included procedures for error detection and recovery. Sequencing and flow control used a system of letters, where the letters were record-oriented. Error control was on these letters, with a complete letter being retransmitted when an error was detected.

A second-generation ARPANET protocol, which became known as TCP (transmission control program), appeared shortly after Cyclades. It offered improvements in virtual-circuit service for internets, using error-detection and recovery procedures which anticipated that some networks in a multinetwork system might not be always reliable.

The TCP sequence numbers were in units of bytes, which allowed finer flow control and more efficient error recovery. This also allowed the fragmentation of data into abitrary-length packets for communication between networks with varying packet sizes. The user interface was also record-oriented, as in Cyclades TS, but error and flow control were performed on a byte basis.

The procedures used for first establishing a connection were simple, and several weaknesses in these connection management procedures soon appeared. This resulted in the adoption of the following:

- A three-way handshake for connection establishment.
- Techniques for initial sequence-number selection.
- Resynchronization for clock-based sequence numbering.

Some of the original TCP functions, such as fragmentation reassembly and TS addressing, have been moved into a separate internet protocol. The priority scheme, which originally used a short interrupt packet, was replaced with a pointer that indicates a point in the data stream requiring service.

The Internetwork Working Group (INWG, Technical Committee 6.1) of the IFIP (the International Federation for Information Processing) has been very active in transport protocol development. Based on ARPANET, Cyclades, and other networks, standards such as an INWG 96 have appeared that are periodically revised and updated.

The more recent trend is to simplify those procedures at the transport protocol level that are already provided by the network, such as flow control. This provides a higher level of efficiency, particularly for public networks with X.25 interfaces.

A number of adaptations resulted from the early ARPANET, Cyclades, and INWIG protocols. Some of these applications are listed below:

- The European Information Network (EIN), which used INWG protocols in a multinetwork multinational environment.
- The MIT TCP-like protocol called DSP, designed for a local network environment, with unique addresses, which can never be reused.
- The Xerox Palo Alto Research Center protocols for local network office automation systems.
- The Lawrence Livermore Laboratory TCP-like protocol based on timers and sequence numbers. It uses a very high-bandwidth local network with small maximum packet lifetimes.
- The U.S. Defense Communications Agency TCP-like protocol used in the AUTODIN II network.

While these systems all have a strong similarity, there are differences which cause a lack of interoperability. The need for standardization of a common transport protocol resulted in ISO (TC97 SC16).

Most computer manufacturers' network protocols have been oriented towards connecting terminals to a central computer. A protocol layer which provides the functions of a transport protocol is usually present in these systems. Typical examples are IBM's SNA and Digital Equipment Corporation's DECNET.

IBM Systems Network Architecture (SNA)

SNA was designed for a number of terminal nodes which access a single or limited number of computer nodes, instead of a number of more equal nodes communicating in a true local area network. This asymmetry shows up in many of the SNA protocols. The transport protocol functions are provided primarily by the transmission control (TC) layer. The connections, which are called sessions, are established between the transmission control layers. A primary TC initiates a connection to a secondary TC, in order to avoid unpredictable timing leading to a race.

System services control points (SSCP) perform such functions as:

- Converting names to addresses.
- Checking access permission.
- Queue requesting.
- Terminating connections.

Sequencing is performed by the level above the TC layer. Flow control is performed by the TC layer, but acknowledgments and error recovery are done at a higher protocol level. Error control uses a hop-by-hop scheme below the transport level, similar to ARPANET.

Normal and expedited logical connections are provided for each session. Both are full duplex, but the expedited channel allows out-of-band signalling between processes. Flow control is only provided on the normal channel.

DECNET

DECNET is patterned after ARPANET in its layering of data link control, logical connections (or virtual-circuits), and user or application-level protocol. A network services protocol (NSP) functions as the transport protocol. There is no distinction between host computers and switching nodes, as there is an ARPANET.

A part of the network services protocol handles the routing of packets and the management of current routing information. The transport protocol section is concerned with the opening and closing connections, and sending and receiving data packets or interrupts. The number of procedural elements, such as flow control, sequencing, and acknowlegments, may be selected by the user. This allows different transport protocol mechanisms to be used as needed. Services can then be used more efficiently.

Addressing can be *generic*—names must be looked up at either the source or destination when the connection is established—or *specific*—the numeric ports are known by the routing algorithms. Error control and flow control use messages, and the source and destination must have the same message size. Flow control is based on a credit system, in which the sender is granted credits for the number of buffers the receiver has available. The addressing can be single level for small networks, or hierarchical for larger systems.

X.25

One of the best-known packet-switching standards is CCITT X.25, which covers three protocol layers:

- Network interface.
- Link control.
- Physical/electrical.

The lowest level is the physical/electrical interface, which, in X.25, follows the CCITT X.21 digital interface standard. The link-control level is compatible with HDLC, although the older binary synchronous protocol (BISYNC) can also be used. The other level of X.25 is the packet or virtual-circuit level. The basic procedures at this level are involved with the creation, termination, and use of virtual circuits which logically connect the host computers to one another in the packet-switched network.

The virtual circuits are identified in information packets which are moved from host to packet switch using the HDLC protocol. The basic X.25 packet format used is shown in Fig. 7-7.

This format shows that the packet level of X.25 uses a flow control scheme similar to the one used at the HDLC link control level. The P(R) field identifies the next sequence number expected to be received, and the P(S) field identifies the one being sent. The M bit indicates that there is more data to be sent that is logically associated with the data packet. This allows sequences of packets to be sent to the destination and logically grouped there as they arrive.

8 bits

0001	Logical

Channel number

P(R)	M	P(S)	0

User data

Fig. 7-7. X.25 data packet format.

These logical channels are full-duplex streams of packets, which are set-up by requests from hosts to packet switches with the call set-up packets shown in Fig. 7-8.

The call set-up packet allows 14 digits of addressing for each source and destination DTE. Destination-only addressing is permitted, but is not often used, because most systems will require the identity of the caller before accepting an incoming call. There are also provisions for special facility requests, such as reverse charging. There are other special packets for accepting calls, closing and resetting virtual circuits, and starting and stopping flow to a virtual circuit.

The X.25 recommendation specifies the interface or protocol to be used by subscribers accessing public networks, but it specifies only the interface between the customer's computer (data terminal equipment or DTE) and its local attachment point to the network (a switching node or DCE, see Fig. 7-9).

The virtual-circuit, or level 3, protocol has many features of a transport protocol, but operates only between the subscriber computer and the local network switching node. To achieve end-to-end service between two subscribers, the network must establish connections and transmit data between source and destination DCEs, using an internal

8 bits	
0001	Logical
Channel number	
Packet type identifier 0000 1011	
Called DTE address length	Calling DTE address length
DTE address ⋮	
00	Facility length
Facilities	
Protocol identifier (4 OCTETS)	
Call user data	

Fig. 7-8. X.25 call set-up packet.

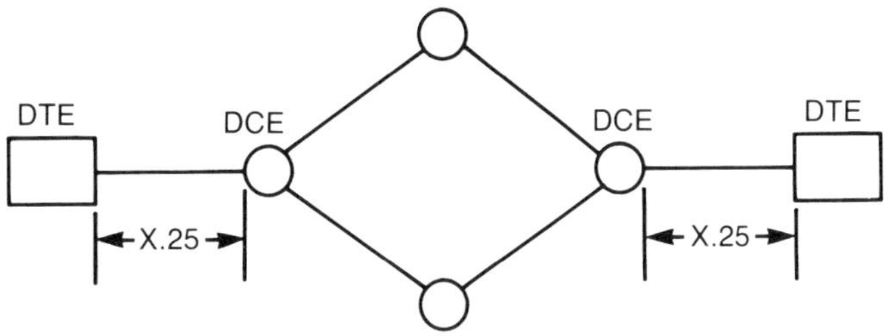

Fig. 7-9. X.25 application.

protocol not specified in X.25. The destination node provides a part of the virtual-circuit path by using X.25 with the destination subscriber.

In some networks, the internal protocol uses a single virtual circuit between source and destination nodes, while in others an independent virtual circuit between each intermediate node is used. End-to-end service requires a series of at least three independent virtual circuits. The outer two links operate under the X.25 protocol, while the inner link (or links) run under the protocol of the local network.

Two logically separate full-duplex data streams are used for each connection: a normal stream and a qualified stream. Both are sequenced and flow-controlled together.

When connections are established by the call request packet, the request is forwarded through the network to the destination subscriber, who returns an accept or reject packet. Simultaneous requests by a pair of subscribers to call each other can result in zero, one, or two calls being set-up, depending on the local network procedures.

While X.25 specifies only the interface between customer and network, it provides a basis for the subscriber-to-subscriber service offered by the network. Several of the level 3 protocol features, such as interrupt and call establishment, can be used for end-to-end operations. Others, such as sequencing and flow control, can only be used locally, as in TRANSPAC, or implemented for end-to-end operations, as in DATAPAC. Call clearing and resets can also be handled in a similar way.

Networks that require high-reliability might need their own error-control procedures in an end-to-end protocol, on top of X.25. An end-to-end flow-control scheme might also be needed, along with an end-to-end transport protocol on top of X.25. A simpler datagram-type service, without connection establishment, sequencing, or error control, could be provided by an end-to-end transport protocol. A datagram service can be less expensive and more efficient to transaction-oriented users who do not require virtual-circuit service.

The interface between packet-switching networks is covered by CCITT recommendation X.75. This standard closely resembles X.25. It specifies a virtual-circuit-like protocol for the link between networks, and a separate virtual circuit used for each internet call. It is concerned with the link between networks, as shown in Fig. 7-10, and not the end-to-end services.

OPTIMIZATION CONSIDERATIONS

Among the key considerations for packet-switched networks are the choice of topology and the assignment of link capacity for the system. The capacity problem is affected by the expected traffic demand and the routing scheme. The routing discipline is influenced by the choice of topology, while the choice of topology is affected by the traffic demand. These interactions describe a classical optimization problem that can be divided into four separated, but related problems:

1. **A capacity assignment problem.**
   Given: The topology, traffic requirement matrix, and routing strategy.

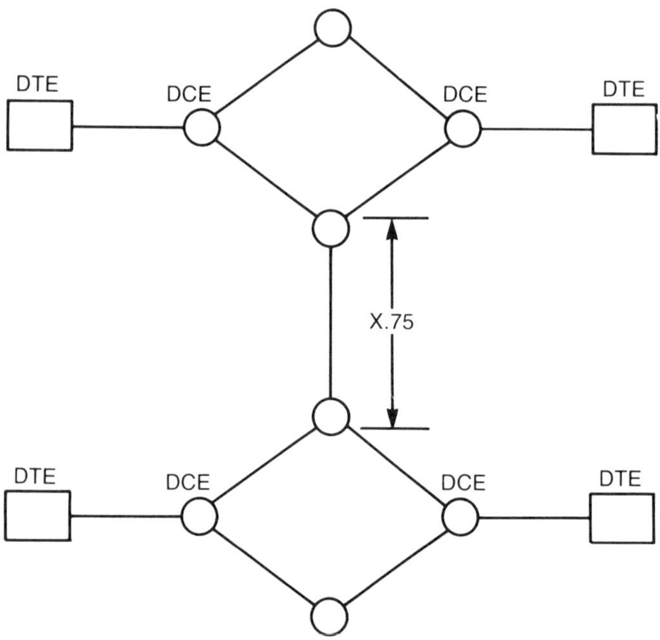

Fig. 7-10. X.75 application.

Select: A capacity assignment that minimizes the average delay, based on a cost function relating cost to units of capacity. The minimization might be subject to a maximum cost, or throughput could be maximized, subject to delay.

2. **A flow assignment problem.**
Given: The topology.
Select: A routing strategy. A fixed routing assignment results in certain flows over each link in the network. If the link capacity is constrained to a fixed set of assigned values, the routing strategy must be adjusted.

3. **A capacity and flow assignment problem.**
Given: The topology, traffic requirement matrix, and cost of the capacity function.
Minimize: The cost for the flow assignments which meet the traffic requirements and limit delay to be less than an allowed maximum. There usually exists a number of local minima, making global solutions difficult, even if simplifying assumptions, such as linear cost for capacity, are made.

4. **A topology, capacity, and flow assignment problem.**
Given: A traffic requirement matrix.
Minimize: The cost of capacity, subject to satisfying traffic, delay, and topology requirements. Among the techniques available for dealing with this problem are branch exchange methods, in which links are inserted or deleted, and *cut set* methods, in which sets of links are examined for capacity.

A cut of links is made which would disconnect the network into two or more parts. The cut is *saturated* if each link in the cut is operating at capacity. If the cut is not saturated, the algorithm will attempt to assign additional traffic on the unsaturated cut. If saturation has been reached, the algorithm will assign the most cost-effective link to join the two parts of the net separated by the cut, and delete the least cost-effective link.

REVIEW EXERCISES

1. Discuss the concept of store-and-forward communications with the aid of a diagram.
2. What is the hop-by-hop acknowledgment method?
3. Show how duplicate pockets can be detected with the aid of a diagram.
4. What is the basic object of flow control? How does it differ from congestion control?
5. Discuss some techniques of congestion control, along with their disadvantages.
6. How will flow control differ between virtual-circuit networks and datagram networks?
7. How is store-and-forward or hop flow control accomplished?
8. Discuss the following types of routing in store-and-forward systems:
    a. Fixed or static.
    b. Dynamic or adaptive.
    c. Distributed.
    d. Centralized.
    e. Isolated.
9. What is the difference between user and system optimization in packet routing?
10. What is the difference between explicit path routing and source routing?
11. Describe the use of virtual addressing.
12. Draw a diagram that describes the basic functions of SNA.
13. What is the advantage of using a datagram service in X.25?
14. Discuss how the following could be optimized in a packet network:
    a. Minimal delay.
    b. Minimal cost.
15. What is the advantage of packet switching over message switching?
16. With the aid of a diagram, discuss the use of negative and positive acknowledgment schemes in a packet network.
17. Describe the use of logical links in a packet network with the aid of a diagram. Include the detection of duplicate packets.
18. Describe three possible methods for congestion control, along with the potential shortcomings of each method.
19. With the aid of a diagram, discuss how cycle time affects dynamic routing. What other problems might exist?

20. Devise an addressing scheme for a system of four connected networks, each of which has eight hosts with 16 ports. There are eight different applications running in each host.

21. What is the function of the M bit in X.25?

Chapter 8

Network Testing and Maintainability

During the process of installation, operation, and maintenance of a digital transmission network, the operator must have the capability to test, monitor, and control the system. This capability should allow the verification of the system objectives. After the system has been commissioned, the components should be monitored and controlled to ensure that the operation and maintenance objectives are met.

The performance standards differ from design objectives in that various sources of degradation are not always included in the design methodology. These include aging, environment, and human errors which affect performance limits during the operation of the system. Real circuits will differ from the hypothetical ideal circuits used in the design methodology because of differing conductor length, media characteristics, and other factors. These differences must be taken into account when specifying and measuring performance standards.

This chapter discusses techniques for testing digital transmission networks for parameters such as bit error rate, jitter, bit count integrity, and equipment reliability. These methods are suitable for both factory or acceptance testing prior to system commission for operation.

During system operation, built-in techniques must be provided for alarm and status indications to allow the identification of transmission problems. This can be accomplished with error coding techniques.

Performance monitors can allow system and equipment margins to be continuously monitored, using an estimation of the bit error rate. Fault isolation techniques can identify the need for maintenance when service has been interrupted.

Because actions taken at one node might affect other nodes or stations, it becomes necessary to incorporate various security schemes to prevent unauthorized actions. In discussing the various schemes used for network security, the emphasis is on developing a conceptual understanding.

TEST METHODS

Performance specifications, or standards, can be verified by testing, either in the factory or in an operational environment. To facilitate the testing process, the specifications and standards should include descriptions of the tests to be used, as well as the recommended test equipment, configurations, and detailed procedures. Commonly used performance parameters of digital transmission systems include:

- Bit error rate (BER).
- Jitter.
- Bit count integrity.

Bit Error Rate Measurement

The error in a digital transmission system can be expressed several ways. The error parameter used in measuring the system performance is normally the same as that used in the system design to allocate performance. The measurement can be made under out-of-service and in-service conditions. In the out-of-service case, the operational traffic is replaced by a known test stimulus or pattern. This can be a pseudorandom binary sequence (PRBS), which simulates the traffic. The received test pattern is then compared, bit by bit, with a locally generated pattern to detect errors. The repetition period of the test pattern must be selected to provide a sufficiently smooth spectrum for the system data rate. The pattern lengths for the most common data rates are listed in Table 8-1.

Because the out-of-service measurement eliminates any traffic, it is most useful in production testing, during installation, or for experimental testing.

A typical configuration for BER measurement is shown in Fig. 8-1. At the receiver, the error measurement can be made for error pulses, average BER, errored seconds, or errored blocks. The bit error rate tester

Table 8-1. Pseudorandom Sequence Length for the Measurement of Error Rate.

Bit Rate	Pattern Length	CCITT Recommendation
Up to 20 Kbps	$2^9 - 1$	V.52
20 to 72 Kbps	$2^{20} - 1$	V.57
1.544 Mbps	$2^{15} - 1$	0.151
2.048 Mbps	$2^{15} - 1$	0.151
6.312 Mbps	$2^{15} - 1$	0.151
8.448 Mbps	$2^{15} - 1$	0.151
32.064 Mbps	$2^{15} - 1$	0.151
34.368 Mbps	$2^{23} - 1$	0.151
44.736 Mbps	$2^{15} - 1$	0.151
139.264 Mbps	$2^{23} - 1$	0.151

might have the ability to force errors at the transmitter and observe them at the receiver to provide an indication of loss of synchronization.

Error-free seconds are another form of error measurement. This is expressed as the percentage of error-free seconds in a measurement period. The measurement can use either synchronous or asynchronous mode. In the synchronous mode, an errored second is defined as a 1 – s interval following the occurrence of the first error. The synchronous mode allows measurements to be made with different instruments on the same link. However, the measurement does not directly provide error-free seconds. Instead, it is a measure of error-free time. In the asynchronous mode, each discrete one second interval is checked for errors, which directly provides error-free seconds. Different measurements are often obtained with different equipment. The use of asynchronous errored

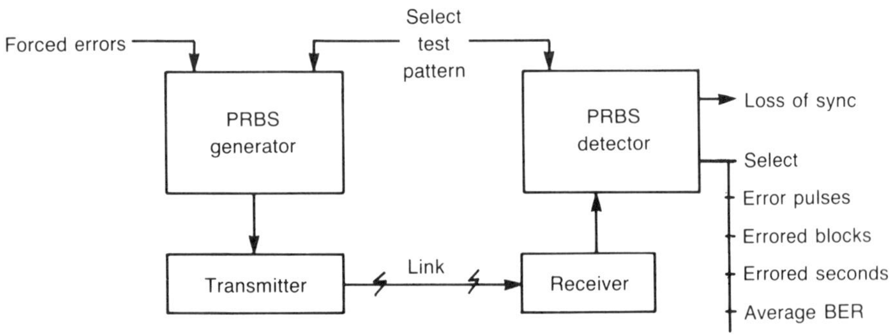

Fig. 8-1. BER measurement.

seconds is advised in CCITT Recommendation G.821, while other standards proposed in North America advise the use of synchronous errored seconds.

In-service error measurements can be performed if the traffic has an inherent repetitive pattern, the line format has some inherent error detection, or the received signal is monitored for certain threshold crossings. The in-service techniques estimate the error rate, and do not provide a true indication. They can be used for performance monitoring during system demonstration, or, if they can be made quickly enough, to allow control of switching functions.

Measured bit error rates require a confidence level in order to be useful. The confidence level states the probability that the measured error rate is within an accuracy factor of the true average BER, or, in terms of the number of errors:

$$\text{Confidence level} = P(np \leq ak_i)$$

where

n = number of trial bits
p = probability of bit error
np = expected number of errors
a = accuracy factor
k_i = number of measured errors

A model for the confidence level can be based on the Bernoulli trials model if the errors are independently distributed. The probability that ak_i or fewer errors occur in n independent trials becomes:

$$P(\leq ak_i \text{ errors in n bits}) = \sum_{k=o}^{ak_i} \binom{n}{k} p^k q^{n-k}$$

where $q = 1 - p$. This expression is difficult to evaluate for n, but approximations can be made for two cases. When n becomes large so that the expected number of errors is also large$_g$ then np becomes much larger than one ($np >> 1$). The approximate expression becomes:

$$P(\leq ak \text{ errors in n bits}) = 1 - \text{erfc}\,[(a - 1)\sqrt{k_i}]\ (np >> 1)$$

where erfc(x) is the complementary error function:

$$\operatorname{erfc}\left(\frac{V}{\sigma}\right) = \frac{1}{\sqrt{2\pi}} \int_{V/\sigma}^{\infty} e^{-Z^2/2}\, dZ$$

For the case where p is small and n is large, then the expected number of errors is small (np ≈ 1) and the probability is closer to a Poisson distribution, and can be expressed as:

$$P(np \leq ak_i) = 1 - e^{-ak_i} \sum_{k=o}^{k} \frac{(ak_i)^k}{k!} \quad (np \approx 1)$$

These expressions can be solved for the probability (confidence level) as a function of the errors measured (k_i) and the actual bit error rate (np). The probability can be fixed, and the BER can be computed as a function of the measured error for 99 percent confidence limits. Plotted curves indicate that the actual BER is less than np/k times the measured BER. If 10 errors are recorded, then the actual BER is within two times the measured BER with a 99 percent confidence (Fig. 8-2).

Jitter Measurements

Jitter can be characterized in three ways:

1. The tolerable input jitter.
2. The output jitter in the absence of input jitter (intrinsic jitter).
3. The ratio of output to input jitter (jitter transfer function).

The basic techniques used to measure jitter are shown in Fig. 8-3. The measurements are all done out-of-service, and are usually combined

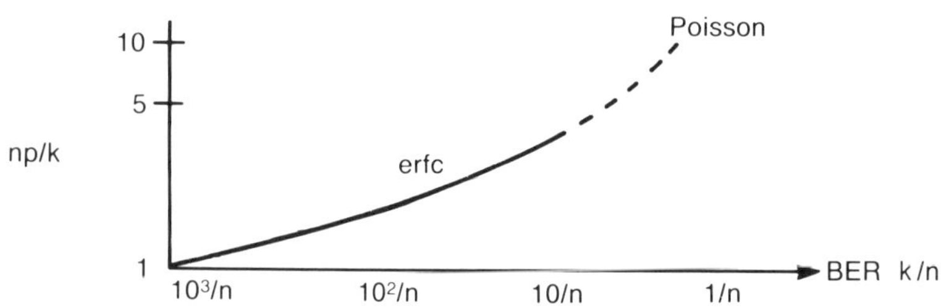

Fig. 8-2. Actual BER 99% confidence level.

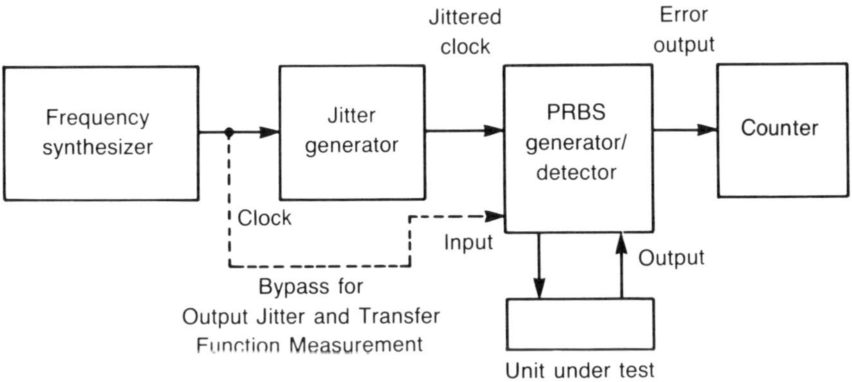

Fig. 8-3. Jitter measurement.

with factory or system acceptance testing. The sources for input jitter testing are connected, and the clock signal produced by the frequency synthesizer is modulated by the jitter generator and used to clock the pattern generator. The output of the pattern generator is then passed through the unit under test from input to output ports. The pattern detector monitors the output port signal and provides an error output to a counter.

The amplitude of the induced jitter is increased until bit errors are detected, and this test is repeated for a range of jitter frequencies. A plot of maximum tolerable input jitter versus jitter frequency can be constructed using the test set-up shown in Fig. 8-3.

The jitter modulation is often sinusoidal, although it is not representative of the type of jitter found in a network. A pseudorandom binary sequence is used for the test pattern, as discussed in the previous section.

Intrinsic jitter and the jitter transfer function use a configuration similar to that used for input jitter, except that a jitter detector replaces the error detector. In order to measure output jitter in the absence of input jitter, the jitter generator is bypassed, and a jitter-free clock is used to generate the PRBS pattern. The received pattern is applied to the jitter detector, which measures jitter amplitude.

The jitter transfer function is found using a PRBS signal modulated by the jitter generator. The gain or attenuation of jitter in the detected PRBS signal is then measured. In both tests, the jitter amplitude, which can be rms (root-mean-square) or peak-to-peak, is measured for the bandwidths of interest. Bandpass, low-pass, or high-pass filters might be required to limit the jitter bandwidth. For the measurement of specified jitter spectra, CCITT Recommendation 0.171 provides test information for these measurements.

Bit Count Integrity Tests

Bit count integrity (BCI) can be a function of several parameters, such as signal-to-noise ratio, clock accuracy, or stability. These tests require observing the conditions under which BCI is lost and then regained. Testing is done out-of-service, and it might be a part of factory tests or system installation.

A multiplexer usually is specified for a certain error rate. To verify this error rate, the multiplexer aggregate data stream is subjected to the specified error rate while measurements are made of the times between the loss of BCI and the time to regain BCI. The measured times are then compared to the specification.

Reliability Tests

Equipment reliability can be verified with a combination of burn-in testing, analysis, and field results. Burn-in tests can be used to verify the mean time between failure (MTBF) specification. Using a number of units under test at one time, it is possible to demonstrate the reliability in relatively short periods of time through the use of sequential testing. The cumulative number of failures is plotted versus the cumulative test time until an accept or reject decision is reached, as shown in Fig. 8-4, or until the maximum allowable test time is reached.

Analysis Techniques

For redundant equipment, direct testing is not a practical way of verifying mean time between outage (MTBO) because of the inordinate length of time that would be required. A recommended means of verifying

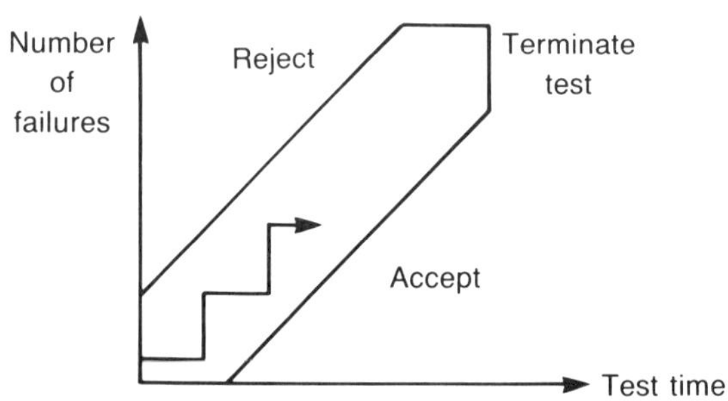

Fig. 8-4. Accept/test plot.

the MTBO is to use analysis and MTBF testing. The analysis would produce a list of failure modes and effects, verify that performance sensors will detect failures, and verify that switching circuits will cause switchover from failed units to standby units. The MTBO can then be calculated from a demonstrated MTBF and predicted redundancy switching.

Reliability can also be monitored and recorded in actual field conditions. The high-failure items can be identified and replaced before failure occurs.

Link Tests

Before acceptance of a cable or radio link, testing is necessary to ensure that the link installation has followed the design criteria. An essential part of this is the verification of equipment interface compatibility and operation in a typical environment. This can be done by operating the equipment in a loop-back mode, rather than over the link. This test period must be long enough to identify cable mismatches, faulty grounds, and other defects in the network.

Another phase of link testing is the actual operation of the transmission equipment over the link. Some design parameters, such as signal-to-noise ratios, can be quickly measured. Error rates can be measured for digital data, and voice-channel measurements can be made for 4 kHz analog signals.

The link can also be stressed to verify the design margins. This can be done using the following procedure:

1. The nominal received signal level (RSL) is determined.
2. A BER test is conducted with a calibrated attenuator inserted in the received signal path and set to yield the threshold BER.

The margin should be determined separately for each received path.

Hysteresis (lag in the response of a signal) can be tested by fixing the attenuation of one branch at a constant value, and then varying the attenuation of a second branch above and below the design value. If the measured margin and hysteresis are approximately equal, the link can be expected to meet performance objectives.

PERFORMANCE MONITORING CONSIDERATIONS

The threshold effect of digital transmission requires a different approach in performance assessment compared to that used in analog transmission. The gradual degradation of an analog signal is transformed directly into degraded user performance, and can be easily monitored.

The gradual degradation of a digital signal has no noticeable effect on system performance until errors appear. After the digital signal has deteriorated to the point where errors are noticed, only a small margin exists between these initial errors and unacceptable performance.

An effective performance monitor must be capable of constantly measuring the margin between the state of the transmission channel and the threshold of that channel. A performance monitor indicating such a margin can allow the system operator to implement diagnostic and maintenance procedures before the actual user performance degrades.

In the design and use of performance monitors, there are several important considerations:

- In-service methods must be used to allow normal traffic and not affect the end user.
- There should be a rapid and observable response to any system degradation.
- The dynamic range should extend from threshold to received signal levels that are significantly higher than the threshold.
- Simplicity should be emphasized to maintain reliability and minimize cost.
- The resolution must be great enough to allow a continuous quantitative measurement of the margin.
- A functional or empirical relationship with the BER should exist.

A number of performance monitoring techniques are available. These are described in the following sections.

Test Sequence Transmission

If channels are available in multiplex equipment, these can be used as test channels. Auxiliary service channels of this nature can be used for the transmission of a pseudorandom binary sequence at a low bit rate. The test sequence is interleaved with the traffic at a fraction (1/N) of the system bit rate. At the receiver end, the BER can be estimated from the ratio of errors detected to the number of transmitted test bits.

There is some overhead required for this technique. The time required to recognize a specified error rate is multiplied by N—the time required to count all errors for the transmitted bits. This results in a relatively long time, even for low error.

Frame Bit and Parity Bit Monitoring

Digital multiplexers use a repetitive frame pattern for synchronization. This pattern is fixed and known beforehand, so an estimate of BER can be made by measuring the frame bit errors. For performance monitoring, multiplexers often provide a digital pulse output for each frame bit error, and only a counter is required to determine the frame bit error rate. In some units, a front panel display of error rate is provided, and the required counting and averaging are done internally.

Parity or check bits can be added to blocks of data or to multiplexer frames in order to provide error detection. At the transmitter, a parity bit is added to each block of data to make the sum of all bits always odd or always even. At the receiver, the sum of bits in each block or frame is compared to the value of the received parity bit. Disagreement indicates that an error has occurred. Parity checking provides an accurate estimate of system error rate for error rates below 10^{-n}, where n is the length of the block or frame.

Some multilevel coding methods place constraints on transitions from one level to another. A received signal can be monitored for differences from these level constraints to provide error detection. The level constraints depend on the code used, for example, a bipolar code should not have two consecutive marks of the same polarity.

Eye Pattern Monitoring

The monitoring of the eye pattern opening allows a qualitative measure of error performance. As the signal degrades, the eye pattern becomes fuzzy, and the opening between levels at the symbol sampling time becomes smaller. Noise and amplitude distortion tend to close the vertical opening, while jitter and timing changes tend to close the horizontal opening.

One technique is to measure the eye closure and compare the measured values with those obtained for the system operating in an ideal environment. The eye closure can be expressed as system degradation decibels by equating the system degradation to $-20\log(1 - \text{eye closure})$. This can be converted to a BER estimate by calibration of the eye pattern monitor.

Another, more general technique is to analyze selected bit patterns. You can compare the received eye pattern to the ideal eye pattern for a selected bit pattern.

Pseudoerror Detection

Pseudoerror detection is a technique that degrades the receiver margin intentionally, and creates a pseudoerror rate. It can be implemented by offsetting either the sampling instant, the decision threshold, or both, from their optimum values, and then counting the number of detected bits (the pseudoerrors) in the offset region. For each type of degradation, the relationship between the actual BER and pseudoerror rate (PER) is fixed. This relationship depends on the amount of intentional offset selected for the pseudodecision circuit. The PER is usually greater than the BER, and can be estimated in a shorter time, especially for low error rates, than by the other methods.

The pseudoerror technique detects channel impairment before actual errors occur. The calibration of PER to BER should be related to the potential sources of degradation for the application.

A block diagram of a pseudoerror detector circuit is shown in Fig. 8-5. If the degradation is additive Gaussian noise with a zero average, then for a transmitted one, the noise density is centered about the received signal at level one.

The probability of pseudoerror can be written using a modification of the expressions for the actual error probability. For coherent binary phase-shift keying (BPSK) or quadrature phase-shift keying (QPSK), the probability of pseudoerror is:

$$\text{PER} = \text{P}\,\{\text{pseudoerror}\} = \text{erfc}\,\sqrt{\text{A}\,(1-\text{h})} - \text{erfc}\,\sqrt{\text{A}\,(1\text{th})}$$

where A is the ratio of the output level to the frame length.

A comparison of BER and PER as a function of the pseudoerror zone height (h) shows that over the range of zone heights, the PER is almost

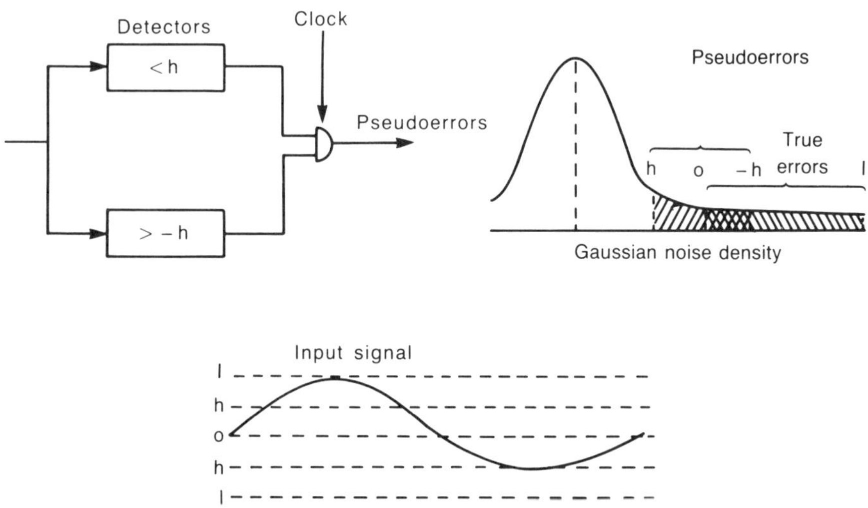

Fig. 8-5. Pseudoerror detection.

parallel to the BER. The pseudoerror rate when h = 0.2 is about two orders of magnitude greater than the ideal error rate. As h increases, this multiplication factor increases even faster, and the time required to estimate the true BER is reduced.

ERROR CONTROL

A fundamental way of improving reliability in a network is to add error control processing at the transmitting and receiving ends. This is normally done through the channel encoder by adding redundancy in such a way that the decoder decision can be based on several received symbols rather than just one.

The selection of an error-control approach requires a review of the performance expected of the approach, the channel environment in which it must operate, and any relevant implementation or system issues that could affect the approach in the particular application. The required information throughput rate and the allowed throughput delay for channel encoding and decoding are important. The modem modulation, symbol-rate, tracking-accuracy, and phase-ambiguity must also be considered.

The phase-ambiguity characteristics are important, because the modem might lock up in response to a signal that is 180° or ±90° out of phase. Differential encoding and decoding can be used with some codes, but performance is generally better when the differential coding is placed outside, rather than inside, the channel coding. The channel codes can also be selected such that the decoder will resolve phase ambiguities without differential coding.

The use of soft receiver quantization, as opposed to hard quantization, is also important. Consider a system that uses binary phase-shift keying modulation. In hard receiver quantization, the demodulator tells the decoder whether the demodulator output for each symbol was positive or negative. In soft receiver quantization, the demodulator also provides additional bits of information related to the degree of confidence the demodulator had in the sign decision. The confidence level is a function of the magnitude of the demodulator output.

The acceptable bandwidth expansion is a factor of this magnitude, because the channel encoders add redundancy which, for a fixed source symbol rate, means a higher channel symbol rate, and, in general, a larger bandwidth requirement. In bandwidth limited systems, only a small amount of redundancy is acceptable. Higher-order modulation alphabet sizes, along with channel coding, can sometimes be used in such a situation. A selective approach might be possible where more redundancy is used for some links in the system.

The characteristics of the bursts on bursty channels are important in terms of:

- The duration and attenuation of the burst.
- The periodic or random characteristics of the duty cycle.
- The guard space between bursts.
- The availability and reliability of the information on the occurrence of a burst that could be furnished to the decoder.

The burst rate and duty cycle of the received data can determine the suitability of using a decoder at a smoothed average rate, rather than at the burst rate.

Other important characteristics include:

- The availability and characteristics of return channels.
- The decoder synchronization time and loss-of-sync requirements.
- The bit, symbol, or message-error probability or error rate required.
- The allowed rate of accepting incorrect messages.
- The number of separately encoded sequences that must be simultaneously decoded.
- The destination-data-sink's vulnerability to bursts of errors from the decoder.
- The possibility of mutual-user, or hostile, jamming.
- Cost, size, weight, and power considerations.

Coding Techniques

The most common error control techniques are forward-error control (FEC), automatic-repeat-request (ARQ), or hybrid FEC-ARQ approaches. In the FEC technique, the decoder automatically corrects as many channel errors as possible. It might make an estimate of the transmitted sequence based on hard or soft decision inputs, without using a communication link back to the transmitting terminal. In the ARQ technique, the decoder detects the errors and uses a communication link to request that the incorrectly received frame be sent again. The request can be repeated until the frame is received correctly.

These repeated transmissions tend to reduce the throughput rate of the system. In an ARQ system, an error occurs whenever the error-detection decoder incorrectly accepts a frame of data with errors. The probability of such undetected errors can be reduced by adding redundancy to the error-detecting code.

The throughput efficiency of an ARQ system is defined as the ratio of the total number of information bits accepted by the decoder per unit time to the total number of bits that could have been transmitted in the same amount of time without ARQ. This ratio is a function of the following:

- The channel error and the ARQ protocol characteristics.
- Data rate.
- Propagation delay time.
- Frame length.

There are three basic types of ARQ protocols: stop-and wait, go-back-n, and selective-repeat. In stop-and-wait ARQ, the source terminal sends one frame at a time and waits for an acknowledgment from the destination terminal that the frame was accepted by the error-detection decoder. If the acknowledgment is there, then the next frame is sent. When the error-detection decoder at the receive terminal detects an error, it provides a negative acknowledgment and the source terminal repeats the frame.

A half-duplex channel can be used for this type of ARQ, because information is sent in one direction at a time. The technique is simple, but inefficient, because of the waiting for an acknowledgment that is required. The use of larger frame lengths reduces the idle-time inefficiency, but as the frame length is increased, each frame becomes more likely to have an error.

Another approach is to use continuous ARQ, in which the source terminal sends frames continuously without waiting for an acknowledgment that the frame was accepted. Suppose that the source terminal could go back some number of frames (n) and begin transmitting the frames again, in sequence, from the point where an error was reported or suspected. This is the go-back-n technique, which can be more effective than the stop-and-wait technique, but becomes inefficient when n becomes large. This problem can be solved by retransmitting only the specific frames that were missed, using the selective-repeat approach. A disadvantage of this approach is the extra buffering that might be required for frame reordering.

ARQ systems are useful in applications where channel errors occur in bursts. If random errors are important, the throughput efficiency will fall rapidly with increasing channel error rates. In this case, a hybrid ARQ approach can be used, where FEC coding is used to correct the randomly distributed errors, and an ARQ scheme is used to reduce the error rate.

FEC codes can be either block or convolutional. Block codes process data in blocks that are independent of one another. A block encoder accepts data in blocks of k symbols, usually binary, and provides output-encoded data in blocks of n symbols. Because redundancy is added, n will be greater than k. The ratio k/n is called the code rate, or rate (R). This is,

$$R = k/n$$
$$\text{where } 0 < R < 1$$

The code rate is different from the data rate of the code, which is the rate at which information is presented to the encoder, usually given in bits per second (bps). The code rate out of the encoder is called the *channel data rate,* and is 1/R times larger than the data rate.

Convolutional codes can be represented that provide n output symbols for each group of k input symbols. The convolutional encoder output will depend not only on the last set of k input symbols, but also on several of the preceding sets of input symbols. In convolutional codes, k and n are smaller than in block codes. The code rate is also defined as R = k/n.

The reciprocal of the code rate can be called the *bandwidth expansion,* because adding coding increases the required channel symbol rate. Codes with low rates can provide greater error detection and correction, but they require a larger bandwidth expansion.

Linear block codes can be described by a $k \times n$ generator matrix, G. In the binary case, all the elements in the generator matrix and the encoder input and output vectors are zeros or ones, and arithmetic is performed using ordinary multiplication rules and bit-by-bit modulo – 2 addition.* The code words are bit-by-bit modulo – 2 sums of the rows of G. In order to guarantee that there are two distinct code words, the rows of G must be linearly independent.

Linear block codes are usually decoded using algebraic or table-lookup techniques based on hard-decision demodulator outputs. Soft-decision implementations can be used with convolutional coding techniques. Another problem of block codes compared to convolutional codes is that the n-way ambiguity, which must be resolved to determine the start of a block, is much larger than required with convolutional codes.

Block codes are often used on channels where only hard receiver decisions are available, and the data is already in a blocked format. The most common application of block codes is for error detection.

---

*In Modulo = 2 addition, $0 + 0 = 0$, $0 + 1 = 1$, $1 + 1 = 0$, $0 \times 0 = 0$, $0 \times 1 = 0$, $1 \times 0 = 0$, $1 \times 1 = 1$, since $1 + 1 = 0$, $1 = -1$, subtraction = addition.

Cyclic Codes and Error Detection

Cyclic codes are a type of linear block code in which each end-around cyclic shift of each code word is also a code word. The generator and parity-check matrices of cyclic codes can be expressed in terms of the coefficients of the generator and parity polynomials. Figure 8-6 illustrates the technique for encoding a cyclic code. A multiple-stage feedback shift register is used, with the feedback tap multipliers based on the coefficients of the generator polynominal. A major advantage of cyclic codes lies in their cyclic properties, which require relatively simple encoder circuits.

A typical application of cyclic codes is error detection. A common example is the cyclic redundancy check (CRC) code. Almost all error-detecting codes are based on the CRC type. This class of codes is characterized by an CRC error burst (of length B) in an n-bit received code word. The error burst may appear as a contiguous sequence, or an end-around shift of a contiguous sequence. The first and last bits, and any number of intermediate bits, are received in error. For a block code with n channel bits, d(min) = minimum distance and k = information bits, the following n-bit channel-error patterns can be detected:

- All CRC error bursts of length n − k or less.
- All combinations of d(min) − 1 or less errors.
- All error patterns with an odd number of errors when the generator polynomial has an even number of nonzero coefficients.
- A fraction $1 - 2^{(n-k-1)}$ of the CRC error bursts of length B = n − k + 1.
- A fraction $1 - 2^{(n-k)}$ of the CRC error bursts of length B > n − k + 1.

The basic cyclic codes selected for error detection usually have a very large block length (n). This basic code is then shortened by deleting the first few information bits. The result is no longer a pure cyclic code, but this modified code is still referred to as CRC code. All of the standard CRC codes are of this type, and have the same minimum distance and error-detection properties as the basic cyclic code.

The encoder for these shortened CRC codes can also be implemented as shown in Fig. 8-6. The decoder computes the end-around shift, and only passes the block of data under specified conditions. One approach is to re-encode the information portion of the received code word, and only pass the block of data when the newly computed parity bits are all equal to the corresponding received parity bits.

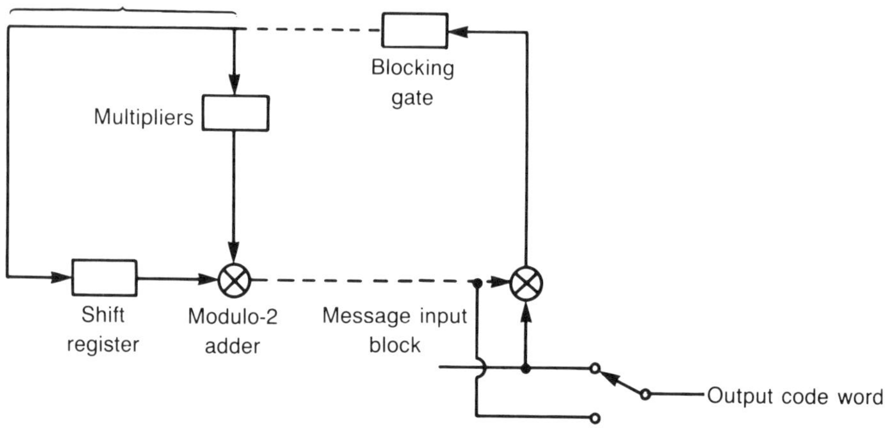

Fig. 8-6. Cyclic encoding.

The polynomials for the most common CRC codes are:

CRC – 12 code $p(x) = 1 + x + x^2 + x^3 + x^{11} + x^{12}$
CRC – 16 code $p(x) = 1 + x^2 + x^{15} + x^{16}$
CCITT CRC code $p(x) = 1 + x^5 + x^{12} + x^{16}$

For additional error-detection capability, the following code can be used:

$$p(x) = 1 + x + x^2 + x^4 + x^5 + x^7 + x^8 + x^{10} + x^{11} + x^{12} + x^{16} + x^{22} + x^{23} + x^{26} + x^{32}$$

Binary Error-Correcting Codes

Two of the most common binary linear-block error-correcting codes are the Hamming and Golay codes. Hamming codes have the following parameters:

$n = 2^m - 1$ $m = 3,4,5,6 \ldots$
$k = 2^m - 1 - m$
$n - k = m$
$d(min) = 3$

where k = input block length
n = output block length

These codes have a minimum distance (d) of three, and are capable of correcting all single errors, or detecting all combinations of two or fewer errors. Hamming codes belong to a class of linear block known as *perfect codes.* A perfect code for correcting x bits has the characteristic that every error pattern of x or fewer errors can be corrected, and no error pattern with more than x errors can be corrected.

A parity bit can be added to the Hamming code to form an *extended* Hamming code with the following parameters:

$$n = 2^m$$
$$k = 2^m - 1 - m$$
$$n - k = m + 1$$
$$d(min) = 4$$

This code is capable of correcting any single error and detecting double errors or any combination of three errors. Table-lookup is normally used for decoding these codes.

The Golay code is another perfect code. This code has a minimum distance of seven, and is capable of correcting any combination of three or fewer errors, or detecting any combination of six or fewer errors. The Golay code is a cyclic code, which can be generated by one of the following:

$$p(x) = 1 + x^2 + x^4 + x^5 + x^6 + x^{10} + x^{11}$$

or

$$p(x) = 1 + x + x^5 + x^6 + x^7 + x^9 + x^{11}$$

An *extended* Golay code can be formed by adding a parity bit to the basic Golay code. The extended code has a minimum distance of eight for the following code words:

- One word of weight zero.
- 759 words of weight eight.
- 2576 words of weight 12.
- 759 words of weight 16.
- One code word of weight 24.

Generally, the minimum distance of any binary linear block code with an odd minimum distance can be increased by one by adding an overall parity bit.

Convolutional Coding

Convolutional codes have the property that each output group depends not only on the k inputs at that time, but also on several preceding input groups. These codes require memory, and use an encoder which accepts data in small groups of k symbols (often k = 1) and provides encoded output data in small groups of n symbols (n > k). These codes allow decoding algorithms that can be used with soft receiver decisions, and they are simple to implement.

In a convolutional code, the encoder provides each of the k input sequences directly as outputs. It would then also provide n – k parity output sequences. Because there is no need to send known tail bits when blocks of data are transmitted, the tail sequence, or trailer, that needs to be transmitted is shorter.

Convolutional codes normally use encoding that is performed with feedforward logic. These codes can also be generated by encoders with feedback logic. However, as with block codes, the bit error rates of equivalent codes are not the same. Generally, a code generated with feedback logic can be expected to have a higher bit error rate than an equivalent code generated using only feedforward logic.

VITERBI DECODING

Viterbi decoding is a path-of-maximum-likelihood decoding approach for convolutional codes. It selects the most likely encoder input sequence based on the particular received sequence. It takes advantage of the path structure that takes place in the trellis or tree representation that occurs.

The Viterbi decoding algorithm can be visualized as a progression through the decoder trellis, or tree diagram, with a hard-decision decoder and a particular received sequence. The branches are monitored for the number of bits in which the received symbols at that branch differ from the encoder output symbols. The Viterbi decoder compares these conditions for the two paths entering each node and eliminates the path with the worst (or largest, in this case) number of differing bits.

Sequential Decoding

Because Viterbi-decoded convolutional codes check all of the possible state transitions at each step, the implementation complexity increases almost exponentially with increasing length. Sequential decoding is an approach that can be used to decode long-constraint-length convolutional codes by checking only some of the branches.*

*See *Principles of Digital Communication and Coding,* A.J. Viterbi and J.K. Omura, New York: McGraw-Hill, 1979.

The number of branches checked depends on the channel characteristics. When a period of reliable data is received, only a few paths are checked, but when a sequence of unreliable data is detected, many more paths are checked. The sequential decoder systematically searches through the coding tree and extends one branch at a time. It bases its decision about which path to add on tests of the already-examined paths.

Feedback Decoding

Feedback decoding is a technique that is simple to implement; however, it does not provide all of the coding benefits that can be obtained with Viterbi or sequential decoding. Interleaving and deinterleaving can easily be included as part of the encoding and decoding processes.

Feedback-decoded convolutional coding systems use hard-quantized received data to compute a sequence in a similar way as for block codes. Some of the bits for every received branch are used to address a ROM whose output bits then provide an estimate of the errors in the data portion of an earlier branch of received bits. When the ROM output indicates that errors have occurred, the errors are removed from the delayed data copy and the sequence is updated as a result of the errors.

The use of this feedback can lead to unlimited error propagation, because a finite number of errors can cause the decoder to make an infinite number of updates. This occurs when the number of ROM address bits is not large enough.*

Figure 8-7 shows the encoder and decoder implementation concept. Internal interleaving and deinterleaving can be achieved by using a shift register for each delay element. Interleaving allows the errors in the burst to be treated as isolated bit errors. A channel error burst is divided so that the bits used in any table lookup are based on only one channel bit error.

The feedback decoding technique can also be used with cyclic block codes. These decoders are sometimes referred to as *Meggit decoders.*

In some systems, the table-lookup decision device is replaced with a threshold device, and the decoding is referred to as threshold decoding.

ERROR CONTROL IN CHANNELS WITH BURST-NOISE

Error-correcting decoders normally use a group of received channel symbols to estimate the original information sequence. Good decoder error-rate performance occurs when there is a high percentage of reliable

*See *Error-Correction Coding for Digital Communications,* G.C. Clark, Jr. and J.B. Cain, New York, Plenum Press, 1981.

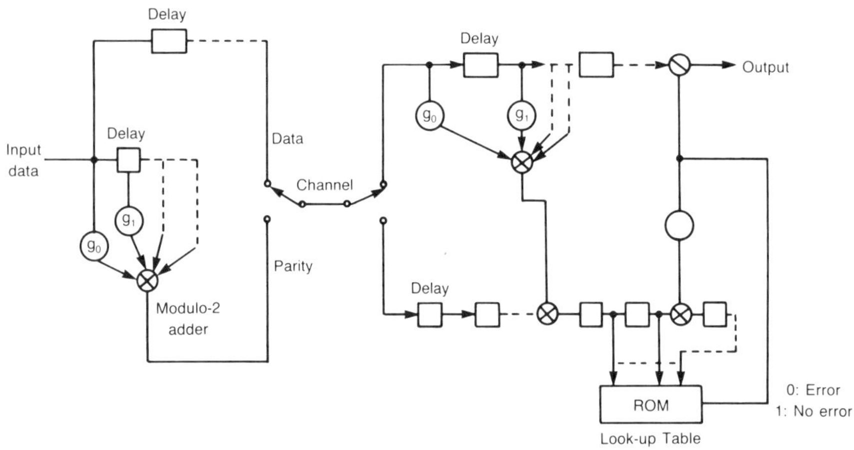

Fig. 8-7. Feedback decoding.

symbols in the group that the decoder uses for its estimate. In bursty channel environments, a major portion of this sequence might be unreliable. Several techniques can be used in this type of environment. One is the ARQ (automatic-repeat-request) approach, which uses an error-detecting code to detect blocks or frames of data that contain errors. It then requests that these incorrect frames be sent again, with the hope that they will be more reliable. Error detection, together with forward error control (FEC), can also be used. FEC can be used to correct as many errors as possible, which reduces the retransmission required.

Some FEC codes are specifically designed to correct bursts of errors. These codes are usually designed to operate on hard-decision channels. Suppose there is an error burst of length B in which the first and last symbols and any number of intermediate symbols are received. Then, for (n,k) linear block codes, the number of parity-check symbols in a code that is capable of correcting all bursts of length B or less is bounded by:

$$n - k \geq 2B$$

The efficiency of a block burst-error-correcting code can be defined as:

$$\text{(efficiency) linear block code} = \frac{2B}{n - k} \leq 1$$

In convolutional codes, the burst-error-correcting efficiency also depends on the number of correctly received channel symbols required between the error bursts. Some convolutional codes are capable of correcting all bursts of length B or less, when there is an error-free guard space of length g on both sides of the error burst. A variety of codes are available that allow burst-error-correcting efficiencies of close to one.

INTERLEAVING FEC CODES

Interleaving is often a good approach in FEC coding in the bursty environment, especially when soft-received decisions are used. This technique involves changing the ordering of the transmitted symbols such that long bursts are not sent to the decoder, employing a random-error-correcting code instead. The interleaving portion requires symbol reordering, or permutation, of the encoded symbols before transmission. An inverse operation is required at the receiving terminal, which reorders the permuted sequence of symbols so that it corresponds to the original encoder output ordering. This is referred to as *deinterleaving.* Generally, the deinterleaving is done on soft-decision data.

If simple hard-decision decoders are used, the interleaving and deinterleaving can be done internally in the encoding and decoding operations. This is often the case with feedback-decoded convolutional codes. Usually, the interleaving and deinterleaving are external to the encoding and decoding operations, and they can be implemented in a single unit.

Block Interleaving

Several interleaving/deinterleaving approaches exist. One of the simplest is block interleaving, in which the interleaver memory space is treated as a rectangular array of storage locations. The data is usually written in by column, and, when the array is full, read out by rows. The deinterleaving is done with an inverse operation, by writing the received input symbols into the rows of another array and reading them out by columns once the array is full. The two arrays are used when data is continuously arriving and symbols are written into one array while they are being read from the other.

The row and column dimensions in the block interleaving memories must be large enough to allow the desired performance. The interleaving approach must provide a separation between any two symbols from the burst that is greater than or equal to the memory span of the decoder. If the memory span is N, then there must be at least (N – 1) reliable symbols not from the burst between any two unreliable symbols from the burst. For linear block codes, the decoder memory span is equal to the block length (n) of the code.

For convolutional decoders, the memory span requirement is more elusive. One approach is to select the smallest value that provides the desired performance. Larger values are required for the higher code rates and other applications where only small error-rate increases, due to bursty channel conditions, can be tolerated.

In addition to the burst error capability of the interleaving approach, other important considerations are throughput delay, synchronization time, and the interleaver and deinterleaver implementation complexity.

Throughput delay is the delay from the time a symbol is written into the interleaver until it is read out of the deinterleaver with a zero channel delay.

Deinterleaver synchronization requires the received symbol sequence to be in accordance with the deinterleaver array mapping. In block interleaving, the deinterleaver can initially use either one of the memory arrays, but it must know which of the memory array locations should be used to store the first symbol. This is usually done with a short *preamble*, or a measurement of node quality.

In order to reduce transmission overhead and implementation, a preamble can be written over the encoded data to be transmitted. The decoder then corrects the inserted errors. Although this technique impairs the error-rate performance of the system, it is useful in low-rate applications. With continuous data, the decoder can be used to determine when the deinterleaver is out of synchronization, and an adjustment can be made. Figure 8-8 shows the basic decoder-aided synchronization concept. The number of deinterleaver synchronization states is a multiple of the block length (for block codes) or the number of channel symbols per branch (for convolutional codes).

Block interleavers and deinterleavers are normally implemented with random-access memories (RAMs). The memory addresses in the array visualization are assigned so that, in interleaving, the symbols are written

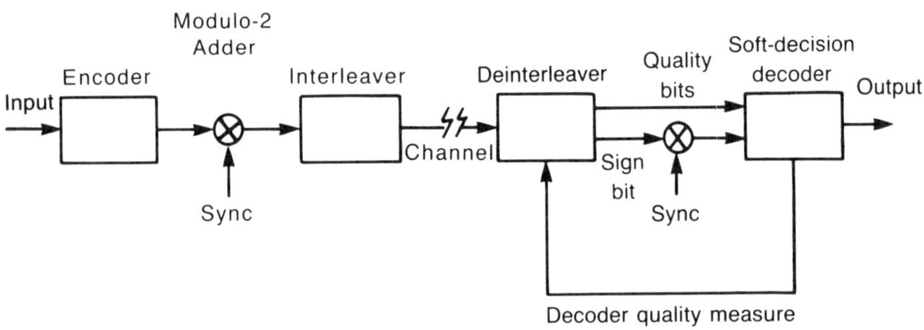

Fig. 8-8. Decoder-aided deinterleaver synchronization.

into RAM in a permuted manner, and read out from a sequence of addresses. In the deinterleaver, the symbols are written into RAM as a sequence of addresses, and read out in a permuted manner. These operations can also be reversed. If the permuted sequence of addresses is randomized, the process is called *random block interleaving.* This technique is useful in applications with intentional interference or unpredictable burst characteristics.

The size of the memory required will depend on the type of decision process used. If q-bit soft-receiver decisions are used (with one bit for the sign and q − 1 quality bits), the deinterleaver memory requirement is multiplied by q.

Block interleaving is useful when the data is already in a block format, or when a random approach is needed. When the data is received continuously or in long blocks, the double buffering required with block interleaving, as well as the large throughput delay and the number of synchronization states, make convolutional interleaving a better approach.

Convolutional Interleaving

The variations of convolutional interleaving are known as synchronous, Ramsey, or helical interleaving. Typically, a series of commutators are placed on the input and output of the interleaver. These are synchronized with each other, and, after each symbol is shifted in, they are sent to the next branch. The deinterleaver commutators are synchronized with each other in a similar way. This is depicted in Fig. 8-9.

The deinterleaver commutators must be synchronized to those of the interleaver. When the commutators are synchronized, there is a constant throughput delay of the channel-symbol time intervals. The deinterleaver disperses unreliable channel symbols such that any two channel symbols in a contiguous input burst are separated by symbols at the output.

Convolutional interleavers and deinterleavers can be implemented with shift-registers or RAMs. The typical RAM implementation approach is to use read and write RAM addresses that are incremented by either one or some other fixed integer amount. Each time a new symbol is re-

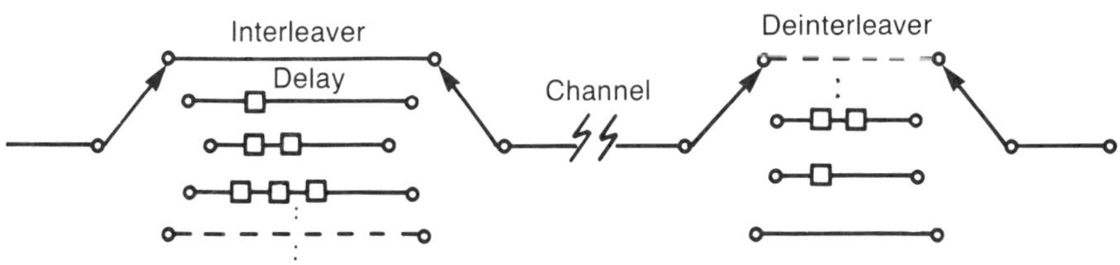

Fig. 8-9. Convolutional interleaving.

ceived by the interleaver or deinterleaver, it is written into the RAM. Then, a symbol is read out.

In the interleaver, symbols are written in at locations whose addresses are increased by the step size of each symbol. They are read out from locations whose addresses are increased by one for each symbol. In the deinterleaver, the opposite occurs. The symbols are written in at locations whose addresses are increased by one for each symbol, and read out from locations whose addresses are increased by the step size of each symbol. This type of constant-address-increment implementation is usually called the *RAM approach.*

THE NEED FOR DATA ENCRYPTION

Network security involves not only communication security, but also authentication and access control measures, as well as physical, electromagnetic-suppression procedural, and personnel security controls. An important development in the area of authentication and access control has been the adoption of the National Bureau of Standards Data Encryption Standard (DES), and the subsequent development of hardware implementing this standard. In this section, the topics of communication security, authentication, and access control are considered. The focus is on the integration of these techniques with computer system security measures to provide a workable framework for network security.

There are several reasons for the need to develop network security measures. The increased use of networks allows remote access to computer facilities, and makes access to these networks easier for intruders. The rapid growth in the quantity and value of information that is vulnerable to breaches in network security, such as that found in electronic funds transfer systems, also enhances the attractiveness of networks to intruders.

Computer systems connected by networks are more likely to incorporate cooperative schemes, such as resource sharing for a user community. The security of the information on a given host then becomes dependent on the security measures used by the network and by the other hosts.

Many of the techniques used for on-site computer system security are directly applicable or easily adaptable to use in the network environment. The major difference is that the security mechanisms incorporated in a computer system accessed via a network can be largely ineffective if the network fails to provide a secure communication path between each user and the computer system.

The interface between network security measures and computer system security measures must be coherent across this interface and permit the security measures to interact synergistically. The design of the communication protocols, especially the end-to-end protocols, is critical, and requires careful coordination with the network security measures for the system to be both effective and efficient.

Networks can range from collections of heterogeneous, autonomous hosts to groups of hosts operating under a single authority and cooperating to provide a coherent interface, as is the case in many distributed systems. The types of methods used for network security will vary depending on the network environment.

The selection of the appropriate network security methods begins with an evaluation of the threat environment and an assessment of risks in that environment. The appropriate techniques are then selected for use in that particular environment. Potential security violations include the unauthorized release or modification of information, and the unauthorized use or denial of use of resources.

Breaches of security related to the release of information are considered *passive wiretapping,* while security breaches of other types are considered *active wiretapping.* The term "unauthorized" is used to imply that the potential violation takes place contrary to some security policy. The intruder can be a wiretapper outside of the user community, or a legitimate user of the network. Communication security techniques are normally used to counter outside attacks, while authentication and access control provide the more difficult protection required in the case of legitimate users.

Principles of System Security

The following design principles have been found to be useful in the development of secure systems:

- Economy of mechanism.
- Fail-safe errors or defaults.
- Complete mediation.
- Open-design concept.
- Separation of privilege.
- Lease privilege.
- Least common mechanism.
- Psychological acceptability.

Economy of mechanism implies the use of the simplest possible design to achieve the desired effect. This is especially important in the development of protection mechanisms, because design and implementation errors that provide unintended access might not be detected during normal use.

Fail-safe defaults require the access decisions to be based on permission, rather than exclusion, while complete mediation requires that each access be tested against an access-control database. Implementing the fail-safe technique requires a selection of data that should be accessible, and the mediation requirement enforces system-wide access control. These requirements tend to be complementary.

An open design implies that the design of the protection mechanisms should not be kept secret. The security mechanisms do not depend on the ignorance of potential attackers, but on the possession of specific, more easily protected keys or passwords. The separation of protection mechanisms from protection keys allows the mechanisms to be reviewed by potential users without the concern that the review itself will compromise the safeguards. This is especially important in the network environment, where standards might be disseminated to a large and diverse group of users.

The concept of open design is not without controversy. The argument is that a hidden design has the advantage of raising the price of penetration, but this approach is generally not acceptable in a common user network environment.

The concept of separation of privilege is based on a protection mechanism that requires two keys for access; the same technique that is used for bank safe-deposit boxes. This principle can be applied to several aspects of network security, including the following:

- The distribution and use of encryption keys.
- The authentication procedures.
- The interaction among the communication security methods.
- The access control mechanisms at the network level.

The concept of least privilege requires that each program and user of the system should operate with the least amount of privileges necessary to perform the required task. This technique tends to reduce the extent of the damage that can result from an accident, error, or default in the system. A typical example is the military security rule of the need-to-know. The application of this principle is important in the implementation of connection-oriented communication security, and often involves the use of selective encryption techniques.

The principle of least common mechanism implies that the amount of mechanism common to more than one user, and depended on by the rest of the users, should be minimized. Each shared mechanism is a potential information path between users, and it must not compromise security. Mechanisms serving all users must operate to the satisfaction of all users. This concept leads to the use of connection-oriented security, and affects the structure of the communications hierarchy regarding encryption techniques.

Psychological acceptability requires that the human interface allow users to routinely and automatically apply the protection mechanisms. This means that the user must be able to easily relate to the protection goals, so that mistakes will be minimized. The application of simple connection models is important in evaluating the suitability of various authentication procedures.

COMMUNICATION SECURITY

Communication security techniques can be grouped into two basic approaches: link-oriented techniques and end-to-end techniques. The link-oriented techniques protect the message traffic independently on each communication link, while the end-to-end techniques provide uniform protection for each message from its source to its destination. These two methods differ in the nature of security provided, and the type of external interface presented to the users of the network.

Link-Oriented Security

Link-oriented measures depend on the data-link control protocols used, such as SDLC and X.25 (level 2). The actual link can be the connection between a host and the communication subnet, or between a terminal and the host to which it is connected. The communication link might be physically unprotected and subject to attack. Link-oriented protection provides security for the message traffic passing over an individual communication link between two nodes. It is independent of the source and destination of the messages.

Generally, it is easier to attack the communication links than the nodes. It is usually easier to secure the terminal and host nodes than to secure nodes in the communication subnet. If all subnet nodes are located near the hosts to which they are attached, they might be given the same level of security as the hosts. Then, if adaptive routing strategies are employed, a subverted packet switch could cause packets to be routed through it more or less independently of the source and destination hosts. Link-oriented protection in the communication subnet has the disadvantage that subversion of one of the subnet nodes can result in exposure of substantial amounts of message traffic.

When the unsecured communication links in a network are within the communication subnet, link-oriented techniques can be useful because they can provide a transparent communication security for the hosts attached to the network. If only some of the communication links between the terminals and hosts, or between the hosts and the communication subnet, must be protected, security for these links can be implemented without affecting the other hosts on the network.

The overall cost of link-oriented measures within the communication subnet can be amortized over all of the users, while the cost of link-oriented protection on terminal-to-host and host-to-communication subnet links can be assessed to the parties that are directly affected. In a common user network, some users might not agree to the need for security measures, and might feel unjustly charged for this service. In other network environments, the subscribers might agree on the use of control of the communication subnet to provide security.

End-to-End Security

Instead of considering a network as a collection of nodes joined by communication links, each of which can be independently protected, a network can be considered as a medium for transporting messages in a secure manner from source to destination.

End-to-end security protects the messages in transit between the source and destination nodes, so the subversion of any communication link between the source and destination does not result in exposure of the message traffic. The end-to-end security can be implemented in the following ways:

- From host to host.
- From terminal to terminal.
- From terminal to process.

End-to-end security measures usually go beyond the communication subnet, and often require a higher level so standardization for the interfaces and protocols. An advantage of end-to-end security measures is that individual users and hosts can employ these measures without affecting other users and hosts.

Connection-Oriented Techniques

A communication network can be considered a vehicle for providing users with connections, or virtual circuits, from source to destination. Security can be connection-oriented, where each connection, or virtual circuit, is protected individually. Connection-oriented techniques represent a refinement of end-to-end measures; the same type of flexibility in selecting the points that act as the ends of the connection exists. Connection-oriented techniques also reduce the chance of undetected cross-talk.

In many systems, these techniques provide the highest degree of communication security, and can be used in a wide array of environments. They are also more naturally suited to the user's concept of security requirements. This is because they rely on the security of equipment at the source and destination of a connection, while link-oriented techniques can require that each node in the communication subnet be secure. In some systems, both measures can be employed to provide a cost-effective level of protection that is higher than can be achieved by using either type alone.

Passive and Active Wiretapping

Assume that an intruder can gain access at some point in a network through which information must pass. In an internetwork environment, this could be a gateway in some intermediate network that provides the communication path between processes, as shown in Fig. 8-10. Although the source and destination networks might be secure, access to the connection could be made as it passes through the gateway.

In passive wiretapping, the intruder observes the messages passing on a connection without interfering with their flow. This observation at the application level of messages is called the *release of message contents* and is the most common type of passive wiretapping. The observation

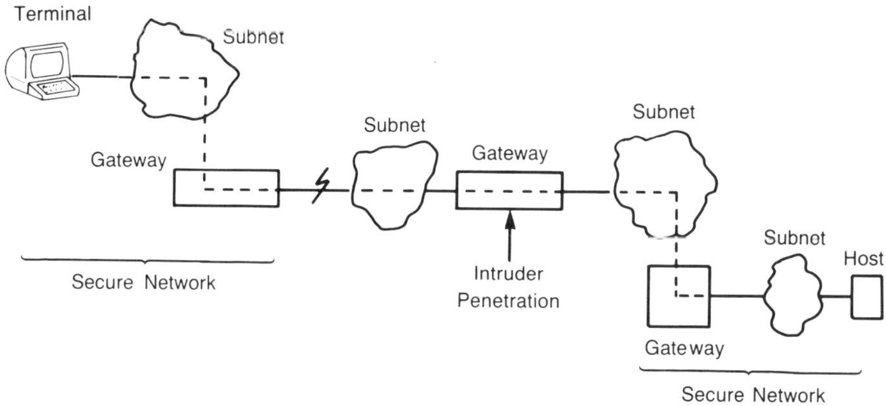

Fig. 8-10. Internetwork system.

can include parts of the message headers, even if the application-level data is unintelligible, which will indicate the location and identities of the communication system. An analysis of the lengths of messages and their frequency of transmission might also be observed. This type of traffic analysis can be used to gain knowledge of the nature of the data being exchanged. Traffic analysis can be blocked by using programs that modulate message destination, length, or frequency of transmission.

Active wiretapping involves the performance of some type of processing on the messages passing the connection. The messages might be modified, duplicated, reordered, or inserted into the connection at a later time, or they might pass through unaffected. False messages might also be inserted into the connection. These acts are known as *message stream modification.*

When messages are discarded or delayed, the action is known as *denial of message service attacks.* The difference between message stream modification and denial of message service attacks is a function of the degree of the attack and the state of the connection. Different countermeasures are used for each type of attack.

Security requires that connections be initiated that emphasize secure identification of the users, terminals, and hosts at each end, and that establish the integrity of the connection. Verification of identity normally involves both authentication and access controls beyond the level of the connection model, but a portion of the identification task is relevant at the connection level.

DATA ENCRYPTION TECHNIQUES

Data encryption is used both as a countermeasure to passive wiretapping and a base for structuring countermeasures to active wiretapping. A *cipher* is an algorithmic transformation which is performed on a symbol-to-symbol basis on any data. Although there are technical differences between the terms "encipherment" and "encryption," the two terms are often used interchangeably to refer to the application of a cipher to data.

Plaintext and Ciphertext

An encryption algorithm implements a cipher. The input to an encryption algorithm is known as *cleartext* or *plaintext*, and the output from the algorithm is referred to as *ciphertext*. The transformation performed on the cleartext to encipher it is controlled by a *key*.

To be useful, the encryption algorithm must be invertible, so there must exist a matching decryption algorithm that reverses the encryption transformation when used with the appropriate key. In a conventional cipher, the key used to decipher a message is the same as the key required to encipher it. This type of key must remain secret, and be known only to users authorized to transmit messages under it and to decipher messages enciphered using it. The concept of a conventional cipher is shown in Fig. 8-11.

In a public-key cipher, the ability to encipher messages with a given key is separate from the ability to decipher the messages. This is done with pairs of transformations, each of which is the inverse of the other, and neither of which is readily derivable from the other. The result is a multiaccess cipher, in which one key is made public for use in enciphering messages for a given user, while a corresponding key is kept secret, for using in deciphering messages sent to the user under the public key. Key distribution and management requires some form of authentication.

One technique that is used in a public-key system to identify the sender requires that the sender encrypt the message under the secret key, and then under the public key of the intended receiver. The receiver then strips off the outer layer of encryption using the secret key, and completes the deciphering using the public key of the sender. The technique is shown in Fig. 8-12.

Public-key systems require that the encryption and decryption transformations be easy to compute and be inverses, and that the key pairs be easy to generate. It also must not be feasible to derive one transformation from the other or to invert the transformations without the correct keys.

Cryptosystems can be classified in the following two ways:

- A *practically secure system* exists if the computational cost makes the task of penetration infeasible.
- An *unconditionally* or *theoretically secure system* exists if it can resist any attack, regardless of the computational power and time required.

Cryptanalytic attacks can be grouped into three hierarchial classes:

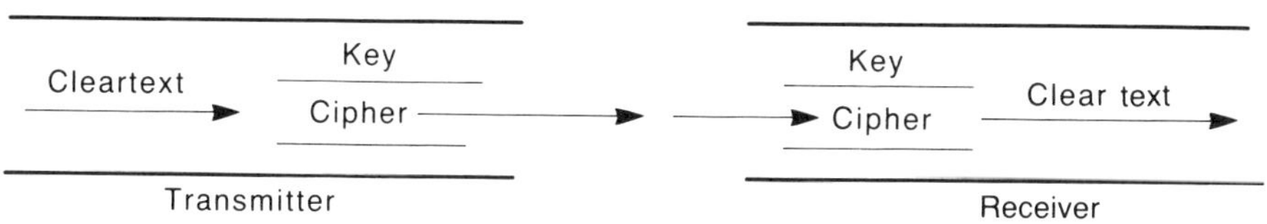

Fig. 8-11. Conventional cypher.

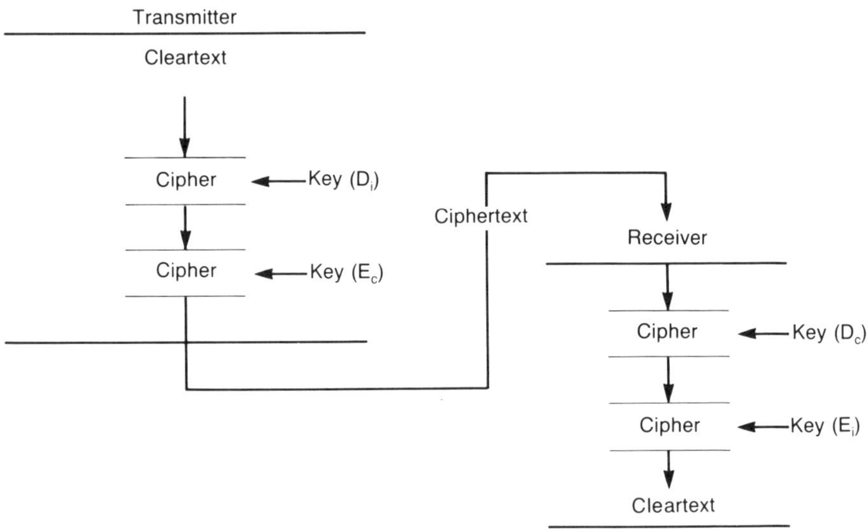

Fig. 8-12. Public-key cipher.

Ciphertext-only. The cryptanalyst uses a knowledge of the statistical properties of the language. This is used to develop the probable words based on the relative frequency of letters or in the use of parity bits in the transmission. Other observed parameters include the use of standard salutations in letter-writing or common variable names in program text.

Known-plaintext. The cryptanalyst matches plaintext and ciphertext. This often occurs in a network environment, because fixed-format messages are used with specific log-in greetings, and there might be system-wide messages in plaintext.

Chosen-plaintext. The cryptanalyst is not only able to match plaintext and ciphertext, but also selects the plaintext. This can be attempted through the network mail.

A cipher for use in a network environment must be resistant to known and chosen plaintext, as well as ciphertext-only penetration.

Stream Ciphers

The two major types of encryption techniques used in nonvoice telecommunications and digital computer applications are stream and block ciphers. The block method enciphers fixed-sized blocks of bits under the control of a key that is approximately the same size as the blocks being encrypted.

The stream method uses bit-by-bit or byte-by-byte transformations on cleartext under the control of a stream of key bits. This is usually done with an easily reversible operation, such as addition by modulo-2. Stream ciphers are structured so that they can operate on a stream of cleartext in real time, enciphering each bit (or byte) as it is generated by combining it with a bit or byte from the key stream.

A *Vernam cipher* is a stream cipher in which the key stream consists of a random bit string as long as the combined length of all messages that are ever transmitted using this stream. This type of cipher is theoretically and practically unbreakable.

Most stream ciphers use pseudorandom bit streams with very long periods, because of the typical volume of communication traffic and the logistic difficulties required to provide each user with enough of the key stream. These stream ciphers are susceptible to cryptanalysis.

Several techniques can be used to generate the key stream. The source of the key bits can be a pseudo-random-number generator started with a small initial key and completely independent of the cleartext stream. Using these independent key streams, changes to individual bits in the ciphertext are not allowed to propagate to other portions of the ciphertext stream.

Transmission errors that affect the value of bits of the ciphertext do not change the ability of the receiver to correctly decipher subsequent transmissions, but undetected insertion or removal of bits from the ciphertext stream still results in a loss of deciphering capability. These ciphers are not often used, because the lack of error propagation reduces the types of mechanisms available to detect length-preserving message-modification penetrations.

An *autokey* cipher is a type of stream cipher in which the key stream is based on the cleartext, ciphertext, or the key stream itself, together with an initial, priming key. Ciphers of this type can be used to detect errors in transmitted ciphertext, because these errors can impede the correct decipherment of subsequent transmissions. In ciphertext autokey (CTAK) ciphers, the transmitted ciphertext is used as input for key-stream generation. These ciphers are self-synchronizing, and recover from transmission errors after a fixed number of correct ciphertext bits are received.

Block Ciphers

Block ciphers transform blocks of bits under the control of a key. They map a set of cleartext blocks into a set of cipher text blocks. If the block size is n bits, the size of the cleartext space, which is the range of cleartext block values, and the size of the ciphertext space, which is the range of ciphertext block values, is 2^n. The mapping must be invertible.

The block cipher, under the control of a single key, requires the defining of one of $2^n!$ permutations on the set of n-bit blocks. It is normally not feasible to implement a block cipher that realizes all the possible permutations, due to the size of the key required and the complexity of the cipher required. The block cipher is usually treated as a classical substitution cipher. If n is seven or eight, the block corresponds to an individual character from a small alphabet. This system is very weak because of the small size of the blocks used.

The cipher can be broken by comparing the frequency distribution of the individual blocks with the known frequency distribution of characters in large samples of cleartext. As the size of the block is increased, the required frequency distribution and analysis becomes infeasible, because the cipher is constructed such that the frequency characteristics of the components of the block are hidden by mixing transformations.

DES

The Data Encryption Standard (DES) is the Federal Information Processing Standard. It is widely used for nonclassified government information, and has become a de facto industry standard as well.

It is essentially a block cipher which operates on 64-bit blocks, using a 56-bit key. Each key defines a permutation on the space of 64-bit blocks. Each bit of ciphertext in a block is a function of the bit of the key and the bit of the cleartext block from which it was generated. A change of one bit in either the key or the cleartext results in ciphertext in which each bit is changed with an approximately equal probability. A change of one in either the key or the ciphertext will result in changes for, on the average, half of the bits of deciphered cleartext. This error propagation is limited to the block in which the error occurs, and decryption of other blocks is not affected.

This mode of DES is known as the *electronic code book* (ECB) because it acts like a conventional code book. The correct deciphering of messages is achieved when both sender and receiver employ the same key and the blocks are properly delimited. Figure 8-13 shows how this mode of DES operates.

The DES is a conventional cipher, and it can be used as part of a key-stream generator for a CTAK cipher. This is known as the *cipher feedback* (CFB) mode of operation. In this mode, the DES is used as a

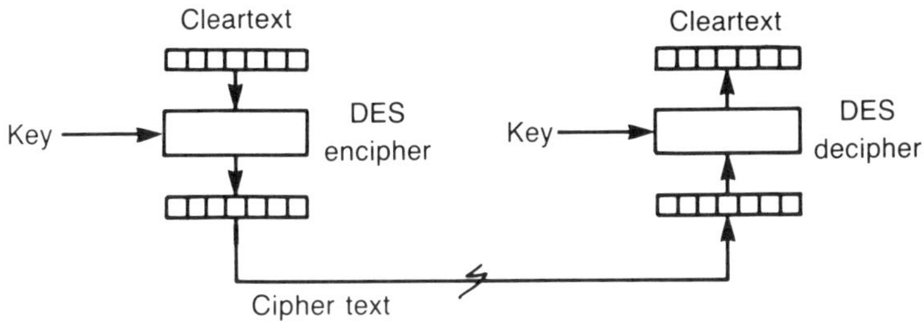

Fig. 8-13. Electronic code book.

self-synchronizing stream cipher which operates on cleartext strings of one to 64 bits in length. The cleartext is combined, by modulo-2 addition, with a matching number of key-stream output bits which are generated by the DES block cipher. Extra DES output bits are dropped. The transmitted ciphertext is loaded into 64-bit shift registers that act as the input to the basic DES at both ends of the system. Figure 8-14 shows how this mode operates with 8-bit bytes.

The sender and receiver must use the same key, and both shift registers must hold the same bit pattern. When an error occurs in the ciphertext stream, a part of the received cleartext will be lost, but the receipt of 64 bits of error-free ciphertext will resynchronize the cipher.

The number of bits actually affected by a single bit error is constant, at 65, while the number of cleartext bits that might be useless because of an error depends on the length of the cleartext bit strings used and the degree of error detection used as higher-level protocols.

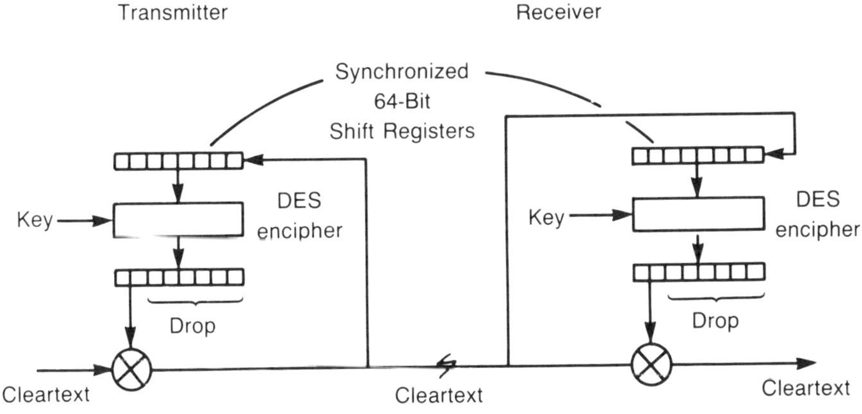

Fig. 8-14. Cipher feedback.

DES is resistant to conventional cryptanalysis, although it can be penetrated with high-powered parallel techniques. Both ECB and CFB modes can be used as a basis for preventing the release of message contents, and can be combined with other countermeasures to achieve additional goals.

AUTHENTICATION

Authentication applies the procedures used for verifying the identity of a principal, including users, terminals, and networks. Personal authentication includes the use of passwords, badges, keys, fingerprints, and voiceprints. Except for the use of encryption keys for authentication purposes, these techniques all rely on the transmission of a stream of identifying bits to the location site performing the authentication. The authentication mechanisms, then, are dependent on communication security.

Measures must be taken to prevent the release of authentication information and to maintain the integrity of the communication paths after authentication has been performed. The first requirement can be achieved with message contents countermeasures, while the second requires message-stream-modification countermeasures.

The Lifetime of Authentication

The use of authentication techniques is dependent on the lifetime of the information transmitted during the authentication procedure. This lifetime can be based on a number of times the information is used, or on a time interval over which the information is acceptable. Fingerprints and passwords might have no set lifetime, while one-time badges, encryption, or physical keys might be given a set time value.

The characterization of authentication methods based on the lifetime of the information transmitted provides a measure of the damage that can result from the exposure of this information. When the authentication information is static and is left exposed, it allows an intruder to develop and test penetration schemes.

Dynamic authentication information can be much harder to penetrate, and might not be useful to the intruder at all. This includes one-time password or encryption key schemes. Some of these might be *chained,* in which the current password or key is transmitted as an epilogue to the previous one. These chained authentications might not provide the same security as the use of true limited-lifetime characteristics, but they are superior to static procedures.

In the network environment, centralized authentication services are important. There are usually accounts on multiple service hosts, and, if the same authentication methods were used at each host, subversion of any one of these would allow penetration of the other hosts. If dynamic authentication consisting of one-time passwords is used, it could be difficult to maintain the password lists on each of the hosts without some form of centralized control.

Personal authentication is often used for both access control and accounting purposes. Central authentication can simplify procedures for individuals whose access is limited to only a single host via the network, because it reduces with the need for multiple or layered authentication procedures.

Because encryption keys are a widely used for of authentication in these environments, the effectiveness of other authentication mechanisms is often overlooked. The inclusion of an encryption module in every terminal can allow a high degree of security, but the cost of modifying existing terminals can be costly. If the users access the network via terminals attached to server hosts, an encrypted communication path from the network through the server host and back to the terminal might be difficult to implement.

Primary keys can be a powerful and inexpensive mechanism, but the distribution of keys at the devices can pose a problem. The concepts of separation of privilege and least privilege suggest that encryption key distribution and personal authentication services be provided independently, because encryption keys are a common mechanism for personal authentication. The solution is a key distribution center for managing authentication information. A secure authentication server host can act as an intermediary, carrying out the user authentication procedures and forwarding the results to the service hosts.

Each authentication server host has a specific domain over which it provides services to users and hosts. The authentication server hosts can be grouped to provide load sharing, and different groups can be provided with boundaries. A trust is set up among the groups, and simple protocols are employed to handle authentication across the boundaries.

Techniques can be employed to minimize the release of authentication information in the event of subversion of an authentication server. If passwords are used, then instead of storing the password at the authentication server, the image of the password, using a one-way transformation, can be stored. The transformation is then submitted as the password during the authentication procedure.

An alternative is to use an authentication server to store the authentication information. The authentication server can act as the user's agent in carrying out the authentication procedures for the host the user wishes to access. The authentication server appears as a user to each service host.

REVIEW EXERCISES

1. For the acceptance of a 10 Mbps system, the actual BER must be less than 1×10^{-8} with a 90 percent confidence. Assuming a large number of trial bits in which errors are distributed, estimate the duration of the test required and the number of errors allowable.
2. A bit error test produces seven measured errors, and there exists a 90 percent confidence that the actual BER is less than 1.5 times the measured BER. If you measure over 10^{10} bits, estimate the minimum measurement period required if the transmission rate is 12 Mbps.
3. Describe three types of input jitter and the techniques that can be used to measure them.
4. Discuss the best way of determining the reliability of equipment that contains microprocessors and other LSI chips.
5. Draw a flowchart for verifying the design margin of a network link that includes hysteresis effects.
6. What is a relatively simple way of determining the BER of a transmission channel? What is the disadvantage of this method?
7. Describe the pseudoerror detection technique.
8. What is the difference between soft and hard quantization?
9. What are the differences between block and convolutional coding?
10. Discuss the following error-correcting codes:

    a. Hamming
    b. Extended Hamming
    c. Golay
    d. Extended Golay
    e. Viterbi
    f. Sequential
    g. Feedback

11. What techniques can be used for error-correction in bursty channels?
12. Describe the use and advantages of interleaving.

13. Can the concept of fail-safe errors ever interfere with the concept of open mediation in security design? Explain.
14. Give some examples of the open-design concept.
15. What is the difference between active and passive wiretapping?
16. What is a public-key cipher?
17. What is the difference between stream and block ciphers?
18. Describe a CTAK cipher.
19. What are the differences between the ECB modes of DES?
20. Describe the use of dynamic authentication.

Chapter 9

Planning and Implementing LANs

Suppose it is decided that a local area network is a possible solution to the heterogenous mix of terminals, computers, and peripherals that have been acquired over the years. How do you start evaluating the feasibility of such a project?

EVALUATING LOCAL AREA NETWORK NEEDS

One of the first steps is to determine how a local area network fits into the organizational structure. To do this, a clear vision of the present, unconnected, informational network must be formed. Key considerations include:

- Which computers, terminals, and peripherals would be connected?
- What data rates and protocols are to be used?
- What information would be generated, stored, and distributed to network workstations and other intelligent devices?
- What information would be protected from general access and require controls?
- Where are the databases located and how can they be interconnected?
- What equipment is projected to be added to the network?

Emerging technologies that integrate video and voice with data transmission should be considered for the last item.* These are considered in Chapter 10.

Local networks can be grouped into three basic types:

1. Terminal-to-terminal networks, which include Telex and facsimile devices.
2. Terminal-to-computer networks, which use protocols such as SDLC and 3270. These are generally low-speed, star-shaped networks, replacing the conventional cabling to a host computer.
3. Computer-to-computer networks, which are generally of the most interest. These networks can connect hundreds of computers at hundreds of kilobits per second across distances of hundreds of meters.

Three major benefits can be identified for networking personal computers. First, local computer networks allow personal computers to share printers, thus reducing the cost-per-user of letter-quality printers in an office. Networks also allow the shared use of laser printers and typesetters. Another peripheral that can be shared is the modem, as well as gateways to other networks. By replacing the need for multiple printers and modems, shared peripherals can, in part, justify the cost of the local network.

Second, shared file systems on large Winchester disks allow group collaboration, and the Winchester disks provide a much faster response time and can be more cost-effective than individual floppy disk systems. Centralizing the disks also allows better maintenance, along with more reliable backup procedures.

Finally, local networks allow cost-effective electronic mail between personal computers. This can be built into the network file system, or it can be accomplished through a gateway into a central electronic mail system.

Network Technologies

Network technologies can be grouped into three basic types: PBX, cable television broadband, and the baseband types such as Ethernet. PBX technologies generally provide only 4.4 kHz of bandwidth. If digital transmission is added, they can support RS-232C or V24 types of terminal communications. PBX is most suitable for terminal-to-computer networking.

---

*"Advanced Local Networks," *Yankee Group Report,* Volume XVI, January 1981.

Broadband networks use cable television technology to provide up to 400 MHz of bandwidth. Because the bandwidth is generally frequency-divided into many small channels, it is most suitable for bundling together many lower-speed lines. Some of the faster broadband networks provide channels of up to 128 kilobits per second.

Digital baseband networks, which operate at about 10 megabaud, can provide their entire bandwidth, if required, between any two points. These networks are most useful for handling the bursts of data which are generated by communications between computers.

These different network technologies can coexist, with each serving a different set of needs in the organization. Interfaces are available between the various technologies, such as gateways to Ethernet.

The International Standards Organization's (ISO)* seven-level network model, Table 9-1, provides a way of defining the compatibility of the layers of network connection and protocol. Protocols such as IBM's SNA, DEC's DECnet, and Xerox's XNS are all higher-level architectures, for levels 3 through 7. An SNA network can include Ethernet as a low-level transmission medium. A variety of local digital networks at levels 1 and 2, such as Ethernet, RS-232C, 3270 or IBM's token-passing network, could exist within SNA.

Most of the problems are found at the higher-level protocols. Consider the example of one vendor's Ethernet sharing a cable with another vendor's Ethernet. While the microcomputers connected by one vendor might communicate with each other, they might not be able to utilize Ethernet file or printer servers from each other, even though both vendors are placing data on the same cable. The problem of higher-level compatibility must be solved before PCs can exchange electronic mail and utilize peripherals on these mixed systems.

The *bottom-up approach* for networking personal computers implies that, if no single network technology can accommodate all of the needs in an organization, it might be better to implement local area networks as the need becomes apparent from the users viewpoint, moving from the bottom of the organization structure.

The higher-lever protocol standards force users to select personal computers and applications before selecting a network. The applications and the PCs then determine the higher-level protocols, and set the choice of local network.

---

*The ISO model sets standards for the exchange of information among systems that are open to one another due to their mutual use of the standards. The standards provide a formal, logical structure for the interactions and functions required to provide communication services to the user.

Table 9-1. The International Standards Organization's Open Systems Interconnect (ISO-OSI) Model.

Layer 7	**Application-User.** Application process and management functions.
Layer 6	**Presentation-Data.** Interpretation, format and code transformation.
Layer 5	**Session-Administration.** Control of sessions between entities.
Layer 4	**Transport-Transparent.** Data transfer, end-to-end control.
Layer 3	**Network-Routing.** Switching, segmenting, blocking, error recovery, flow control. (CCITT X.25).
Layer 2	**Link-Establish.** Maintain and release data links, error and flow control (Bisync, HDLC).
Layer 1	**Physical-Electrical.** Mechanical, functional control of data circuits (RS-232C, RS-449, CCITT X.21).

This application-driven approach implies a bottom-up decision making. Because there seems to be no single network that will satisfy the diversity of needs in an organization, a decision might be deferred. The bottom-up approach addresses specific groups of users with their unique needs, rather than, for example, wiring an entire building. In a system of multiple local networks, compatibility can be achieved using gateways between the networks. The bottom-up approach can be summarized in three steps:

1. Implement the personal computers and applications required.
2. Identify the need for and the benefits of local networks.
3. Select the network that offers the appropriate high-level protocols.

Local area network technology is changing rapidly, and many new products are available. Complex decisions need to be made before the network of choice is selected. The methodology presented here is designed to aid in the selection of a network that will not hamper growth options and yet satisfy the greatest number of the desired requirements within the current and projected budget restrictions.

Because there are many different networking products available, choosing the best solution is a difficult task. If you do not recognize and quantify local network requirements, proper network selection can be a difficult and confusing task. Instead of initially comparing all of the available products, it is much more effective to first assess the needs and requirements of the organization. Once this is complete, the next step involves familiarizing and educating yourself in local networking technologies, followed by an initial recommendation of those technologies which appear to be most suitable. An evaluation of specific products needs to be completed, before making a final selection.

Network Planning

Comprehensive network planning begins with a thorough assessment of specific needs. Network users might have special needs, such as specific graphics requirements, high volume printing, or printing on special forms. The use of common printers, each loaded with a different form, can be an effective strategy for minimizing hardware and maximizing efficiency in the network.

The sharing of hardware peripherals, such as printers, requires a consideration of the duty cycles involved. A device with a recommended duty cycle of 55 percent should not be utilized 75 percent of the time, or there will be an excessive amount of downtime and repairs.

The following steps are representative of a typical local network implementation:

1. Perform a needs assessment to define the design criteria.
2. Investigate the generic local networking technologies and compare costs.
3. Request vendor information and research recent products.
4. Perform a preliminary comparison of the viable generic solutions.
5. Prioritize future requirements.
6. Develop a request-for-proposal based on the highest priority requirements.
7. Evaluate vendor responses and develop a ranking matrix with costs, comparing the design criteria to the associated rank values.
8. Request final bids from the vendors with the highest ranking.
9. Select the final network vendor(s) and negotiate contracts.
10. Plan pilot installation, acceptance testing, training, and support.
11. Begin full installation after the successful pilot installation.
12. Perform system tuning/optimization based upon the initial traffic statistics.
13. Plan for future growth and document the project accomplishments.

NETWORK PROFILES

There are six profiles that can be used to define the local network design criteria:

- The user profile.
- The usage profile.
- The geographic profile.
- The applications profile.
- The hardware profile.
- The special requirements profile.

These profiles allow a description of the present and potential local network users and their environments. Most profiles should be prepared for several time periods, because some information will remain the same while other factors might be constantly changing.

The *user profile* includes a listing of all the departments that use computer resources. This listing includes the number of people within each user group their job titles, job descriptions, and related information. Written surveys can be used to determine the major characteristics of the user group. These are combined with structured meetings with the department heads of the groups.

The *usage profile* is concerned with how the current computer resources are utilized. This profile includes determining the amount of access to outside resources and the typical peak periods for this access. A listing of applications, programs, software packages, and terminal emulations in use is also included, as are the peak periods for communications, printing, database inquiry, and file transfers. This measurement can be done in terms of the number of transactions per day and per the peak hours, the hours of operation, the file server input/output transactions, the print transactions per type of printer, the number and size of records stored, and the retention and access guidelines.

There are two key considerations in the development of the usage profile. The first is the system sensitivity to downtime (SSDT), which is a rating of the effect of downtime. A high SSDT means that downtime has a severe effect upon operations. The other is the maximum acceptable response time (MART) of the network application.

The *geographic profile* is concerned with the physical distribution of local network users. This can be done for the present, the near future, the distant future, and the far distant future. A code number can be used to describe specific departments and buildings in an installation. Each department or building can be further subdivided using codes.

The *applications profile* is concerned with the use of the information processing resources in completing the tasks of each department. Some applications, such as order fulfillment and payroll, have a real-time priority over other applications, such as human resources or fixed assets management. The applications profile is also concerned with the extent to which local network downtime affects operations.

The *hardware profile* is a listing of each user group and its computer hardware configurations. The listing includes the manufacturer, model, amount of main memory, amount of disk storage, operating system, tape backup facilities, and software packages. Peripherals, such as printers, plotters, digitizers, and high resolution monitors, should also be listed.

Disk drives should be categorized into family types. This should also be done for the different sizes and densities of tape backup units. Modems should be listed in terms of speed, Bell compatibility, and software compatibility. Other information listed would include communications protocols and network applications to which access is needed.

In addition to the hardware features, the special requirements of the network software environment must be considered. The following questions must be answered:

- Does the network support file locking and record locking?
- Are remote-access and print-spooling functions included?
- What other software is required for electronic mail?

Communications Programs

Consider one of the most popular microcomputers, the IBM Personal Computer (PC). By examining one of its available communication packages you can determine just what services it offers to the typical user. This is not the PC's only communications resource, but it is one that performs a modest service at a cost of about $150. There are other products available that exceed this capability, but they also require a greater investment.

This package is called the Asynchronous Communications Support program. In order to utilize this card and its embedded software, the following minimum equipment is required:

- 64K bytes of memory with at least one diskette drive.
- An asynchronous communications adapter and operating disk.
- A full-duplex telephone modem or direct cable connection to a host computer.

This communications program enables the IBM PC to function as a terminal that can access hosts that are running under TSO and VM/370 operating systems. The means of connection can be by common carrier lines using the telephone modems or by direct cable. Another option in this program is the ability to link up with another IBM Personal Computer. The same minimum hardware would be required for both the sending and receiving units.

The adapter hardware board occupies one of the five available system expansion slots and utilizes RS-232C start-stop (asynchronous) protocol at transmission speeds from 50 to 9600 bits per second.

The actual operation of the support software consists of two phases: terminal selection and terminal operation. Following initialization of the communications program, terminal-select processing begins. This involves a series of menu presentations which are used to determine a choice of terminal parameters. For the interface between two personal computers, only the line bit rate needs to be specified. After they are specified, the descriptors can be saved on a disk for future use.

Once the terminal parameters are set, terminal operation is initiated. The user entries, as well as the text received from the linked device, are displayed on the screen. Transmission errors are reported at the bottom of the screen. A control key is used to indicate an upload or download. In upload, files are sent to the recipient, while in download they travel in the opposite direction.

Most communications programs allow extensions to the standard options. The user can devise further capabilities, such as protocol enhancements or unique communications programs that are appropriate for the application in use.

Consider the pace of technological change occurring in microcomputer packaging and performance. In spending time attempting to assimilate the effect of all of these developments, there will be virtually no opportunity to focus on the particular application needs where small computers are concerned. How can rational decisions be made about the use of these products if the technological target is moving too swiftly for measured analysis?

One technique is to employ a freeze-frame approach, as utilized in other specialties. The communications capability of one system are viewed from a relatively practical level.

In order to guard against installing an obsolete network, the sources of future growth must be recognized and quantified. This growth must be realistically considered over the expected lifetime of the network.

Many environments exist in which almost every user has a microcomputer. Common areas, such as those used for training, must also be considered.

The Needs Assessment

The initial data collection is a part of the needs assessment process. The information must be analyzed for important patterns and trends. The most important criteria to be gained as a result of the needs assessment process are the requirements of the user community and the priority of needs that must be serviced by the network. The heaviest users must be identified, and their needs examined in relation to the needs of the complete operation.

The needs assessment indicates the specific networking requirements, as well as the overall requirements of the system. These requirements will drive the selection process, and become a part of the requests for vendor proposals.

The needs assessment should also include an analysis of business and organizational factors. The organizational factors include the willingness to use state-of-the-art technology, while business factors include the company's position within its industry, as well as the likelihood that it will significantly increase its market share.

The needs assessment is an important step in the process of selecting a local network product which is responsive to the needs of the user organization.

The initial information gathering can be done using a checklist* similar to that shown in Fig. 9-1.

The information gathering will eventually form the basis for a more formal requirements document, which can then be used to identify the alternative solutions. This document provides a checklist of the most common items. It can be expanded or contracted as required. A typical outline for such a document is shown in Fig. 9-2.

Another task is preparing an alternatives analysis report. This involves constructing a decision matrix and listing the advantages and disadvantages for each alternative solution. The requirements assessment outline can be used as a guideline in developing this report. The structure of a typical report is shown in Fig. 9-3.

TECHNOLOGY EVALUATION

The needs assessment should quantify the needs and requirements of the network for the present, as well as for the following two years.

**Guidelines for the Selection of Local Area Networks,* by G.B. Ennis, L.J. Gardner and M.K. Graham, Washington, D.C.: National Bureau of Standards, July 1981 (Pub. No. ICST/LANP-81-5).

Organization: Date:
Person(s) contacted:
Position(s): Telephone(s):

A. Interfaces.

☐ Organizations that must be involved in order for the network to function.
Organization Building Function

☐ Volume and frequency of paper flow between organizations.
Organization Drawings Reports Documents Other

☐ Volume and frequency of data flow between organizations in units per time interval.
Organization Records or Files Tapes Disks Other

B. Computing Equipment Capabilities/Capacities.

☐ Current network capability.
☐ Maintenance.
☐ Types of computers accessed.
☐ Single terminal access.
☐ Access through other computers.
☐ Organizational sharing.
☐ Sharing controls.
☐ Size of organization.
☐ Percent of organization members using terminals.
☐ Types of users.

☐ Types of terminal devices.
Device Location Qty Baud Rate Data Type Dial/Dedicated

☐ Types of dedicated or dial-up lines existing between computers.
Source Destination Baud rate Dial/Dedicated

☐ Utilization levels of each terminal/device.
☐ Database management system in use.
☐ Query language.

C. System Operations and Utilizations.

☐ Operational sequence flow diagrams.
☐ Applications in use.
☐ Response time requirements.
☐ Support time requirements.
☐ Security requirements.
☐ Environment of physical equipment.

Fig. 9-1. Networking requirements checklist.

D. Expansion and Growth Projections.

- ☐ History of past studies, or reports on productivity improvements and system upgrades.
- ☐ Potential for automation.
- ☐ Automation requirements.
- ☐ Terminal/device requirements, present and future.
- ☐ Growth factors.
- ☐ Desired/expected productivity improvements.
- ☐ Future use/status of present equipment.
- ☐ Past growth patterns.
- ☐ Current problems.
- ☐ Desired improvements.

Fig. 9-1. Continued from page 231.

- I. Description of current method of operation
- II. Basic requirements
  - A. Overview of new operating methods
  - B. Processing logic
    1. General description
    2. Data flow
    3. Usage frequency and timing
- III. Data requirements
  - A. Data storage structure layout
  - B. Data dependency and data currency requirements
  - C. Accessibility requirements
  - D. Data elements
    1. Identity
    2. Relationships
    3. Size
    4. Frequency of Access
  - E. Peak access periods and volumes
    1. Daily
    2. Weekly
    3. Monthly
    4. Yearly
- IV. Operator interaction requirements
  - A. Remote access or control
  - B. Geographic distribution
  - C. Other interaction requirements
- V. External systems interfaces

Fig. 9-2. Requirements assessment document outline.

- A. Data volumes
  - 1. Average
  - 2. Peak
- B. Flow times
- C. Frequency
- D. Medium

VI. Performance requirements

- A. System availability
- B. Response time
- C. Data accessibility
- D. Frequency of operation
- E. Record retention duration
- F. Backup frequency
- G. Auditing
- H. Security

VII. Special operational requirements

VIII. Growth and expansion requirements

- A. Data storage
- B. External interfaces
- C. Number of terminals to be supported
- D. CPU throughput
- E. Geographic dispersion
- F. Estimated percentages
  - 1. Three years
  - 2. Five years

IX. Implementation requirements

- A. Schedule
- B. Equipment and human resources
- C. Existing systems
- D. Languages and operating systems
- E. Software portability
- F. Assumptions
- G. Responsibilities
- H. Converison
- I. Testing
- J. Acceptance criteria

Fig. 9-2. Continued from page 232.

The needs assessment analysis should reveal two important items. One is a quantification of the support requirements for the user community, and the other is a prioritization of the individual needs that must be serviced by the local area network.

I. Introduction and background
II. Summary of recommendations
III. Alternatives considered
    A. Assumptions
    B. Alternative descriptions and qualifications

IV. Trade-off study results
    A. Requirements
    B. Weights
    C. Scoring alternatives

V. Expected system costs

VI. Recommended solution
    A. Selection criteria/justification
    B. Preliminary system
        1. Definition
        2. Specifications
    C. Functional flow
    D. Expected expansion

VII. Preliminary schedule and plan
    A. Phase I—system selection and preliminary design
    B. Phase II—system installation and testing
    C. Phase III—system operation and support

Fig. 9-3. Alternatives analysis report outline.

The next step is to evaluate which LAN technology to implement. This requires an understanding of local network technology. The viable local communications solutions for most companies include using facilities provided by the telephone company or installing a new local area network. The three types of local area network technologies involve various technologies, as follows:

- The private branch exchange (PBX) for data-only or integrated voice/data.
- Baseband signaling using twisted-pair wiring or coaxial cable.
- Broadband signaling using coax or fiber-optic cable.

The important technical factors to be considered include:

- Configuration alternatives.
- Types of microcomputers supported.

- Typical device speeds and maximum network speed.
- Signaling medium and capacity per cable.
- Maximum network distance.
- Support for gateway and bridge processors.
- Support for video and voice as well as data communications.
- Installation.

PBX Technology

PBX-based local networks generally employ star or tree configurations while using in-place wiring as the signaling medium. These networks are suitable for installations that have been renting telephone equipment. There is the opportunity to provide support for integrated voice and data workstations, as well as to support a variety of data devices by purchasing new PBX facilities. A comprehensive cabling plan should be considered for any new installation, because the installation cost is small compared to the cost of changing dedicated cabling each time a new data device is installed.

The PBX acts like a large automated switching matrix. It is similar to a telephone switchboard, except that the PBX does not have physical wire connections between users. Time division sampling techniques are used to sample each conversation and convert the analog signal into a digital representation. By synchronizing the paths of the digital signals from the various extensions, the PBX establishes a virtual circuit connection.

The PBX-based local network can be used with intelligent or standard terminals. Microcomputers can be connected to central databases using terminal emulation software. These microcomputers can also be used as integrated voice/data workstations. They support voice, data and facsimile communications, but generally not video. Each network cable supports one voice channel with control signals, and one data channel.

The maximum network distance for microcomputers is 20 meters without modems or repeaters. A limited-distance dataset is normally used to connect the microcomputer to the PBX switch.

The PBX network's central-point configuration is a source of system failure, so many centralized PBX products use an additional processor for backup, and provide electrical backup provisions. Others use a distributed architecture or redundant processors for each node. (Voice/data network sources include American Telecom, ATTIS, Ericsson, GTE, Harris, Intercom, Mitel, Northern Telecom, Nippon Electric, Rolm, and Siemens. Data-only network sources include Develcon, Gandalf and Micom.)

The cost per port for a typical voice/data PBX can range from several hundred to well over a thousand dollars for voice and data transmission. The cost per port for a typical data-only PBX is about half as much.

The first PBXs functioned much like a switchboard operator. They were purely mechanical in nature, occupied a large amount of space, kept no usage statistics, and could handle only voice (analog) transmissions. PBXs now use electronic switching, and accommodate digital communications. Many models handle interterminal communications, route electronic mail, control peripheral devices, store and forward voice messages, and direct calls over the most cost-effective routes. Others allow users to switch terminals among computers, using the same techniques with which calls are transferred between phone extensions.

The newer PBXs use many of the same microprocessors that microcomputers use. They track which lines are overcrowded or underutilized, and provide diagnostic test capabilities. A twisted-pair cable is used for all devices, including telephones, data terminals, printers, microcomputers, and facsimile devices. Analog telephone sets are connected to a line card using one path for the analog voice signal, and a separate path for digital signal control. The microcomputers are usually attached to the time division multiplexer (TDM) bus using an add-on data module. The TDM bus samples each line card, or data module, and, by aligning the time sample of two line cards or data modules, it creates a communications path through electronic switches.

Data traffic can be multiplexed in either the telephone set or at the line card within the PBX switch. If the telephone set has an internal digitizer, the voice is multiplexed with the data onto the telephone cable using time-division and two or three twisted-pair cables. The voice and data paths are separated at the switch. This technique is used in the Intercom IBX, the Northern Telecom SL-100, and the Rolm CBX-II.

If the telephone station does not have a digitizer, the analog and digital signals travel through separate cable pairs from the telephone set to the switch. The analog voice signals are then digitized in the line card of the PBX switch.

Microcomputers connected in a PBX network can be switched to a local host computer, another local microcomputer acting as a file server, or an outward dial trunk on the public switched telephone network. The connection can also be made to an X.25 packet assembler/disassembler (PAD) gateway for connection to an X.25 public data network (PDN) such as Telenet, Tymnet, or Uninet. Multiple microcomputers can share one leased line with the X.25 PAD multiplexing a number of data streams. Remote microcomputers can be connected to a statistical multiplexer through a leased data line into the private branch exchange.

Many PBX switches allow a direct connection to a T1 transmission line, which operates at 1544 megabits per second. The T1 link can be divided into voice-grade and data channels, and can be very cost effective compared to the cost of individual voice-grade lines. All of the leading PBX switches support asynchronous data traffic up to 19.2 Kbps, which is the most common requirement for microcomputers today.

The AT&T ATTIS PBX System 85 uses T1-compatible switching. This system uses pulse code modulation (PCM), creating digitized voice data at 64 Kbps. The maximum number of time slots per processor is 512, with a maximum of 16 processors supported. Separate voice and data signal paths are used, and the cost per station is about $1000.

The Rolm CBX-II PBX uses a proprictary switching technique with a sampling rate of 12 kHz. There is no consistent companding technique, so proprietary telephone sets are required to use all of the data switching features. A data terminal interface (DTI) is available as part of the telephone set. A proprietary submultiplexing scheme is used, in which several data streams can be combined into one voice path to reduce the requirements on the TDM bus. A protocol converter is available for use as an SNA gateway processor. There is also an X.25 PAD gateway.

The Northern Telecom SL-1 uses a T1-compatible internal switching technique with 64 kHz sampling. Equipment is available for an X.25 PAD gateway and SNA gateway, based on protocol converters.

The Northern Telecom SL-1 and the ATTIS System 85 use a port-doubling configuration, in which voice and data traffic travel over separate cable pairs. Rolm and Intercom use true multiplexing techniques to combine voice and data traffic over the same two cable pairs.

The Intercom IBX supports direct digital connection to Bell's T1 transmission link, and allows more than 4000 simultaneous conversations. The connection cost is about $1000 per connection when 25 percent of the voice stations also support data. The Rolm CBX-II and Northern Telecom SL-1 connection cost is about 10 percent less based upon the same data mix.

The Rolm and Northern Telecom PBX architectures are considered to be mature, because they are based upon hardware introduced in the late 1970s. The ATTIS and Intercom architectures are much more recent, and tend to be more expensive.

The advantages of PBX local area networks include proven technology and resource availability. They are the least expensive alternative for users with an existing telephone switch. PBX local networks typically support data rates from 300 bps to 9600 bps, with 56 kilobits per second rarely utilized. The disadvantages of using PBXs include limited device capacity, transfer rates, and bandwidth, which makes them ineffective for heavy volume requirements.

PBX local networks are best suited to low speed and low volume traffic, such as communicating word processors, communicating copiers, microcomputers, interactive minicomputers, terminals, and printers. These networks support message store-and-forward applications, protocol conversion, and connections to value-added X.25 packet data networks such as Telenet, Tymnet and Uninet.

PBX-based solutions are adequate for moderate numbers of communicating microcomputers and asynchronous terminals. They are not commonly employed for data entry and synchronous data devices communicating at 9.6 or 56 kilobits per second.

Baseband Technology

Baseband technology employs signaling techniques, in which each station sends digital signals on a communications channel that is shared by all of the network stations. Each station listens to all network traffic, but responds only to those messages that are addressed to it.

Baseband networks are available which support the star, ring, and bus topologies. These networks use twisted-pair telephone cable, 50-ohm coaxial cable, or Ethernet coaxial cable. In some environments, the twisted-pair telephone cable might already be in place to support the star configuration.

Baseband networks are generally used for a small population of microcomputer workstations. The microcomputers are typically provided with baseband transceivers in the form of expansion boards. A microprocessor on the board is usually dedicated to managing the network protocol. These systems usually operate at speeds from 2.4 to 56 Kbps, with a maximum network speed of 10 Mbps. They support one data channel, with ten to 100 devices sharing that channel by circulating the data, which can be in the form of packets. Some networks support digitized voice, as well as data, transmission. They do not usually support analog facsimile devices or video transmission, although some support digital facsimile devices.

The total transmission distance is usually less than 20 kilometers, with each individual segment separated by less than 1500 meters. The microcomputers are usually much closer than this because of the high cost of baseband repeaters.

Baseband local networks such as Datapoint's Attached Resource Computer have been in use since about 1975. The initial application was the connection of intelligent workstations.

Ethernet-compatible components are available from many sources, including 3Com, Digital Equipment Corporation, Ungermann-Bass, and

Xerox. Baseband local networks based upon twisted-pair trunk cables are available from Corvus and others. The cost per port ranges from $500 to $1000 each.

Baseband local networks allow a mix of more types of traffic and applications than is possible with PBX networks. A typical application is a cluster of microcomputers sharing a database and providing electronic mail services.

Baseband networks allow the sharing of information among users on a highly interactive basis such as that found in engineering design groups. The cost of baseband technology is similar to that of broadband technology, depending upon the data rates and station configuration. They are limited in maximum cable distances, and have less growth capacity than broadband networks.

Baseband local networks use a time-division scheme to apportion the single stream of high speed digital bits among the users. The network typically employs a ring topology, and operates at speeds ranging from 19.2 Kbps to 10 Mbps.

Many baseband networking products are available, with Ethernet-compatible products representing the largest segment. Ethernet trunk cables normally do not exceed 1500 meters without using a local bridge. Some baseband products use twisted-pair wiring in addition to RG-62, RG-59, RG-11 and Ethernet coaxial cable. Existing telephone wiring cannot normally be utilized, because most baseband local networks typically require a ring configuration. Telephone wiring supports only a star topology, which is rarely used for baseband. Baseband cabling costs are similar to broadband costs when more than 15 nodes are used.

In addition to the network medium, there are the strengths and weaknesses of the different access methods to consider. The general categories include token-passing, and the different versions of carrier-sense multiple access (CSMA): collision detection and collision avoidance (CSMA/CD and CSMA/CA). The CSMA methods are best suited for networks with an aggregate network utilization of less than 30 percent, and terminal devices utilization of between 10 and 40 percent. Carrier-sense multiple access local networks are best for asynchronous terminals, and should not be used for synchronous terminals with use rates higher than 30 percent, or for supporting digitized voice applications mixed with any type of data traffic.

The token-passing access method should be used for terminals with use rates greater than 30 percent. Token passing allows device access at a regular rate. It is suitable for scientific/engineering workstations, realtime process control, factory automation, and some office automation applications. Token passing tends to be inefficient when a small group of devices is highly utilized in a network.

The following are typical baseband network products:

- The 3Com EtherSeries, which uses a bus topology and operates at 10 megabits per second with CSMA/CD access. It can support 1000 devices, with an average price of about $600 per connection.
- The Corvus Systems Omninet network, a baseband network which uses twisted-pair cabling. It employs a bus topology, and operates at 1 Mbps with CSMA/CA. The network supports up to 63 users, with an average price per connection of $800.
- Datapoint's ARCnet, which uses baseband techniques as the primary method of connecting microprocessor-based workstations. ARCnet operates at 2.5 Mbps, and supports up to 255 devices. ARCnet supports both bus and star topologies and uses token passing. The average price per user device is $600.
- Digital Equipment's Decnet, an Ethernet-compatible baseband local network which uses a tree network topology. The network supports up to 1024 user devices, and the trunk channel operates at 10-Mbps. The CSMA/CD access method is used, and protocol conversion capabilities are available for X.25 and SNA/SDLC devices. The average price per connection is about $700.
- The IBM PC cluster, a coaxial baseband network which uses the CSMA/CA access method. It operates at 375 Kbps, and supports up to 64 users. Per station costs are about $1000.
- The Nestar Plan, which uses RG-62 coax in a tree topology, and operates at 2.5 Mbps. Token passing is used, and protocol conversions to bisynchronous 3270 and SNA/SDLC are available. The average price per user station is about $600.
- The Orchid Technology PC-Net, a baseband local network for IBM and IBM-compatible microcomputers. The network uses RG-59 and RG-11 coax in a linear bus topology. The CSMA/CD access method is used with transmission at 1 Mbps. Average connection cost is $700.
- The Ungermann-Bass NET-ONE, a baseband system for IBM and compatibles. The interface device is offered as an expansion board. Ethernet cable or RG-59 cable can be used in a linear bus network configuration. The network operates at 1.3 Mbps using CSMA/CD access. The average price per connection is $600.

Baseband implementation costs are reasonable for small numbers of devices. Baseband supports high data transfer rates, and is effective for applications such as intelligent workstations sharing database information. Supporting voice transmission can be difficult and costly compared to PBX. Intelligent terminal devices are required for voice transmission, because the device must constantly monitor the network for messages. Baseband networks usually support lower-speed devices, have less aggregate network growth, and cover less distance than broadband networks.

Broadband Technology

Broadband technology supports tree and bus configurations, and uses single or dual 75-ohm coaxial cable. These configurations operate with devices using speeds of 2.4 Kbps to 3 Mbps. The maximum channel speed is typically 5 Mbps. Frequency division is utilized to allow simultaneous transmission of many conversations on a single physical channel. The different devices or user groups connected to the network are assigned frequency ranges called *bands.* The transmission is analog, and digital signals require conversion using modems.

These networks provide the high bandwidth necessary to support hundreds of voice, video, and data channels within the network. Broadband components are based on community antenna television (CATV) technology, which is relatively mature. The maximum geographic distance is 50 kilometers. Broadband is especially suitable to facilities with a number of buildings in a campus-like environment. The cost per port is approximately $700 to $1,000. Components are available from a number of vendors, including 3M/Interactive Systems, Applitek, Codex, Concord Data Systems, TRV, Sytek, Ungermann-Bass, and Wang.

High-volume and large-bandwidth applications are the area of choice for broadband technology. This includes integrated voice and data communications, as well as video requirements. The broadband networks, with their large bandwidths and high transfer rates, can support most types of communication, and allow multiple data channels for data and video. Difficulties include adding stations in dense areas, the analog signaling requirement and the initial expense for network installation. A user can prewire a building with coaxial cable for the maximum capacity, and save considerably compared to installing coaxial and twisted-pair cable as needed.

Broadband local networks offer the highest bandwidth capacity, but they are also the most costly for initial implementation even though the technology is based upon community antenna television hardware. Over the long term, broadband networks are cost-effective for users with a high volume of voice, video, and data communications. They are the only technology that can be used for such applications as full-motion, full-color video.

Broadband local networks can be implemented as single and dual-cable configurations. Some networks, such as Ungermann-Bass' Net/One and Interactive Systems' LAN/1, are available in either a single or dual-cable implementation. Others are available only as a single-cable implementation or only as a dual-cable implementation.

The dual-cable broadband systems, such as Wang's Wangnet or Ungermann-Bass' Net/One, are generally more expensive than single-cable broadband implementations such as Sytek's Localnet 20. The dual-cable implementations require two coaxial cables with two connections and two interface circuits per user. Increasing the cost are the additional space required for the cable and mounting hardware, the requirement of isolating the signals in the terminal equipment, and the additional time required for cable installation.

All broadband local networks require separate transmit and receive paths for bidirectional operation. The radio frequency signals propagate through the trunk cable to the head-end hardware, which controls the signal distribution throughout the network. This hardware provides the required modulation, demodulation, addition, and frequency translation functions to the network.

Broadband networks support the T1 data rates that are generally used between Telco central offices. Data rates range from 9.6 Kbps to 20 Mbps. The channels are usually divided into bands of 6 MHz, which can be subdivided using access schemes such as CSMA/CD or CSMS/CA. Token-passing channel access can also be used. This allows broadband local networks to support Ethernet and other baseband configurations within a frequency band of the broadband configuration.

The maximum throughput on the main data channel ranges from 128 Kbps to 20 Mbps, with a maximum user device transmission rate of 19.2 Kbps to 2.5 Mbps. A limit of ten thousand station devices is offered, along with a maximum geographic distance of 10 miles.

Protocol conversion using a gateway processor can be used for conversion from asynchronous ASCII to either IBM 3270 bisynchronous protocol or X.25 bit-synchronous high-level data link control (HDLC) protocol.

Broadband local networks are best suited to applications that require large bandwidth and high-volume communications, such as the following examples:

- Integrated voice and data workstations.
- Central-processor-to-central-processor file transfers.
- Response-time-critical, interactive applications.
- High-volume, high-speed print stations, including laser printers.

- High-speed data workstations, such as those needed for computer aided design and computer aided manufacturing (CAD/CAM) applications.
- Video applications.

The major disadvantages of broadband networks are the difficulty and cost of design, implementation, and expansion, especially in densely populated areas.

Major differences can exist among broadband networks in their support for coax-attached terminals. Some only support IBM 3270-type CRTs, while others, such as Wang, only support Wang workstations. The IBM broadband network for microcomputers, PC-Net, is based upon the Sytek network technology.

Broadband local networks provide enough bandwidth to support complete voice, video, data, and facsimile transmission. However, the cable and cable interface hardware require an extensive undertaking. In environments with large volumes of data and some video, such as universities and hospitals, they are the best solution.

PACKET TECHNOLOGY

Packet switching is becoming an increasingly attractive alternative to dialed telephone and leased-line data links. Unlike a leased line, which is dedicated to a single user, packet-switching networks allow a number of data users to share a high-speed network. The result is fast, error-free, reliable, and low-cost communications.

The operation of a packet network is not unlike that of a railroad system. Each group of information is placed in a container (the railroad car) and carried to the next station. The information is taken out of the first container and placed into another, for the trip to the next station, or node. The process ends when the information arrives at the final destination.

An actual packet-switching network transmits information in small groups, usually less than 128 characters, for minimal end-to-end delay. Small-volume users simultaneously share the facility, which results in a lower cost per bit of information transmitted. The user is not burdened with the task of network operation, or the cost of support.

Message switching is not usually performed in real time, which requires large storage facilities at each node, because each message is stored in its entirety before being delivered. This storage can result in delays.

Before the blocks of characters are sent, the control and destination information is added, and the packet is assembled. At the proper destination, this information is removed as the packet is disassembled.

The control and destination bits are discarded, and the data is sent to the receiving terminal or other device.

The packet assembler/disassembler (PAD) can be owned by either the user or the network. The PAD has many of the characteristics of a statistical multiplexer, because it allows terminals and devices to share one leased phone line for network access.

The connection to the packet network requires several steps:

1. The user connects to the nearest node in the network via a dedicated or leased phone line.
2. The originator sends a call-request packet to the call port.
3. The call request forces the network to assign a logical channel number, which identifies the data and the address to which the data is routed.

The connection is automatic and transparent to the terminals connected to the network.

The packet network is less vulnerable to line failure than a leased data link. If a link fails, the packets can be rerouted on other links. The packet network is not sensitive to the transmission error problems that occur in dial-up networks. Error checking is done at each node to ensure that the message is received correctly. In a packet network, the user pays for the phone line from the device to the nearest node. A fee is assessed for each packet sent, and for the connection time.

Packet switching provides a flexible data communications system. It is not necessary for the user to design, implement, and support a data network linking geographically separate locations. A connection is made via the packet-switching network to outside value-added services.

NOVELL NETWARE

The Novell NetWare includes a proprietary network as well as a software operating environment which is used on top of other vendors' local networks. Local area network architectures from IBM, ATTIS, and Apple are supported.

The NetWare/S-Net is a star-based baseband network connecting up to 24 microcomputers using dual twisted-pair cable, as shown in Fig. 9-4. The microcomputers are connected to a file server, which uses the Motorola MC68000 microprocessor to control workstation access to the disk subsystem as well as printers. IBM PC, PC-XT and AT microcomputers are supported, as well as IBM compatibles and the Texas Instruments Professional.

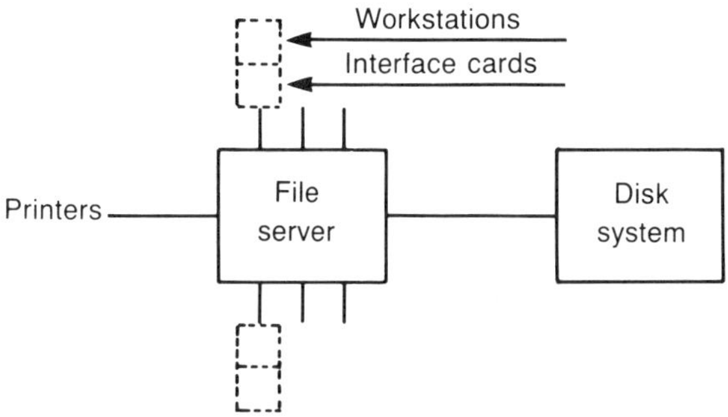

Basic configuration

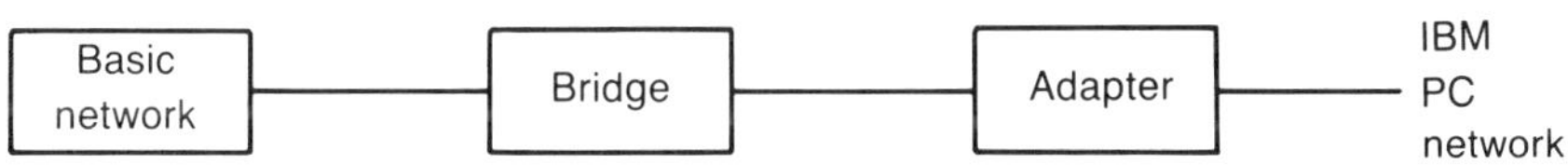

Advanced configuration

Fig. 9-4. Novell Netware/S-Net.

Each file server in the network can support up to 500 megabits of storage and five printers. Multiple file servers can be connected to expand the network's size and geographic coverage. Each connected microcomputer requires an interface card.

This network offers a true file server configuration, and the microcomputers intercept an application program's service request to the server's hard disk as the workstations open, read, and close files. Other networks interrupt only when they need to read and write to the server's hard disk. The file server's hard disk is divided into directories, which appear as individual hard disk drives to the user. A system manager is used to assign passwords allowing read/write or read-only access to the directories.

The NetWare/S-Net server allocates disk sectors based upon microcomputer requests. This is done with a special version of the MS-DOS operating system. Other networks might use a standard MS-DOS operating system. Other networks might use a standard MS-DOS operating system, and disk sectoring is left to the workstations.

The network software tracks the opening of files, and can restrict a second user if the file is already in use. Other file servers depend upon the application program as well as network hardware to prevent two users from simultaneously updating the same data.

IBM'S PC NETWORK

IBM's PC Network* is a broadband network that uses one frequency channel for the transmit signals, and a second frequency channel for the receive signals. Each channel operates at 2 Mbps.** The network uses the CSMA/CD technique, which is implemented at the transport layer to control station access to the network.

The PC adapter card uses a microprocessor, two communications processors, and 16K of random access memory. The first five layers of the seven-layer open systems interconnection (OSI) model, starting from the physical layer through the session layer, are implemented in the network adapter hardware. The sixth and seventh layers of presentation and application are supported with the PC Network software.

The IBM PC Network allows IBM microcomputers to be networked together, with an AT acting as a shared file server as well as a stand-alone device. The network hardware configuration is illustrated in Fig. 9-5 and consists of:

- A central translator unit, which is required for each group of eight computers connected to the network.
- A PC Network adapter card for each microcomputer connected to the network.
- Cabling and connectors, including base expanders.

Eight microcomputers can be attached to the initial tap, or base, unit, and up to 72 microcomputers can be connected using a maximum of eight base expander modules. Drop cables are available in lengths up to 200 feet for connecting the microcomputer to the expander module. This can be extended to support up to 255 micros over a radius of several miles

---

*IBM'S first local network was the PC Cluster. The PC cluster appeared to be IBM's response to market pressure for a local network product. But the product was considered technically poor. IBM's most recent local network is the 4 Mbps token ring, which will run on shielded twisted pair cable (see Chapter 10).

**The 2 Mbps PC Network could use gateways between the PC Network and the Rolm CBX-II. The PBX capabilities of the IBM-Rolm CBX-II product would allow an effective networked and integrated PBX environment using the internal T1 capabilities of the CBX-II along with submultiplexing for data. To be effective, the PC Network should support both communications gateways and modem pooling.

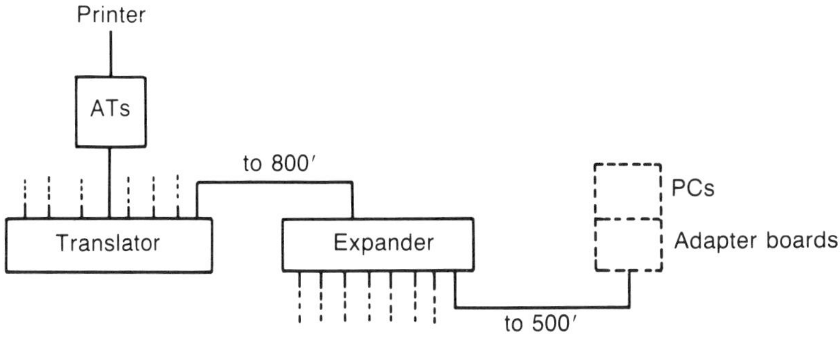

Fig. 9-5. IBM PC-network.

in a custom engineered configuration. The software required is MS-DOS version 3.1 and the PC Network Control Program.

Devices which act as file servers or have shared printers attached to them must have a hard disk. Other microcomputers need only a floppy disk drive, because they use the network as a virtual hard disk.

The file-sharing capabilities allow the PCs to segment and share a hard disk, as well as a directory or file within a segment of the hard disk. The network software includes password protection of all shared files, including read-only and read/write access. The software also spools reports only to printers for which the user is authorized. Up to three print servers are supported, with a queue size limitation of 99 files.

Most of the microcomputers on the network will not require printers, or even printer interface boards. Each user has access to three printers without having even one serial or parallel printer interface board.

The main menu, which appears when the user logs on, also advises if there are any messages waiting. When a message is broadcast to a user, a status line at the bottom of the screen flashes. The user can temporarily suspend an application, handle the message, and then return to the application.

The messaging programs are menu-driven, and include the ability to display, file, or print messages. Distribution lists can be stored, and messages can be forwarded to another user.

The translator costs approximately $600, while the network adapter cards cost about $700 each. A mix of 20 microcomputers can be networked at a cost of approximately $20,000. Based on a three-year life without depreciation, this can be broken down to about $1.25 per user per working day. Factoring in the benefits of accelerated depreciation, the cost drops to about $.60 per day. This figure does not include maintenance, administration, and support of the network.

The cost of the network interface hardware, including the broadband wiring, is easily justified in view of the potential savings. Other benefits involve productivity gains caused by information sharing and the new applications which are possible in this environment.

AT&T ISN

The AT&T Information Systems ISN is an office communications architecture based on twisted-pair wiring. The user is likely to have the necessary wiring already in place. Figure 9-6 illustrates the possible connections in a typical configuration.

The network uses AT&T's Premises Distribution System (PDS) as the signaling medium. PDS can support voice, data, video, and facsimile. Fiber-optic cable can be used in addition to twisted pairs. PDS can be used with almost any PBX switch product. Almost any PBX will also operate using the IBM Cabling System with Type-2 cable. The cost per station is about $100 to $150 for twisted-pair cable, and $150 to $300 for the combination of twisted-pair and fiber-optic cables.

The network uses twisted-pair cable to connect terminals, microcomputers, host computer ports, print servers, and file servers to a packet controller. The packet controller acts as a data packet switch, processing up to 48,000 packets per second, to control and manage the traffic flow in the network.

Terminal devices can be connected to a concentrator, which multiplexes up to 40 devices into an 8.6 Mbps data stream. The concentrators are connected to packet controllers which can be located up to 1 kilometer apart using fiber-optic cable. The packet controller can be connected to an ATTIS System 85 or System 75 PBX via the 8.6 Mbps fiber data stream.

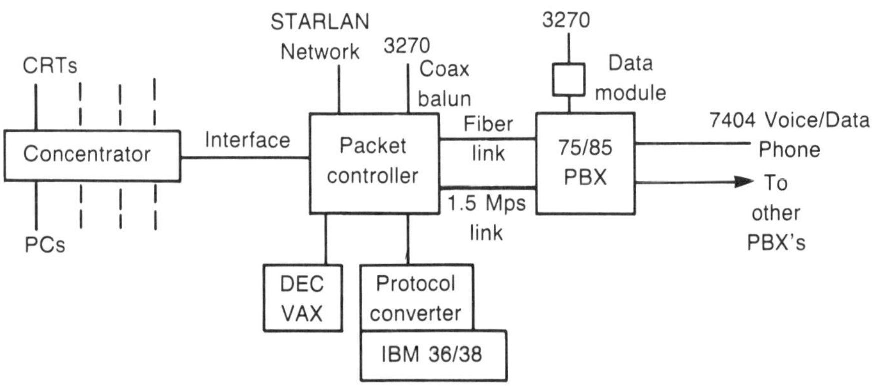

Fig. 9-6. AT&T ISD.

ISN supports asynchronous communications, and a 7404 Digital Voice Terminal allows simultaneous voice and data transmission through a digital port on the System 75/85 PBX. Data modules allow a user to switch IBM 3270 data messages from asynchronous terminals to IBM-compatible host computers using the System 75/85 PBX. The data modules are available in several models, ranging in price from $800 to $1600.

Synchronous support for IBM's Systems Network Architecture and a high-speed transmission trunk for connecting packet controllers as remote nodes are also available. For networks with more than 75 devices, the average cost per connection is $400 for asynchronous devices, $700 for STARLAN* attached devices, and $1200 for IBM-synchronous devices.

AT&T offers several local networking solutions:

- ISN with 8 Mbps throughput in a star topology, integrating the System 75/85, fiber-optics and the PDSA cabling scheme.
- STARLAN, a 1 Mbps network based on CSMA/CD access techniques.
- Ethernet, the industry standard baseband local network, with a channel speed of 10 Mbps.

An adapter on the ISN packet controller supports IBM synchronous communications; 3270 BSC and 3270 SDLC cluster controllers can be used at speeds of 9600 bps and 19200 bps. Another adapter allows the direct connection of 3270 terminals. Keyboard commands can be used to switch cluster controller ports to different applications and host computers. A balun (a type of transformer) is used to interface the 3270 device's coaxial cable to a single twisted-pair copper cable using a 2.36 Mbps data rate. This allows terminal movement without expensive cabling changes.

The data modules connect 3270 devices to a System 75/85 PBX by first converting the 2.36 Mbps data stream to 64 Kbps. This 64 Kbps data stream is switched through the PBX in the same manner as other circuit based services. The protocol used between the data module and the PBX is Digital Communications Protocol (DCP), a protocol which is proprietary to AT&T. System 34/36/38 terminals would require a gateway.

Gateways can be used to connect to a STARLAN or Ethernet local network. PBX networking is possible through the Electronic Tandem

*STARLAN is a local network implementation which emulates Microsoft's MS-Net and MS-DOS version 3.1 operating environment.

Network (ETN) and Distributed Communications Systems (DCS) products.

An ISN implementation should support T1 and Dataphone Digital Service (DDS) transmission channels for effective remote networking. The use of the Digital Multiplexed Interface (DMI) will allow multiline host interfaces to be reduced to a single high-speed 1.544 Mbps data stream. Networking with the DMI interface and T1 transmission links can be an effective method for both local and remote requirements.

An important advantage of ISN is the ability to build networks by interconnecting it with a System 75 or System 85 PBX, as well as additional remote ISN environments.

Several differences exist in the areas of premise wiring and office communications architecture between AT&T and IBM. Both offer twisted-pair wiring with a fiber option, but AT&T uses the traditional four-pair per station of nonshielded, 22 to 26 gauge wire, while IBM uses nonstandard shielded twisted-pair cabling for data, and four pairs of conventional telephone wiring in their Type-2 cabling. The PC Network is broadband based, and requires coaxial cable.

As the communications industry continues with deregulation, many users might return to the dependability of AT&T products. AT&T has many products in place today and it will promote ISN as a local communications architecture because ISN uses existing telephone wiring.

With the convergence of data processing, communications, and office automation, vendors are striving to provide more integrated solutions. Local networks represent a commitment to a facilities architecture and a business strategy. Parts of the solution can be obtained from different vendors, because all the pieces are interconnected. Difficulties arise when competing technologies are nurtured in different parts of the same organization. The coexistence of competing architectures usually leads to difficulties.

THE APPLETALK LOCAL NETWORK

AppleTalk is a baseband network that uses a bus topology. It can be used for connections up to 1000 feet with twisted-pair wiring to support up to 32 devices. The network operates at 230 Kbps using the CSMA/CA technique. The frame format is based on the synchronous data-link control (SDLC). The connection cost is low, being about 20 percent of the cost of an IBM PC-Net connection. The interface hardware is a part of the communications built into each Macintosh. This includes a Zilog 8530 communications microprocessor with interface driver and receiver chips.

The AppleTalk protocol architecture has the relationship to the seven-layer open systems architecture of the International Standards Organization as shown in Table 9-2.

At the physical layer, shielded twisted-pair wiring with baseband signaling is used. The data link layer uses the AppleTalk link access protocol (ATLAP). Each node on the network has ATLAP facilities for packet assembly and disassembly. The microcomputers on the network compete for access to the network bus through the link layer.

Contention is resolved through CSMA/CA, in which each device with data to send listens to the network. If a device is sending, the other units avoid transmitting and wait until the channel is free. To avoid data collisions, the following collision avoidance scheme is used:

1. After a free channel is detected, each device waits 400 microseconds plus a random interval.
2. A line reservation signal is sent.
3. Each device is held, within these limits, until the time they are allowed to begin the collision-avoidance reservation cycle.

This technique can become overloaded rather easily compared to other methods, and it is the same access method used by IBM in its first attempt at a network, the PC Cluster.

The network layer uses a high-level protocol called the datagram delivery protocol (DDP). It manages the transmission of packets among units called *sockets*. These are logical network units that link the local Macintosh applications to the networking functions. DDP manages the node-to-node message delivery on a single network and the socket-to-socket delivery for internet connections.

At the transport layer, the routing maintenance protocol (RTMP) is used for locating communications paths between nodes within the network. This protocol is integrated with the zone information protocol

Table 9-2. The Relationship of the AppleTalk Protocol Architecture to the ISO-OSI Architecture.

ISO-OSI Architecture	AppleTalk Protocols
Applications Layer	
Presentation Layer	Printer Access Protocol Filing Protocol
Session Layer	Name Binding Protocol
Transport Layer	Routing Table Protocol Transaction Protocol (Socket-to-Socket Delivery, Internet)
Network Layer	Datagram Delivery Protocol (Node-to-Node Delivery)
Link Layer	Link Access Protocol
Physical Layer	Media

(ZIP), which is used to identify the location of nodes in the network. The AppleTalk transport protocol (ATP) manages the delivery of packets between sockets, controlling the packet sequence and preventing packet loss. ATP uses a transmission identification frame for each packet. A data stream protocol is used to manage the full-duplex data transmission between sockets.

In the fifth, or session, layer, a name binding protocol is used to control the translation between the object-oriented names of the network nodes and the numeric addresses used by the network.

In the presentation level, a printer access protocol controls the print server functions, and a filing protocol controls the file server functions.

An automatic network addressing scheme is used, which eliminates the need for a dedicated network control station. Each node has an eight-bit network address. When a device is connected to the network, it transmits a network address bid. If no other device answers this transmission, the originating device assumes the address. If another device answers the network address bid, a new address is calculated and transmitted. The initiation and operational management of the network, from the user's view, appear to be simple.

AppleTalk is an open architecture, and other vendors supply gateways for other local network architectures, such as the PC Network and Ethernet.

AppleTalk is an inexpensive local network for Macintosh microcomputers. Typical applications are those which mix high resolution text with graphics using laser printers.

THE IBM TOKEN RING

The major parts of the IBM token-passing ring LAN include a 3274 cluster controller to support peer-to-peer communications and a plug-in communications card for the PC. Both the controller and the card incorporate a five-chip token-ring LAN set that Texas Instruments developed for IBM. IBM's token-ring development started in the early 1970s at its research labs in Zurich. It demonstrated a token-ring network in Geneva in 1983 that used network interface units as large as the PC itself. Other LAN vendors can use these chips in developing compatible products. Proteon, for example, has its 10 Mbps ProNet Lan, which is designed to be compatible with the token ring.

IBM's broadband PC Network is expected to be supported as a low-end LAN for users who need to communicate among a limited number of PCs at no more than 2 Mbps. Future emphasis will be on token-ring technology which fits in well with SNA.

The token ring will run on the IBM cabling system. Initially available at 4 Mbps using shielded twisted-pair wiring, in the future it could reach 16 Mbps using metallic cable. A fiber-optic version of the token ring could be capable of achieving speeds of up to 100 Mbps. This could be used for transmitting voice via SNA protocols.

If an XT is used as the server, it limits the number of nodes the server can support to about 10. An AT can probably support about 16 to 20 nodes. An APPC/PC applications interface is offered, which implements the LU 6.2 subset protocols for program-to-program communications. This interface allows users to develop programs that support peer-to-peer communications.

NETBIOS is also offered, and it has a sizable and growing base of available applications. Its addressing scheme is easy to use, but it was not developed for internetworking, and the number of nodes that can communicate across a gateway are limited. It also does not talk directly to mainframes.

APPC/PC tends to be less efficient as an applications interface, but it allows peer-to-peer communications between applications running on S/370 (with CICS), S/36, S/38, Series/1, and PCs. It can operate interactively or in a background mode, and it is supported on both the token ring and SDLC adapters.

The user has several options in building a token-ring network. The low cost, short term solution is to use Type-3 wiring based on twisted-pair telephone wire, which might already exist in the user's building. Two pairs are used for data, one pair for voice, and one pair for 3270 traffic.

Type-3 cabling limits the number of nodes on the network to 72, and limits the distance between wire closets and workstations to 330 feet, or 150 feet if the two-wire closets are connected on the ring. The distance limitation is based on the signal quality falling off as the distance increases while the noise level remains the same.

A media filter is required to attach a PC with the token-ring adapter to the Type-3 media. The filter reduces the amount of signal radiation, and allows the token ring to support 4 Mbps data rates by eliminating frequencies that could radiate from one pair to another. A jumper cable is used to connect the Multistation Access Unit (MAU) to the Type-3 wire.

The Type-3 cabling is at its limits in supporting 4 Mbps, while Type 1 and Type 2 are designed for high-speed data transfer for large processors. An eight-foot attachment cable connects the PC to Type 1 or Type 2 cabling. In connecting two wire closets on the same ring, coax cabling (Type 1) must be used. Type 1 and Type 2 media cannot be mixed.

The MAUs can be used to link up to eight nodes on the network, and MAUs can be connected together to expand the ring. MAUs can be installed in a 19 inch rack in the wiring closet, or in a housing attached to a wall or tabletop.

Another adapter is used for 3270 traffic on Type-3 cabling. The 3270 coax-to-twisted-pair adapter (CTPA) is a combination balun-and-media filter.

There are two low-level and two high-level application programming interfaces. The lower-level interfaces are for IEEE 802.2 data link control and IEEE 802.5 direct physical control. The higher-level interfaces are NETBIOS and APPC/PC, which can be run concurrently on the token-ring, without requiring an adapter card for each node.

The applications interfaces perform the functions found in layers three through five in the OSI model, and are implemented in software programs, rather than in ROM on the adapter card, as was done with the PC Network. Implementing the applications protocols in software allows more flexibility for incorporating protocols such as SNA.

A token-ring-to-PC Network program is available, which uses a dedicated AT or XT for running the interconnect program. Network applications communicating across the link use NETBIOS. The program provides limited access to nodes between the two networks.

An asynchronous communications server program is also available for low-speed communications over switched lines. The program runs on a PC, XT, and AT in a non-dedicated mode, and supports two dial lines per server. Multiple asynchronous servers are supported on the token ring. Communications out of the ring can be done through the Rolm CBX II, a PBX, or public switched network, using modems. The program manages outbound calls and accepts incoming calls for asynchronous communications programs running on the PCs. It requires exclusive use of the asynchronous communications adapters, and might limit performance of other programs running on the same PC.

A PC Network SNA 3270 Emulation Program can also be used on the token ring to provide access to host applications that support 3278 Model-2 devices. The PC running this program is connected to protocol converters, such as the 3708, 3710, or 7171, or to the Rolm CBX II using a Rolm DataCom Module for the interface. The CBX II link supports data rates to 9.6 Kbps, while the protocol converters can operate at rates up to 19.2 Kbps. Access to 3270 devices is available in four different configurations:

- A stand-alone configuration, in which a PC is attached with a SNA/SDLC line to a host. This configuration emulates the 3274 controller functions with a 3278 or 3279 terminal and 3287 printer.

- A gateway, which acts as a communication server for up to 32 PCs on the token ring or PC Network using a SNA/SDLC line to the host.
- A network station configuration, where each station acts as a communications node on either network by emulating a 3278 or 3279 terminal and a 3287 printer. A gateway is used to access the host.
- A combined gateway and network station configuration, which emulates the functions of the 3274 controller, 3278 and 3279 terminals and the 3287 printer.

TRANSMISSION MEDIA

There are several concerns associated with data communications transmission media. The most important factors that must be considered in communications system design include the issues of design objectives for the eventual configuration, topological structure, transmission facilities, protocol methodology, switching techniques, interface characteristics, and communication hardware. The most likely transmission services include wire, coaxial cable, fiber-optics, microwave, and satellite.

Wire

Wire is used for transmission rates of up to 9600 bps, while microwaves and satellites offer a wide variety of differing speed channels. Coaxial cable is used as an interface mechanism between local loops and wideband communication systems, and is an important element in many local area networks. Microwave systems are used in common carrier, long distance circuits, and in wideband communications installations installed by private users for limited area coverage.

A common-carrier circuit is generally a voice-grade telecommunications facility, using either private or switched lines which are widely available throughout the world. Multiplexing allows the user several circuits on the same cable.

The one type of communication service that relieves the user from concerns about the physical media involves leasing facilities from a value-added carrier. The costs for such services vary widely, because the facilities are often customized for specific usage, irrespective of distance. They are a good choice for relatively long distances with special data handling requirements.

Coaxial Cable

Coaxial cable can provide a variety of digital and information services to the system user. It is composed of a conductive cylinder with a wire in the center and insulation filling the space between the cylinder and the wire. Coaxial cable can transmit at a much higher frequency than wire, allowing megabit throughput speeds while remaining relatively immune to noise. It is inexpensive relative to its transmission capacity, and supports both point-to-point and broadcast operation.

Fiber Optics

Until the early 1970s, attenuation problems limited the use of fiber-optics in data communications to distances up to 200 feet. This has been improved to the point where attenuation now is about the same as coaxial cable, with substantially greater bandwidth. Fiber-optic costs remain higher, however. Existing problems currently being resolved include connection techniques and splicing methodology, along with the overall cost factors.

Performance with optical fiber is typically up to 50 megabits per second, with special implementations achieving throughputs of one gigabit per second. In addition to improved throughput, other major advantages include a large reduction in electromagnetic interference, reduced electrical grounding problems, and very low error rates.

Microwave

Microwave transmission employs the high end of the radio frequency range, and is often used by common carriers for long-distance communication links. The bandwidth is high, and the media is free space. A line-of-sight path between installations is required, with relay towers at about 30-mile intervals along the transmission path.

Satellite

A transmission medium that has achieved wide acceptance is satellite communications. With the numerous commercial satellites orbiting the earth, costs have become competitive with land-based common carriers when communication distances exceed 500-700 miles. One of the main advantages of satellite communications is the availability of extremely high bandwidth with a low incremental cost per bit per second.

A disadvantage is the delay time due to long distances, which impacts response time and satellite maintenance. Maintenance is minimized, however, with the use of transponder redundancy to reduce the chance of transmission interruptions.

Satellite communication is inherently broadcast, with a single transmission branching out to multiple recipients. A typical satellite can supply over 12,000 voice channels, and can serve the entire United States.

REVIEW EXERCISES

1. Discuss six major considerations of evaluating network requirements.

2. Describe the bottom-up approach for networking personal computers. What is its drawbacks?

3. Diagram a flow chart for a typical local area network implementation.

4. Develop a network criteria checklist based on network profiles.

5. What organizational factors are important to the success of the network?

6. Construct a decision matrix for the three major LAN technologies.

7. Discuss the use of T1 transmission lines in a PBX implementation.

8. What are the major advantages and applications of:
    a. PBX
    b. Baseband networks
    c. Broadband networks

How do packet switching and T1 transmission fit into this mix?

9. Compare the following networks for an application involving 24 microcomputers which will need to exchange primarily text. Consider costs, expansion, and support to other networks.
    a. Netware/S-Net
    b. IBM PC Network
    c. AT&T ISN
    d. AppleTalk
    e. IBM Token Ring

10. Repeat Exercise 9 for an existing building wired for telephones at each computer site, and a new installation subject to fast expansion.

Chapter 10

Future Developments

The world has entered a new Information Age, with a global telecommunication network that today forms the infrastructure for an information-based society. Telecommunications is one of the fastest-growing industries, due to the demands of society, the rapid growth of technology, and the declining costs of equipment and services. The telephone network will continue to be the workhorse of the telecommunications industry. The global telephone network includes over half a billion devices, which handle an average of two billion calls each day.

The demand for data, video, and other telecommunication services is causing major changes in telephone communications. The use of microelectronics has resulted in low-cost memory and computing power packaged as devices such as microprocessors. These technological advances have created an environment for more efficient, low-cost communications. In addition, the computer and microelectronics industries have penetrated the telecommunication industry with the wide use of digital communication systems. In the future, the differences between the telephone, computer, and other home or office devices will be less distinct. The telephones of the future will be much more like intelligent terminals, integrating features that are either not available now, or are provided by separate facilities.

The integration of services will be due to the use of digital technology, which will extend all the way to the actual user. The use of completely digital networks has led to the concept of the integrated services digital network (ISDN).

Digital transmission will play an even more important role in the evolution of telecommunication networks. While switches and terminals in the past have remained analog, the new technology and declining transmission costs allows the development and use of new types of networks and services. The use of digital switches has resulted in the integration of switching and transmission systems, commonly called an integrated digital network (IDN).

In addition to these technological advances, changes have also been due to the change in government regulation of the telecommunication industry in the United States. Technological advances during the 1960s and 1970s were often impeded by public policy. The use of innovations were limited by the U.S. regulatory structure, and other common and specialized carriers were at a disadvantage due to AT&T's monopolistic powers. The deregulation of the telecommunication industry, and the divestiture of the Bell System in the 1980s has brought far-reaching changes to the telecommunication network.

Outside of the United States, most telecommunication systems are owned and operated by a government ministry or administration. Instead of the multiple public and private networks found in the United States, most countries have only a few networks. Canada and the United Kingdom allow competition in their telecommunication networks, and several countries, including Japan, West Germany, and France, are moving towards possible deregulation.

THE DEVELOPMENT OF STANDARDS

A major concern is the development of standards in the United States and the rest of the world. With competition and deregulation, the need for standards is greater, but possibly more difficult to attain, than in the past. In the United States, AT&T traditionally determined communication standards, which were followed by other telecommunication suppliers.

The divestiture of the Bell System and the emergence of new carriers and networks has made standards even more important in order to avoid incompatibility and fragmentation in telecommunication systems. The implementation of new international networks, such as the ISDN, will have to accommodate all providers of services.

The breakup of the Bell System has also meant the loss of a single point of contact for planning and providing end-to-end service to customers. This has created restrictions on end-to-end service, potential increases in cost, and more complex implementation procedures, as well as a general uncertainty about future standards and regulation.

The Computer and Communications Industry Association has formed the Corporation for Open Systems, which will dedicate itself to testing network products for compatibility with the International Standards Organization's Open Systems Interconnect model, commonly known as OSI. The CCIA changed its name from the Computer Industry Association ten years ago. The National Bureau of Standards X.400 Special Interest Group is also involved in the formation of a not-for-profit corporation dedicated to X.400 product-compatibility testing. The X.400 standard, which addresses such issues as the interconnection of messaging networks, is incorporated into the seven-layer OSI model at the two uppermost layers, the application and presentation layers. The Corporation for Open Systems will test for X.400 compatibility, as well as for the other parts of the model, in a way similar to the way in which the packet networks now certify outside vendors' products as X.25 compatible.

The European Computer Manufacturers' Association (ECMA) has indicated an interest in supporting IBM's Logical Unit 6.2 (LU 6.2) and using it as part of the OSI model. LU 6.2 is designed for program-to-program communications.

In the Corporation for Open Systems, many of the initial members are supporting the IBM DISOSS format with gateway or interconnection products. There is a need to connect with IBM systems, and it can be done more easily with an open architecture like OSI rather than proprietary SNA products. The most useful parts of SNA are LU 6.2 and DISOSS, which could be merged into OSI.

OSI Networks

The goal of making equipment compatible with OSI has resulted in the development of related OSI networks, such as the Manufacturing Automation Protocol (MAP) and the Technical & Office Protocol (TOP). General Motors and Boeing have been the major forces behind the development of these networks since 1980.

MAP is a broadband token-bus network designed for the manufacturing environment. It was developed to link the various "islands" of information that are found in factory systems. These include:

- Mainframe computers for materials requirements planning (MRP).
- Supermini or microcomputers for computer-aided design.
- Real-time mini or microcomputers for quality control.

- Programmable controllers (PCs) for scheduling and dispatching parts on the manufacturing line.
- Robots to perform such tasks as welding and painting.
- Numerical control (NC) machines for drilling holes and milling parts.

MAP is designed to offer gains in productivity through complete integration. General Motors plans to install MAP in all of its plants. However, the initial version of MAP can be expected to undergo major changes. In the application layer, the protocol, which was called the Manufacturing Message Format Standard (MMFS), is to be superseded by the Electronics Industries Association standard, EIA 13 93, which will be known as RS-511. As a result, equipment for the implementation of MAP might bypass MMFS frequently. To quickly meet any upgrade changes to MAP in a way that is as inexpensive as possible for users, changes are required that affect only the software.

Two configurations can be used. The first involves the implementation of layers three through seven in software, with layers one and two, and an HDLC interface, on a Token Interface Module (TIM), which communicates under X.25. The other involves the implementation of layers five through seven in software, with a MAP interface board for layers one through four.

By 1990 it is expected that over 6000 MAP networks will be used for manufacturing and process control. Many of these might be MAP carrierband networks rather that broadband networks. Motorola is expected to support this configuration with VSLI chips and carrierband modems.

The use of MAP carrierband, single-channel subnetworks allows the factory system to be implemented in phases, rather than as a completely integrated network. The broadband approach is viewed as a potential plant safety problem, because complete isolation of independent systems is difficult. An equipment malfunction, which normally would not be critical, could affect another control loop and interrupt the overall plant operation.

The T1 Telecommunications Standards Committee

Divestiture of the Bell System and the resulting influx of new carriers, networks, and services has increased the need for standardization. The American National Standards Institute (ANSI) has established the T1 Telecommunications Standards Committee to develop standards for network interfaces. The technical aspects of services, switching, signaling, transmission, performance, operation, administration, and maintenance of telecommunication networks are covered, as shown in Table 10-1.

EMERGING DIGITAL SERVICES

New services are emerging from the fields of data processing, such as broadcast and interactive video, which are a departure from the traditional services of voice and data. The integration of telecommunications with data processing has resulted in such services as facsimile, telex, videotext, and electronic mail, which are carried with digital transmission.

Video services, such as teleconferencing, interactive CATV, and direct broadcast by satellite are emerging. Some of these, such as teleconferencing, are now being provided via analog transmission.

Facsimile

Facsimile allows the transmission of documents using public telephone or data networks. Three classes of facsimile terminals have

Table 10-1. The Organization of the T1 Telecommunications Standards Committee.

Technical Subcommittee	Working Groups
Customer premise equipment/carrier interfaces	Analog interfaces Digital interfaces Special interfaces Editing
Integrated services digital networks (ISDN)	ISDN architecture services ISDN switching/signaling protocols ISDN physical layer
Internetwork operations administration	Internetwork planning/engineering Internetwork operations testing support systems
Performance objectives	Administrative systems 4 kHz voice Voice-band data Digital circuit Digital packet Wideband Wideband analog
Carrier-to-carrier interfaces	Common channel signaling Carrier interfaces Digital network synchronization Hierarchical rates, formats
Specialized areas	Specialized video, audio Specialized voice, data Advanced technologies, services Environmental standards

been standardized by the CCITT for use over the public telephone networks:

Group	Minutes to transmit a standard page
1	6
2	3
3	1

Group 3 terminals operate with 2.4 Kbps or 4.8 Kbps modems (CCITT Rec. V.27), or 7.2 Kbps or 9.6 Kbps modems (CCITT Rec. V.29). The early standardization of facsimile terminals has resulted in more rapid growth and acceptance compared to other emerging services.

The future will bring a convergence of facsimile with other forms of communications. Mixed-mode terminals, for example, can use an optical character reader (OCR) to read text on the page, and facsimile to transmit any graphical information.

The facsimile industry has changed every three years. In 1978, the leading machines were analog devices built in the United States which sent at a rate of two to six minutes per page. Most of these were incompatible devices. The Japanese pushed for standards, so that all the newer machines are compatible.

Teletex

Teletex involves the communication of character-coded text between offices for word processing and editing. A teletex terminal includes:

- A keyboard for input.
- Facilities for storing, sending, and receiving characters.
- Devices for display and hard-copy output.

Teletex transmission can be provided by data or telephone switched networks using a transmission rate of 2.4 Kbps or greater, or by unused channels in broadcast television.

The CCITT Series-S recommendations for the basic teletex functions include the allowable characters, text dimensions and positioning, control functions, and data transport.

Videotext

Videotext is an interactive system for the display of alphanumeric text and basic graphics. Using a telephone line and keyboard, the subscriber can access and interrogate data banks. The data can be displayed on the user's television receiver. Services that can be offered as videotext systems include news, games, advertising, shopping, working, and banking at home. Several public and private videotext systems are available in the United States, Canada, Europe, Japan, and Australia.

The transmission rate is limited by the use of the switched telephone network, and development has focused on bandwidth-efficient picture coding techniques, including the digital coding techniques of alphamosaics, alphageometrics and alphaphotographics. In the near future, the limitations of the analog telephone network will be eliminated with the use of a 56 or 64 Kbps digital channel as a part of the integrated services digital network ((ISDN).

IBM has filed with the FCC an interference specification for a device called the IBM Voice Communications Adapter. This device acts like a modem in that it interfaces to the telephone system. It is more than a modem, however, because it has voice digitizing functions. The Voice Communications Adapter is a plug-in card for the PC that includes a Bell-compatible 300/1200 baud modem with voice digitizing and storage capability. According to documentation, it can answer the telephone and take messages.

This device would allow voice mail for the PC, because it would facilitate the transfer of voice-annotated text. The logical addition to digitized voice storage capability would involve combining this device with the PC, and adding the other functions required to make an integrated voice/data workstation. Other products, such as Rolm's Juniper and Cygnet Technologies' CoSystem, use telephones with the PC and provide office automation functions such as creating and updating calendars, electronic mail, and telephone directories.

Electronic Mail

In the past, postal services have been distinct from electronic communications. Even in countries where postal, telephone, and telegraph services are provided by a single government agency, these services have been treated separately. The evolution of voice and data network technology has resulted in the advent of interactive electronic mail services. The users of these services exchange messages through terminals which are part of a network. The messages are stored until the user logs on and requests them.

The United States Postal Service has developed Electronic Computer-Originated Mail (E-COM), which is a form of electronic mail in which a customer can send a text message via telephone lines to certain post offices. These receiving offices produce a hard copy, which is delivered by first-class mail. Canada has a similar electronic mail service, called

EnvoyPost, which uses the postal service and the TransCanada Telephone System. Other electronic mail (E-mail) services are available in the United States, such as Telemail and Tymnet. These employ packet-switching technology. In the Canadian E-mail market, there is MCI Mail, OnTyme, EasyLink, CompuServe, and Telemail, in addition to Telecom Canada's Envoy 100, and CNCP's EOS system.

In 1978, computer-based messaging systems (CBMS) were not considered serious electronic mail systems, and were used only by leading-edge high-tech firms. Today, almost every Fortune 500 company, and thousands of smaller ones, have at least one group using a CBMS. Many of the larger companies have thousands of employees with electronic mail systems. The point of psychological acceptance for E-mail has been reached. The industry has arrived, and people are getting down to the business of implementing it. In companies across the country, CBMS services of various types are being explored and implemented.

Most users are looking for many types of capabilities, most of which are not provided on any single system. New arrangements providing gateways between systems have appeared, which allow users to combine services like CompuServe's databases, MCI Mail's offnet delivery services, and Dow Jones' financial information.

Software is also available for interconnecting PC programs to E-mail services. These communications programs allow the user to develop a business form using a PC program such as Lotus 1-2-3. After the form is filled out, the communications software allows it to be passed into an electronic mail system.

Almost every system looks the same, and many companies run applications in which personal computers and hosts are so well integrated that is will soon be difficult to tell which one of them has control of the application. A program such as Microsoft Access, for example, can be used with a group of PCs to automate the sending of weekly sales reports to the head office for consolidation and final reporting. Another common application is a computer conferencing system to hold periodic electronic meetings.

Electronic mail applications will grow to sizable proportions in the near future. The situation is not unlike the personal computer prior to the IBM PC; the industry was dominated by products such as the Apple II, 8-bit CP/M micros, and software like VisiCalc. Most of today's electronic mail services will have to undergo changes in order to meet the needs of future users.

Advances will occur in the following four major areas:

1. The capability to integrate PC application files into a CBMS.

The line-oriented CBMSs will be phased out, as more services allow applications with PC files beyond mailbox storage and transfer.

2. The use of gateways. A user who signs onto one system also has access to other services without leaving the initial service. The user receives a single bill, as in Telecom Canada's iNet. This type of service gives users access to hundreds of different database or communication services, along with the ability to devise a menu for a specific network application.

3. This area is closely related to gateways. The development of front-end communications software. An example of this type of software already in use is the Instant Mail Manager by Kensington Microware for Western Union's Easylink.

4. The development of electronic data interchange applications. This includes business forms generation capabilities which have formerly been line-oriented in most systems.

The continued integration of PC applications programs will allow users to develop forms for such applications as sales management, shipping, billing, and customer services. Electronic mail is entering a phase of detailed implementation, the major focus being integration with PCs.

Interconnections are becoming more common, such as MCI Mail connecting to subscribers of CompuServe's Easy Plex and InfoPlex E-mail systems. This allows users to trade messages via a direct connection of the three systems.

MCI Mail is essentially an electronic mail delivery service, with a minor role in information services. CompuServe offers a diverse collection of business-oriented timesharing services, consumer-oriented electronic information services, and electronic messaging services. EasyPlex is just one of several ways to send and receive messages on CompuServe. Others include the bulletin board systems (known as Special Interest Groups) and the CB-radio type of chatting mode, which can be used to pass messages between two or more online users in real time. EasyPlex is a store-and-forward service which is included at no charge to all subscribers.

MCI Mail provides another way for CompuServe subscribers to get their messages out using nonelectronic options such as overnight letters or telex. CompuServe also has telex, but it must be used with InfoPlex. The sender must know the recipient's unique address, because the MCI Mail directory is not available while on CompuServe. CompuServe's subscriber directory does not offer the same convenience as the MCI directory.

In the MCI system, users need only enter the last name of the recipient at the **TO:** prompt. If there is only one subscriber with that last name, the system inserts the full name, city, and ID number in the space. If there are several possibilities, the system lists them in alphabetical order and asks the sender to choose the one desired.

CompuServe dominates the online information service industry, and is far ahead of such services as The Source, Dow Jones News/Retrieval, and Viewtron. MCI ranks with AT&T, GTE, RCA, and ITT as one of the dominant communications carriers. In the electronic mail industry, MCI is in the top half for both the number of subscribers and the volume of messages. Western Union's EasyLink has a greater volume of messages, but CompuServe has the largest number of mailboxes, although many subscribers might not use this free service.

CompuServe also allows subscribers to use AT&T's Message Access Service, which allows E-mail subscribers to call an operator on an 800 line and ask for their messages to be read to them.

Telex subscribers might have several problems when trying to pass messages from one network to another. The telex networks of TRT, Western Union, ITT World Communications, RCA Global Communications, MCI, and FTC Communications are fully interconnected, but it is not easy to pass from one to another. When many of the public and private E-mail carriers are interconnected, subscribers will need only one mailbox to receive messages from any system. The one selected will be dictated by price and service, not by the size of the service.

MCI Mail offers low prices and reliability is generally good. The network offers the financial databases of the Dow Jones News/Retrieval service available as a menu option, but there are no other similar services offered.

CompuServe offers basic messaging, and specializes in online information services. MCI Mail also offers less than EasyLink's FYI and InFact services and ITT's Dialcom service.

The X.400 Recommendation

Most electronic mail systems will be interconnected using the X.400 recommendation of the CCITT. Work on a directory standard is needed before it can interconnect most systems. GTE's Telemail service in the United States is connected through a partial X.400 gateway to the Envoy 100 network operated by Telecom Canada. Envoy 100 and Telemail subscribers send messages between the United States and Canada as an option beyond normal services. An X.75 gateway is provided by GTE

Telenet to Canada's Datapac network, and Envoy 100 appears as a host system on Datapac.

A potential drawback of this type of interconnection is the need for a common directory of the two systems' subscribers and addresses. This requires an addressing standard to run on the X.400 network.

MCI Mail has its complete directory on-line, making partial addresses easy to find. EasyLink, which is available through Tymnet, has both a printed and an online directory, and Western Union prints the Telex/TWX/EasyLink telephone book.

There is a need for a single mailbox that can be used by multiple carriers, which would eliminate the need for users to check several sources for messages. The concept of such a unified messaging service could be based on the Unix operating systems, and would have to support the international message handling systems (MHS) standards. AT&T has its message transport architecture, which is ASCII-based, while MHS is binary.

In the United States, every carrier competes with every other carrier for customers, while in other countries there are nearly always monopoly services. In the United States, therefore, there are competitive reasons to keep other carriers from access to subscribers, rather than interconnecting. In other countries, interconnections with other national systems do not reduce the competitive advantage. ITT Dialcom already has interconnections with systems in Canada, Australia, South Korea, Puerto Rico, Singapore, Britain, Hong Kong, Denmark, The Netherlands, The Republic of Ireland, New Zealand, Japan, and West Germany. Because these countries use the X.400 standard, any carrier can theoretically interconnect, but ITT will have an advantage.

Another trend is the growth of offnet delivery services, such as General Electric Information Services Company's (GEISCO) Quikgram, which is an overnight delivery extension to the Quikware electronic mail service. GEISCO prints out the message on stationery with the customer's logo on the letter and envelope, and the U.S. Postal Service does the actual delivery. The service allows customers to create, store, and update mailing lists so that a letter can be sent to all or some names on the lists.

This service is similar to Western Union's Mailgram service. Both services use uppercase text only, and regular postal employees deliver the message. In the future, letter-quality service will allow users more control over the format of the document.

GEISCO is also providing interfaces to in-house E-mail systems, such as IBM's PROFS, Digital Equipment Corporation's ALL-In-1, and IBM's DISOSS systems. Almost half of all in-house, E-mail systems use one of these implementations.

Wang Information Services Corporation is licensing GEISCO's Quick-Comm service for a portable terminal with a printer and modem. This system is designed for mobile employees, such as salespeople. The terminal weighs only six pounds, and it can be used as both a remote printer and an electronic typewriter. It has 24-character display, and the printer operates at 16 characters per second using a 24 × 18 dot matrix of pins. Thermal paper, or plain paper with a thermal ribbon, are required.

The terminal uses a 14.3K RAM, and holds about nine pages of text. The modem is a 300 bps Bell 103 compatible unit. The terminal is priced at about $600.

Video Teleconferencing

Video teleconferencing allows the users at two or more facilities to have real-time, interactive, visual contact. Typically, the images that are transmitted consist of graphics, slides, or speakers. If the movement of the image can be limited, bandwidth compression techniques can be used while still achieving sufficient resolution.

Most video teleconferencing services use digital encoding, bit-rate reduction, and digital transmission to achieve lower costs. Bit rates range from 1.5 to 6.3 Mbps. AT&T's Picturephone Meeting Service has used rates from 1.5 to 3 Mbps. This service is part of the high-speed switched digital service (HSSDS) offered by AT&T between major cities. Similar video teleconferencing services are offered by other carriers, using satellite and terrestrial networks.

Standards for video teleconferencing have been based on video broadcasting standards, such as those established by the National Television Systems Committee. The trends in video are expected to result in lower bit rates (for lower costs), a single international standard, and the integration of video with voice and data signals.

Satellite Business Systems offers its Video Network Services (VNS), which is a video teleconferencing service that provides full-motion, television-quality broadcast video via satellite using a point-to-multipoint configuration. Their earlier Videolink service digitized the video signal and used data compression techniques, but did not provide full-motion video. The newer service transmits an analog video signal. Videolink also used only point-to-point company-owned meeting rooms in major U.S. cities.

VNS allows large companies to disseminate information to geographically dispersed locations almost simultaneously. It uses small aperture earth stations, in the range of 1.8 to 2.8 meters, and customers are able to download software programs to personal computers, but it does not allow interactive data communications. Audio is the only type of signal that VNS can return from a remote site to the original point of broadcast, and this is done using terrestrial, not satellite, communication. The technology to offer two-way data communications via satellite is available, but costs need to be reduced.

Interactive satellite data communications networks will probably be based on advanced high-speed data communications techniques which combine both data processing and telecommunications technologies. While 19.2 Kbps is being used as the data transmission speed for these small-aperture earth stations, future systems will use T1 technology at speeds up to 1.544 Mbps. T1 speeds allow small-aperture earth stations to be used virtually at any site, because they eliminate the terrestrial tails of a satellite network that result in increased data transmission errors.

Cable television (CATV) and direct broadcast by satellite (DBS) are common in the United States and Europe. The transmission of video signals for television is expected to remain analog for the near future, but two-way cable television, based on digital transmission, is already in use. Subscribers are provided with a low-speed digital connection for these interactive services in addition to the normal one-way video channels.

THE INTEGRATED SERVICES DIGITAL NETWORK

The evolution of the switched telephone network and the growth digital communications has resulted in the emergence of the concept known as the integrated services digital network (ISDN). The concept is based in the belief that end-to-end digital connectivity allows a wide range of integrated voice and nonvoice services.

ISDN can use the current integrated digital networks (IDN) that employ 64 Kbps switched systems. Services can include voice, data, facsimile, teletext, and videotext. The CCITT has been active in defining and standardizing the ISDN concept. The complete transition from existing networks to a comprehensive ISDN is expected to take place over the next 10-20 years.

As shown in Fig. 10-1, the ISDN concept uses two basic types of communication channels, the B channel at 64 Kbps for the transmission of digital voice and data and the D channel at 16 Kbps for out-of-band signaling to support the B channel services. Without video services, two B channels and a D channel are required for a total of 144 Kbps. Adding more B channels allows higher speeds, and moves the D channel up to 64 Kbps.

The weak link in most applications is the local loop, which consists primarily of metallic two-wire cable. Several techniques can be used to

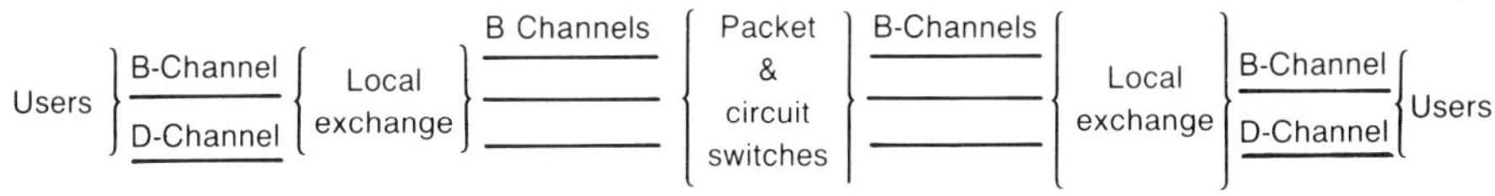

Fig. 10-1. ISDN.

provide full-duplex digital transmission over these two-wire loops. One of these is time-compressed multiplexing (TCM). In this scheme, the loop is shared between the two transmission paths by transmitting bursts of data in each direction at a rate somewhat higher than twice the nominal rate. TCM has sufficient bandwidth for all services except video. In the United States, a 56 Kbps circuit-switched digital capability (CSDC) has been used with TCM for the local loop, and IDN for the long-haul link.

CATV networks using coaxial cable offer video services independent of ISDN plans. Subscriber demand for switched video service or two-way video, as well as the use of low-cost, high-bandwidth fiberoptics, will be important factors in the emergence of video into ISDN. ISDN in the United States will also be influenced by the new competitive market caused by the government deregulation of telecommunication services. Several ISDNs are likely to emerge from competing services. Standards for interfacing these networks will be necessary for a national ISDN. In other countries, national telecommunication organizations have already developed standards for ISDN.

The CCITT I series recommendations from the 1984 CCITT Plenary Assembly deal exclusively with ISDN. Specific performance parameters that have been addressed are availability and error performance (Rec. G.821), and slip rate performance (Rec. G.822). These parameters apply to voice and data services, with either circuit switching or packet switching. The major difficulties lie in prescribing the proper transmission performance allocations for the wide variety of services and bit rates envisioned by ISDN.

Integrated System Architectures

An example of an integrated system architecture is Cyber Digital's MSX, which is an integrated voice/data system that allows users to access data systems without the use of modems. Dissimilar asynchronous devices communicate with each other through automatic data flow control and protocol conversions.

The system supports asynchronous devices at speeds up to 19.2 Kbps and synchronous devices up to 64 Kbps in a circuit-switched mode. Asynchronous packet-switched data is supported in the X.25 format. The basic configuration is a star-topology local area network, as shown in Fig. 10-2.

A proprietary, distributed microprocessor design is used with parallel processing. The architecture is based on six types of printed circuit boards:

- A main processor unit (MPU).
- A time switch unit (TSU).
- An integrated service terminal (IST).
- A T1 interface unit (T1-U).
- A voice interface unit (VIU).
- A data voice unit (DVU).

The MPU uses an 8086, 16-bit microprocessor and addresses two megabytes of onboard dynamic RAM storage. The basic software occupies about one megabyte of memory. The MPU originates the 12.8 Mbps packet/data bus, and provides the required interface, real-time clock, error detection and correction, and an RS-232-C interface for a service terminal.

The TSU uses a Z-80, 8-bit microprocessor to control the 32.7 Mbps circuit bus, providing 512 TDM, 64 Kbps circuits for trunks, voice, and data. The TSU also provides the system clock, tone generation, and digital conferencing.

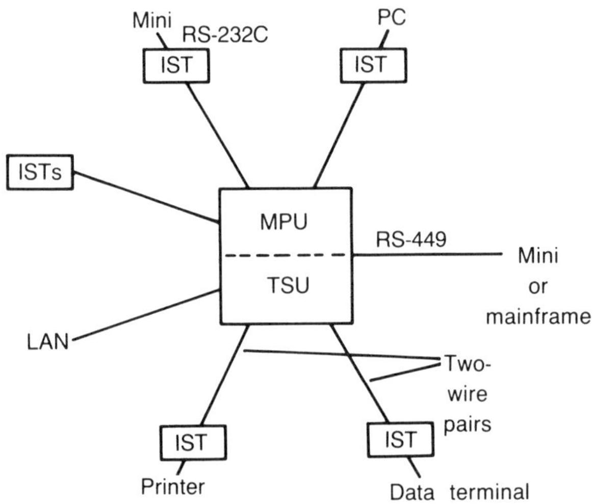

Fig. 10-2. An integrated system architecture.

The T1-U uses a Z-80, 8-bit microprocessor to support two 1.544 Mbps T1-D3 circuits providing 24 or 48 digital trunks. The T1-U provides a direct T1 connection to digital telephone central offices, fiber-optic, digital microwave, and digital satellite systems. The T1-U also provides one X.25 input/output port (DTE or DCE) with an RS-449 interface. The T1-U can be configured with software to use either 24 or 48 time slots, with 24 time slots per T1 trunk. The complete range of analog-telephone central-office trunking is supported using a D3 Channel Bank connected to one T1 circuit.

The VIU uses a Z-80, 8-bit microprocessor to provide a two-wire interface to standard analog telephone equipment. Each VIU supports 16 dual-tone multifrequency dialing (DTMF) or rotary dialing telephones, and requires 16 time slots.

The DVU uses a Z-80, 8-bit microprocessor to support eight ISTs. Each DVU port uses time-division multiplexing to support data, voice, and control signaling. A codec (encoding/decoding device) is located in each IST for digital voice transmission in a PCM format at 64 Kbps. Each DVU requires 16 time slots.

Software is stored on a floppy disk that is used in conjunction with a 10 megabyte Winchester disk. Redundant boards and disks can also be used and configured as required.

The system is non-blocking, with 36 hundred-call-seconds (CCS) of traffic for trunks or standard analog telephones, and 72 CCS of traffic for ISTs: 36 CCS voice and 36 CCS data.

Communications

The system uses a star-topology local area network to provide asynchronous and synchronous data, digitized voice, text, graphics, and messaging by employing store-and-forward modes over standard two-pair twisted wiring. HDLC (high level data link control) and MDPSK (modified differential phase shift keying) are used, and X.25 and T1 gateways are available.

Three data buses are used for transmitting digital information:

- A circuit bus, which is a 32.7 Mbps, 8-bit, time-division multiplexed bus with 512 time slots, of 64 Kbps for voice and data.
- A packet/data bus, which is a 12.8 Mbps, 8-bit, bidirectional bus that carries all control and signaling information, as well as up to 64 Kbps of packet-switched data in the X.25 format.
- A Shugart Associates Standard Interface (SASI) bus, which is an 8-bit, parallel, 10 Mbps bus to connect to the disk storage devices.

Asynchronous data to or from an IST or ISU is routed via the circuit or packet/data bus. An X.25 serial input/output port with an RS-449 interface is provided on each T1 interface unit (T1-U). The packet/data bus supports multiple X.25 ports using dynamic allocation of the total 64 Kbps bandwidth. Data can be submultiplexed over T1 channels or other digital trunks in 8 Kbps increments.

An integrated service terminal (IST), is a type of digital telephone having 12 or 20 push buttons. It is used with printed circuit board options such as asynchronous or synchronous data option boards with RS-232-C or RS-449 connectors. Other options include an LCD display, and each IST is an intelligent terminal with its own microprocessor and memory.

The software allows routine administration through user-friendly English-language commands with prompts and help functions. The system can continue to operate without service degradation when faults occur through the use of redundant elements. Costs range from $200 to $700 per line, depending on the features and options required.

DIGITAL TRANSMISSION TECHNOLOGY

The future of digital transmission in telecommunication networks depends largely on cost considerations. Digital transmission for voice and video requires a greater bandwidth, and often a greater cost, compared to analog transmission techniques. Two factors are expected to change this situation. One is the more widespread use of fiber-optic cables, and the other is the development of more efficient coding schemes for analog signals. In the local area and short-haul environments, digital radio and fiber optics will become more competitive with metallic cable systems. In long-haul applications, fiber optics and digital radio will become more competitive with satellite transmission. Costs are independent of distance with satellite transmission, so for very long-haul applications, satellite transmission will remain the least expensive.

The use of digital transmission techniques in satellite systems, such as digital speech interpolation (DSI) and time-division multiple access (TDMA) will make these systems even more cost-effective compared to analog transmission techniques. Terrestrial systems are characterized by costs that are directly dependent on distance and right-of-way requirements. They have a longer system life and a greater transmission capacity than satellites, however. Submarine cables using fiber optics might be more cost-effective than satellite transmission in the future.

Digital Speech

The present standard for digital speech in telephone networks is PCM at 64 Kbps. When transmission costs are high or bandwidth is limited, as in long-haul terrestrial networks or satellite links, reduced-rate coding for speech allows more channels. The bit rate for speech can be 32 or 16 Kbps, or lower. Encrypted voice typically operates at rates of 16 Kbps and less, using modems over the switched telephone network.

Local loops often use low bit rates for speech, because of the limited bandwidth available in existing metallic cables. The bandwidth is even more constrained if digital speech and data are provided simultaneously, as in ISDN.

Any replacement for 64 Kbps PCM in public switched networks must provide:

- A speech quality comparable to PCM.
- The capability to maintain speech quality with multiple conversions.
- The ability to handle other signals, such as voice-band data.

New standards will probably use 32 Kbps, and one of the following schemes:

- Adaptive differential PCM (ADPCM).
- An adaptive delta modulation (ADM).
- Nearly instantaneous companding (NIC).

The performance of ADPCM improves over that of PCM for transmission line error rates of 10^{-4} and higher. The voice-band data performance at rates up to 2.4 Kbps (CCITT V.26 modems) is similar for PCM and ADPCM. Voice-band data at 4.8 Kbps (CCITT V.27 modems) can be acceptable, but is degradated compared to 64 Kbps PCM. Higher than this, it becomes unacceptable. Dual-tone multifrequency (DTMF) signaling and Group 2 facsimile is satisfactory with 32 Kbps ADPCM.

Lower rates, such as 16 Kbps, can be used for more limited speech networks, especially those that are controlled and private. Coding techniques for 16 Kbps include adaptive predictive coding (APC), subband coding (SBC), and adaptive transform coding (ATC).

The Digital Access and Cross-Connect System (DACS) is designed for use in digital telephone networks. It is capable of terminating up to 128 DS-1 signals and providing digital connections to any 64 Kbps channel. It eliminates the need for digital/analog and analog/digital conversion of channels, and allows direct digital rerouting, and dropping and inserting using electronic switching.

The switching can be initiated with a standard terminal, or remotely, with a data link. DACS combines multiplexing, network control, and testing in a manner which greatly reduces digital network operation and maintenance. Future plans include the wider national networking of DACS and the addition of a 2.048 Mbps capability for international gateways.

Fiber Optics

Advances in fiber optics are expected to continue. In a single decade, the fiber optics industry has gone through three generations of technology:

- The first-generation systems used multimode fibers and short-wavelength sources of 850 nm.
- The second-generation systems used graded-index fibers at wavelengths of 1300 nm.
- The third-generation systems use single-mode fibers and wavelengths of 1300 and 1500 nm.

AT&T began field trials with fiber optics in Atlanta in 1976 and Chicago in 1977, with systems of 45 Mbps. AT&T also began using a fiber-optic link in 1983 between New York and Washington, D.C. This was the first part of the Northeast Corridor FT3C 90 Mbps system, which was completed in 1984, and links Boston, Massachusetts and Richmond, Virginia, with a total length of 776 miles. Other intercity fiber-optic routes will use third-generation technology with 432 Mbps.

Other carriers, such as MCI, are installing fiber-optic cables along railroad right-of-ways. Some of these will be single-mode fibers, operating at a bit rate of 405 Mbps with planned expansion to 1 Gbps. Other 400 Mbps and 565 Mbps systems have been installed in the United Kingdom and Japan. Future systems are likely to use single-mode fibers operating at rates of 565 Mbps and higher.

In the future, transoceanic cables will use optical fibers rather than coaxial cable. The TAT-8, which will link North America with Europe, is made up of six single-mode fibers, four active and two backup, with automatic switching. A transmission rate of 274 Mbps is planned which will provide four times the capacity of its predecessor, the TAT-7, which used copper coaxial cable. Fiber-optic submarine cable systems are also planned to link Japan and the United States.

Advances in fiber-optic communications will occur in the following areas:

- New processes for manufacturing optical fibers, resulting in lower costs and improved properties.

- Integrated optical circuits, which combine the transmitter and receiver functions.
- Longer wavelength sources of 1500 nm or higher, for lower losses.
- Single-mode fibers with higher data rates, for longer transmission distances.
- Wavelength-division multiplexing, for increased data transfer.
- Power transmission over fibers, using techniques such as infrared radiation.

Digital Radio

In the past, digital radio was characterized by transmission rates of 90 Mbps or less, and routes were limited to a few hundred miles. Long-haul costs were high compared to analog radio, which employs techniques such as single sideband which is bandwidth-efficient.

Recent digital terminal equipment, such as multiplexers, are economical, and the cost of a digital transmission system is usually less compared to an analog transmission system for short distances. Digital radio is used in the United States and Japan for intercity applications. Digital switches, such as AT&T's No. 4 ESS, can be used with digital radio in these applications.

The growth of digital radio is due to the rapid spread of digital cable systems. Both T-carrier types and fiber optics can be easily interconnected via digital radio.

The future in digital radio will include improvements in spectral efficiency, multipath fading at high transmission rates, and reliability. A spectral efficiency of 4.5 bps/Hz has been achieved with 64 QAM, resulting in upgraded service in the United States and Canada.

Other coding and modulation techniques might also become popular, such as the Ungerboeck codes for higher bandwidth efficiency. These modulation or coding schemes must be able to perform in the presence of multipath fading and other forms of degradation. New types of adaptive equalizers, such as those that use transversal equalization, can allow transmission rates of 100 Mbps. Improved reliability can occur with the replacement of TWTs with solid-state devices.

Digital Multiplexing

In telephone networks, reduced rates are possible using multiplexers and existing digital transmission facilities, including T-carrier, fiber optics, and digital radio to increase the channel capacity. Using 32 Kbps coding, multiplexers allow up to 48 voice channels in 1.544 Mbps or 60 voice channels in 2.048 Mbps. These units interface directly with PCM multiplexers, and use transcoding to digitally convert from PCM to the 32 Kbps code.

Digital speech interpolation (DSI) is another form of multiplexing used to compress the bit rate for speech transmission. Two PCM multiplexed signals are compressed into a single 1.544 Mbps or 2.048 Mbps transmission signal. Improved speech compression is possible with variable-rate ADPCM. The variable coding rate limits the degradation that can occur under heavy traffic.

Other improvements necessary for ISDN standards include upgrading to 64 Kbps and phasing out bipolar coding on T-carrier systems. The bipolar scheme places constraints on the density of ones, because at least a single one is required every eight bits. This affects the available data rate. The use of bipolar with eight-zero substitution (B8ZS) eliminates this problem, and provides a cleaner 64 Kbps channel for ISDN.

EXTENDED FRAMING FORMAT

The extended framing format extends the multiframe structure from 12 to 24 frames, and redefines the 8 Kbps framing overhead in 1.544 Mbps PCM multiplex equipment (Bell DS-1 and CCITT Rec. G.733). A comparison of the DS-1 framing format and the extended framing format is shown in Table 10-2.

The 8 Kbps overhead channel uses three separate patterns:

- The 2 Kbps framing relies on the framing bit of every fourth frame to form the 2 Kbps pattern 001011—001011. This pattern is used to provide the frame and multiframe synchronization. Frame synchronization identifies each 64 Kbps PCM channel of each frame, and multiframe synchronization locates the frame.
- A 2 Kbps cyclic redundancy check (CRC) is contained within the framing bit position of frames 2, 6, 10, 14, 18, and 22 of each multiframe. Check bits in the CRC are used to detect errors in the extended multiframe. The CRC can be used for end-to-end performance monitoring, false-framing protection, protection switching, automatic restoration after alarms, line verification, and the measurement of error-free seconds.
- A 4 Kbps data link begins with the first frame of every multiframe; every other 193rd bit is part of the 4 Kbps data link. Using the X.25 level-2 protocol, the data link can be used for the transmission of alarms, status, supervisory signals, network configuration, performance, and maintenance testing.

PACKET SWITCHING

Packet-switching services in the United States are expected to grow

Table 10-2. A Comparison of the Extended Framing Format with the DS-1 Format.

	Extended Frame Format, F (Framing Bits)				DS-1 Format (Framing Bits)		
Frame Number	Framing	Data	Error Detection	Signaling Channel	Frame Synch.	Multiframe Synch.	Signaling Channel
2	-	-	CB		0	-	
3	-	D	-		-	0	
4	0	-	-		0	-	
5	-	D	-		-	1	
6	-	-	CB	A	1	-	A
7	-	D	-		-	0	
8	0	-	-		1	-	
9	-	D	-		-	1	
10	-	-	CB		1	-	
11	-	D	-		-	0	
12	1	-	-	B	0	-	B
13	-	D	-		-	1	
14	-	-	CB		0	-	
15	-	D	-		-	0	
16	0	-	-		0	1	
17	-	D	-		-	1	
18	-	-	CB	C	1	-	A
19	-	D	-		-	0	
20	1	-	-		1	-	
21	-	D	-		-	1	
22	-	-	CB		1	-	
23	-	D	-		-	0	
24	1	-	-	D	0	-	B

tenfold by the mid 1990s. Due to user demand for data, image, text and voice services, much of the future growth in data transmission will be absorbed by packet services, rather than through the increased use of leased-line data networks.

The actual quantity of data transmitted is growing much faster than the overall costs of transmission. This is due to several factors:

- Rapid increases in data transmission speeds in both SNA leased networks and ASCII transmission.
- The transfer of heavy traffic customers to packet switching, which allows ten times the traffic for the same cost.
- Improvements in data communications protocols.

During the next decade, a major transfer of data traffic into leased wideband facilities such as T1 and packet-switched facilities, from leased voice-grade networks will occur. SNA is expected to be upgraded for improved X.25 and T1 transmission. The trend in upgrading to faster modems, multiplexers, packet nodes, and other hardware in order to reduce spending on leased transmission channels will continue.

The growth in X.25 hardware will continue, both in the U.S. and internationally. The X.25 market is expected to be close to one billion dollars per year by 1990, with many specialized products.

Packet network facilities such as Tymnet are becoming more accessible with X.25-to-X.75 gateways. Connections between local telephone companies and international packet-switching networks can allow a local call to get to public database and messaging services. The public systems available through the Tymnet link includes CompuServe, Western Union EasyLink, MCI Mail, NewsNet, Dialog, the Official Airlines Guide, and Dow Jones News/Retrieval.

There are several requirements for database and electronic mail services in the home sector:

- A low-cost type of data transport is needed.
- A low-cost data terminal must be available.
- There must be a variety of useful and low-cost services available.

The first requirement depends on the number and location of packet switches and PADs so a connection can be available as a local call. The second requirement is taking place in the personal computer marketplace. There are many information services, which are at present dominated by business usage. This is expected to increase as more businesses analyze the price of packet-switching network access versus the price of leased lines.

Much of the present situation is due to the environment. The local telephone company monopoly still controls most of the end-user economic viewpoint of the public voice network, including leased lines and packet switching, which are regulated. This could change with a few tariff reductions.

Most voice calls average four minutes each, while data connections average 15 minutes. Without packet systems, data communications could soon overload the voice network. Most future intra-state to local packet networks will be in the form of X.75 gateway connections.

REVIEW EXERCISES

1. Discuss the factors contributing to the growth of telecommunication networks.
2. What is a major factor in the growth of electronic mail?

3. What features will be provided by advanced electronic mail systems?

4. What is the advantage behind the ISDN concept? How can ISDN be implemented over metallic pairs?

5. What characteristics are important in digital speech transmission?

6. What advances in fiber-optic transmission are expected?

7. Describe the extended framing format.

8. What factors will affect the growth of packet switching?

Glossary

ABR—Automatic baud rate detection. The receiving device automatically senses the baud rate of an incoming message, and sets its own baud rate accordingly.

ACK—A transmission control character transmitted by a receiver as an affirmative response (acknowledgment) to the sender.

acknowledgment—A response sent to indicate receipt of a particular message or portion (block) of a message.

acoustic coupler—A device that converts electrical signals into audio signals, enabling data to be transmitted over the public telephone network via a conventional telephone handset.

adaptive equalization—A process in a receiver in which received symbols are used to continuously update the settings of a filter used for equalization.

address—A coded representation of the origin or destination of data.

aliasing distortion—The error in reconstructing a sampled analog signal when the signal is sampled at a rate that is less than twice the signal bandwidth. Also called *foldover distortion*.

ALOHA network—A radio-linked local area network developed at the University of Hawaii.

alternate mark inversion coding—A bipolar line coding scheme in which spaces are encoded as zero signal levels and marks are encoded as nonzero levels which alternate between positive and negative for successive marks.

American National Standards Institute—ANSI. An organization concerned with standardization in areas of commerce and technology, such as electronics, data processing, and communications.

American Standard Code for Information Interchange—ASCII. A popular standard seven-bit data code supported by ANSI.

American Wire Gage—A standardized system for the specification of wire sizes.

amplitude dispersion—See *dispersion*.

amplitude distortion—Distortion in a transmission system caused by nonuniform gain or attenuation with respect to frequency. Also called *attenuation distortion*.

amplitude modulation—A modulation scheme in which the amplitude of a constant-frequency sinusoidal carrier is varied as a function of the baseband signal.

amplitude-shift keying—A form of amplitude modulation in which the amplitude of the carrier must assume one of several discrete levels.

analog loopback—A loopback procedure in which a device's analog transmission is looped back to its analog receive input. Local analog loopback can be used to the local modem; remote analog loopback tests the modem and transmission line. See *loopback*.

analog transmission—A transmission using varying, continuous waveforms to represent information, values of which must be interpreted by the receiver, which estimates the values by approximation.

angle modulation—A general category of modulation techniques which includes both phase modulation and frequency modulation.

anomalous propagation—A propagation condition that results from abnormal changes with altitude in the atmospheric index of refraction.

applications layer—The portion of the ISO/OSI model that is concerned with the interface between the applications software and the presentation layer.

ARPA—Advanced Research Projects Agency of the Department of Defense.

ARPANET—One of the earliest of the packet-switched networks; developed and funded by ARPA.

ARQ—Automatic request for repetition. The ARQ character sequence allows for automatic retransmission in the event of an error.

ASCII—American Standard Code for Information Interchange. Pronounced "askee." This is a seven-bit-plus-parity code supported by ANSI to allow compatibility between data services.

asynchronous data transmission—An operating mode in which there is no intentional bit synchronization between the transmitting and receiving devices. Start-stop operation is the most common form of asynchronous transmission, where start and stop bits are used to indicate the beginning and end of each character.

asynchronous transmission—A transmission mode in which each character is individually synchronized using start and stop elements. The time intervals between transmitted characters can be of unequal length.

attenuation—A reduction in the strength or power of a signal.

auto-answer—The ability of a device such as a modem to answer an incoming call automatically.

autodial—The ability of a modem to originate and dial an outgoing call without a telephone. The call can be initiated remotely, by keystrokes at a terminal or by a computer.

auto log-on—The ability of an autodial modem to cycle through a handshaking procedure with a remote computer automatically.

balanced transmission—A method for the transmission of baseband data in which each signal circuit consists of a pair of conductors, and the signal consists of a differential voltage between the two conductors. The voltage with respect to ground on one conductor of the pair will be mirrored or balanced by a voltage of equal magnitude of opposite polarity on the other conductor.

band splitter—A multiplexer designed to split the available bandwidth into several independent narrower band subchannels, each suitable for data transmission at a fraction of the total channel data rate.

bandwidth—The range of frequencies that can pass over a given circuit. Usually, the greater the bandwidth, the more information can be sent through the circuit in a given amount of time.

bandwidth-distance product—The product of bandwidth and distance which is used to specify a limit on a transmission media such as an optical fiber's bandwidth and repeater spacing.

baseband—A signalling technique in which the signal is transmitted in its original form, not changed by modulation.

baseband data—The normal or unmodulated form of a data signal as generated by digital circuits.

baseband LAN—A local area network which transfers data in baseband form only. This is in contrast to broadband LANs, which handle modulated data signals.

baud—The unit or symbol rate in modulation. Corresponds to a rate of one symbol or unit interval per second.

Baudot—A data transmission code in which five bits represent one character.

Baudot code—A term used to refer to any of several similar five-bit data codes commonly used in older teletype equipment. These codes are actually very different from the five-bit codes developed by Baudot for the British Post Office telegraph system in 1874.

BCC—Block check character. The result of a transmission verification algorithm accumulated over a transmission block, and normally appended at the end. See *CRC, LRC.*

BEL—A control character used when there is a need to use an alarm or attention device.

Bell 103—A family of 300 bps FSK modem standards developed by the Bell System. These, along with compatible models, have become the 300 bps modems in most widespread use today.

Bell 113—Same as Bell 103, but provides originate-or-answer capability only.

Bell 201—A family of 2400 bps four-level DPSK modem standards developed by the Bell System.

Bell 202—A family of FSK modem standards developed by the Bell System. These modems operate at 1200 bps on dial-up lines, at 1400 bps on leased lines with C1 conditioning, and at 1800 bps on leased lines with C2 conditioning.

Bell 208—A family of 4800 bps eight-level PSK modem standards developed by the Bell System.

Bell 209A—A 9600 bps modem standard developed by the Bell System. This modem uses a combination of PSK and ASK called *quadrature amplitude modulation.*

Bell 212A—A 1200 bps four-level PSK modem standard developed by the Bell System. This modem can also operate in a 300 bps mode which is compatible with the Bell 103 standard.

Bell 43401—A Bell publication which defines requirements for data transmission over limited-distance dc-continuous private metallic circuits supplied by the telephone company.

BERT—Bit Error Rate Testor or test.

bias distortion—A condition in which there is a significant difference between the nominally equal lengths of received marks and spaces.

binary synchronous communication—BSC/BISYNC. A half-duplex, character-oriented synchronous data communications protocol originated by IBM in the 1960s.

biphase coding—A line coding scheme in which a one is represented as a high-to-low signal transition occurring in the middle of the bit cell, while a zero is represented as a low-to-high transition. This is also referred to as *Manchester II coding.*

bipolar—A pseudoternary signal, conveying binary digits, in which successive marks are of alternate polarity (positive and negative) but equal in amplitude, and in which spaces are of zero amplitude. Also called *alternate mark inversion.*

bipolar coding—Line coding schemes which involve both positive and negative voltages referenced to ground. This is in contrast to unipolar coding, which uses either all-positive or all-negative voltages.

bipolar N-zero substitution—BNZS. A form of bipolar transmission in which all strings of N zeros are replaced with a special N bit sequence of bipolar violations.

bipolar violation—A mark that has the same polarity as the previous mark in the transmission of bipolar signals.

Bisync—See *binary synchronous communication.*

bit—A binary digit; the basic unit of digital communication. A positive voltage bit indicates a zero; a negative voltage bit, one.

bit count integrity—Refers to the preservation of the precise number of bits (or characters or frames) that originated in a message or unit of time.

bit error rate—The ratio of the number of bits incorrectly received to the total number of bits transmitted.

bit interleaving—A method of time-division multiplexing in which each channel is assigned a time slot corresponding to a single bit.

bit-oriented protocol—A type of data-link control protocol that does not use control characters. The data need not even be in character form, because its nature is completely transparent to the data-link control protocol.

bit stuffing—See *pulse stuffing.*

block check character—Refers to a character appended to a message or transmission block for the purpose of error detection.

block mode—A mode in data transmission where the data keyed in by a terminal is stored until a particular key (usually send) is pressed, then all the data is sent as a block.

block parity—An error-detection scheme in which codes such as LRC and VRC are used together to permit the precise location of a single bit error within a block of data.

bps—Bits per second. The unit of data transmission rate.

bridge—Equipment which allows the interconnection of LANs, allowing communication between devices on separate networks using similar protocols.

bridge tap—In a telephone line local loop, a length of unused wire attached to one of the conductors (usually from an unused connection) that affects the characteristics of the line.

broadband LAN—A LAN in which use of the links is shared through frequency-division.

BS—Backspace. A format effector which moves the active position one character backward on the same line.

BTF—Bulk transfer facility; a file transfer protocol developed by a group at ETH Zurich.

buffer—A storage device used to compensate for a difference in the rate of data flow or timing when transmitting data from one device to another.

buffered timing—A form of timing used with independent clocks in which buffers compensate for the differences in clock rates between pieces of equipment.

bulk encryption—The process in which two or more channels of a telecommunications system are encrypted by a single unit of crypto-equipment.

bunched frame structure—A TDM frame structure in which the frame alignment signal occupies contiguous bit positions. Also called *burst frame structure.*

burst error—An error condition in which a number of contiguous or closely spaced bits all become corrupted.

burst frame structure—See *bunched frame structure.*

bus—One or more conductors used for transmitting signals, data, or power. A bus normally provides a common connection between several locations.

bus topology—A LAN architecture in which the output drivers and input receivers of every node are connected directly to a linear bus.

busy token—A unique bit pattern used in token-passing access control schemes to indicate that a data packet or message immediately follows.

byte—A binary element string operated upon as a unit and usually shorter than a computer word. Eight-bit bytes are most common. Also called a *character.*

CAN—Cancel. A character indicating that the data preceding it is in error, and should be ignored.

carrier—A wave suitable for modulation by an information-bearing signal which is to be transmitted over a communication system.

carrier detect—An RS-232 interface modem signal that indicates to the attached terminal that the modem is receiving a signal from the remote modem. Same as *received line signal detector.*

carrier-sense multiple access with collision detection—An access control scheme in which each station monitors the transmission medium for the presence of a carrier signal from another location. If none is detected, the station can begin transmitting its message, while simultaneously monitoring the channel to ensure that the message does not collide with messages from other stations that might have begun transmitting at approximately the same time. Upon detection of a collision, all transmitting stations cease transmission, wait for a random length time interval, and then—if the channel is available—retransmit the aborted message. By requiring each station to wait for a random time interval before attempting to retransmit, one station will usually begin before the other(s), and they will sense the busy channel and postpone their own retransmission attempts, thus minimizing the probability of repeated collisions.

catenate—To join two strings of text together end-to-end.

CCITT—Consultative Committee for International Telegraphy and Telephony. An international consultative committee that sets international communications standards.

CCITT V.21—International recommendation defining standards for modems operating asynchronously to 200 or 300 bps, full-duplex, on the dial network. Similar to *Bell 103.*

CCITT V.22—International recommendation defining standards for modems operating synchronously (with asynchronous terminal interface) at 1200 bps, full-duplex, on the dial network. Similar to *Bell 212.*

CCITT V.23—International recommendation defining standards for modems operating asynchronously at 600 bps or 1200 bps, half-duplex on the dial network and full-duplex on a leased four-wire line. Similar to *Bell 202.*

CCITT V.24—International recommendation defining interchange circuits between data communications and data terminal equipment. Similar to, and operationally compatible with, EIA *RS-232C.*

CCITT V.26—International recommendation defining standards for modems operating synchronously at 2400 bps, half-duplex on the dial network and full-duplex on a leased four-wire line. Similar to *Bell 201.*

CCITT V.27—International recommendation defining standards for modems operating synchronously at 4800 bps, half-duplex on the dial network and full-duplex on a leased four-wire line. Similar to *Bell 208.*

CCITT V.28—International recommendation defining electrical characteristics for interchange circuits defined in CCITT V.24. Similar to, and operationally compatible with, EIA *RS-232C.*

CCITT V.29—International recommendation defining standards for modems operating synchronously at 9600 bps, full-duplex, on a leased four-wire line. Similar to *Bell 209.*

CCITT X.25—International recommendation defining a standard communication protocol for access to a packet switching network.

cesium clock—An atomic clock using the cesium element to produce a stable, accurate timing source.

channel—A single path provided from a transmission medium either by physical separation (multipair cable) or by electrical separation (frequency or time-division multiplexing).

channel vocoder—A vocoder in which the vocal tract filter, is estimated by samples taken in contiguous frequency bands within the speech signal.

character—A symbol, such as a letter or number, used to express information; expressed as a series of digital bits including start and stop bits.

character interleaving—A method of time-division multiplexing in which each channel is assigned a time slot corresponding to a single character. Also called *word interleaving.*

character-oriented protocol—A data-link control protocol that uses special characters to frame the data characters and to control their exchange between communicating stations.

character parity—An error-detection scheme in which an extra bit is added to each character. The value of the extra bit is set so that the total number of one-bits in each character is either always even or always odd.

Cheapernet—A CSMA/CD local area networking system similar to Ethernet, but which uses less expensive cabling in exchange for a smaller maximum network size.

cipher text—The apparently random text that results from encrypting a message.

circuit—The electrical path between two endpoints over which one-way or two-way communications can be provided.

circuit-switched routing—A communications technique in which a circuit connection between the communicating parties is established and maintained for the duration of the conversation or data exchange. Packet switching and message switching are alternative techniques.

clipping—In speech interpolation, the loss of speech segments due to overload or delay in speech detection. Also see *overloading.*

clock—Equipment for providing a time base used in a transmission system to control the timing of functions such as the duration of signal elements or sampling.

closed system—A microcomputer system in which direct access to the system bus is not provided. Thus, the user is prevented from adding expansion cards and special interfaces to the basic computer. All peripherals must be connected through I/O ports provided by the manufacturer. The Apple Macintosh is an example of a closed system.

cluster—A terminal configuration in which two or more terminals are connected to a single line or single modem.

coax—Coaxial cable consisting of a central conductor surrounded by insulation and covered by a wire mesh or metal sheathing.

coaxial cable—A metallic communications cable consisting of an inner conductor surrounded by and insulated from a concentric outer conductor.

coded mark inversion—A two-level code in which binary zero is coded so that both amplitude levels are attained within the bit duration, each for half the interval. Binary one is coded by either of the amplitude levels for the full bit duration in such a way that the levels alternate with each occurrence of a one.

codirectional timing—A form of timing for synchronous transmission in which the timing is provided along with data by the data terminal equipment.

coherent detection—Detection using a reference signal that is synchronized in frequency and phase to the transmitted signal. Also called *synchronous detection.*

collision detection—CD. The ability of a transmitting node to detect simultaneous transmission attempts on a shared medium.

Comite' Consultatif Internationale de Telegraphique et Telephonique—A committee of the International Telegraph Union (ITU) concerned with standardization in data communications. The name of this committee is often anglicized as the "Consultative Committee in International Telegraphy and Telephony."

companding—The process of compressing a signal at the transmitter and expanding it at the receiver to allow signals with a large dynamic range to be sent through a device with a more limited range.

composite link—The line or circuit connecting a pair of multiplexers or concentrators; the circuit carrying multiplexed data.

composite signal—The data signal on the trunk side of a multiplexer. This signal is a combination or composite of a number of individual user data signals that have been combined by the multiplexer.

concatenate—Synonymous with *catenate.*

concentrator—A device used to divide a data channel into two or more channels of lower than average speed, dynamically allocating the channel space according to demand in order to maximize the throughput. Also called a *statistical multiplexer.*

conditioned diphase—A two-level code in which diphase is applied to a conditioned NRZ signal.

conditioned line—A privately owned or leased telephone circuit which has been tuned to improve its performance for data communications applications.

conditioned NRZ—A two-level nonreturn-to-zero code in which the presence or absence of a level change is used to signal a binary number.

conditioning—A special treatment of voice-band data circuits provided by telephone companies. AT&T provides, for example, C-type conditioning, which controls phase and amplitude distortion, and D-type conditioning to limit noise and harmonic distortion.

console—The part of a computer used for communication between the operator and the CPU.

constant carrier—A condition in a modem where the Data Carrier Detect (pin 8) is held high, regardless of whether a carrier signal is present or not.

contention—The conflict that arises when two or more data sources simultaneously attempt to put data onto the same physical medium. This will cause the loss of data if not detected, and can cause damage to driver and receiver circuits if they are not designed to withstand the increased voltage or current levels that can occur.

continuously variable slope delta modulation—CVSD. A type of delta modulation in which the size of the steps of the approximated signal is progressively increased or decreased to make the approximated signal closely match the input analog wave.

contradirectional timing—A form of timing for synchronous transmission in which the timing of the data terminal equipment is slaved to the timing from the data circuit terminating equipment.

conversational mode—A mode in data transmission where a device talks to another device character-by-character, as opposed to block mode, where blocks of data are used.

correlative coding—See *partial response.*

CPU—Central processing unit. The portion of a computer that directs the sequence of opcrations and initiates the proper commands to the computer for execution.

CR—Carriage return. A format effector that moves the active position to the first character position of the same line.

CRC—Cylical redundancy check. A method of checking the accuracy of a block of data. The sending device calculates a number based on each bit in a block and sends it at the end of the block. The receiving device performs the same calculation and sends back an ACK if it gets the same number, or an NACK, if it does not.

CRC-12—A twelve-bit cyclic redundancy checking scheme which uses $X^{12} + X^{11} + X^3 + X + 1$ as the generator polynomial.

CRC-16—A 16-bit cyclic redundancy checking scheme which uses $X^{16} + X^{12} + X^5 + 1$ as the generator polynomial.

CRC-CCITT—A 16-bit cyclic redundancy checking scheme which uses $X^{16} + X^{12} + X + 1$ as the generator polynomial.

crosstalk—The interference that occurs when a signal transmitted on one circuit or channel of a transmission system creates an undesired effect in another circuit or channel.

cryptographic equipment—Scrambling devices based on digital logic for encrypting communications.

CSMA—Carrier-sense multiple access. A contention technique which allows multiple stations to gain access to a single channel.

CSMA/CD—Carrier-sense multiple access with collision detection. A contention technique which allows multiple stations to successfully share a broadcast channel by avoiding contention via carrier sense and deference, managing collisions via collision detection and packet retransmission. See *CSMA* and *collision detection.*

CSU—Channel service unit for DDS.

CTS—Clear to send. A modem interface control signal from data communication equipment (DCE) that indicates to the data terminal equipment (DTE) that it may begin data transmission.

current loop—A method of interconnecting terminals and transmitting signals, where a mark (binary one) is represented by a current on the line and a space (binary zero) is represented by the absence of current.

cyclic redundancy checking—An error-detection scheme which treats an N-bit message as an Nth order polynomial, and divides it by a generator polynomial to produce a quotient and a remainder. This remainder is then appended to the message and transmitted. At the receiver, another remainder is computed from the received data bits and compared to the received remainder. If errors have occurred during transmission, the two remainder values will not agree.

DAA—Data access arrangement. Data communications equipment furnished or approved by a common carrier, permitting attachment of privately owned data terminal and data communications equipment to the common carrier network, normally the dial network.

DAP—Data access protocol. A file transfer protocol developed by Digital Equipment Corporation (DEC).

data above voice—A hybrid transmission scheme that places a data signal above the voice spectrum in a cable or radio system. Also called *data over voice.*

data bits—The bits in an asynchronous character that are actually data. In ASCII, there are typically seven data bits. There is also a start bit, one or two stop bits, and perhaps a parity bit.

data circuit-terminating equipment—DCE. The interfacing equipment sometimes required to couple the data terminal equipment (DTE) into a transmission circuit or channel and from a transmission circuit or channel into the DTE.

data code—The scheme for using various bit patterns to represent alphabetic, numeric, punctuation, and control characters.

data communications equipment—As used in EIA RS-232-C and related documents, this normally refers to modems or other equipment fulfilling a similar role. *Data circuit-terminating equipment* is a more specific terminology which has essentially the same meaning.

data compression—A means of representing data in a more compact form, with fewer bits, in order to save storage space or transmission time. Redundancies are removed, but no information is lost. After retrieval or reception of the compressed data, it can be expanded back into its original uncompressed form.

data encryption standard—DES. A standardized technique for encrypting data which is supported by the National Bureau of Standards for use throughout the commercial realm and nondefense areas of the government.

datagram—A packet that includes a complete destination address specification, which is usually provided by the user, along with the data it carries. It is a one-way construction much like a telegram.

data in voice—A hybrid transmission scheme that places a data signal in the middle of the voice spectrum in a cable or radio system.

data integrity—A performance measure based on the rate of undetected errors.

data link control layer—The second layer of the ISO-OSI model. This layer is concerned with the establishment of an active link between stations, control of byte synchronization, block framing, error detection and correction, and the regulation of the data flow rate over the link.

data over voice—See *data above voice.*

dataphone—A trademark of AT&T and the Bell System which identifies the data sets or modems manufactured and supplied for use in the transmission of data over the regular telephone network.

Dataphone Digital Service—DDS. A communications service of the Bell System in which data is transmitted in digital rather than analog form, eliminating the need for modems.

dataset—A Bell System term which is synonymous with *modem.*

data terminal equipment—DTE. Equipment consisting of digital devices that convert the user information into data signals for transmission or reconvert the received data signals into user information.

data transparency—An environment provided by a data-link control protocol in which any arbitrary sequence of data bits can be sent without interfering with normal link operation. Data transparency is required when the data to be transmitted might contain bit sequences which could be interpreted as communications control characters. In character-oriented protocols, transparency can be provided by means of escape sequences or fixed-length frame structures.

data under voice—A hybrid transmission scheme that places a data signal under the voice spectrum in a cable or radio system.

dBm—Power level in decibels relative to one milliwatt.

dBm0—Power level in dBm referred to or measured at a point of zero relative level.

DBU—Dial back-up unit.

DC—Device Control. A category of control characters primarily used for turning on or off a subordinate device.

DCD—Data Carrier Detect. An RS-232 signal to a device connected to a modem that indicates the modem is receiving a signal. Usually carried on pin 8.

DCE—Data communications equipment. The equipment that provides the functions required to establish, maintain, and terminate a data transmission connection.

DDCMP—Digital Data Communications Message Protocol. A byte-oriented synchronous protocol developed by Digital Equipment Corporation that supports half-duplex or full-duplex modes, and either point-to-point or multipoint lines in a DNA (Digital Network Architecture) network.

DDD—Direct distance dialing. The switched dial-up network. See *PSTN.*

DDS—Dataphone Digital Service. A communication service of the Bell System in which data is transmitted in digital form so modems are not required.

decision feedback equalizer—An equalizer that uses a feedback loopback operating on the detector outputs to cancel intersymbol interference due to previous symbols.

dedicated circuit—A circuit designated for exclusive use by two users.

delay distortion—The distortion of a waveform made up of two or more different frequencies, caused by the difference in arrival time of each frequency at the output of the transmission system.

Delta modulation—A form of DPCM in which the magnitude of the difference between the predicted value and the actual value is encoded by one bit only, where only the sign of that difference is detected and transmitted.

dial network—A network that is shared among many users, any one of whom can establish communication between desired points using a dial or push-button telephone.

dial-up—The use of the standard telephone network (PSTN) by dialing.

dibit—A data element which contains two bits.

differential phase-shift keying—DPSK. A method of phase-shift keying in which each symbol is a change in the phase of the carrier with respect to its previous phase angle.

differential pulse code modulation—DPCM. A process in which a signal is sampled, and the difference between the actual value of each sample and its predicted value (as derived from previous samples) is quantized and converted, by encoding, to a digital signal.

digital channel bank—Refers to PCM multiplexer equipment used in the North American digital hierarchy.

digital speech interpolation—DSI. A form of digital multiplexing for voice that uses speech interpolation.

digital termination system—A form of local loop or local distribution in which digital radio is used to connect users to a long-haul communication network.

DIP—Dual in-line package. An electronic component package characterized by two rows of external connecting pins which are inserted into the holes of the printed circuit board.

diphase—A two-level code generated by the modulo-2 addition of an NRZ signal with its associated clock signal.

DIP switch—A dual in-line package housing a group of small adjacent switches designed to be mounted on a PC board.

direct access adaptor—See *DAA*.

direct distance dialing—DDD. A telephone service which enables the telephone user to call other subscribers outside the local area without operator assistance.

dispersion—The spreading, separation, or scattering of a waveform during transmission. Also called *amplitude dispersion.*

distortion—Any departure from a specified input/output relationship over a range of frequencies, amplitudes, or phase shifts during a time interval.

distributed frame structure—A TDM frame structure in which the frame alignment signal occupies noncontiguous bit positions.

doppler—A shift in the observed frequence of a signal caused by variations in the path length between the source and the point of observation.

double sideband signal—A signal which contains both the upper and lower sidebands produced by the modulation process. This is in contrast to single sideband or vestigial sideband, in which one of the sidebands is either completely or partially removed.

drift—An undesirable progressive change in frequency with time. Also called *frequency drift* or *wander.*

DSR—Data set ready. A modem interface control signal from the DCE which indicates to the attached terminal equipment that the modem is connected to the telephone circuit.

DSU—Data service unit, in DDS.

DTE—Data terminal equipment. Equipment acting as data source, data sink, or both.

DTMF—Dual-tone multifrequency; ordinary tone dial.

DTR—Data Terminal Ready. A modem interface control signal from the data terminal, indicating to the modem that the terminal is ready for transmission.

dual-tone multifrequency signaling—The generic name for the tone signaling method used on push-button or Touchtone telephones.

dumb terminal—A terminal that has no processing capability.

duobinary—A three-level coding scheme that uses controlled amounts of intersymbol interference to achieve transmission.

duplex—A type of transmission that affords simultaneous operation in both directions.

EBCDIC—Extended binary-coded decimal interchange code. An eight-bit character code used primarily in IBM equipment.

echoplex—A method of checking data transmission accuracy, where the received data characters are returned to the sending end for comparison with the original data.

echo suppression—A technique used by telephone companies to ensure that speakers will not have to listen to an echo of their own words returned by the coupling between the remote ends of the receive ad transmit paths. A speech detector in the outbound path causes an attenuator to be switched into the inbound path whenever outbound speech is present.

effective earth radius—The radius of a hypothetical earth for which the distance to the radio horizon, for rectilinear propagation, is the same as that for the actual earth assuming a uniform vertical gradient refractive index.

elastic buffer—A storage device designed to accept data timed by one clock and deliver it timed by another clock.

Electronic Industries Association—EIA. An organization of companies involved in the electronics industry. The EIA establishes standards such as RS-232-C and RS-449.

EM—End of medium. A control character used to identify the physical end of data recorded on a medium.

emulate—To imitate a computer system using a combination of hardware and software that allows programs written for one computer to run on another.

encoder—A device that generates a code, usually consisting of binary numbers, to represent individual characters or signal samples.

encryption—A means of securing data by transforming it into what appears to be a random sequence of characters.

ENQ—End of enquiry. A transmission control character used as a request from a remote station.

envelope delay—The amount of delay experienced by the various frequency components of a signal when traversing a communications channel. Also known as *group delay*.

envelope delay distortion—In a given passband of a device or a transmission facility, the maximum difference of the group delay time between any two specified frequencies. Also called *group delay distortion.*

envelope detection—A form of demodulation in which detection is based on the presence or absence of the signal envelope.

EOT—End of transmission. A transmission control character used to indicate the conclusion of the transmission of one or more text strings.

EPSS—Experimental Packet-Switched System. A packet-switched network developed by the British Post Office.

equalization—The process of reducing frequency distortion and/or phase distortion of a circuit by the addition of networks to compensate for the difference in attenuation and/or time delay of the various frequencies in the transmission band.

error-free blocks—A measure of error performance based on the percentage or probability of data blocks that are error-free.

error-free seconds—A measure of error performance based on the percentage or probability of seconds that are error-free.

ESC—Escape. A control character used to provide additional control functions. It alters the meaning of a limited number of contiguously following bit combinations.

ETB—End of transmission block. A transmission control character used to indicate the end of a block of data.

ETH—Eidgenossishe Technische Hochscule, Zurich.

Ethernet—A baseband local area network specification developed jointly by Digital Equipment Corporation, Xerox and Intel to interconnect computer equipment using coaxial cable and transceivers.

ETX—End of text. A transmission control character which terminates a text string.

exponential delta modulator—A type of delta modulator that uses an RC circuit as an integrator to provide an exponential response to a constant input.

extended binary-coded decimal interchange code—EBCDIC. A data code developed by IBM. In most newer systems, ASCII has replaced the use of EBCDIC.

extended framing format—A framing format for 1.544 Mbps digital channel banks introduced by AT&T.

external reference synchronization—A form of network synchronization in which the timing or frequency reference is obtained from a source external to the communication network.

eye pattern—An oscilloscope display of a digital signal used to examine performance.

fade margin—The amount by which a received signal level can be reduced without causing the system or channel output to fall below a specified threshold.

fading—The variation, with time, of the intensity and/or relative phase of any frequency component of a received signal due to changes in the characteristics of the propagation path with time.

failure—The inability of an item to perform its required function.

failure rate—The average rate at which failures can be expected to occur throughout the useful life of an item.

falltime—The time it takes for the falling edge of a pulse-type signal to decrease from 90 percent to full scale to 10 percent of full scale.

FAP—File access protocol. A file transfer protocol that allows parts of a file to be transferred. Also used as a generic term for the transfer portion of an FTP.

far-end crosstalk—FEXT. Crosstalk that is propagated in a disturbed channel in the same direction as the propagation of a signal in the disturbing channel. The receiving terminals of the disturbed channel and the energized terminals of the disturbing channel are usually remote from each other.

FCC—Federal Communication Commission.

FCC Rules Part 68—The section of FCC rules concerned with data-access arrangements.

FDX—Full-duplex.

FE—Format effectors. A category of control characters mainly used for the control of the layout and positioning of information on printing and/or display devices.

FF—Form feed. A format effector which advances the active position to the same character position on a pre-determined line on the next form or page.

fiberoptics—A technology that uses light as an information carrier. Fiber-optic cables act as light guides, and are a direct replacement for conventional coaxial cable and wire pairs. The glass-based transmission occupies less physical volume for an equivalent transmission capacity, and the fibers are immune to normal electrical interference.

Figures Shift—FIGS. A physical shift in a terminal using Baudot code which enables the printing of number, symbols, or uppercase characters.

firmware—A computer program or software stored permanently in PROM or ROM or semi-permanently in EPROM.

flat fading—Fading in which all frequency components of the received radio signal vary in the same propagation simultaneously.

flooding—A routing scheme in tree topology LANs in which each intermediate node repeats each received message onto all of its outbound branch links.

flow control—The control of incoming data to a buffer or similar device, which stops the data before the buffer overflows. It can involve a signal, such as an x-off character, to stop the transmitting device.

FMP—File maintenance protocol. A generic term for some of the higher-level functions of an FTP, such as directory management and renaming.

foldover distortion—See *aliasing distortion.*

formant vocoder—A vocoder in which the vocal tract filter is estimated by the frequencies and amplitude of the spectral peaks, or formants.

Fourier series—Refers to a mathematical technique for computing the frequency spectrum of a periodic signal.

Fourier transform—A mathematical technique for computing the frequency spectrum of a time-limited periodic signal.

fractional frequency difference—The algebraic difference between two normalized frequencies. Also called *relative frequency difference* or *normalized frequency difference.*

frame—A set of consecutive time slots in which the position of each slot can be identified by referring to a frame alignment signal. The frame alignment signal does not necessarily occur in each frame.

frame acquisition mode—A mode of operation in TDM frame synchronization in which the frame alignment signal is detected. Also called *frame search mode.*

frame acquisition time—The time that elapses between a valid frame alignment signal being available at the receiver terminal equipment and the frame alignment being established. Also called *frame alignment recovery time.*

frame alignment—The state in which the frame of the receiving equipment is correctly phased with respect to that of the received signal.

frame maintenance mode—A mode of operation in TDM frame synchronization in which the frame alignment signal, after detection, is continuously monitored to ensure that frame alignment is maintained.

frame reacquisition time—The time that elapses between a loss of frame synchronization and the recovery of the frame alignment signal.

frame search mode—See *frame acquisition mode.*

free-space loss—The signal attenuation that would result if all obstructing, scattering, or reflecting influences were sufficiently removed such that they would have no effect on propagation.

frequency—The number of cycles per second at which an analog signal occurs, usually expressed in hertz (Hz). One hertz is one cycle per second.

frequency accuracy—The degree of conformity to a specified value of frequency.

frequency deviation—In frequency modulation, the peak difference between the instantaneous frequency of the modulated wave and the carrier frequency of the modulated wave.

frequency diversity—A method of radio transmission used to minimize the effects of fading, where the same information signal is transmitted and received simultaneously on two or more independent carrier frequencies.

frequency division multiplexer—A device that divides the available transmission frequency range into narrower bands, each of which is used for a separate channel.

frequency drift—See *drift.*

frequency-selective fading—Fading in which not all frequency components of the received radio signal vary simultaneously.

frequency-shift keying—FSK. A method of frequency modulation in which frequency is made to vary at significant times by smooth as well as abrupt transitions. Typically a one-bit is represented as one frequency, and a zero as another frequency. Also called *frequency-shift signaling.*

Fresnel zones—A cigar-shaped shell of circular cross-section surrounding the direct path between a transmitter and a receiver. For the first Fresnel zone, the distance from the transmitter to any point on this shell and on to the receiver is one half-wavelength longer than the direct path. For the second Fresnel zone, it is two half-wavelengths, and for the third it is three half-wavelengths.

FS—File separator. A control character used to separate and qualify data logically. It normally delimits the data items known as files.

FTP—File transfer protocol. A network protocol for moving files from one host to another.

full-duplex—Simultaneous, two-way, independent transmission in both directions.

fully connected mesh—A network topology in which every node has a direct connection to every other node.

gateway—A special node that interfaces two or more dissimilar networks, providing protocol translation between the networks. Also used to describe the hardware and software used to provide this node.

generator polynomial—In CRC schemes, the polynomial which is divided into the message polynomial to produce the quotient and remainder.

graded-index fiber—An optical fiber which has a refractive index that gets progressively higher toward the center, causing light rays to be continually refocused inward.

ground—An electrical connection to the earth.

ground start—A telephone signaling method where a station determines that a circuit is ground at the other end.

group—In frequency-division multiplexing, a number of voice channels (generally 12) occupying a 48 kHz frequency band.

group delay—See *envelope delay.*

GS—Group separator. A control character used to separate and qualify data logically. It normally delimits the data items known as groups.

half-duplex—Transmission in either direction, but not both directions simultaneously.

half-duplex circuit—In North American usage, a half-duplex circuit is capable of transmitting in either direction, but only in a single direction at one time. As defined by the International

Telecommunications Unions, a half-duplex circuit is inherently capable of full-duplex operation, but is restricted to transmitting in one direction at a time due to the limitations of the terminal equipment.

handshaking—The exchange of predetermined signals between two devices for purposes of control.

HDLC—High-level data link control. The International Standards Organization physical link protocol. Various manufacturers have their own form of HDLC, the most common of which is IBM's SDLC (synchronous data link control).

header—The control information prefixed in a message text, such as the source or destination address, sequence number, or message length or type.

hertz—Hz. A measure of frequency or bandwidth in cycles per second.

hexadecimal number system—The number system with the base of sixteen. In hexadecimal, the first nine digits are 0-9 and the last six digits are represented by the letters A-F.

high-density bipolar N—HDBN. A form of bipolar transmission that limits the number of consecutive zeros to N by replacing the (N + 1)th zero with bipolar violation.

high-information delta modulation—A form of delta modulation in which the step size is doubled for consecutively identical bits at the coder output, and halved for consecutively opposite bits at the coder output.

host—The main or central computer which supports a number of terminals communicating with it. In the case of a large mainframe with a number of remote terminals, the host-terminal relationship is clear. In the case of several personal computers connected via modems and a telephone circuit, it is less obvious which computer is the host and which is the terminal. The distinction will depend on the specific role that each takes in executing the communications protocol being used.

HT—Horizontal tabulation. A format effector which advances the active position to the next pre-determined character position on the same line.

Huffman coding—A type of data coding scheme used to achieve data compression by using short code words to represent frequently used characters, and longer code words to represent rarer ones.

hybrid transmission—A type of transmission that carries FDM voice and digital data on the same medium.

IEEE-488—Institute of Electrical and Electronic Engineers-488. An IEEE standard parallel interface bus consisting of eight bidirectional data lines, eight control lines, and eight signal grounds, which provides connections to IEEE-488 devices.

IEEE-802—Standards for the interconnection of local area networking computer equipment. The IEEE-802 standard deals with the physical and link layers of the ISO Reference Model for OSI.

IFIP—International Federation for Information Processing.

in-band signaling—Telephone system signaling which is transmitted over the same path and within the same frequency band used for the voice signal.

independent clock synchronization—A form of network synchronization based on the use of clocks that are independently timed or constrained within certain limits of accuracy.

in-service testing—A form of testing in which operational traffic is not interrupted.

instantaneous companding—A form of companding used in delta modulation in which changes in step size are made at a rate equal to the sampling rate.

integrated digital network—IDN. A network in which connections established by digital switching are used for the transmission of digital signals.

integrated services digital network—ISDN. An integrated digital network in which the same digital switches and digital paths are used to establish connection for different services, such as telephone and data.

intelligent terminal—A terminal that can do some data processing on its own, separately from the host computer.

interleave—To send blocks of data alternately to two or more stations on a multipoint system, or to put bits or characters alternately into the time slots in a time-division multiplexer.

intermodal dispersion—See *multimode dispersion.*

interrupt—A mechanism by which elements of a computer system can request service from the central processor. Often, this is more efficient than a polled approach, in which the CPU must periodically interrogate each element to inquire whether or not it requires service.

intersymbol interference—The extraneous energy from the signal in one or more signaling intervals that tends to interfere with the reception of the signal in another signaling interval.

intramodal dispersion—See *material dispersion.*

INWG—International Network Working Group, IFIP Working Group 6.1.

IS—Information separator. A class of control characters used to separate and qualify data logically. Specific characters are defined for different applications.

ISO—International Standards Organization.

ISO 3309—The international standard which defines the procedural elements used in the HDLC bit-oriented data-link control protocol.

ISO 4335—The international standard which defines the procedural elements used in the HDLC bit-oriented data-link control protocol.

ISO 6159—The international standard which defines the procedural elements to be used in unbalanced operating configurations.

ISO 6256—The international standard which defines the procedural elements to be used in balanced operating configurations.

isochronous communications—Communications in which the transmitter and the distant receiver use data clocks which have the same nominal rate, but are not truly synchronous.

isochronous TDM—Time-division multiplexing in which the individual user terminals each generate their own clock. These clocks are not mutually synchronized, but they are running at the same nominal rate. The isochronous multiplexers must provide some buffering and rate smoothing to compensate for the slight differences in the user clock rates.

ITB—Intermediate block character. A transmission control character that terminates an intermediate block. A block check character (BCC) usually follows. Use of ITBs allows for error checking of relatively small transmission blocks.

ITI—Interactive Terminal Interface. A Telenet product.

jitter—The short-term variations of the parts of a digital signal from their ideal positions in time.

jumbogroup—In frequency-division multiplexing, a number of voice channels (generally 3600) composed of six mastergroups.

jumper—A patch cable between two circuits.

justification—See *pulse stuffing.*

Kbps—One thousand bits per second.

k-factor—The ratio of effective to true earth radius.

KSR—Keyboard-send-receive. A printer with a keyboard that can send as well as receive data.

leased line—A private telephone line leased from the phone company.

leased line service—Dedicated telephone circuits that can be leased from the telephone company on a monthly basis. Leased lines offer an advantage over the regular switched-line service in that they can be specially selected and conditioned to optimize them for data transmission.

LED—Light-emitting diode. A semiconductor light source that emits visible light or invisible infrared radiation.

LF—Line feed. A format effector which advances the active position to the same character position of the next line.

linear predictive coding—A voice code technique based on the prediction of speed samples from a linear weighted sum of previously measured samples.

line conditioning—Extra cost options on private telephone lines to allow higher speed or higher quality data transmission than an ordinary 3002 line.

line driver—A signal converter which conditions a digital signal to ensure transmission over an extended distance.

line-of-sight—Radio propagation in the atmosphere along a path that is unobstructed by the earth or opaque objects.

line turnaround—The reversing of transmission direction from sender to receiver or from receiver to sender when using a half-duplex circuit.

loaded line—A telephone line equipped with loading coils to add inductance in order to minimize amplitude distortion.

loading coil—An induction device used in telephone local loops over 1800 feet long that compensates for wire capacitance and boosts voice grade frequency.

loading factor—In a quantizer, the ratio of peak to rms amplitude for the input signal.

local area network—LAN. A network that is in a localized geographical area, such as an office, building, or complex of buildings. LAN communications technology provides a medium through which many nodes can be connected.

local line, local loop—A channel connecting the subscriber's equipment to the line terminating equipment in the central office. Usually consists of a metallic circuit using either two-wire or four-wire cable.

longitudinal parity—An error detection scheme in which an extra character is added to each block of data. The value of each bit in this character is set so that the total number of one-bits in each bit position is either always even or always odd.

loopback—A procedure for testing modems in which a transmission is sent back to the originating modem and compared to determine if the modem is transmitting and/or receiving the data correctly. See *analog loopback* and *digital loopback.*

lowpass filter—A circuit which attenuates high frequency signals more than low frequency signals.

LRC—Longitudinal redundancy check. An error detection scheme where the check character consists of bits calculated on the basis of odd and even parity of the characters in the block.

Manchester coding—A line coding scheme in which a one is represented as a high-to-low signal transition occurring in the middle of the bit cell, while a zero is represented as a low-to-high transition. This is also called *biphase coding.*

mark—The presence of a signal. In telegraph communications, a mark represents the closed condition or current flowing. A mark impulse is equivalent to a binary one.

marking distortion—A bias distortion in which received marks appear longer than received spaces.

mastergroup—In frequency-division multiplexing, a number of voice channels, typically 300 or 600, consisting of five or ten supergroups.

master-slave synchronization—A form of network synchronization in which a master clock is distributed and used to control other clocks, devices, or nodes.

material dispersion—In an optical fiber, the dispersion caused by the variation in propagation velocity with the wavelength of light. Also called *intramodal dispersion.*

mean time between failure—MTBF. For a specific interval, the ratio of total operating time to the number of failures in the same interval.

mean time between outages—MTBO. For a specific interval, the ratio of total operating time to the number of outages in the same interval.

mean time to repair—MTTR. The total corrective maintenance time divided by the total number of corrective maintenance actions during a given period of time.

mean time to service restoral—MTSR. The mean time to restore service following system failures that result in a service outage. The time to restore includes all time from the occurrence of the failure until the restoral of service.

medium—A substance regarded as the means of signal transmission.

message switching—A technique in which a complete data message is transmitted to a switching center, where it is stored until the necessary links become available to forward the message to either its final destination or to the next switching center.

microbending—Refers to minute curvatures in an optical fiber caused by external forces. Because the principle of total internal reflection is not fully satisfied at such bends, additional loss in the fiber is introduced.

midpoint equalization—A combination of postequalization and preequalization used at intermediate points in a circuit.

minimum-shift keying—MSK. A type of digital modulation that uses offset QPSK with sinusoidal pulse shaping. Also, a special case of FSK in which continuous phase is maintained at symbol transitions using a minimum difference in signaling frequencies.

modem—A contraction of modulator/demodulator. The term is commonly used when the modulator and the demodulator are associated in the same signal-conversion unit.

modem eliminator—A device which interfaces between a local terminal that normally requires a modem. It functions as an imitation modem in both directions.

modified duobinary—A form of duobinary coding whose spectral shape has no dc component.

modulation—The process of varying certain characteristics of a carrier in accordance with a message signal.

modulation index—In FSK, the ratio of the frequency deviation of the modulated signal to the bandwidth of the modulating signal.

modulator—A device that performs modulation.

multiframe—A set of consecutive frames in which the position of each frame can be identified by reference to a frame alignment signal.

multimode dispersion—In an optical fiber, the dispersion resulting from the different arrival times of optical rays that follow different paths. Also called *intermodal dispersion.*

multimode fiber—A fiber that supports propagation of more than one mode at a given wavelength.

multipath fading—The fading that results when signals reach a receiving antenna by two or more paths.

multiplexer—A device used for the division of a transmission facility into two or more subchannels, either by splitting the frequency band into narrower bands (frequency division), or by allotting a common channel to several different transmitting devices, one at a time (time division).

multipoint line—A single communications line or circuit interconnecting several stations. The use of this type of line usually requires some kind of polling mechanism to address each terminal with a unique address code.

mutual synchronization—A network synchronizing arrangement in which each clock in the network exerts some degree of control on all others.

NAK—Negative acknowledgment. A transmission control character transmitted by a receiver as a negative response to the sender.

narrowband coder—A voice coder with a transmission rate that can be accommodated by 3-kHz telephone channels using modems.

narrowband FSK—A form of FSK in which the modulation index is much less than one.

near-end crosstalk—NEXT. Crosstalk that is propagated in a channel in the direction opposite to the direction of propagation of the circuit. The receiving terminals of the disturbed channel and the energized terminals of the disturbing channel are usually near each other in the circuit.

negative pulse stuffing—In time-division multiplexing, the controlled deletion of bits from channel inputs so that the rates of the individual channel inputs correspond to a rate determined by the multiplex equipment. The deleted information is transmitted via a separate overhead channel.

NETRJE—Network remote-job entry protocol, in ARPANET.

NETRJS—Network remote-job entry service developed by UCLA for ARPANET.

network—A series of nodes connected by communications channels.

network interface controller—A communications device that allows the interconnection of information processing devices to a network.

network layer—The portion of the ISO-OSI model which is concerned with the routing of data from the source terminal to the destination terminal.

network service—An application available on a network, such as file transfer.

NEXT coupling loss—For near-end crosstalk, the ratio of power in the disturbing circuit to the induced power in the disturbed circuit.

NJCL—Network Job Control Language.

node—A station.

noncoherent detection—Any form of detection that does not require a phase reference.

nonreturn-to-zero—NRZ. A two-level code in which each level is held for the duration of a signal interval.

nonvolatile—In a device, the ability to retain parameters if power is interrupted. This can be accomplished by a backup battery, which keeps the circuitry energized.

normalized frequency—The ratio between the actual frequency and its nominal value.

NRZ—Nonreturn-to-zero pulse code. Pulses in alternating directions for successive one-bits with no change from existing bias for zero-bits.

null modem—A device that connects two DTE devices directly by emulating the physical connections of a DCE device.

numerical aperture—NA. A number that expresses the light-gathering characteristics of an optical fiber, expressed by the sine of the maximum angle (with respect to the fiber axis) at which an entering ray will experience total internal reflection.

NVT—Network virtual terminal.

NWG—Network Working Group; a committee drawn from members of ARPANET which designed the higher-level protocols for ARPANET.

Nyquist bandwidth—As first described by Nyquist, the minimum channel bandwidth required for transmission without intersymbol interference.

Nyquist rate—As described by Nyquist, the sampling rate (equal to twice the signal bandwidth) that permits the samples of a signal to completely determine the signal waveform.

offset quadrature phase-shift keying—OQPSK. A form of QPSK in which the in-phase and quadrature bit streams are offset in time by one bit period.

on-off keying—A form of modulation which involves switching the carrier off and on in a pattern corresponding to the sequence of data bits.

open system—A computer system which provides direct access to the system bus, permitting the owner/user to add expansion cards and special interfaces to the basic computer. The IBM PC is an example of an open system.

optical fiber—A thin cylinder having a central core of one transparent material of high refractive index surrounded with a cladding of another transparent material of lower refractive index.

OSA—Open System Architecture. The reference model developed by ISO.

outage—A condition in which a user is deprived of service due to failure in the communication system.

out-band signaling—Telephone system signaling which is transmitted outside of the frequency band used for the voice signal.

out-of-service testing—A form of testing in which operational traffic is interrupted and replaced by a test pattern.

overhead—That part of a transmission that is not data, such as control, handshaking, parity, or synchronization characters.

overhead bit—A bit other than a data bit, check bit, framing bit, or parity bit.

overloading—The error introduced in quantization when the input signal amplitude exceeds the allowed amplitude range of the quantizer. Also called *clipping.*

PABX—Private Automatic Branch Exchange. An automatic exchange installed on the users premises that allows the transmission of calls to and from the public telephone network.

packet—A group of binary digits, including data and call control signals, which is transmitted as a whole. The packet information is arranged in a specific format.

packet radio—A digital radio designed to handle multiple users who share a common high-speed channel and transmit data in bursts called *packets.*

packet switching—A switching technique in which data traffic is broken up into short groups of approximately 100 to 2000 bits each. These packets are then sent using store-and-forward techniques.

PAD—Packet assembler/disassembler. An interface device that assembles and disassembles packets for a network.

parallel—A form of data transmission in which a line is used for each data bit or piece of information. These lines are usually sent simultaneously.

parallel interface—An interface which permits parallel transmission, or the simultaneous transmission of the bits making up a character or byte, over separate channels or different carrier frequencies of the same channel.

parallel transmission—A type of data transmission that allocates a data line for each bit in a word. The transmission is often unidirectional.

parity bit—A noninformation bit added to an asynchronous character or byte for error checking. In even parity, the parity bit is a mark or space used to make the count of marks in the character even. In odd parity, this total is odd.

parity check—The addition of noninformation bits to data, making the number of ones in a group either always odd or always even. This permits the detection of errors in blocks that have a single error.

partial response—A multilevel coding scheme that uses selected amounts of intersymbol interference to increase the transmission rate in a given bandwidth.

path profile—A graphic representation of a propagation path showing the objects that might cause obstruction or reflection.

PDTE—Packet-mode data terminating equipment. A DTE that generates packets, as opposed to characters.

phase delay—In the transfer of a single-frequency wave from one point to another in a system, the time delay of the part of the wave that identifies its phase.

phase modulation—A modulation method where a sine wave signal or carrier has its phase changed in accordance with the information to be transmitted.

phase-shift keying—PSK. A form of digital modulation in which discrete phases of the carrier are used to represent a digital signal.

physical layer—The portion of the ISO-OSI model which is concerned with defining the mechanical, electrical, functional, and procedural characteristics of the physical link between two communicating devices.

piezoelectric effect—An effect in certain materials, such as quartz, in which electrical energy causes vibration and, conversely, mechanical vibration induces electrical energy.

pixel—The smallest unit of a graphics or video display, the characteristics of which can be coded into an electrical signal.

plesiochronous—The relationship between two signals such that their corresponding significant instants or transitions occur at nominally the same rate, any variation in rate being constrained within a specified limit.

point-to-point—A connection between two, and only two, devices.

polar—A two-level signal using balanced, symmetric, positive and negative levels.

polling—A method of controlling multipoint lines in which each station on the line has a different address. The computer calls each address in sequence to see if it has data to send.

port—An interface on a computer configured as data terminal equipment and capable of attaching a device for communication with a remote data terminal.

positive pulse stuffing—In time-division multiplexing, the provision of a fixed number of dedicated time slots used to transmit either information from the individual channel inputs, or no information, according to the relative bit rates of the channel input and the TDM channel output signals.

positive-zero-negative pulse stuffing—A combination of positive and negative pulse stuffing, in which the two stuffing states are indicated by uniquely coded signals and the state of no stuffing is indicated by a third signal.

postequalization—The equalization of a circuit performed at the receiver.

power fading—A fading caused by anomalous propagation conditions characterized as slowly varying in time.

preequalization—The equalization of a circuit performed at the transmitter using a form of predistortion.

presentation layer—The portion of the ISO-OSI model concerned with providing the necessary services to interface a variety of applications to the communications system without requiring modifications to the applications software.

preset equalization—A form of automatic equalization where a test sequence is used to fix the settings of the equalizer.

private line—A telephone line owned or leased from the phone company for the exclusive use of the owner or leasee.

PI—Protocol interpreter.

PROM—Programmable read-only memory. A nonvolatile memory chip that allows a program to reside permanently in hardware.

protocol—A set of rules and conventions that allows the orderly and meaningful exchange of information between or among communicating parties. Both hardware protocols and software protocols can be defined.

protocol converter—A device for translating the data transmission code and/or the protocol of one network or device to the corresponding code or protocol of another network or device, allowing equipment with different conventions to communicate with one another.

pseudoerror detector—A BER estimation technique that uses modified decision regions in a separate decision circuit to degrade the receiver margin intentionally, and reduce the time required to estimate the BER.

pseudorandom sequence—A sequence of numbers or bits that exhibits properties of a random signal. Although it appears to lack a definite pattern, there is a sequence that repeats after some time interval.

PSTN—The public switched telephone network. The common dial network.

public key encryption—An encryption system which uses one key for encryption and a separate key for decryption. The encryption keys for a number of different users can be published in a public directory and used by anyone wishing to encrypt a message and send it to one of the listed users. Each user has a different decryption key which is kept private to insure that only the intended recipient can decrypt the message.

pulse-code modulation—A process in which a signal is sampled, and the magnitude of each sample is quantized independently of other samples and converted by encoding to a digital signal.

pulse stuffing—A process for changing the rate of a digital signal in a controlled manner such that it can be in accord with a rate different from its own inherent rate, usually without loss of information. Also called *bit stuffing* and *justification.*

pulse-stuffing jitter—The jitter caused by the removal of stuffed bits at the demultiplexer and the inability of a clock recovery circuit to eliminate completely the resulting gaps in the information signal.

quadbit—A symbol which contains four bits of information.

quadrature amplitude modulation—QAM. The independent amplitude modulation of two orthogonal channels using the same carrier frequency.

quadrature partial response—QPR. The use of partial response filtering on the two orthogonal channels of a QAM system to increase the bandwidth efficiency.

quadrature phase-shift keying—QPSK. A form of PSK in which four discrete phases, separated by 90 degrees, are used to represent two information bits per signaling interval.

quantization—A process in which the continuous range of values of a signal is divided into nonoverlapping, but not always equal, subranges. To each subrange, a discrete value of the output is uniquely assigned. When the signal value falls within a given subrange, the output has the corresponding discrete value.

quantization noise—An undesirable random signal caused by the error of approximation in a quantizing process.

quantizing distortion—The distortion resulting from the process of quantizing.

quartz clock—A clock fabricated from quartz crystal.

queue—A waiting line or area.

radio refractivity—One million times the amount by which the refractive index of the atmosphere exceeds unity.

raised-cosine filter—A filter with a specific characteristic that produces no intersymbol interference at the sample times of adjacent signaling intervals.

RAM—Random access memory. A semiconductor read-write volatile memory where the data stored is lost if power is removed.

raster—A scanning pattern used in generating graphic images on a screen.

received line signal detector—A modem interface signal defined in RS-232 which indicates to the attached data terminal equipment that it is receiving a signal from the distant modem.

receiver—A device that converts electrical or optical signals used for transmission back to information signals.

recurrence coding—A data compression technique in which the sending system replaces strings of three or more identical characters with a special sequence consisting of a special character, a character count, and one of the original characters.

redundancy check—A technique of error detection involving the transmission of additional data related to the basic data in such a way that the receiving terminal, by comparing the two sets of data, can determine to a certain degree of probability if an error has occurred in transmission.

relative frequency drift—The frequency drift divided by the nominal frequency value. Also called *normalized frequency drift.*

reliability—The probability that an item will perform its intended function for a specified interval under stated conditions.

remote station—Data terminal equipment in a distant location.

repeater—In local area networks, a device that increases the signal of a single LAN segment by joining it to another, so that packets sent on one segment can be repeated or copied onto the other, expanding the local environment.

response time—In communications, the elapsed time between the generation of the last character of a message at a terminal and the receipt of the first character of the reply. It includes terminal delay and network delay.

return-to-zero—RZ. A two-level code in which each level is held for a fraction, which is usually half, of the signaling interval, and then returned to a reference level for the remainder of the signaling interval.

RG-58—A specific type of coaxial cable having a nominal characteristic impedance of 50 ohms.

RG-59—A specific type of coaxial cable having a nominal characteristic impedance of 75 ohms.

ring indicator—A modem interface signal defined in RS-232 which indicates to the attached data terminal equipment that an incoming call is present.

ring interface unit—A device used in ring-topology LANs for interfacing a terminal to the ring. By using the properly designed ring interface unit, potentially unreliable terminals can be used without jeopardizing the entire network.

ringing—Refers to oscillations that occur after a level transition in a digital signal. Ringing is usually caused by an impedance mismatch or an improperly terminated signal line.

risetime—The time it takes for the rising edge of a pulse-type signal to increase from 10 percent of full scale to 90 percent of full scale.

RJ-11—An interface between the telephone line and a customer's device consisting of a modular six-wire plug and jack. The standard connection for a single line phone.

RJ-16—A six-wire jack for exclusion-key telephones. (USOC 502 or 2502). This jack is used with modems that do not incorporate voice-data switches. The exclusion key of the telephone is the voice data switching device. The modem plugs into the RJ-16 and the phone into an RS36 jack. The telephone company wires the two jacks together.

RJ-21—A 50-wire jack for up to 25 lines.

RJ-27—A programmable 50-wire jack for up to eight lines.

RJ-36—See *RJ-16.*

RJ-41—An eight-wire jack that has a fixed resistance, unless used with an exclusion key phone. It provides 8 dB attenuation to provide a maximum output of −4 dBm. When programmable with an exclusion key phone, it is programmed to the telephone company to provide optimum conditions at the central office.

RJ-45—An interface between the telephone line and customer's devices consisting of an eight-wire modular plug and jack. The RJ-41 is similar physically.

RJEP—Remote job-entry protocol.

RO—Read-only. A device with no transmission capability.

ROM—Read-only memory. A non-volatile semiconductor memory with a predefined data content, which is permanently stored.

RS-232-C—A specification published by the EIA that specifies the mechanical and electrical characteristics of the interface for connecting DTE and DCE. It defines interface circuit functions and their corresponding connector pin assignments. The standard applies to both asynchronous and synchronous, serial binary data transmission at speeds up to 20 Kbps in full or half-duplex mode. RS-232-C defines 20 specific functions. The physical connection between DTE and DCE is made through plug-in, 25-pin connectors. RS-232-C is functionally compatible with the CCITT Recommendation V.24.

RS-422—A standard operating in conjunction with RS-449 that specifies electrical characteristics for balanced circuits with their own ground leads.

RS-423—A standard operating in conjunction with RS-449 that specifies electrical characteristics for unbalanced circuits using common or shared grounding techniques.

RS-449—A general-purpose 37-pin and 9-pin interface for data terminal equipment and data circuit-terminating equipment employing serial binary data interchange.

RTS—Request to send. A physical modem interface control signal from DTE, requesting clearance to transmit.

rubidium clock—An atomic clock using the element rubidium to produce a stable, accurate timing source.

RVI—Reverse interrupt. A transmission control character transmitted by a receiving station to request termination of the current transmission because of a higher-priority message it must send.

satellite transmission—A transmission path in which the data is transmitted to a satellite and relayed back to the receiving unit. Because of the vast distances involved, satellite transmission involves delays up to 800 ms in receiving replies to handshaking signals, so modems have to have special options to work with satellites.

scintillation—In radio propagation, a random fluctuation of the received field about its mean value. The deviations usually are relatively small.

SDLC—Synchronous data link control. An IBM communications line discipline or protocol associated with SNA. SDLC provides for control of a single communications link or line, accommodates a number of network arrangements, and operates in half-duplex or full-duplex over private or switched facilities.

secondary channel—A logical channel using the same physical path as the main channel, but independent of it. It usually runs at a low data rate (150 bps), and is used for control signals on HDX systems.

secure voice—Refers to telephone communications that are protected through the use of an encryption system.

serial interface—An interface that requires serial transmission, or the transfer of information in which the bits composing a character are sent sequentially. It implies only a single transmission channel.

serial transmission—A method of data transmission in which each bit of information is sent sequentially on a single data channel.

server—A processor that provides a specific service to the network, such as the following processors: routing (which connects nodes and networks of like architectures), gateway (which connects nodes and networks of different architectures by performing protocol conversions), terminal, printer, and file servers, which provide an interface between compatible peripheral devices on a LAN.

session layer—The portion of the ISO-OSI model which is concerned with providing file management and bookkeeping functions needed to support intersystem communications.

settability—The degree to which frequency can be adjusted to correspond with a reference frequency.

short-haul modem—A signal converter which conditions a digital signal to ensure reliable transmission over continuous private-line metallic circuits.

signal constellation—The signal magnitudes and phases of a digital modulation scheme when displayed by a phasor diagram.

signal-to-distortion ratio—The ratio of the amplitude of the desired signal to the amplitude of the distortion.

simplex—Refers to permitting the transmission of signals in either direction, but not simultaneously.

simplex circuit—In North American usage, a simplex circuit can transmit in only one direction. As defined by the ITU, however, a simplex circuit is capable of transmitting in either direction, but only in a single direction at one time.

simplex transmission—Data transmission in one direction only.

single-mode fiber—An optical fiber with a core radius close to a wavelength of light, so that only one mode can be propagated.

single sideband—A form of amplitude modulation in which one of the two sidebands are removed prior to transmission.

slip—The irretrievable loss or gain of a set of consecutive bits without loss of alignment. Also called *timing slip.*

slope overload distortion—In quantization, the distortion that results when the slope of the input signal exceeds the slope of the quantizer.

slotted ring—An access control scheme sometimes used in LANs with ring topologies. A number of tokens, separated by fixed-length slots for data packets, circulate continuously around the ring. The fixed spacing between the tokens eliminates the need for complex token-recognition hardware.

SNA—Systems Network Architecture. A network architecture developed by IBM.

SOH—Start of header. A transmission control character used as the first character of a heading of an information message.

space—Absence of signal. In telegraph communications, a space represents the open condition, or no current flowing. A space impulse is equivalent to a binary zero.

space diversity—A method of radio transmission employed to minimize the effects of fading by the simultaneous use of two or more antennas spaced apart.

spacing distortion—A bias distortion in which received spaces appear longer than received marks.

speech interpolation—A voice multiplexing scheme in which the gaps and pauses occurring in one voice channel are filled with speech bursts from other voice channels to reduce the bandwidth or transmission rate.

stability—The rate at which a device changes from its nominal frequency over a selected period of time.

standard refraction—The refraction resulting from a gradient of radio refractivity equal to −40 N/km. Also corresponds to atmospheric refraction with k equal to 4/3.

star topology—A LAN topology in which links to all of the other stations radiate from a central hub station.

start bit—In asynchronous transmission, the first bit or element in each character, normally a space, which serves to prepare the receiving equipment for the reception and registration of the character.

statistical multiplexing—A form of concentration in data multiplexing in which time slots are allocated to whichever terminals are active at any one time.

STAT MUX—A statistical multiplexer.

step-index fiber—An optical fiber that has an abrupt change in refractive index at the boundary of the core and cladding.

stop bit—In start-stop transmission, the last bit or element in each character, normally a mark, to which is assigned a minimum duration, during which the receiving equipment is returned to its rest condition in preparation for the reception of the next character.

store-and-forward—A technique used in message switching, in which a message is transmitted to a switching center, where it is stored until the necessary links become available to forward the message to either its final destination or to the next switching center along the way.

streaming—A condition that occurs particularly in polling systems where one device monopolizes the line, because a fault keeps it sending spurious signals.

STX—Start of text. A transmission control character which precedes a text and which is used to terminate a heading.

SUB—Substitude character. A control character used in place of a character that has been found to be invalid or in error.

subrefraction—Refraction for which the refractivity gradient is greater than that for standard refraction. Also correspond to atmospheric refraction with $k < 1$.

supergroup—In frequency-division multiplexing, a number of voice channels, typically 60, occupying a 240 kHz bandwidth and composed of five groups.

supermastergroup—In frequency-division multiplexing, a number of voice channels, typically 900, occupying a 3872 kHz bandwidth and composed of three 300-channel mastergroups.

superrefraction—Refraction for which the refractivity gradient is less than that for standard refraction.

switched circuit—A circuit that can be temporarily established at the request of one or more of the connected stations.

switched network—The public switched telephone network. The dial-up telephone network.

syllabic companding—A form of companding in which the step sizes are controlled by the syllabic rate of human speech.

SYN—Synchronous idle. A transmission control character used by a synchronous transmission system in the absence of any other character (the idle condition), to provide a signal.

synchronous data link control—IBM's bit-oriented data-link protocol, which is very similar to ISO HDLC.

synchronous data transmission—Data transmission in which the transmitter and distant receiver are synchronized by the same bit clock, which is either sent in parallel with the data or embedded.

synchronous TDM—Time-division multiplexing in which the data clocks of the individual user signals are all derived from a master clock which is provided by the multiplexer.

systematic drift—Frequency drift in an oscillator resulting from slowly changing physical characteristics and causing frequency changes that, over a long period of time, tend to be in one direction.

system gain—The difference, in decibels, between the transmitter output power and the minimum receiver signal level required to meet a given performance objective.

system rise time—The time for the system response to a step function to rise from 10 percent to 90 percent of maximum amplitude.

tail circuit—A feeder circuit or an access line to a network node.

TC—Transmission control. A category of control characters designed to control or facilitate the transmission of data over telecommunication networks. Typical TC characters include: ACK, DLE, ENQ, EOT, ETB, ETX, and NAK.

TDM—A time-division multiplexer.

telco—Telephone company. Usually, the company serving the location of concern.

TELEX—Teleprinter exchange. A teleprinter dial network offered by Western Union and International Record Carriers; it uses Baudot code.

TELNET—Telecommunications network. The ARPANET virtual terminal protocol.

terminal—A point in a system where data can be entered and/or read.

time accuracy—The degree to which a clock agrees to a specified standard time.

time assignment speech interpolation—TASI. A form of speech interpolation typically used with analog voice transmission.

time base error—See *time interval error.*

time-division multiplexer—TDM. A device which derives multiple channels on a single transmission facility by connecting terminals one at a time at regular intervals. It interleaves bits in bit TDM or characters in character TDM from each terminal.

time interval error—TIE. The error in time that accumulates when a frequency source is used as a clock.

time to loss of frame alignment—After proper frame alignment occurs, the time to the loss of frame synchronization, usually specified as a function of BER.

timing slip—See *slip.*

TIP—Terminal interface processor. An ARPANET switch that allows terminals to be connected to the network.

token passing—A popular access control technique used in LANs with ring topologies.

transcoder—A device that performs direct digital-to-digital conversion between two different voice encoding schemes without returning the signals to analog form.

transitional coding—A coding scheme used to convert asynchronous data to synchronous transmission by transmitting the data values and data transition times.

transmitter—A device that converts information signals to electrical or optical signals for transmission.

transmultiplexer—A device that transforms frequency-division multiplexed signals (group or supergroup) into corresponding time-division multiplexed signals that have the same structure as those derived from PCM multiplexing. This type of equipment also carries out the inverse function.

transport layer—The portion of the ISO-OSI model which is concerned with the interface between the relatively hardware-oriented lower layers and the relatively software-oriented upper layers.

transversal filter—An equalizer that uses a tapped delay line with weighting coefficients at each tap to reduce intersymbol interference.

tribit—A data element that contains three bits.

trunk—A single circuit between two points, both of which are switching centers or individual distribution points. A trunk usually handles many channels simultaneously.

TTD—Temporary text delay. A control sequence which is sent by a sending station in the message transfer state when it wants to retain the line, but is not ready to transmit.

turnaround time—The actual time required to reverse the direction of transmission from sender to receiver or from receiver to sender using a half-duplex circuit. It is a combination of propagation effects, modem timing, and computer reaction.

twisted-pair cable—A communication cable consisting of two insulated conductors twisted together.

TWX—Teletypewriter Exchange Service. A teletypewriter dial network operated by Western Union. ASCII-coded machines are used.

unavailability—The propability or fraction of time that a system is down.

unbalanced transmission—A method for the transmission of baseband data in which each signal circuit consists of one signal conductor and a ground return.

unipolar—A two-level code using a single polarity for one level and zero voltage for the other level.

USOC—Universal Service Ordering Code, for telephones.

USOC-500—Standard telephone, rotary dial.

USOC-502—A rotary dial telephone with an exclusion key. The exclusion key, which is a voice/data switch, is normally one of the buttons on which the handset rests. It is pulled up to be activated. There are two ways to wire a 502 telephone. The telephone can control the line, and a call is made or answered by lifting the handset and dialing. The exclusion key must be pulled to go into the data mode. Alternatively, the modem can control the line, and the exclusion key is used to originate or answer a voice call. The modem is in the data mode when the telephone is hung up, so if the modem is the auto answer type, it can answer a call without any action by an operator.

USOC-2500—Standard telephone, touch-tone.

USOC-2502—A touch-tone telephone with an exclusion key. Operation is the same as the 502.

VDT—Video display terminal. It consists of a monitor, keyboard and communication capability.

vertical redundancy check—Synonymous with *character parity.*

VF—Voice frequency. An analog signal within the range of transmitted speech on a telephone line (300—3300Hz). The voice band of a telephone line.

V.5—CCITT recommendation for the standardization of modulation rates and data signaling rates for synchronous data transmission in the switched network.

V.6—Same as V.5, for leased telephone circuits.

V.15—CCITT recommendation for the use of acoustic coupling for data transmission.

V.16—CCITT recommendation for modems for the transmissions of analog data.

V.19—CCITT recommendation for modems for parallel data transmission using telephone signaling frequencies.

V.21—A 200 bps full-duplex FSK modem recommendation by CCITT.

V.22—A 1200 bps full-duplex two-wire modem standard by CCITT for use in the switched telephone network.

V.23—A CCITT modem recommendation for half-duplex FSK modems operating at either 600 bps or 1200 bps.

V.24—A list of CCITT definitions for interchange circuits between data terminal equipment and data communication equipment.

V.25—A CCITT recommendation for automatic calling and/or answering equipment on the switched telephone network.

V.26—A CCITT 2400 bps modem standard for use on four-wire point-to-point circuits in the switched telephone network.

V.27—A CCITT 4800 bps modem standard for leased circuits.

V.29—A CCITT 9600 bps modem standard for use on leased circuits.

V.35—A CCITT recommendation for data transmission at 48 Kbps using 60-108 kHz group band circuits.

V.36—A CCITT modem recommendation for synchronous data transmission using 60-108 kHz group band circuits.

V.41—A CCITT recommendation for code-independent error control systems.

V.50—CCITT standard limits for transmission quality of data transmission.

V.52—CCITT recommendation for characteristics of distortion and error-rate measuring apparatus for data transmission.

V.53—CCITT recommendation for limits on the maintenance of telephone circuits used for data transmission.

V.54—CCITT recommendation for loop-test devices for modems.

V.55—CCITT specification for an impulsive-noise measuring instrument for telephone-type circuits.

V.56—CCITT recommendation for comparative tests for modems for use over telephone-type circuits.

V.57—CCITT recommendation for a comprehensive data test set for high data signaling rates.

virtual circuit—A circuit-like service which uses the software protocols of a network, enabling two end points to communicate as through a physical circuit. A logical transmission path. The network nodes provide the addressing information needed in the packets that carry the source data to the destination. The advantages of virtual circuits over physical circuits include the resolution of speed mismatch between the data-generating and data-consuming end points, data retransmissions in case of transient communication errors, and the transformation of the information that traverses the circuits.

vocoder—A type of voice coder that is based on a model of the human speech mechanism in which the source of sound is separated from the vocal tract. A speech analyzer determines the source of sound and vocal tract characteristics and formats this information into a bandwidth that is much smaller than the speech signal itself. A speech synthesizer converts the formatted information back into artificial speech sounds.

VRC—Vertical redundancy check. An error detection scheme in which the parity bit of each character is set to one or zero so that the total number of one-bits in the character is odd or even.

VT—Vertical tabulation. A format effector which advances the active position to the same character position on the next predetermined line.

VTP—Vertical terminal protocol.

WACK—Wait before transmit. A character sequence that allows a receiving station to indicate a temporary-not-ready-to-receive condition to the transmitting station.

waiting-time jitter—In a pulse stuffing multiplexer, the jitter occurring because of the delay between the time a stuff is needed and the prescribed times that stuffing is allowed.

wander—See *drift.*

watchdog timer—A response timer that can be used to ensure that a station will become locked up waiting for an expected response that never arrives.

WECO—Western Electric Company, a manufacturing division of AT&T.

white noise—Noise with a frequency spectrum that is continuous and uniform over a wide frequency range.

wideband coder—A voice coder with a transmission rate that exceeds the rate that can be accommodated by 3 kHz telephone channels using modems.

wideband FSK—A form of FSK in which the modulation index is much greater than one.

word interleaving—See *character interleaving.*

xmodem—A character-oriented protocol which is widely used in computerized bulletin board systems.

x-off—Transmitter off. The communication control character used to instruct a terminal to suspend transmission.

x-on—Transmitter on. The communication control character used to instruct a terminal to start or resume transmission.

X.1—CCITT recommendation for international user classes of service in the public data network.

X.2—CCITT recommendation for international user facilities in public data networks.

X.3—CCITT recommendation defining PADs.

X.4—CCITT specification which defines the general structure of signals of the International Alphabet No. 5 code for data transmission over public data networks.

X.20—CCITT recommendation for the interface between data terminal equipment and data circuit-terminating equipment for synchronous services on public data networks.

X.21—CCITT recommendation for the interface between data terminal equipment and data circuit-terminating equipment for synchronous operation on public data networks.

X.24—CCITT definitions of interchange circuits between data terminal equipment and data circuit-terminating equipment on public data networks.

X.25—CCITT recommendation that defines the interface between a packet-mode DTE and a packet-mode DCE.

X.28—CCITT recommendation that defines the interface between a start/stop-mode DTE and PAD.

X.29—CCITT recommendation that defines the interface between a packet-mode DTE and the PAD.

X.95—CCITT recommendation for network parameters in public data network.

X.96—CCITT recommendation for call progress signals in public data networks.

zero-bit insertion/deletion—A technique used in bit-oriented protocols to separate runs of six or more contiguous ones so they are not mistaken for flags or aborts.

zero-forcing equalizer—An equalizer in which the weighting coefficients of a transversal filter are selected to force the equalizer output to zero at sampling instants on either side of the desired signal.

Bibliography

Abramson, N., and Kuo, F. F., Eds. *Computer-Communications Networks.* Englewood Cliffs: Prentice-Hall, 1973.

Acampora, A.S., *et al. Performance of a Centralized-Bus Local Area Network.* Proceedings of Localnet 1983. New York, 1983.

Advances in Cryptology: Proceedings of Crypto 82. New York, 1983.

Allison, D.R. "A Design Philosophy for Microcomputer Architectures", *Computer,* Vol. 10, No. 2, 1977.

Altman, L., ed. *Microprocessors.* New York: Electronic Magazine Book Series, 1975.

Anderson, D.A. "Design of Self-Checking Digital Networks Using Code Techniques." PhD thesis, Report R-527, University of Illinois, October, 1971.

Andrews, M. *Principles of Firmware Engineering in Microprogram Control.* London: Computer Science Press, 1980.

AT&T Compatibility Bulletin No. 142. *The Extended Framing Format Interface Specification.* Parsippamy, NJ.

Avizienis, A. "Fault-Tolerant Computing—An Overview." *Computer,* January-February 1971.

Baum, A. and Senzig, D. *Hardware Considerations in a Microcomputer Multiprocessor System.* COMCON Paper, San Francisco, February 1975.

Bell, C., and Newell, A. *Computer Structures.* New York: McGraw-Hill, 1970.

Bell, Trudy E. "Long-distance Fiber-Optic Networks, Direct Broadcast Satellites, and Low-Cost PBXs Bring Increased Communications Capacity to Customers." *IEEE Spectrum.* January 1984.

Blahut, R.E. *Theory and Practice of Error Control Codes.* Reading, MA: Addison-Wesley, 1983.

Bosworth, Bruce. *Codes, Ciphers and Computers.* Rochelle Park, NJ: Hayden 1982.

Breuer, M.A., and Griedman, A.D. *Diagnosis and Reliable Design of Digital Systems.* Woodland Hills, CA: Computer Science Press, 1976.

Brooks, F.P. *An Overview of Microcomputer Architecture and Software.* Micro Architecture, EUROMICRO 1976 Proceedings.

Burton, D.P. "Handle Microcomputer I/O Efficiently." *Electronic Design,* Vol. 13 (June 21, 1978).

Burzio, G. "Operating Systems Enhance uCs." *Electronic Design,* Vol. 13 (June 21, 1978).

Camenzind, H.R. *Electronic Integrated System Design.* New York: Van Nostrand Reinhold, 1972.

Carne, E.B. "New Dimensions in Telecommunications." *IEEE Communications Magazine,* Vol. 20, No. 1 (January, 1982).

CCITT Yellow Book, Vol. IV.4. "Specifications of Measuring Equipment." 1981.

CCITT Yellow Book, Vol. II.2. "Telegraph and Telematic Services Terminal Equipment." 1981.

CCITT Yellow Book, Vol. VIII.1. "Data Communication Over the Telephone Network." 1981.

CCITT Yellow Book, Vol. III.3. "Digital Networks—Transmission Systems and Multiplexing Equipment." 1981.

Chandy, K.M., and Reiser, M, eds. *Computer Performance.* Amsterdam, Netherlands: North-Holland Publishers, 1977.

Childs, R.E. Multiple *Microprocessor Systems: Goals, Limitations and Alternatives.* Digest of Papers COMPCON, Spring, 1979.

Chu, Y. *Computer Organization and Microprogramming.* Englewood Cliffs, NJ: Prentice-Hall, 1972.

Clark, G.C., Jr., and Cain, J.B. *Error-Correction Coding for Digital Communications.* New York: Plenum Press, 1981.

Cooper, Edward. *CATV/Broadband Overview for Data and Telecommunications Managers.* TR-81052, November 1981. SYTEK Inc., 1981.

Crick, A. "Scheduling and Controlling I/O Operations." *Data Processing,* May-June, 1974.

Crochiere, R.E., and Flanagan, J.L. "Current Perspectives in Digital Speech."

IEEE Communications Magazine, Vol. No. 1 (January, 1983).

Crossett, J.A. *Monitor and Control of Digital Transmission Systems.* International Conference on Communications, 1981.

Dal Cin, M. *Performance Evaluation of Self-Diagnosing Multiprocessor Systems.* Conference of Fault-Tolerant Computing, Toulouse, France, June, 1978.

"Demultiplexing Considerations for Statistical Multiplexers." *IEEE Transactions on Communications,* Vol. COM-20, No. 3, June 1982.

Denning, Dorothy. *Cryptography and Data Security.* Reading, MA: Addison-Wesley Publishing Co., 1982.

Digital Equipment Corporation. *Introduction to Local Area Networks.* 1982.

Digital Equipment Corp., Intel Corp., and Xerox Corp. *The Ethernet: Data Link and Physical Layers.* September 1980.

Dowsing, R.D. "Processor Management in a Multiprocessor System." *Electronic Letters,* November, 1976.

Drucker, P.F. *The Age of Discontinuity: Guidelines to Our Changing Society.* New York: Harper & Row, 1968.

Duke, David A., Keck, Donald B. "Single-Mode Fiber Optic Features." *Telecommunicatios,* Vol. 17, No. 12, December 1983.

Eastman, C., Lividini, J., and Stoker, D. "A Data Base for Designing Large Physical Systems," *NCC: AFIPS,* 1975.

Eastman, C.M., and Henrion, M. GLIDE: *A Language for Design Information Systems.* SIGGRAPH 1977 Proceedings, published as *Computer Graphics,* 11 (2), 1977.

Eckhouse, R.H., Jr. *Minicomputer Systems.* Englewood Cliffs, NJ: Prentice-Hall, 1975.

Eckman, D.P.. *Automatic Process Control.* New York: John Wiley & Sons, Inc., 1958.

Encarnacao, J., *et al. The Workstation Concept of GKS and the Resulting Conceptual Differences to the GSPC Core System.* SIGGRAPH 1980 Proceedings, published as *Computer Graphics,* 14 (3), July 1980.

Engel, S., and Granda, R. *Guidelines for Man/Display Interfaces.* Technical Report TR 00.2720. Poughkeepsie, NY: IBM, 1975.

English, R.E. "Systems Management of a CAD/CAM Installation." *CADCON East 84,* June 13, Boston.

Enslow, P.H., Jr., ed. *Multiprocessors and Parallel Processing.* New York: John Wiley and Sons, Inc. 1974.

Farnbach, W.A. "Bring Up Your uP Bit-By-Bit." *Electronic Design,* Vol. 24, No. 15 (July 19, 1976).

Faux, I.D., and Pratt, M.J. *Computational Geometry for Design Manufacture.* New York: John Wiley, 1979.

Feher, Kamilo. *Digital Communications.* Englewood Cliffs, NJ: Prentice Hall, 1981.

Feiner, S., Nagy, S., and van Dam, A. *An Integrated System for Creating and Presenting Complex Computer-Based Documents.* SIGGRAPH 1981, Proceedings published as *Computer Graphics,* 15 (3), August 1981.

Fields, A., Maisano, R., and Marshall, C. *A Comparative Analysis of Methods for Tactical Data Inputting.* Army Research Institute, 1977.

Foley, J.D. "Evaluation of Small Computers and Display Controls for Computer Graphics." *Computer Group News,* Vol. 3 No. 1 (January/February 1970).

Foley, J.D. "Managing the Design of User-Computer Interfaces." *Computer Graphics World,* December 1983.

Foley, J.D., and Wallace, V.L. *The Art of Natural Graphic Man-Machine Conversation.* IEEE Proceedings Vol. 62, No. 4 (April 1974).

Foley, J.D., Wallace, V., and Chan, P. *The Human Factors of Interaction Techniques.* The George Washington University, Institute for Information Science and Technology Technical Report GWU-IIST-81-03, Washington, DC, 1981.

Foster, C.C. *Computer Architecture.* New York: Van Nostrand Reinhold Company, 1970.

Franklin, M.A., Kahn, S.A., and Stucki, M.J. *Design Issues in the Development of a Modular Multiprocessor Communications Network.* Sixth Annual Symposium on Computer Architecture, April 23-25, 1979.

Freedman, M.D. *Principles of Digital Computer Operation.* New York: John Wiley and Sons, Inc. 1972.

Freeman, R.L. *Telecommunications Transmission Handbook,* 2nd ed. New York: Wiley, 1981.

Friedman, A.D., and Memon, P.R. *Fault Detection in Digital Circuits.* Englewood Cliffs, NJ: Prentice-Hall, 1971.

Fuchs, H. *Distributing a Visible Surface Algorithm Over Multiple Processors.* Proceedings 1977 ACM National Conference.

Fuchs, H., Duran, J., and Johnson, B. *A System for Automatic Acquisition of Three-Dimensional Data.* Proceedings of the 1977 NCC.

Garland, H. *Introduction to Microprocessor System Design.* New York: McGraw-Hill, 1979.

Garrett, M.A. "Unified Nonprocedural Environment for Designing and Implementing Graphical Interfaces to Relational Data Base Management Systems." Ph.D. dissertation, George Washington University, 1980.

Gear, C.W. *Computer Organization and Programming.* New York: McGraw-Hill, 1974.

Germann, J.J. *Using Special Processors to Enhance Engineering Workstations.* CAD/CAM West 84, February 7-9, 1984, San Francisco.

Geyer, K.E., and Wilson, K.R. *Computing with Feeling.* Proceedings of the IEEE Conference on Computer Graphics, Pattern Recognition and Data Structure, May 1975.

Gibson, J.E. *Nonlinear Automatic Control.* New York: MCGRAW-Hill, 1963.

Giloi, W. *Interactive Computer Graphics—Data Structures, Algorithms, Languages.* Englewood Cliffs, NJ: Prentice-Hall, 1978.

Glasgal, Ralph. *Techniques in Data Communications.* Dedham, MA: Artech House, 1983.

Goldberg, Adele, and Robson, David. *A Metaphor for User Interface Design.* Palo Alto, CA: Xerox Palo Alto Research Center, 1979.

Gloge, D.C., *et al Characteristics and Operation of the TF4E-432 Mb/s Repeater Line.* International Conference on Communications, 1984.

Gonzalez, M.J., and Ramamoorthy, C.V. "Parallel Task Execution in a Decentralized System." *IEEE Transactions on Computers,* December, 1972.

Gooch, R.P. *DCEM: A DSI System for North America and Europe.* International Conference on Communications, 1982.

Grant, E., and Leavenworth, R.S. *Statistical Quality Control.* New York: McGraw Hill, 1972.

Grimsdale, R.L., and Johnson, D.M. "A Modular Executive for Multiprocessor Systems." *Trends in On-Line Computer Control Systems,* April, 1972.

Groff, G. K., and Muth, I.F. *Operations Management: Analysis for Decisions.* Homewood Ill.: Irwin, 1972.

Guedj, R., *et al,* ed. *Methodology of Interaction.* North-Holland, Amsterdam, 1980.

Hamilton, M., and Zeldin, S. "Higher Order Software—A Methodology for Defining Software." *IEEE Transactions on Software Engineering,* SE-2, 1, March, 1976.

Hanau, P.R., and Lenorovitz, D.R. *Prototyping and Simulation Tools for User/Computer Dialogue Design.* SIGGRAPH 1980 Proceedings, published as *Computer Graphics,* 14 (2), July 1980.

Hansen, W. *User Engineering Principles for Interactive Systems.* Proceedings 1971 Fall Joint Computer Conference.

Harris, J.A., and Smith, D.R. *Hierarchical Multiprocessor Organizations.* Fourth Annual Symposium on Computer Architecture, March 23-25, 1977.

Hayes, P., Ball, E., and Reddy, R. "Breaking the Man-Machine Communication

Barrier." *Computer,* Vol. 14 No. 3 (March 1981).

Helmers, C.T., ed *Robotics Age, in the Beginning.* Rochelle Park, NJ: Hayden, 1983.

Herot, C.F., *et al. A Prototype Spatial Data Base Management System.* SIGGRAPH 1980 Proceedings, published as *Computer Graphics,* 14 (2), July 1980.

Hill, F.J., and Peterson, G.R. *Digital Systems: Hardware Organization and Design.* New York: John Wiley, 1973.

Hnatek, Eugene R. "Current Semiconductor Memories." *Computer Design,* April, 1978.

Hordeski, M.F. "Digital Control of Microprocessors." *Electronic Design,* December 6, 1975.

Hordeski, M.F. "Innovative Design: Microprocessors." *Digital Design,* December 1976.

Hordeski, M.F. *Fundamentals of Digital Control Loops and Factors in Choosing Pneumatic or Electronic Instruments.* Presentation at the SCMA Instrumentation Short Course, Los Angeles. April 6, 1977.

Hordeski, M.F. "Balancing Microprocessor-Interface Tradeoffs." *Digital Design,* April 1977.

Hordeski, M.F. "Future Microprocessor Software." *Digital Design,* August 1977.

Hordeski, M.F. "Radiation and Stored Data." *Digital Design,* September 1977.

Hordeski, M.F. "Microprocessor Chips." *Instrumentation Technology,* September 1977.

Hordeski, M.F. "Fundamentals of Digital Control Loops." *Measurements and Control,* February 1978.

Hordeski, M.F. "Using Microprocessors." *Measurements and Control,* June, 1978.

Hordeski, M.F. *Illustrated Dictionary of Microcomputer Terminology.* Blue Ridge Summit, PA: TAB, 1978.

Hordeski, M.F. *Microprocessor Cookbook.* Blue Ridge Summit, PA: TAB, 1979.

Hordeski, M.F. *Selecting Test Strategies for Microprocessor Systems.* ATE Seminar Proceedings, Pasadena, CA, January 1982.

Hordeski, M.F. "Selection of a Test Strategy for MPU Systems." *Electronics Test,* February 1982.

Hordeski, M.F. *The Impact of 16-Bit Microprocessors.* Instrumentation Symposium Proceedings, May 1982 (Research Triangle Park, N.C.: Instrument Society of America).

Hordeski, M.F. *Diagnostic Strategies for Microprocessor Systems.* ATE Seminar Proceedings, Anaheim, CA, January 1983.

Hordeski, M.F. *Microprocessors in Industry.* New York: Van Nostrand Reinhold, 1984.

Hordeski, M.F. *The Design of Microprocessor Sensor and Control Systems.* Reston, VA.: Reston, 1984.

Hordeski, M.F. *CAD/CAM Equipment Reliability.* Western Design Engineering Show and ASME Conference, San Francisco, December 5, 1984.

Hordeski, M.F. *Specifying and Selecting CAD/CAM Equipment.* CADCON West, Anaheim, January 14-17, 1985.

Hordeski, M.F., *A Tutorial on CIM/Factory Automation.* Western Design Engineering Show and ASME Conference, Anaheim, December 12, 1985.

Hordeski, M.F. *CAD/CAM Techniques.* Reston, VA: Reston, 1986.

Hordeski, M.F. *Microcomputer Design.* Reston, VA: Reston, 1986.

Hornbuckle, G.D. *The Computer Graphics/User Interface.* IEEE Transactions HFE-8 (1), March 1967.

Houtzel, A. *The Graphics Side of Group Technology.* CADCON East, Boston, June 13, 1984.

Hudry, J. "Man-Machine Interface Issues." *Computer Graphics World,* April 1984.

Intel Corporation. *8086 User's Guide.* Santa Clara, CA, 1976.

Irani, K., and Wallace, V. "On Network Linguistics and the Conversational Design of Queueing Networks." *Journal of the ACM,* Vol. 18 (October 1971).

Ishiguro, T., and Inuma, K. "Television Bandwidth Compression by Motion-Compensated Interframe Coding." *IEEE Communications Magazine,* Vol. 20 No. 6 (November, 1982).

Ito, T., Nakagawa, K., and Hakamada, Y. *Design and Performances of the F-400M Trunk Transmission System Using a Single-Mode Fiber Cable.* International Conference on Communications, 1982.

Jackson, M.A. *Principles of Program Design.* New York: Academic, 1975.

Johnson, S., and Lesk, M. "Language Development Tools." *The Bell System Technical Journal,* 57 (6,2) July-August 1978.

Jones, J.C. *Design Methods.* New York: Wiley-Interscience, 1970.

Kamae, T. "Public Facsimile Communication Network." *IEEE Communication Magazine,* Vol. 20 No. 2 (March, 1982).

Kaplan, M., and Greenberg, D. *Parallel Processing Techniques for Hidden Surface Algorithms.* SIGGRAPH 1979 Proceedings, published as *Computer Graphics,* August 1979.

Katayama, S., Iwamoto, M., and Segawa, J. *Digital Radio-Relay Systems in NTT.* International Communications Conference, 1984.

Kay, Alan C. "Microelectronics and the Personal Computer." *Scientific American,* Vol. 237 No. 3 (September 1977).

Kennedy, J.R. *A System for Timesharing Graphic Consoles, FJCC.* Washington, DC: Sparton Books, 1966.

Kilgour, A.C. "The Evolution of a Graphic System for Linked Computers." *Software—Practice and Experience,* 1, 1971.

Klingman, E.E. *Microprocessor Systems Design.* Englewood Cliffs, NJ: Prentice-Hall, 1977.

Knapp, J.M. "The Ergonomic Millennium." *Computer Graphics World,* June 1983.

Klipec, B. "How to Avoid Noise Pickup on Wire and Cables." *Instruments and Control Systems,* December, 1977.

Knuth, D.E. *The Art of Computer Programming.* Volume I: *Fundamental Algorithms.* Reading, Mass.: Addison-Wesley, 1973.

Kohonen, T. *Digital Circuits and Devices.* Englewood Cliffs, NJ: Prentice-Hall, 1972.

Konheim, A.G. and Pickholtz, R.L. "An Analysis of a Voice/Data Integrated Multiplexer." *IEEE Transactions on Communications.* January 1984.

Kostas, D.J. "Transition to ISDN—an Overview." *IEEE Communications Magazine,* Vol. 22 No. 1 (January 1984).

Kriloff, H. *Human Factor Considerations for Interactive Display Systems.* In *Proceedings ACM/SIGGRAPH Workshop on User-Oriented Design of Interactive Graphics Systems,* S. Trem, ed. ACM 1976.

Kuck, D.J. *The Structure of Computers and Computations.* Volume 1, New York: John Wiley and Sons, Inc., 1978.

Kwakernaak, H., and Swan, R. *Linear Optimal Control Systems.* New York: John Wiley & Sons, Inc, 1972.

Lampson, Butler W. *Bravo Manual.* In *Alto User's Handbook.* Palo Alto, CA: Xerox Palo Alto Research Center, November 1978.

Lawrence, S., and Marcus, L.S. "Designing PC Boards with a Centralized Database." *Computer Graphics World,* March 1984.

Leahy, W. *Data Base Management—Automated Graphics Generation.* CADCON East, Boston, June 12, 1984.

Leininger, M. *Present and Future Developments in Robotic Applications.* Automated Manufacturing, Greenville, SC, March 1984.

Leventhal, L.V. *Microprocessor: Software, Hardware, Programming.* Englewood Cliffs, NJ: Prentice-Hall, 1978.

Lidinsky, W.P. *LANs, Internetworking and Public Networks.* Symposium on Local Area Networks, Sydney, Australia, December 14-16, 1982.

"Linking Up to Boost the Electronic Office." *Business Week,* March 1983.

Local-Area Subnetworks: A Performance Comparison. Proceedings of IFIP 6.4 International Workshop on Local Area Networks.

Lorin, H. *Parallelism in Hardware and Software.* Englewood Cliffs, NJ: Prentice-Hall, 1972.

Lunden, J.W. *Intellignet Vision: Rapid Advances in Industrial Automation.* Automated Manufacturing, Greenville, SC, March 1984.

Madnick, S.F., and Donovan, J.L. *Operating Systems.* New York: McGraw-Hill, 1974.

Martin, Donald P. *Microcomputer Design.* Chicago: Martin Research Ltd., 1975.

Martin, J. *Design of Man-Computer Dialogues.* Englewood Cliffs, NJ: Prentice-Hall, 1973.

Martin, W.A. *Computer Input/Output of Mathematical Expressions.* Second Symposium or Symbolic Algebraic Manipulation, ACM, March 1971.

Mazur, T. "Microprocessor Basics: Part 4: The Motorola 6800." *Electronic Design,* July 19, 1976.

McCool, M. *Interfacing CAD/CAM with ATE.* ATE West Proceedings, January 1983.

McGlynn, D.R. *Microprocessors.* New York: John Wiley and Sons, Inc., 1976.

McKay, C.W. *An Approach to Distributing Intelligence Among a Network of Cooperative, Autonomus, Functional Computing Clusters.* Automated Manufacturing, Greenville, SC, March 1984.

McKenezie, K., and Nichols, A.J. "Build a Compact Microcomputer." *Electronic Design,* May 10, 1976.

McManigal, D., and Stevenson, D. "Architecture of the IBM 3277 Graphics Attachment." *IBM Systems Journal,* Vol. 19 No. 3 (1980).

McNamara, John E. *Technical Aspects of Data Communications.* 2nd ed. Bedford, MA: Digital Equipment Corp., 1982.

McNichol, J., Barber, S., and Rivest, F. *Design and Application of the RD-4 and RD-6 Digital Radio Systems.* International Conference on Communications, 1984.

Meditch, J.S. *Stochastic Optimal Linear Estimation and Control.* New York: McGraw-Hill, 1969.

Metcalfe, R.M., and Boggs, D.R. "Ethernet: Distributed Packet Switching for Local Computer Networks." *Communications of the ACM,* Vol. 19 No. 7 (July 1976).

Meyer, J.D. "Commercial Machine Vision Systems." *Computer Graphics World,* October 1983.

Meyrowitz, N., and Moser, M. *BRUWIN: An Adaptable Design Strategy for Window Manager/Virtual Terminal Systems.* Proceedings of the 8th Annual Symposium on Operating Systems Principles (SIGOPS), Pacific Grove, CA, December 1981.

Midwinter, J.E. *Development of High Bit Rate Monomode Fibre Systems in the UK.* International Conference on Communications, 1982.

Miller, N. "Bus-oriented Graphics Systems." *Computer Graphics World,* May 1983.

Miller, R.B. *Response Time in Man-Computer Conversational Transactions.* FJCC, AFIPS Conference Proceedings, Vol. 33, Montvale, NJ (AFIPS Press, 1968).

Moran, T. "The Command Language Grammar: A Representation for the User Interface of Interactive Computer Systems." *International Journal of Man-Machine Studies,* 15, 1981.

Moss, D. "Multiprocessing Adds Muscle to uPs." *Electronic Design II,* May 24, 1978.

Motorola Semiconductor. *MC68000 Microprocessor User's Manual.* Austin, TX: Motorola, 1979.

Motorola Semiconductor. *M6800 Microprocessor Applications Manual.* Phoenix, AZ: Motorola, 1975.

Mouthaan. *Long-Wavelength Optical Transmission Systems in Europe.* International Conference on Communications, 1982.

Murrill, P.W. *Automatic Control of Processes.* Scranton, PA: International Textbook Co., 1967.

Myers, G.J. *Reliable Software Through Composite Design.* New York: Petrocelli Charter, 1975.

Myers, G.J. *Advances in Computer Architecture.* New York: John Wiley and Sons, Inc., 1978.

Newman, W.M., and Sproull, R.F. *Principles of Interactive Computer Graphics.* 2nd ed. New York: McGraw-Hill, 1979.

Newton, R.S. *An Exercise in Multiprocessor Operating System* Design. Agard Conference on Real-Time Computer-Based Systems, Athens, Greece: NATO Advisory Group on Aerospace R & D, May 1974.

Nick, J.R. "Using Schottky Three-State Outputs in Bus-Organized Systems." *Electronic Design News,* Vol. 19, No. 23 (December 5, 1974).

Nielson, D."The Role of Radio in Local Area Data Distribution." *Journal of Telecommunication Networks,* Vol. 1, No. 1 (Spring 1982).

Norton, F.J. *CADD, Human Relations, and the Management Process.* CADCON West, San Francisco, February 7-9, 1984.

Novitsky, M.P. *MRP in the Process Industry.* Automated Manufacturing, Greenville, SC, March 1984.

Nunn, M. *CAE/CAD/CAM Testability—An Overview.* CADCON West, San Francisco, February 7-9, 1984.

Obenzinger, Mark, M. *The Personal Computer Market: a Profile for Growth.* New York: Lehman Brothers Kuhn Loeb Research, January 1983.

O'Brien, Michael T. *A Network Graphical Conferencing System.* RAND Corporation, Santa Monica, CA, 1979 (N-1250-DARPA).

Olmstead, K. "The Future Factory—A First Report." *Test and Measurement World,* December 1983.

Oppenheim, A.V., and Schafer, S. *Digital Signal Processing.* Englewood Cliffs, NJ: Prentice-Hall, 1975.

Ottinger, L. *Using Robots in Flexible Manufacturing Cells/Facilities.* Automated Manufacturing, Greenville, SC, March 1984.

Patel, J.H. *Processor-Memory Interconnections for Multiprocessors.* Proceedings of the Sixth Annual Symposium Computer Architecture, April 23-25, 1979.

Patterson, D.A., and Sequin, C.H. *Design Considerations for Single-Chip Computers of the Future.* IEEE Transactions C-29, February, 1980.

Pearson, D.J. "Graphics Workstation Intelligence." *Computer Graphics World,* January 1983.

Peuto, B.L., and Shustek, L.J. "Current Issues in the Architecture of Microprocessors." *Computer,* February 1977.

Pferd, W. "A New Boost with Automated Data Capture." *Computer Graphics World,* March 1983.

Pinto, J. "ARTIFICIAL Intelligence and Robotics in the Future Factory." *Test and Measurement World,* December 1983.

Preiss, R. "Storage CRT Display Terminals: Evolution and Trends." *Computer,* Vol. 11 No. 11 (November 1978).

Proakis, John G. *Digital Communications.* New York: McGraw-Hill, 1983.

Quereshi, Shahid. "Adaptive Equalization." *IEEE Communications Magazine,* March 1982.

Renfrow, N. *Tools for Facilities Management.* CADCON East, Boston, June 12, 1984.

Riker, D.C. "Digital Transmission in the MCI Network." *IEEE Communications Magazine,* Vol 22 No. 10 (October 1984).

Riley, J. *Process Control for a PWB Facility.* Automated Manufacturing, Greenville, SC, March 1984.

Roberson, R.E. *Automated Manufacturing and Management Decision Information.* Automated Manufacturing, Greenville, SC, March 1984.

Rodgers, R.C. "Peripherals for Programmable Controllers." *Computer-Aided*

Engineering, November/December 1982.

Ross, C.A. *Automation Policies, Practices and Procedures.* Automated Manufacturing, Greenville, SC, March 1984.

Roth, G. "Integrated Test Functions Aid in Process Control." *Test and Measurement World,* December 1983.

Schaeffer, E.J., and Williams, T. J. *An Analysis of Fault Detection Correction and Prevention in Industrial Computer Systems.* Purdue Laboratory for Applied Industrial Control, Purdue University, October 1977.

Schmidt, W.C. "The Promise of Automatic Digitizing." *Computer Graphics World,* April 1983.

Seybold, J. "The Xerox Professional Workstation." *The Seybold Report,* Vol. 10 No. 16 (April 1981).

Sheingold, D.H. *Analog-Digital Conversion Handbook.* Norwood, MA: Analog Devices, 1972.

Shepherd, M., Jr. *Distributed Computing Power: Opportunities and Challenges.* National Computer Conference, 1977.

Shneiderman, B. "Human Factors Experiments in Designing Interactive Systems." *Computer,* Vol. 12 No. 12 (December 1979).

Shoch, J.F., *et al.* "Evolution of the Ethernet Local Computer Network." *Computer,* August 1982.

Sigsbly. B. "ATE in the Future Factory." *Test and Measurement World,* December 1983.

Skrokov, M.R., ed. *Mini and Microcomputer Control in Industrial Processes.* New York: Van Nostrand Reinhold, 1980.

Sneeringer, J. "User-Interface Design for Test Editing: A Case Study." *Software-Practice and Experience,* Vol. 8 (1978).

Sobel, H.S. *Introduction to Digital Computer Design.* Reading, MA: Addison Wesley, 1970.

Socci, V. "Microprocessors in Distributed Graphics." *Computer Graphics World,* May 1983.

Soucek, B. *Microprocessors and Microcomputers.* New York: John Wiley & Sons, Inc., 1976.

Sproull, R.F., and Thomas, E.L. "A Network Graphics Protocol." *Computer Graphics.* Vol. 8 No. 3 (Fall 1974).

Stone, Harold. *Critical Load Factors in Two-Processor Distributed Systems.* IEEE Transactions on Software Engineering, SE-4 (3), May 1978.

Stone, H.S. *Introduction to Computer Architecture.* New York: McGraw-Hill, 1975.

Stover, R.N. "Automating Data Base Capture for CAD/CAM." *Computer Graphics*

World, March 1983.

Takikawa, K. *Simplified 6.3 Mbit/s Codec for Video Conferencing.* IEEE Transactions on Communications. Vol. COM-29, December 1981.

Tanenbaum, Andrew S. *Computer Networks.* Englewood Cliffs, NJ: Prentice-Hall, 1981.

Tasar, O., and Tasar, V. *A Study of Intermittent Faults in Digital Computers.* AFIPS Conference Proceedings, Vol. 46, Montvalue, NJ. (AFIPS Press, 1977).

Taylor, A.P. "Getting a Handle on Factory Automation." *Computer-Aided Engineering,* May-June 1983.

Texas Instruments. *TMS 9900 Microprocessor Data Manual.* Dallas, Texas: Texas Instruments, 1978.

Texas Instruments. *The TTL Data Book for Design Engineers.* Dallas, Texas: Texas Instruments, 1973.

Texas Instruments, *The Microprocessor Handbook.* Houston, Texas: Texas Instruments, 1975.

Thomas, T.B., and Arbuckle, W.L. *Multiporcessor Software: Two Approaches.* Conference on the Use of Digital Computers in Process Control, Baton Rouge, LA, February, 1971.

Thompson, J.E. *European Collaboration Picture Coding Research for Two Mbit/s Transmission.* IEEE Transactions on Communications, Vol. COM-29, December 1981.

Thurber, K.J., and Masson, G.M. *Distributed Processor Communication Architecture.* Lexington, MA: Lexington, 1979.

Tippie, J.W., and Kulaga, J.E. *Design Considerations for a Multiprocessor-Based Data Acquisition System.* IEEE Transactions on Nuclear Science, August, 1979.

Toong, H.D., and Gupta, A. "An Architectural Comparison of Contemporary 16-Bit Microprocessors." *IEEE Micro,* May 1981.

Torrero, E.A. "Focus on Microprocessors." *Electronic Design,* September 1, 1974.

Torrero, E.A. ed. *Microprocessors: New Directions for Designers.* Rochelle Park, NJ: Hayden Book Co., 1975.

Ungerboeck, G. *Channel Coding with Multilevel/Phase Signals.* IEEE Transactions on Information Theory, Vol IT-28, No. 1, January 1982.

Vacroux, A.G. "Explore Microcomputer I/O Capabilities." *Electronic Design,* May 10, 1975.

van Dam, A. "Some Implementation Issues Relating to Data Structures for Interactive Graphics." *International Journal of Computer and Information Sciences,* Vol. 1 No. 4 (1972).

Vandenbrouche, L. *Selecting CAD/CAM Displays.* CADCON West, San Francisco, February 7-9, 1984.

van den Bos, J. *Definition and Use of Higher-Level Graphics Input Tools.* SIGGRAPH 1978 Proceedings, published as *Computer Graphics,* 12 (3), August 1978.

Wallace, V.L. *The Semantics of Graphic Input Devices.* Proceedings SIGGRAPH/SIGPLAN Conference on Graphics Languages, published as *Computer Graphics,* 10 (1), April 1976.

Warner, J.R. "Device-Independent Tool Systems." *Computer Graphics World,* February 1984.

Warnock, J. *The Display of Characters Using Grey Level Sample Arrays.* SIGGRAPH 1980 Proceedings, published as *Computer Graphics,* 14 (3), July 1980.

Wegner, W. Ed. *Research Directions in Software Technology.* Cambridge, MA: MIT Press, 1978.

Weisberg, D.E. "Performance and Productivity in CAD." *Computer Graphics World,* June 1983.

Weller, D., and Williams, R. *Graphic and Relational Data Base Support for Problem Solving.* SIGGRAPH 1976 Proceedings, published as *Computer Graphics,* 10 (2), Summer 1976.

West, J. *Emerging Importance of Engineering Workstations in Manufacturing.* CADCON East, Boston, 1984. (New York: Morgan-Grampian. June 13, 1984.)

Westerhoff, T. "Software in the Future Factory." *Test and Measurements World,* December 1983.

Wilde, D.J. *Optimum Seeking Methods.* Englewood Cliffs, NJ: Prentice-Hall, 1964.

Williams, R. *On the Application of Relational Data Structures in Computer Graphics.* Proceedings 1974 IFIP Congress (North-Holland Publishing Company).

Wolf, J.K., Michelson, A.M., and Levesque, A.H. *On the Probability of Undetected Error for Linear Block Codes.* IEEE Transactions on Communications. Vol. COM-30, February 1982.

Woodruff, G. *Automated Inspection of PWBs.* Automated Manufacturing Greenville, SC, March 1984.

Wong, E., and Youssefi, K. *Decomposition—A Strategy for Query Processing.* ACM Transactions on Data Base Systems, September 1976.

Yourdon, E., and Constantine, L.L. *Structured Design.* New York: Yourdon, 1975.

Zaks, R. *Microprocessors.* Berkeley, CA: Sybex, 1979.

Zambuto, D.A. *Robotic System Needs for Nonstandard Components Assembly in Electronics Manufacturing.* Automated Manufacturing, Greenville, SC, March 1984.

Zilog Corp. *Z8000 User's Guide.* Cupertino, CA: Zilog Corp.

Zimmerman, H.H., and Sovereign, M.G. *Quantitative Models for Production Management.* Englewood Cliffs, NJ: Prentice-Hall, 1974.

Index

Q

R

S

T

U

V

W

V

X

Edited by Marianne Krcma